# THE POSTIE AND THE PRIEST

A Look At Father Bob Maguire
Through His Letterbox

A biography by Ron Burrows

WIPF & STOCK · Eugene, Oregon

Wipf and Stock Publishers
199 W 8th Ave, Suite 3
Eugene, OR 97401

The Postie and The Priest
A Look at Father Bob Maguire Through His Letterbox
By Burrows, Ron
Copyright©2011 Mosaic Press
ISBN 13: 978-1-62564-331-5
Publication date 7/30/2013
Previously published by Mosaic Press, 2011

## Table of Contents

Chapter 1: That Can't Be Right . . . . . . . . . . . . . . . . . . . . . . . . . 6
Chapter 2: Father Bob And The Mobile Priest . . . . . . . . . . . . . . . . . . 8
Chapter 3: The Divide. . . . . . . . . . . . . . . . . . . . . . . . . . . . . . . . . . . 14
Chapter 4: James 836133 . . . . . . . . . . . . . . . . . . . . . . . . . . . . . . . . 22
Chapter 5: Creepy Catholics and the Post Office Fleas . . . . . . . . . . 30
Chapter 6: Vatican Who? . . . . . . . . . . . . . . . . . . . . . . . . . . . . . . . . . 39
Chapter 7: The Wheel of Life . . . . . . . . . . . . . . . . . . . . . . . . . . . . . 44
Chapter 8: Abbe Pierre . . . . . . . . . . . . . . . . . . . . . . . . . . . . . . . . . . 56
Chapter 9: Love and Best Wishes . . . . . . . . . . . . . . . . . . . . . . . . . . 61
Chapter 10: The Peanut Farm . . . . . . . . . . . . . . . . . . . . . . . . . . . . . 69
Chapter 11: Brother Alex . . . . . . . . . . . . . . . . . . . . . . . . . . . . . . . . 73
Chapter 12: You've Gotta Have Two Men . . . . . . . . . . . . . . . . . . . 78
Chapter 13: Nathan Stirling . . . . . . . . . . . . . . . . . . . . . . . . . . . . . . 86
Chapter 14: Betrayal . . . . . . . . . . . . . . . . . . . . . . . . . . . . . . . . . . . . 93
Chapter 15: Chuck A Buck . . . . . . . . . . . . . . . . . . . . . . . . . . . . . . 98
Chapter 16: Father Smooch . . . . . . . . . . . . . . . . . . . . . . . . . . . . . 106
Chapter 17: The Cause . . . . . . . . . . . . . . . . . . . . . . . . . . . . . . . . . 115
Chapter 18: Father Bob: Star Of The Wireless . . . . . . . . . . . . . . . 124
Chapter 19: . . . And Television. . . . . . . . . . . . . . . . . . . . . . . . . . . 132
Chapter 20: The Mad Micks . . . . . . . . . . . . . . . . . . . . . . . . . . . . . 135
Chapter 21: God Is Good . . . . . . . . . . . . . . . . . . . . . . . . . . . . . . . 145
Chapter 22: Shiny Suburban Catholics . . . . . . . . . . . . . . . . . . . . . 148
Chapter 23: You're In the Army Now . . . . . . . . . . . . . . . . . . . . . . 156
Chapter 24: The Moon, The Morgue, and The Man . . . . . . . . . . . 167
Chapter 25: The Grin . . . . . . . . . . . . . . . . . . . . . . . . . . . . . . . . . . 171
Chapter 26: They Died On Our Watch . . . . . . . . . . . . . . . . . . . . . 181
Chapter 27: Christmas Eve . . . . . . . . . . . . . . . . . . . . . . . . . . . . . . 189
Chapter 28: A Priest For All Religions . . . . . . . . . . . . . . . . . . . . . 192
Chapter 29: The Three Flags . . . . . . . . . . . . . . . . . . . . . . . . . . . . 199

Chapter 30: Back to the Desert . . . . . . . . . . . . . . . . . . . . . . . . . . . 204
Chapter 31: The Tail Wags the Dog . . . . . . . . . . . . . . . . . . . . . . . 214
Chapter 32: Hot In The City . . . . . . . . . . . . . . . . . . . . . . . . . . . . 220
Chapter 33: St Patrick's Day . . . . . . . . . . . . . . . . . . . . . . . . . . . . 222
Chapter 34: The Last Supper . . . . . . . . . . . . . . . . . . . . . . . . . . . 232
Chapter 35: Good Friday . . . . . . . . . . . . . . . . . . . . . . . . . . . . . . 239
Chapter 36: Post Mortem . . . . . . . . . . . . . . . . . . . . . . . . . . . . . . 246
Chapter 37: Catherine Of Siena . . . . . . . . . . . . . . . . . . . . . . . . . 253
Chapter 38: Tractoring . . . . . . . . . . . . . . . . . . . . . . . . . . . . . . . . 258
Chapter 39: The Beekeeper . . . . . . . . . . . . . . . . . . . . . . . . . . . . . 262
Chapter 40: The Fool-In-The-Grey-Flannel-Suit . . . . . . . . . . . . . . 270
Chapter 41: The-Man-in-the-Middle . . . . . . . . . . . . . . . . . . . . . 272
Chapter 42: The Icon File . . . . . . . . . . . . . . . . . . . . . . . . . . . . . . 277
Chapter 43: Flash In The Mud . . . . . . . . . . . . . . . . . . . . . . . . . . 279
Chapter 44: Chiko . . . . . . . . . . . . . . . . . . . . . . . . . . . . . . . . . . . 289
Chapter 45: The Roman Catholic Thing . . . . . . . . . . . . . . . . . . . 292
Chapter 46: The Roaming Catholics . . . . . . . . . . . . . . . . . . . . . . 301
Chapter 47: Cuban Cigars . . . . . . . . . . . . . . . . . . . . . . . . . . . . . 306
Chapter 48: Exponential Growth . . . . . . . . . . . . . . . . . . . . . . . . 309
Chapter 49: The Gladstone Bag . . . . . . . . . . . . . . . . . . . . . . . . . 311
Chapter 50: Father Bob And The Clerical Cliche . . . . . . . . . . . . . 316
Chapter 51: More Tea Vicar? . . . . . . . . . . . . . . . . . . . . . . . . . . . 324
Chapter 52: The Hard Sell . . . . . . . . . . . . . . . . . . . . . . . . . . . . . 332
Chapter 53: Follow Me . . . . . . . . . . . . . . . . . . . . . . . . . . . . . . . 346
Chapter 54: The Fish 'n' Chip Eaters . . . . . . . . . . . . . . . . . . . . . . 350
Chapter 55: The Civil-Bloody-War . . . . . . . . . . . . . . . . . . . . . . . 358
Chapter 56: Broken Rites . . . . . . . . . . . . . . . . . . . . . . . . . . . . . . 364
Chapter 57: The Flat Daddy . . . . . . . . . . . . . . . . . . . . . . . . . . . . 371
Chapter 58: The Unknown God . . . . . . . . . . . . . . . . . . . . . . . . . 372

'Is it possible, in the final analysis, for one human being to achieve perfect understanding of another? We can invest enormous time and energy in serious efforts to know another person, but in the end, how close can we come to that person's essence? We convince ourselves that we know the other person well, but do we really know anything important about anyone?'

Haruki Murakami

# Chapter 1: That Can't Be Right

*"Watch him. The bastard's mad."*

When I first began delivering mail to Sts Peter and Paul's Church in South Melbourne, I took that address quite literally and delivered mail to the church. I rode my bike into the grounds and up to the front steps. On the first occasion I walked quietly, almost reverently, past the baptismal font and paschal candle, looking with wonder at the magnificent stained-glass windows, gently calling out: "Is there anybody there?" It makes me laugh now to think of my naivety. I placed the bundle of mail on the altar and rode off thinking to myself: *'That can't be right.'*

For a week or two, I simply left the mail on the nearest pew. I came to enjoy going into the church. It was not really a religious experience though, more like a quiet interlude away from the traffic. I wanted to sit down on a pew and relax but was afraid that I would either fall asleep or be 'sprung' so I stood, just inside the door, and soaked up the silence instead. It was Father Bob who eventually set me straight, telling me that there was a letterbox near the front door of the rectory. I missed my daily visits to the church where I could be on my own for a few moments away from the noise of the street. There were a few times when I would have appreciated that sanctuary too. If I had told Bob, he probably would have said: 'That's alright Father, just keep leaving the mail on the pew. I'll send the dog over to collect it.' And what a dog it was.

Father Bob had a big black incongruous poodle. 'Watch him,' he used to say, 'the bastard's mad.' I handed Bob a bundle of mail outside the rectory one morning as the dog, with his red tongue hanging out, ran round and around the bike panting and closely watching the wheels. We talked for a while then I started to ride off, standing up on the pedals to get the bike moving. The dog barked once then sprang up and bit me sharply on the arse. Bob, usually a master at keeping a straight face, had trouble that day. That dog has long since died but Father Bob managed to get a 'replacement' that looks to be a clone. This one has a much better temperament than his predecessor though and the two of us get along well. It is indicative of the generous nature of Father Bob Maguire that, years later, he would consider giving the nod to the local postie to write his biography, but he *is*, after all is said and done, a champion of the underdog. Then again, maybe he was simply seeking atonement for the actions of his mad dog all those years ago.

The welfare of the battlers takes precedence in Bob's life. He looks upon them as his personal responsibility and is penniless as a consequence. He feeds and fends for 'those that live on the hungry side of town and for the reckless ones whose bad trip left them cold', people like those portrayed in the Johnny Cash song *Man in Black*. He has even been known to slip the poor old postie $100 at Christmas, with his usual: 'I'd better fix you up with that hundred quid I owe you, Father.'

This is the story of a priest with panache who has become a household name written by a postie who hasn't. It is also the story of how I fulfilled my dream of writing Father Bob's biography, of how I gathered the threads of the story together whilst still working as a postie and of the drama that unfolded as Father Bob and I tried to get the manuscript published.

# Chapter 2: Father Bob And The Mobile Priest

*"Oh, no he's not just the postman. He's really a priest."*

When you take Daylight Savings Time into account, it is relatively early as I ride out of the Disaster Centre aka the South Melbourne Delivery Centre. It is 8.15am or 7.15am God's Time, as Father Bob might say. The weather forecast is for a maximum of 38 degrees with strong northerly winds and a late afternoon change. I pedal up Cecil Street past the South Melbourne Market wondering for the umpteenth time about the viability of so many fruit and vegie stalls at one location. I'm also thinking about the manuscript because partway through the round I will be visiting Father Bob for my first 'official' visit as his biographer-on-a-bike.

There is a bloke, with a young woman beside him, sitting in the shade on a bench on Father Bob's front verandah when I arrive about an hour later. Before I go inside to visit Bob we talk for a while. The young woman sits as still as a Flat Daddy, a life-sized cardboard cutout that the Americans bizarrely substitute for a real daddy who has gone off to fight in Iraq or Afghanistan, as the man begins to tell a story about a cat he once had. He was living rough at the time, he said, sleeping on the streets, or in parks, and had been scrounging for food in a rubbish bin when he came across a ginger cat. "One of her legs was crushed, and she was barely alive," he said. So he took the cat to a local vet and asked him if he could look after her and find her a home, saying that he would pay as soon as he got some money. He returned to pay the vet some time later only to discover that the cat, now in excellent health apart from a crooked leg, was waiting for him.

"She's as bright as a button," the young vet told him, "and has a real personality. She's different to your average moggie. I can't quite explain it. I couldn't find her a new home though so unless you take her I'll have to put her down."

"But I haven't got a home either," the man responded "How can I look after her?"

The vet shrugged sympathetically. "I'm sorry, mate, but I've done all I can."

The man's story is suddenly interrupted. A volunteer worker has been cooking breakfast for a few homeless people at the back of the rectory. One of them, after eating his fill, is on his way singing raucously as he ambles down the path. The storyteller and I look at each other and laugh and it is then that I see a barely perceptible movement from his younger friend. The corners of her mouth twitch ever so slightly.

The storyteller continues, his brown eyes shining: "I took the cat with me. I christened her Cherie. My Cherie: 'my love'. I got the name from the cartoon Pepé Le Pew, the skunk and a cat named Cherie, the love of his life. She was my love." Pepé looks down at his hands for a moment. "For a while there, we slept in a burnt out car. She used to follow me around like a dog and if I stopped to talk to someone she would 'drop' and remain lying beside my feet until it was time for us to move on. All the street people loved her. She really was just like a dog. We lived together for fifteen years. She was all I had. I had hardly any money for myself but I had to feed her, share whatever I had. She was my responsibility. I had to stay out of trouble with the police too. There would be no one to feed her if I got banged up. She couldn't hunt with her crook leg. We went bush and lived in a deserted farmhouse. Now and then I used to pinch a sheep from a neighbour's paddock and butcher it. She loved the meat," he confides almost whispering.

"What happened to her?" I ask after a few quiet moments.

"She died of old age about six months ago," he says sadly. "Matilda knew her," he indicates his friend beside him who doesn't respond. "I won't get another one for a while."

Pepé is not doing it as hard now, he tells me. He lives in a Ministry of Housing flat in South Melbourne; he says that he has come to "borrow a few quid from Bob," one of many colourful people who rely on Father for regular subs.

Father Bob has a kind, round, suntanned face with dark brown eyes and thick rubbery lips. Most of his hair has deserted him although he still has a white 'border' around the sides and back which highlights his suntanned scalp. He has a penchant for Hawaiian shirts, not tucked into the trousers. From a photograph that I've seen of him he is not as corpulent as he once was. The snapshot that he showed me depicted a young chubby priest wearing a white cassock. We are sitting in his study discussing the weighty subject of his father's predilection for alcohol: the usual sort of thing that priests discuss with their posties. It is welcome then when a visitor, who is also a customer on my round, lightens the mood. I have been delivering mail to Chris Apostalidis for as long as I have to Father Bob although we've only ever been on a 'G'day, mate' basis.

"You think Ron's just the postman, don't you?" Father Bob asks

Chris, who looks at me and pulls a face. I raise my eyebrows and shrug.

Father Bob Maguire grins mischievously. Before speaking again he glances out the window of his study. It is a bugger of a day for posties and parrots alike, I think to myself, noticing that someone has taken away the birdbath that used to sit under the eucalypt near the tap. The large windows of the study, where we are sitting, look out onto the garden, a large area of patchy lawn shaded by eucalypts.

"Oh, no he's not just the postman," says Bob. "He's really a priest." He times his story, swivelling in his chair to look at our guest steadily. "He came to me one day and asked: 'Will you ordain me as a priest, Father?' And I said: 'Yes, you can be the Mobile Priest. You go round delivering the letters and if you come across someone who has just staggered out of the brothel, you say: 'I absolve you from your sins in the name of the Father.' I'm never going to be able to get near a person like that, so you, as the Mobile Priest, can look after him. You ride along a bit further and somebody else brings a baby out to you in the street for baptism.'" I'm caught up in the story imagining a need for holy water and a basin strapped to the bike.

The laughter pushes us all back in our chairs. Chris is still chuckling as he leaves. Father Bob is grinning too as he glances out the window again. There are a couple of large photographs on the wall beside the window. Bob tells me that the priest depicted in one is Helder Camara, a Brazilian Catholic Archbishop, "who tried to put Vatican Two into operation, not only in his own parish, but in his diocese. He became the face of Latin American Liberation Theology," he explains to me.

"You must think highly of him to have his photo on the wall," I say wondering what Vatican Two is or was.

"Yes, he was doing good things but was knocked orf eventually by headquarters. He got caught short because the international leadership changed. John Paul the first died and then JP2, who was frightened stiff of Communists, came in. He thought that the Latin American Church was falling into Communism just as the German Pope now is frightened that the Roman Catholic Church is falling into Anti-Europeanism."

He tells me that the other black-and-white photograph is of the original street people taken at the time when Open Family came into being, a motley bunch as you would imagine but somehow appealing and intriguing. I decide to leave alone this avenue to the Open Family story for another time so that I can concentrate on Father Bob's early history. I am about to ask him another question when his secretary, Annette, comes in and says that there is someone at the door to see him. Whilst Bob is out of the room I open my notebook and write a description of the church and its surrounds.

Sts Peter and Paul's Church is an impressive bluestone church with a recently renovated dark-grey slate roof. There is a half-moon driveway, serviced by two entrances off Montague Street, which sweeps past the front steps of the church through the parvis. Wedding and funeral vehicles predominantly use this arc. A pair of modern glass doors positioned inside the double outer-doors protects against draughts in winter and keeps the heat out in summer. "So youse don't have to suffer like Jesus did," Father Bob once observed.

The rectory, where we are now, is on the other side of the driveway with a footpath leading out into Dorcas Street. A white statue of the Virgin Mary stands near the path. A diminutive Irish lady who often attends Mass at noon sometimes stands and talks to the statue. They are both the same height. Before leaving she kisses the first two fingers of her right hand and then tenderly places her fingers on Mary's head.

The school on the other side of the church was once called St. Peter and St. Paul's Catholic School, but some years ago it had to amalgamate with a couple of other schools in the neighbourhood because of dwindling enrollments. I remember riding into the school with the mail not long after the name change. A competition had been organised to find a new name and 'Galilee' was chosen. A teacher walking by asked whether I liked the new name.

"I love it. I think that it's a magnificent idea to name a school after a Melbourne Cup winner," I replied. "It's one of the few Cup winners that I have actually backed too."

"We didn't name the school after a racehorse!" the indignant teacher huffed. She straightened her body and puffed out her chest like a pigeon. "Galilee is where Jesus grew up, don't you know!" She glared at me, wiping the spittle from the corners of her mouth, before stalking off across the quadrangle.

Smiling at the memory I focus on the present as Bob comes back into the room. He sits down, takes off his glasses, and knuckle-massages his eyes. "It's all too much for me," he says. Although we haven't been talking for long the interruption has taken up a fair bit of time and we decide to call it a day. The story about Bob's father will have to wait. Bob checks his diary so that we can arrange another appointment for the following Friday and we say our goodbyes.

I ride away from the church, humming softly as the tyres sing along in the sticky tar of the footpath. I cross Montague St, ride along Dorcas and turn left into Nelson Road, a wide, curving tree-lined thoroughfare with broad nature-strips and two-storey Victorian style houses on both sides. Some parts of the streetscape have been destroyed over the years by slack building regulations and careless development. Victorian houses have been demolished and replaced by houses that do not fit, but generally speaking it is still a lovely street. A grey two-storey weatherboard in Nelson Road, on the other side of Park Street, with a wide front verandah is my favourite. The weatherboards could be cedar that has greyed from the weather over time. Its appearance has barely changed over the years but there is no denying its appeal. A massive eucalypt in the narrow front yard is a feature in the garden with the branches within reach from the second-storey verandah. The garden doesn't really need anything else, although I'll definitely be searching for a birdbath that looks as if it just *belongs* under that tree when I buy the place. The front fence would probably collapse if anyone leant on it and has been like that for some time. I'll have to do something about that too.

An early model, low-slung, Citroen, that always seems to stay at home sits out in the street in front of the house. A stay-at-home yacht on a trailer sits behind, but not connected to, the car. I always look at the place as a package: the house, the car, and the boat. Flicking through the mail as I approach I stop near the gate where the letterbox would be if there were one and stretch a red rubber band around the mail and fling the bundle onto the front verandah like a paperboy delivering newspapers. It lands with a satisfying plop.

A couple of houses past the weatherboard, I stop, lean the bike against a fence, and step onto a shady verandah to deliver a registered letter. The roar of a vacuum cleaner is barely audible above the thumping stereo. I go through the motions of knocking on the door in between the heavy beats from the sub-woofer then write out a card and poke it into the letterbox.

Astride the bike once again, delivering mail in a detached manner, I cross the road to deliver the even numbers and make my way back down Nelson Road towards Dorcas Street. The bloke on the right has already begun to wander about. Thankfully, Rene keeps the bike and letters straight and out of harm's way. Rene is good at navigation and order, keeping track of logical things like letterboxes and people's names while the bloke on the right can't even remember his own name never mind the moniker of the bloke on the left; he can't even tie his shoe laces and is always getting lost. One good thing about this job is that Rene, who, incidentally, christened himself *Rene Descartes*, can quietly look after the mail while the bloke on the right keeps the bloke on the bike smiling. I was quite young when I first became aware of the bloke on the right; he used to get me into all kinds of strife at school. That's when he got the name *Ronny*. He has never been able to remember Descartes' name and rarely pays attention to anything he says. Even at that young age Ronny would laugh with delight as Rene chastised me for looking out the window, daydreaming as I listened to Ronny, instead of listening to the teacher. Divided almost at conception the Cauliflower-twins like to maintain their own independence.

    I ride on, my earlier buoyant mood gradually fading as the heat sucks the enthusiasm out of me. An old lady beating against the hot northerly wind, like a sailing boat, is blown off course on the black ribbon of tar as the wind tugs at her wispy white hair; nevertheless she manages a smile as she tacks past lugging her plastic bags of groceries up the street.

# Chapter 3: The Divide

*"The bloody past will only drive me mad! You'll have me locked up in a lunatic asylum, delving into my past, trying to find my mother."*

Jan Ullrich, the big German who has been riding in the Tour De France for the last few years, might appreciate a sprocket similar to the one that the bike mechanic has fitted to my bike but my skinny old legs are protesting. I'm out of the saddle going up the Cecil Street hill (more like a hillock really) on the way to the start of the round. There are three and a half hours of riding to go yet, including the time that I will spend at Father Bob's. I do a stage of the Tour every day – the only problem is it's the same bloody stage day in day out!

Father Bob's cluttered desk is large enough to easily accommodate a priest on one side and a postie on the other but I've got it to myself this morning; Bob is not back yet from an earlier appointment. I'm lounging back reading the blurb on the back of one of Father Bob's books when he enters the study and says without formality: "We'd better get on with it, Your Grace." He tells me that his mother was a practising Catholic even though his father much preferred grog to God. Bob begins to talk about his early life when his mobile phone buzzes in his pocket. This is something that I will have to get used to it seems because it buzzed a couple of times during the first interview too. "Bob Maguire," he says as he slits open one of the envelopes that I've just placed on his desk.

"Most of my family was swept away into the cemetery," Bob says, getting back to his story after dealing with the phone call. "Swept away and erased!" he exclaims. "I was only sixteen years old. That was right at the time that I should have been forming lasting relationships and social connections."

I am caught up by Bob's dramatic use of language, already distracted, going over those two sentences in my head: 'Most of my family was swept away into the cemetery. Swept away and erased!' Hang on, what is Bob saying?

"I never knew my mother. I've got no early memories of her," he says as Descartes pokes me with his cattle prod. I sit up straight and tune in.

"That seems a bit odd," I frown. "You were a teenager when she died. I've got memories of my mother back to when I was about three. My first memory is of being perched up in the little pillion seat behind her on her bike."

"Yes," Bob responds loudly and emphatically, perhaps a little too loudly, "but you probably lived a peaceful existence. Was your father raging-drunk most of the time, railing against your mother? She had a stroke. I remember her being partly paralysed down one side. There's not much more to the poor woman. Poor Annie, God rest her soul." Father shakes his head and compresses his lips. "She was home all day and night with no money. She used to take me with her on the tram down to Ansell's in Chapel Street to pawn her wedding ring." I swallow and remain still as Bob contemplates.

"The bloody past will only drive me mad! You'll have me locked up in a lunatic asylum, delving into my past, trying to find my mother. All these repressed memories," he says, putting his glasses back on and fixing me with a doleful stare as if I were Freud's apprentice. Then he picks up another envelope from the mail on the desk, opens it and returns to the subject of his family.

"We were all short," states Bob as if starting anew. "My father was only 5 feet 5 inches tall."

'As if this had anything to do with anything,' say Rene Descartes.

His earliest and fondest memory, he says, is of his lovely sister, Kathleen, taking him to "the pictures at The Fleapit," also known as The Empress Theatre, in Chapel Street St Kilda.

"We hardly ever went to the pictures. The name of the film we went to see that day was 'Song of Russia.' I remember the music: it was a Tchaikovsky piano concerto. I don't seem to have many childhood memories," he says as he rubs a hand reflectively across his chin. "I think Robert Taylor starred in the show." Bob softly hums a few bars of the music.

"That's when you joined 'Peter's Pals!' he exclaims jubilantly. "It's all coming back to me now. The names of the birthday boys and girls were flashed up onto the screen and you went up and received a certificate or something. I was a Sunbeamer with Corinella too. I remember getting a green certificate."

Frank pads into the study, goes over to Father and 'kisses' his hand.

"Go and see your Uncle Ron!" commands Bob imperiously.

Frank wanders around the big desk, 'kisses' my hand, and then slumps into a leather armchair. Two long legs stretch out over the front of the seat; his head, with his tongue hanging out the side of his mouth, rests on the arm of the chair. On the first occasion that I visited, Bob was calling the big black poodle Rocky. Today though, it seems, his name is Frank.

"Kathleen used to take me across town to 'Windy Hill,' the Essendon Football ground," continues Father Bob. "She was making a valiant effort to take the youngest, and a boy, out to events that he would enjoy. Those were the days of the famous Dick Reynolds, Jack Dyer and Billy Morris. Then poor Kathleen died from tuberculosis and I was devastated. That was the end of the footy matches for a few years too," he says pensively.

"Then a few years after that," says Bob ripping through his past with a chainsaw, "a local priest, Jimmy McKew, took an interest in me and used to take me to the Richmond footy matches. He'd pick me up in his big black Pontiac. His family had money. It was an upwardly, socially mobile, Catholic family. We would get to the ground and he would say: 'Wait here,' and he'd leave me in the outer whilst he went into the Members." Bob smiles fondly at the memory. "Then he died suddenly and it was all over. No more football matches again. This is what's happened to me all my life," he adds philosophically, "I'd just get up and running and it would all fall over."

"Can you tell me about your school days, Father?" I ask blindly missing the opportunity to find out what else had fallen over. Rene just shakes his half of the cauli.'

"Yes", he continues with barely a pause. "Our Lady of Lourdes Armidale was my first school. This was during the forties. We had to carry around lumps of rubber, a piece of black solid rubber that we could stick in our mouths, so that we wouldn't bite our tongues off, in case the Japanese bombed us."

"Hell," I murmur. Frank lifts his head and looks at me with his big brown eyes.

"They dug trenches we could all run into if the man came over to drop bombs on us. It was just around the corner in the lovely park where we would normally have gone to play footy or cricket."

"It would have been a scramble to try to get everyone into the park. Couldn't they have dug the trenches in the school grounds?" I ask Father Bob.

"We never had much room at school," he explains, taking off his glasses to massage his eyes again. "Catholic schools were small," he says suppressing a yawn but then gives in and yawns as he speaks. "Whether we should have had Catholic schools or all gone to the State schools, I don't know. Sometimes I think we'd all be better off if we had community schools. It would give everybody equal access."

"What were you like as a teenager?" I ask trying not to yawn. "That seems to be the time when a lot of us go off the rails." 'Easily led astray,' is what teachers used to write about me, amongst their other lies and misconceptions. I realise only when editing the manuscript that Bob had not said much at all about his school experiences, lumps of black rubber and trenches in "the lovely park". Who were his friends? What were his teachers like? Was he a good and obedient student?

"Teenage years." Bob underlines the words and once again I'm impressed with the way he structures his spoken sentences. There is no umming and arring; even the commas fall into place. "We knew we were in danger of falling into delinquency, which was the term used in those days. There was a general consensus: a warning system that said if you're not gainfully employed, or you are behind the eight-ball as far as money is concerned, or the ability to fulfill your dreams then you might well end up a juvenile delinquent. If you got into that category you were buggered."

Bob smiles and raises his eyebrows. "Some of us were wise little boys in those days and tried to stay out of the pit. Don't stray from the herd. So we went around to the head of the herd, the parish priest, and said: 'We do not want to stray from the herd, Father. We would like a place where we can get together now that we are grown up boys, and the church has got a house around the corner with a billiard table and other amenities. We would like to be able to assemble there.' Now, this was wisdom before our time." Father Bob inclines his head as he looks at me. Then he says flatly: "He knocked us back."

Before I have time to interject and ask why, Bob has moved on to tell a story about his oldest living relative in Australia, his 86 year-old cousin Molly Langman, a pious Roman Catholic from Fairfield. Bob moves from one topic to another with nary a thought for segue. Stories seem piled up inside him in no apparent order, waiting for an opportunity to escape. How will I move the reader from Bob's herd and the billiard table to his pious aunt? 'I'm sure you'll come up with something,' says Rene Descartes drily.

Bob continues with hardly a breath, making the point that "Molly is a practising Mick. The women in my family may well have been devotional Catholics. My father, as far as I know, was not a practising Catholic. My brother is not a practising Catholic. My sister, however, was."

Father Bob glances at his watch. "Get out!" he exclaims theatrically. "I've gotta go to Mass."

I laugh and thank Bob; it's time to get back on the pushbike and deliver the rest of the mail. I've got extra mail today too. Absenteeism is rife on Mondays and Fridays. We are short of posties today so those of us who turned up have to do extra. If there aren't enough relieving posties to fill the gaps, vacant rounds are divided up amongst the group. This punishment for coming to work is called a 'divide.'

I cross to the other side of Dorcas Street, which is also a divide. Dorcas Street divides those who live in Nelson Road who have, from those who live in Nelson Road who do not have. Today I cross the divide and deliver to the many have-nots. Most of the houses, although not all, in this section of Nelson Road are Ministry of Housing places where the poorer residents, who do not own their own homes, live. The street curves from the corner of Dorcas Street, where an old pub called the Star and Garter that began in 1877 still stands (now luxurious apartments), down to City Road. There is a large Ministry of Housing area within the borders of Dorcas Street, Nelson Road, City Road and Pickles Street.

The Housing Commission, as it was called when these houses were designed and built, succeeded to some extent, in building houses that would not appear out of place with their richer cousins on the other side of 'the divide.' Today, although hardly opulent, these two-storey houses on narrow blocks in Nelson Road would be described as town houses.

After delivering to Coventry, Normanby, Smith and Iffla Streets I end up back in Dorcas Street where my divide ends. I open the front gate of a single storey Victorian house, not far from the corner, and back my bike in a few metres until I reach a solid two metre high gate. I open the gate, back my bike in and shut the gate behind me. I roll the bike down the narrow path that runs between the house and the high paling fence. Leaning it against the fence I step onto a tiny back verandah and then in the side door to the kitchen.

I walk in as if I own the place and greet my old mate Eric who is already pulling two bottles of homebrew from the fridge. The amount of beer stockpiled in the back shed would be enough to slake the thirst of Pantagruel. As usual the nasal sounds of a race-caller are emanating from the radio that sits on top of the fridge. Eric has always been a keen punter and the races are usually on during the day whether he is punting or not. I telephoned him the other day; he wasn't home but the race-caller was there. I could hear him in the background of the recorded message. I sit down in my usual place at the kitchen table whilst Eric decants the beer into a jug and then fills two pewter pots. This used to be my routine every day for nearly fifteen years when this divide was part of my usual round.

Eric, a quietly spoken bloke, retired from work at the Melbourne Metropolitan Board of Works about the same time as I started work as a postie at the Disaster Centre. We met out the front of his house one day when the tar on the footpath was softening and the northerly wind was grounding the birds. Eric invited me in for a beer and suggested that I back the bike in and leave it in the narrow sideway, behind the side-gate, so that it couldn't be seen from the street. His wife, May, prepared four *Uneeda* biscuits, with half-inch thick pieces of cheese on top for me. I was the only one who ate. This would also become part of the daily routine. 'And is the reason you put on so much weight over those years,' sniffs Descartes sitting in judgment. Eric and I drank three bottles, pushing the beer down fairly fast, because I still had to finish the round and get back within my allocated round time. Our friendship grew from that day and within weeks we were knocking back three bottles every day. After about ten years, which would have been around the time that May died of Alzheimer's, we cut our quota back to two; I was worried about getting pulled over by the police and breath-tested as I drove home.

It became common knowledge amongst the posties, over the years, that I was having a beer with Eric every day. I suspect that a couple of the bosses (we had a few different ones during my time there) might even have known but chose to ignore it for reasons unknown. For the last couple of years, since this section was removed from my round, I've been visiting on my way home from work. There's something tantalising about forbidden hops though.

Eric and I talk and laugh about this as we sit at the kitchen table and quaff his homebrew. The divide doesn't seem such a bad thing after all. Work is what you make it I think as I push my bike back along the narrow sideway (it's 3 feet 1 inch wide according to Eric) to the street. Eric follows me out and then chuckles as I shy clear of the bees buzzing around the big lavender bush near the front gate. "They won't sting you unless you swipe at them," he says. He gently puts an outstretched hand into the bush. Tiny feet walk onto his index finger and smiling again he proffers his hand. After a couple of moments the bee flies back to the nectar and I say goodbye and ride back to the office.

The Disaster Centre has disastrous Feng Shui. I noticed it the first time I drove into the joint in my car: the entrance is in direct line with the exit. Today as I ride in from York Street through the car park I frown yet again at the dichotomous nature of the place. The driveway, with strategically placed speed-humps, divides the facility, in effect making it two buildings sharing the one roof. Under this corrugated iron roof three groups of posties are split into two major divisions. On the left-hand side the superior group, South Melbourne, is accommodated. Port Melbourne and Albert Park share the building on the right-hand side. These two groups each have their own territory although there is no physical wall dividing them.

The next day, I telephone Molly Langman hoping to be granted an interview. There is no answer so I leave a message detailing my request but she doesn't respond.

When I next see Father Bob, he says: "She mightn't be answering. She's probably sick of it too, worn out with it all. She's old. Don't forget that Terry Monagle has already been over there asking questions. She'll be wondering what the hell is going on. I'll go over there sooner or later with a peace offering," says Father resignedly.

Terry Monagle writes a column about Catholicism for *The Age*. He has had books about religion published and has won awards for his writing. I met Terry in Father Bob's study one morning not long ago. I had just stepped onto the front verandah with a bundle of mail in hand that morning when Father Bob came to the door. It had been a couple of years since I had last asked him if I could write his biography. On the two previous occasions (both a couple of years apart) he said that he didn't want anyone to write a biography about him, but there was no harm in trying again, is what I thought. The idea of writing Bob's biography had become an obsession. Once again I put it to him.

"He's in there now," Bob said, inclining his head toward the door.

"Who?" I asked, but I had already twigged. The dream was over.

"My biographer, Terry Monagle. Come in and meet him," said Bob as he walked back inside.

After Father Bob introduced us we made small talk for a couple of minutes. Terry said that he had been writing the biography for about six months. I remember feeling as if I had taken a direct hit but managed to smile as if everything was hunky dory. Then Bob said casually: "Ron wants to write my biography too."

Terry pursed his lips and his eyes seemed to bore into me.

"They will be two completely different stories," said Bob to Terry. "Ron's will be more of an anecdotal type of yarn."

I remember a feeling of weightlessness as I rode around delivering the rest of the round that day.

Father Bob brings me back to the present by proffering a sepia photograph and 'introducing' me to his paternal forebears.

Bob's father, James, is standing next to his father, James, at the back. Bob's grandma, Ellen is pictured in the front with the other five children. According to family legend Grandpa Maguire was somewhat of a legend himself. He liked a wee dram (I can sense Descartes is about to make a smart arsed comment about my liking for the Scotch mist but I block the bastard out) and was quite likely to stagger into the front garden reciting Shakespeare at full volume after getting home from the pub. According to Bob, his favourite well-rehearsed lines were by Iago in Othello:

*Who steals my purse steals trash; 'tis something, nothing;*
*'T'was mine, 'tis his, and has been slaves to thousands;*
*But he that filches from me my good name robs*
*me of that which not enriches him, and makes*
*me poor indeed.*
*(Othello, III, iii, 157-61)*

Can I see the effects of Grandfather James's alcoholism on his children in the photo? Or is everybody masked by his or her Sunday best expression? Was Grandpa's penchant for performance passed down to Bob without his weakness for whisky I wonder? The pulpit is, after all, a raised platform not unlike a stage, smaller but no less demanding of our attention. The programmers of the television and radio stations hold Bob in high esteem because of his ability to pull in an audience and keep them watching or listening. Bob says that his father, James, also loved reciting Shakespeare so Father Bob's theatrical persuasion has probably been passed on through genes going back for many generations.

When I mention the high regard that the media has for him, Bob says matter-of-factly: "That's the reason why I perform for them like a trained monkey, although the result hardly seems worth the effort sometimes." He stifles one of his yawns and says: "That's it! End of the penny section."

As I walk down the path to where the iron horse is standing I decide that at our next session I will ask Father Bob to tell me a bit more about his father. I smile to myself thinking it must have been easy for his mother not to call him James but find out later that Annie and James had indeed continued the tradition: Bob's elder brother is named James.

## Chapter 4: James 836133

*"Earnings: three pounds, five shillings. And you're gonna tell me he drank the lot."*

It's a sunny Tuesday morning with a light breeze blowing. Ideal conditions for delivering if you've got anything to deliver. The Cauliflower-twins and I are sitting on the footpath in Bank Street, just around the corner from the barbershop waiting for my depot bag: there's only so much mail you can carry in the basket of a bike. I've gone too hard early in the round and will now have to wait for the driver to arrive. There's a milk bar on the corner of Park and Ferrars so I spring back onto the bike and dash around to buy *The Age*. Back in Bank Street, I'm only just out of the saddle and settling down to read the paper when I hear the rattle of a diesel motor approaching. The contract driver pulls up and apologises for keeping me waiting. "I got caught up in the bloody traffic at Southbank," he says with a shrug. We stand around talking for a couple of minutes and then he rattles off with a big puff of black smoke belching out the exhaust pipe.

When I eventually step onto the front verandah at the rectory with the mail Father Bob comes to the door and says that although we haven't scheduled an appointment for today he has a little bit of time to spare. After handing Father Bob his mail, I sit down opposite him in his study, glance at the pile of papers and books all over the desk, and ask, with the subtlety of Inspector Plod: "What can you tell me about your father?"

Bob groans theatrically. Frank lifts his head from the armrest of his chair and studies Bob with a concerned look in his big brown eyes. He jumps down out of the chair and walks over to Bob who gives him a consoling pat.

Father Bob must have been waiting for me because he has a World Atlas that has that well-consulted look sitting on the desk in front of him. He tells me that his father was a Merchant sailor and that he wrote comments in this Atlas, as he served aboard the S.S Corinthian, out of Glasgow, bound for New York or Quebec or some other exotic port. Bob hands it to me as I lounge back in my chair with my right ankle resting on my left knee. Leafing through the Atlas I notice that James was not the first person to write in it: his father held that distinction. He wrote: 'This Atlas was presented to James Patrick Maguire by his father on his 12th birthday, July 3rd 1895.' Later James (Bob's father) inscribed his own name in this atlas/journal: 'Jas. Maguire S.S "Corinthian" Boston. Phila. Portland. Halifax. St John's, Newfoundland. Montreal. Quebec. New York.' My immediate reaction is a feeling of pity. I feel for this man whose life was ruined by grog because at the time he wrote in the Atlas he was obviously proud of all the foreign ports that he had visited. The First World War interrupted a lot of adventures and his was one of them. The last entry in his atlas was as concise as the Oxford Dictionary: 'Returned home Oct. 1916. Joined Navy same date.' James served on six warships during his stint in the Royal Navy but he never wrote in his atlas again.

I have been doing my homework leading up to today's impromptu interview and know a bit about James. As a young man he was a fine musician; he won a prize at school for violin playing and after leaving school he used to play the piano for pints of beer in the local pubs. Family legend has it that his poor old mother was brave enough to go into the pubs to try to haul him out. Rebellious, he tried to run away to sea several times to escape the clutches of his mother.

Father Bob's cousin, Francis, who still lives in Scotland, tells me that he had noticed for years that in the sideboard in his mother's living room there was a broken lock. He says that he offered to replace it, but his mother immediately said: "No. That is to remain. Your Uncle James was looking after Jo (Francis' elder sister) while your father and I got a night out. He broke into the cupboard and stole the one bottle of whisky that your father had put in it!"

'Och weel, whisky dosnae do anyone any good sitting in the bottle,' quips Rene flippantly.

James was 'transported' to the colonies in 1923, apparently succumbing to pressure from his parents and siblings, who were unable to come to terms with his alcoholism. After sailing from the Northern to the Southern Hemisphere, he met and married a girl, named Annie McLaughlin from his hometown of Springburn in Glasgow. However this fairy tale beginning to life in Melbourne foundered. James kept drinking even as the children kept coming. Five children were born during the hard times. The Great Depression could also have been a term to describe the family's circumstances; alongside poverty sat alcoholism, then death sat in on the game and as Father Bob said, swept his family away into the cemetery. Swept them away and erased them! Marguerite Annie was only 7 months old when she died of Meningococcal Encephalitis in 1929. Bob was born on 14th September 1934 at Thornbury so never met his sister with the beautiful name. Kathleen, to whom Bob was devoted, died of tuberculosis in 1946. James, Bob's father, died in 1948, his mother, Annie, followed suit in 1950.

Bob wrote a short piece about his parents not long ago and posted it to his Blog. That's right, Father Bob is a digital priest; you can also find him on Facebook as well as Twitter! He pointed out that his father, Jim, landed in Australia 'just down the road at Station Pier in 1923.' He had travelled the world in the Royal Navy and Merchant Navy for many years. Bob says that his father never got back to Scotland. He writes: 'Jim never did well in Australia. Despite being talented, he had alienated his family and friends in Glasgow. He drank too much.'

Nor did his mother, Annie, ever get back to Scotland. Bob says that he got used to hearing the words: 'The Old Country.' He tries to make light of it by saying: 'Tough thing leaving kith and kin (long before Kath and Kim!).' It's sad though because as Bob says Annie was never seen or heard of again by her family. There were no letters or phone calls because 'Jim and Annie were desperately poor.' There must have been many families affected in this way. My maternal grandparents suffered the same fate. They arrived in Australia from England with two young children in tow four years later than Bob's parents and shifted from house to house during the Great Depression, often doing moonlight flits.

As Frank wanders over to me, Bob says that he has felt hurt by his father's behaviour since he was a boy. He wants to know why his father self destructed whilst his family battled to survive. He yawns and I have to clench my jaw to stop myself from doing the same. As he sits opening the mail we discuss the circumstances that could have brought about his father's downfall. According to one family legend James's ship had been torpedoed during the war and after that he was unable to cope. Subsequent research, says Father, failed to reveal any evidence of this happening. There is no record of any of the six ships on which he served during World War One being torpedoed. We reckon that there are probably lots of reasons for him hitting the grog during wartime, but Bob wishes that he had 'dried out' after he moved to Australia and got married. It can't be easy though, being addicted to alcohol.

Father Bob and I agree to have another session at the end of the week because my 'little bit of time' is up. Frank, with his head held high like some sort of canine butler, escorts me to the door.

"Goodbye, Your Grace," says Father as I head along the path to my always-patient bicycle.

I've usually got Friday on my mind and now there is more reason than ever. Before I know it I'm pedalling along 'the divide' towards

Sts Peter and Paul's Church again. It seems that Dorcas Street has now also become the divide between my 'day job' at the Disaster Centre and my new role as Father Bob's biographer.

Before going through his mail Father Bob picks up a little book from his desktop and flourishes it, waving it from side to side like I used to wave one of those little Aussie flags at the Bendigo Easter Fair when I was a kid. "This is my father's *Continuous Certificate of Discharge*. I showed it to you, but you ignored it."

"No I never did!" I laugh indignantly.

We look through the *Continuous Certificate of Discharge*, a small black book, which is filled out by the Master of each ship that a seaman sails in and which the seaman must carry at all times. It acts as a passport and visa and without it a sailor can't do anything much on shore. Inside the book is an 'Identity and Service Certificate,' with a passport size photograph and his service number: 836133. Next to the photograph there is a space for a thumbprint with the following words: 'Left Thumb Print. Compulsory in the case of Asiatics, Africans and other coloured seamen.'

"You had him on board The Corinthian," says Father Bob sternly, acting the part of cross-examiner.

"Yes. That was my intelligence from Francis," I reply like an indignant witness.

"There's no Corinthian in here," he says brandishing the book again and eyeballing me sternly. "All of the documents for each ship have been stamped with 'Very Good' for behaviour too. You're saying he went off like a bottle of stale milk." He peruses the document. "The Corsican is in here. Maybe he was on the one that rescued the people from the Titanic. What was that called?" he almost barks.

"Gee, I don't know off the cuff like this." Even Rene Descartes fails the test.

"The Carpathian!" he says loudly, as if I should have known it.

Bob continues looking through the Certificate of Discharge at a few notes that his father has made in the back of this little black, dilapidated book, reading out the names of the ships. "Here's the Kowhia. That's the one I told you about. It used to be tied up in the Maribyrnong River."

"Yes. I checked that out but it's gone now."

"That's a shame. We could have made a shrine out of it." Bob extracts a loose sheet that is folded in the back of the book: "Account of Wages. Jimmy McGuire, spelt M-c-G-u-i-r-e. February. Earnings: three pounds, five shillings. And you're gonna tell me he drank the lot."

"I'm not saying that," I splutter. No answer. Bob's mobile phone buzzes and as he answers it I reflect on the story of James. He seems to come across as a two-dimensional figure with a weakness for grog. We are told that he was a good violinist and that he worked at The Herald office as a proofreader after the Great Depression but I can't get any more out of Bob.*

*Four years after this interview, as a guest columnist in *The Age*, Bob elaborates a bit: he says that his father who was a heavy drinker "had to cope with 6 o'clock closing at Young and Jacksons and at the Erica Hotel near our home in Prahran. He was a regular traveller on the number 6 tram from the city to Glen Iris." The adage 'like father, like son' does not apply in Bob's case. In this column he writes: 'Lots of secondary school students in the 1950's had voluntarily pledged to abstain from alcohol either for life or until 25 years of age. My mate Paul and I took the 25 option. We stuck to it, too, which was made easy by being confined to a 'dry' campus at the priest training facility at Werribee. We ended the alcohol zero tolerance phase of our lives with a glass of Porphyry Pearl at Russell Collins Cafeteria. It was an important occasion for me. Don't read too much into this but social drinking and eating at Triaca's Latin, Codognotto's Society and Massoni's were memorable experiences of controlled euphoria. Latin speakers, as we were, took seriously the adage 'in vino veritas.' "

"I'd like to go to Scotland to retrace my father's steps," says Father Bob quietly, after slipping his moby back into his pocket.
"I hope you get there some day. You don't seem to have holidays but maybe you could go after you retire."
Bob is non-committal. Then he says: "We've lost his medals as well."
"What do you think happened to them?"
"Buggered if I know. The other thing that is missing is a decorative plate that you hang on the wall. It was dark green with a cottage painted on it. I often wonder where the hell that went. I think there was a jug and saucer that you sit on the mantelpiece too. That's about all we 'ad," he says. When Bob says 'That's about all we 'ad' I'm reminded of the four Yorkshiremen in a Monty Python skit sitting around their private club drinking posh French wine trying to outdo each other with horrific tales of their childhood poverty. When one complains of having to live in a tiny house with great big holes in the roof, another responds saying his family had to live in a corridor. This is greeted with a groan and

'Ohhhh we used to *dream* of livin' in a corridor!' Eventually one of the Yorkshiremen claims that his family had to live in a shoebox in the road and eat cold gravel for breakfast. Despite making this bizarre connection I feel quite sad for Bob. The melancholy missing medals and lost plate and 'that's about all we 'ad' seem to hint at other things lost or missing in Bob's life.

He sits quietly reflecting and then begins to talk about his beloved sister Kathleen, perhaps the most significant loss in Bob's life. "And then my dear Kathleen fell in love with Ted Whatever-his-name-was, the American marine. There's a letter from him. He was posted from Melbourne to Sydney then wound up hospitalised. He sent back a letter to my sister that said: 'Dear Kathleen, just to let you know I've been diagnosed with TB and I hope it hasn't effected you." Bob slams a book down onto the desk. "She was already dead with it!"

We are still for a few moments then, each with our own thoughts. I don't know what Bob is thinking but I am looking at the photo of Kathleen on Father Bob's mantelpiece and thinking how pretty she was.

"Ted had a marine ring. I remember that," says Father flatly. "They loved getting things off the bloody Yanks." He shakes his head and yawns. "Anything else for today?"

"What about your brother, Jim, what does he do?"

The priest stops tearing open envelopes, looks up, and growls: "I dunno, sits on his arse counting his money I suppose." He says that they aren't very close and only see each other once a year. "We never got off to a good start when we were young," he comments matter-of-factly.

"If it's OK with you I'll ask Jim what he can tell us about your dad."

Father Bob assents and I ride away from the rectory in a sombre mood but it's a lovely sunny day to be out and about and I am soon looking forward to having a beer with Eric after the round.

I contact Father Bob's brother, James M Maguire (Jim) who was born in 1926 and lives in Queensland with his wife Betty, by phone. We talk about Bob for a few minutes and as if in retribution for comments from Bob about him sitting on his arse counting his money, he says of Bob: "He's an elusive character: very slippery." He is proud of his younger brother's achievements though, stressing how hard it was for Bob because of their father's alcoholism. Jim tells me that the family was forced to move six times that he remembers. He says that *Legacy* assisted Annie and her young son and indeed supported them financially, as well as in other ways, right into Bob's years in the Seminary. Not much here, I think to myself. Two short paragraphs. Perhaps it is what's not said, the missing lives lived, that speaks loudest.

Riding down Dorcas Street towards Bob's a few days later, I think about James pinching the bottle of Scotch. Aren't Catholics supposed to forgive those who trespass against them? Francis' mother couldn't forgive the young James for breaking into her sideboard and knocking off a bottle of Scotch for God's sake! Decades later she maintained her anger, wanting the lock to remain broken so as never to forget his betrayal. Or were there darker transgressions for which the lock served as a symbol? Was the sideboard locked because James had previously helped himself? Even so . . .

I am just about to step off the front verandah after giving the mail to Father Bob's secretary when the man himself, with his dog at his side, asks me to come in. The three of us, Bob and I, with Frank in step, troop into the study and sit in our respective chairs. In this second impromptu session Father Bob and I decide to wind up the family side of his story.

"You've got my cousin over in Scotland going like nobody's business," he says with a chuckle. "You know more about my mother now than I've known for seventy-three years." This seems most unlikely. "Francis has done a genealogy study and unearthed family connections that go back to the dark ages. He has done a good job with that."

Frank who is sitting up straight in his chair looks from Bob to me.

"There's another McLachlan involved who we haven't done justice to," says Father Bob, "and that's Jack, who was Annie's brother. He was a good bloke. He was one of the Rats of Tobruk. They fought the Africa Corp, Rommel and his tanks. He brought back a German cap and a rifle cleaning kit, a little metal box with a chain and brushes and oil in it. Now bugger me, I had that around here. I think the police took it, from Barnabus, an ex feral I've been mentoring for years, as possible stolen property.

Barnabus is not the real name of the man who Father Bob has been mentoring but Bob says that he does not want the man's name printed in the biography. Barnabus is a Greek form of the Aramaic, Barnbhuah, the biblical name of a disciple of Paul. This name seems to sit well with Bob.

"God knows where that rifle cleaning kit is now," says Bob. "If you go near the police they can't be bothered." Bob does an impersonation of a copper giving someone the brush-off, then says wistfully: "I'd like it back: Uncle Jack's rifle cleaning kit."

If only there were a way to get it back, I think, as I look at Father Bob.

"I remember that after Uncle Jack came back from Tobruk," says Father, "he used to ride a motorcycle and work at the Fairfield Infectious Diseases Hospital."

"My Uncle Jack had a motorbike too, a Norton with a sidecar," I tell Bob. I tell him about the time in the mid 1950's when I was about 8 years old. We were returning from Rockbank one morning where we had been rabbiting. I distinctly remember Uncle Jack's rabbit-skin motorbike gloves that came up to his elbows. I was in the sidecar with Darky, the dog. He was a good rabbiter, that dog. We were on our way home, crossing the railway crossing in Anderson Road in Sunshine, when Darky spotted a rabbit near the railway lines. He jumped out of the sidecar as we rode across the crossing and took off at full pelt along the railway lines after the rabbit.

"Yeah," Bob laughs, and then he thinks for a while. "*My* Uncle Jack got married late in life to a divorced woman, which was frowned on in those days," he says. "I don't think we went to the church for the wedding. The Micks weren't supposed to attend such ceremonies."

Just the mention of the two words, Uncle Jack, is enough to conjure up memories of the 'What-about-the-time' nature. Father Bob and I swap Uncle Jack stories for a while and I'm about to tell another one about when my Uncle Jack had a job as a shit-carter after the war when I realise what time it is. Strewth! I've been here for nearly forty minutes. It's time to leave. I'll have to pedal hard for the rest of the round, otherwise there will be questions asked when I get back to the Disaster Centre.

"God's speed, your Grace," Bob says as I pat Frank and hurriedly depart.

Speed can be a dangerous thing, I think as I ride along the footpath on the heavy pushbike, especially on the corners. If one goes around too hard one might just end up with a pedestrian on the handlebars, whether it's God's speed or someone else's.

# Chapter 5: Creepy Catholics and the Post Office Fleas

*"This place is infested with Creepy Catholics."*

After leaning the bike against the fence, I take the registered mail out of the bag, check to make sure that my voice recorder is functioning properly and walk up to the front verandah. Father Bob with Frank at his heels opens the security door for me and I follow him into his study. Frank settles himself in his chair and like a chairman opening a meeting looks at me expectantly so I ask Bob about his cousin John who is a Catholic priest in Scotland, now gravely ill. After a brief résumé of his cousin he tells me that the Catholic Church in Scotland is a bit peculiar. "It's always had a very mixed relationship with the Scots, because of the *bloody Protestants!"*

"Maybe the Proddies object to it because it is a *Roman* Catholic Church. The Scots would see themselves as Scots, not Romans, wouldn't they?"

"I dunno. The Roman Connection has been a pain in the arse for 1600 years," growls Father Bob. I straighten up, glancing at the picture of Kathleen on the mantelpiece as I do so. 1946 would have been a hard year for Bob.

"Everyone wants to say that they're Roman Catholics, The Roman Pope and the Roman Cardinals love to describe themselves as the Romans. Here in Australia, we're saying: 'Listen, darling, just forget the Roman thing, alright?" says Father Bob like an old queen. "Just be the Australian Catholic Church. 'Oh, no,' they say, 'you can be the Catholic Church in Australia.' See? That's the Roman thing. It's like the McDonalds franchise. We're all wearing the same bloody uniforms. Now the Scots have to ask themselves what they want. Do they want the Brits down south or do they want the influence of the Roman Pope?"

"Eggs Benedict," I grin.

"Eh?" Father looks genuinely confused.

"The Pope. Isn't his name Benedict?"

"Oh, yes," says Bob screwing up his face. "He can't even use his own name. They like putting on all the bullshit. The Iranians now are wearing suits with no ties. That would do us, suits with no ties. All this flowery bullshit with sticks and hats," he grimaces. "They can't even talk properly. I don't know what they are on about half the time." He waves his arms in a pontifical manner and affects a high-pitched mumbling voice. "Mumble, mumble, world peace, mumble, mumble."

It sounds a bit more like Eggs's predecessor, Pope John Paul. Bob probably hasn't had time to 'study' the new man yet. I laugh at his antics. This sure beats delivering mail and I marvel at my luck at having this opportunity to banter with Bob. Knowing that I still have to finish the round is in the back of my mind, and that's where I keep it too despite snide remarks from Rene Descartes. What has me preoccupied though is Father Bob's mum. We've managed to flesh out James's skeleton (not much meat on the bones though) but what about his mum? Off the top of my head all I can remember about her is that she used to take young Bob with her on the tram to pawn her wedding ring. We can't leave it like that. She's barely a sliver of a sentence, surely there's more to her than that? The problem is that although Father Bob has agreed to have his life story told he is reluctant to tell it! Rather than talk about his early life he simply changes the subject. His brother, James's words come back to me: "He's an elusive character: very slippery." I manage to filch a snippet of information whilst listening to Father Bob talk to John Safran on JJJ one Sunday night. Bob confesses that he kept one of his mother's jumpers for twenty years after she died but Safran doesn't discuss it further which disappoints me.

"Are you going to follow Eggs Benedict's line and conduct the Mass in Latin from now on?" I ask Bob whilst still thinking about how much he loved his mum.

"Nah," says Bob. "You don't have to. It's optional. You can put it on, in addition, for four or five creepy Catholics. This place is infested with Creepy Catholics." One could be forgiven for thinking that he was now on the side of the Bloody Protestants. "You don't know they are there," he says. "They are a bit like fleas in that you forget about them until they bite. All institutions have fleas. Your institution, around the corner, the Post Office, has its fleas. They are irritating, and can be fatally so, if allowed to get control."

Unfortunately, I think, the Post Office Fleas have already taken control. After 'Little Johnny' and the Liberal Party introduced 'WorkChoices' the Post Office Fleas took full advantage. Some of the posties have got bites all over them. I've been flea-bitten too. During the campaign opposing WorkChoices I knocked off work and attended the big rally in the city where we marched to show our opposition. I was put on a 'Code of Conduct,' a pathetic little ceremonial show of strength by the head Flea. There was nothing dramatic, no slashing the buttons off my uniform and drumming me out of the service or anything of that nature. My crime was simply documented and I was then supposed to be a good boy for the next year. The union secretary, Joan Doyle, came out and terrorised the poor old Flea and that was it. WorkChoices has gone now but unfortunately the Post Office Fleas are still biting.

"Who are these Creepy Catholics?" I ask, intrigued.

"I suppose creepy in the sense that they give *me* the creeps. They don't necessarily give anyone else the creeps."

"What do you mean?" I persevere.

"You might go into church and find two or three Roman Catholics kneeling in the pews," Father Bob slowly enunciates the word 'pews' using a high falutin' voice, "and *you* might say: 'that's very impressive' but I'd be saying to myself: 'have they nothing else to do?' Not because they are kneeling in prayerful posture," (posture is pronounced slowly and in a toffee voice) "but I've seen them and I know exactly what they have left behind at home."

"Mmm." My mind wanders then, takes a fork off Bob's track, and again I end up on the path that leads back to his mum. We have even less information about Bob's mother than we have for his father I lament. There is no one back in Scotland to tell us about her early life. What we do have though are two sepia photographs of her, taken in 1946, which would probably have been snapped with a Box Brownie and which I examined last night. There is nothing striking about either of the photos but there is a lot of information in a photo if you look. Both are posed shots. In the first one, twelve-year-old Bob is standing to the left of, and slightly behind, his mum who is sitting on a wooden chair. There is a pool of shadow directly beneath the pair indicating that it was taken close to noon. It's a warm day in 1946. What have you been doing this morning Bob? I recall Bob saying: 'We were all short.' That was an accurate assessment. Bob is wearing dark shorts with a light short-sleeved shirt and a sleeveless jumper. Two short legs poking out of the bottom of his short-pants end in a pair of dark, short socks and dark coloured shoes. He is looking directly into the lens and smiling.

Despite the fact that his mother is wearing medium sized heels, her short legs only just allow one foot to touch the concrete. Her left ankle crosses her right with her foot dangling a few inches from the ground and she is wearing a smock that is tied around the waist; the lower part is open revealing a calf-length dark skirt. Beneath the smock she is wearing a jumper, with the sleeves pushed up. Her arms are crossed in a relaxed fashion on her lap. She looks to be a short dumpy lady with a kind face. Her head is tilted slightly to the right. The sun, which is in front of her and slightly off to her right, shines onto her grey hair and casts a gentle shadow across her face and left shoulder. She is wearing round glasses and is not smiling although she does look quite content. The photographer has positioned them, or they have positioned themselves, at the entrance to the sideway which leads to the back of the house. Bob is standing with his left arm hanging down in line with a down-pipe, which has a saddle-bracket hanging skewiff. His right arm is down behind his mother's chair, which is sitting just forward of the entrance to the sideway, with a high open gate made of palings, hinged to the fence, hanging open. There is a brick, which was probably used to prop open the gate, lying near the fence.

In the second photo, Annie is standing in front of and to the right hand side of Kathleen who is leaning slightly back, with both legs together, against the down pipe. Kathleen, who is about a half-head taller than her mother, is wearing an attractive, flowery summer frock with half-sleeves; it is buttoned down the front and reaches a few inches past her knees. She is wearing white sandals. Her head is tilted somewhat to her right, towards her mother, who is standing straight with her arms hanging down and with her left hand open. Her right hand is closed but her index finger is pointing stiffly downwards. The sun is casting that same gentle shadow across their faces and left shoulders yet leaving their hair shining in the light as they look into the lens. Both of them are smiling. Was it Bob's father who took these two photos?

This is about all we really have on Bob's mother, Annie, a couple of family snapshots where she manages to look happy despite all she is going through. The worst part about this photograph is that it was taken in 1946.

I hope that marrying an alcoholic did not destroy her whole life. There would have been some joyous occasions, especially the births of her children, but well and truly tempered by two World Wars and the Great Depression, not to mention the deaths of two of those children. The Wars and the Depression took their toll on thousands of people who lived through them. Annie's life was harder than most, to and from the pawnshop, and, it would seem, without the support of her family in Scotland. Annie was a God fearing mortal woman who stood by her husband through difficult times. It is sad that Bob remembers so little of her and has no keepsakes apart from these two photos.

"See," says Father, after taking off his glasses and massaging his eyes, as I stumble back onto the track he is carving out, "to *know all* is probably one of the saddest jobs of the Parish priest. You know lots of things. I don't know that much now," he amends, "but we *used* to know because we were knockin' on doors and goin' into people's 'ouses. That was considered to be the great sign of effective Parish priesthood. You knew people. Then Vatican Two said: 'Hey, why don't you get the parishioners to look after one another. They can knock on each others bloody doors and keep tabs on each other much better than you can.' Apart from that," adds Father, "people won't be unnerved if they go to the door and lo and behold the bloody Parish priest is standing there dressed up like a sore toe and the woman has to yell out to her husband in the kitchen to put his stubbies away because the aristocrat has come to visit. Or," laughs Bob, "he might join in the drinking." I laugh as well.

"Post Vatican Two, they said: 'Why don't you go and become part of the neighbourhood?' so a few of the boys did that and I suppose some of 'em went too far, hence the series *Father Ted*, drunk and disorderly most of his life apparently. He was not nearly so chatty and sociable as the *Vicar of Dibley*, the Anglican equivalent."

"Two different outlooks on religion," I say. "Both probably written by a Bloody Protestant."

"Yes," laughs Bob. "The drunken Irish priest and the sober, or socially drinking only, woman priest in the Anglican Church.

"We knocked on doors here, or *tent flaps* when the church first started, until Vatican Two tended to de-clericalise the church. That's what I miss. I'm old now but I wish to God the whole outfit was staffed by laypeople who would be doing layperson-friendly things."

Bob drops that subject as if he has just been bitten by one of the Post Office Fleas and starts scratching at another itch. "You are going to come up against a barrier," he says, "with this biography. There's no story in my life to tell. It's like blogging. Lets say people are interested in the contents of Ron Burrows's left hand pocket. We could go on all day about that because people are so far out into space, cyberspace, that they hunger and thirst for trivia."

"They love it," I say trying to think of exactly what I have got in my left hand pocket: the keys to the green depot bins for my depot bags. "I also think that they will love hearing about your life. Not that it's trivial," I hurriedly add.

"What's this book going to be, a comedy style of thing?" asks Father Bob. "No. I'll start off with a little bit of the Maguire genealogy, which goes back a couple of hundred years, and then…" I don't get a chance to finish my sentence. Father Bob shakes his head and interrupts: "Let's go *forward* 200 years to 2207. What will be the result of what we are doing now?"

"That's a long way off," I say considering what it might be like. "Maybe with global warming going the way it is the planet will blow up."

"Put that in the book," says Bob emphatically. "We've all been blown up and we are all in outer space, as specks of carbon and we are looking at one speck of carbon interviewing another, saying I wonder what it was like back there. What happened, when we blew up in . . .?" Father Bob is chopped off this time. His mobile phone buzzes, so we now know one thing that *he* keeps in his left hand pocket. Unfortunately his little story ends abruptly. Mobile phones can be a curse.

I will have to wind this up shortly and get on with my work, I say to myself, but before leaving I decide to ask Father Bob about 'Open House,' a meals program, which is run by the Church.

Bob willingly changes subject. He gestures towards the rear of the building. "The homeless are being fed in the backyard of the Church as we speak. Now I feel like telling off the old sheila who's feeding them for keeping them waiting outside until ten o'clock."

"What time do they start arriving?" I ask.

"I don't know. I haven't got a bloody clue. They've been coming here for years and they've probably settled for that, but I would have thought…" Father Bob trails off and sighs. "Then again I'm talking from a civilised point of view. If you're going to eat, then you eat at the start of the day but if you have no day and you have no start I don't suppose that it worries them. I just feel for them. I hope we are not institutionalising our care for them. They're in more need of social 'food' too. But maybe they don't want to be social. Why should they be social?" Bob asks. "You've got the mental illness that's allegedly going around. It's a reasonable response to an unreasonable situation." That sounds vaguely familiar to me. Bob could be referring to R.D. Laing's view that schizophrenia is a sane response to an insane world.

"We're driving the poor buggers mad with the way we are living in the big city, a way which doesn't include them," says Father Bob.

"There seems to be a fair amount of conviviality amongst them," I say. "I've seen them out in the yard. It's a social occasion for them, a get-together. It's probably comforting having other people, who are in a similar predicament, to talk to after spending a lonely cold night in a park or shop doorway."

"Yes, they're a bit like your birds," says Bob, "they fly around on their own but once in a blue moon they like to get together and have a chatter. So if we are doing that at least we are keeping people in touch with one another. If they are still in touch with one another they mightn't feel the urge to act outside the herd."

Father Bob must have seen me, on hot days, filling up the birdbath outside his study window after dropping off the mail.

Unfortunately it's time to leave. "I'd better be off, Father," I say reluctantly. "Thanks for your time."

"Alright, Your Grace," says Father Bob smiling as Frank nimbly hops down from his chair and shows me to the door.

As I ride around delivering the remainder of my mail, I replay the interview in my head. This is the second time that Father Bob has mentioned Vatican Two. I'll have to find out all about it. As well, Bob has given me the name and address of two very old friends whom he met when he was a little boy attending Our Lady of Lourdes Catholic School in Armidale. I'll give them a ring when I get home to see if I can arrange an interview, I think as I head up Nelson Road towards the Albert Park boundary of St Vincent Street.

Despite the mundane nature of the job if you don't concentrate it's easy to put mail in the wrong box and I've done just that. I look around to see if anyone is watching me. There always seems to be some bugger watching. I go back, pull mail out of a letterbox and put it in the correct box next door. I always feel a bit of a dill whenever this happens. Concentrating now I ride on, telling myself that it is important that the mail goes into the correct boxes but my mind soon starts wandering. I smile as I think about Father Bob's Creepy Catholics and the Post Office Fleas.

The bike, like an olden days milk carthorse, stops, seemingly of its own volition. I hop off and lean it against the fence to take mail into one of the houses where the mail has to be put through the slot in the front door. There are quite a lot of these along Nelson Road but only along the section where the 'haves' live. Most of the 'have-nots' have letterboxes. I once asked a lady at number wifty wif, who shall remain nameless, if she would mind putting a letterbox on the front fence. She replied in an indignant toffee tone: "We've been getting our mail put through the door since the 1800's!" As I'm walking back to the iron horse a small truck roars past. The little driver, Halfman, sticks his head out the window and yells: "Get on with it you old poof!" I laugh and wave, wondering if the lady heard him before she shut the door.

I smile as I continue my 'stage.' The Cauliflower-twins are keeping me amused. Ronny is on about fleas and wombats. Rene, always looking for a connection, notes that wombats have fleas but otherwise ignores Ronny, methodically picking and flicking his way up the street, pleased that he has set the round up in a more efficient way today. Later as we turn from Dorcas Street into Ferrars Street Ronny loses interest in wombats and fleas, pointing out my reflection in a shop window as I ride past. Descartes who only had eyes for the next letter in the bundle until now dredges up the wombat from his home in the past: he recalls that it was the wombat that became a flea! Rene also makes a connection between the wombat and a postie who everyone called Blurter. I smile as I am carried back to earlier days at the Disaster Centre on the back of Rene's flea.

Rene is a bit like Father Bob; he always has a story to tell from the past. This one's about a manager at the Disaster Centre who everyone called The Wombat. He was a thickset bloke with a walrus moustache that hung untidily over his top lip. His white shirts were immaculate, with knife-edge creases. His trousers were always hanging low beneath his generous gut looking for all intents and purposes as if they were about to fall down. His eyes drooped sleepily as if he might be at his best when no one else was about.

Not long after The Wombat's appointment as head Flea at the Disaster Centre, he arranged for the carpenters to build him a new office upstairs within the confines of the lunchroom. This lunchroom, which doubled as a conference room was a huge window-less area lit by dozens of fluorescent tubes, and was not very popular with the staff. Some of the posties even preferred to eat at their desks. The Wombat had an office built within this room, with windows running the full length of one wall. Through these windows he had a breathtaking view of the empty lunchroom. I don't know what he did up there all on his own, away from the action, but he obviously liked his solitude. As far as anyone knew he lived alone, yet he bought a loaf of bread to take home every day. For some time he was known as The-Wombat-Who-Eats-A-Loaf-Of-Bread-A-Day.

Every Friday morning, any postie who happened to be on light duties because of a work related injury, or who was currently on a programme called: 'Get-Back-to-Work,' had to report to Doctor Wombat's surgery. Sick call was compulsory. Employees had to troop up stairs to The Wombat's office, one at a time, discuss their situation and sign a form, which he also signed. Doctor Wombat would sit back in his chair, a concerned look on his face as each patient's circumstances were discussed. In his impeccable white shirt, he even looked like a doctor. The patients, whilst ridiculing the farcical nature of The Wombat's sick call, didn't mind too much though, because it got them away from sorting for a few minutes. This playacting . . .

Rene stops me as I'm about to shove a couple of letters into the wrong box again telling me that story time is over. He sniffs and says that I should now forget about fleas and wombats and start thinking about the mail 'and which letter goes in which box'. Besides, he adds with his usual measure of logic: 'this story has got nothing whatsoever to do with Father Bob'.

## Chapter 6: Vatican Who?

*"Bob doesn't buck the system; he doesn't buck Jesus in any way.
He has a great feeling for people, especially the poor.
A lot of priests could learn a lot from him."*

"We were not supposed to fraternise with the boys on the trams but I would have felt a total disaster if I hadn't known every boy on the tram." So says Pat Harman with a girlish giggle when my wife, Ladybugs, and I meet Father Bob's old friends. Fairly innocuous stuff, but remember that this was sixty years ago. Pat was not supposed to fraternise with the boys yet she knew every boy on the tram. She not only knew them all she went out with one!

"I used to 'see' Paul Garland who was Dux of the College. The boys on the tram used to dump their kit bags right where you'd fall over them but Paul Garland used to hang on to his case." 'Mr. Goody-two-shoes,' sneers Descartes. Pat doesn't say this brazenly; she says it sheepishly and blushes when she glances at her husband of fifty years. Brian merely smiles.

Paul Garland was Bob's best mate and Pat was Paul's girlfriend. Brian, the man who Pat subsequently married was also Bob's mate. Pat and Brian were friends before they even started school, where they met and became friends with Bob. The dynamics of the relationship changed after Brian and Pat got married and Bob and Paul enlisted at the Seminary.

"I think that was cruel," Pat shakes her head, "to go through school and then go straight into the priesthood."

My wife, Ladybugs, is sitting in an armchair opposite me as Pat tells us a story about their early marriage. Brian and Pat's first house was a great big weatherboard at Dimboola, she tells us. They heard that Bob, on leave from the Seminary at Werribee, wasn't going anywhere for his holidays so they decided to invite him up to Dimboola to stay for a while. Brian went down to the Post Office to ring-up and when he got home he told Pat that they were coming. Pat asked Brian whom he meant by 'they.' He told her that 'they' was Bob and Paul.

"Well! I nearly fell on the floor," declares Pat.

"The old boyfriend eh?!" I exclaim. Ladybugs catches my eye and frowns.

Pat giggles, "What was I going to talk to him about?" It is very easy to imagine Pat as a young woman because she is still slim and has a girlish laugh. She tells us that there was a big *Metters* wood-fired stove in the house but she had not yet used it; the cooking of a roast in honour of Bob and Brian's visit would be the first time. Pat lit up and to everyone's dismay smoked the kitchen out. They found out later, she says, that the flue was blocked.

Pat says that the four of them all got on well together and she remembers how much fun they had just sitting around the kitchen table talking and joking. That's what life was like sixty years ago I suppose. They would have been lucky to have a wireless.

"I used to go to bed when they started doing exorcisms though," Pat adds casually.

"They used to perform exorcisms?!" I ask, amazed. I look across at Ladybugs who raises her eyebrows and opens her mouth in mock horror.

"They were learning about exorcism at the Seminary at that time," says Brian, "and this was before Vatican Two."

Vatican Two! This time Ladybugs glances in *my* direction. I shrug imperceptibly. On the day that Father Bob mentioned Vatican Two for the second time, I told her that I was going to Google it but somehow just never got around to it. She has reminded me a couple of times since but I still haven't done it. It's not good enough really. Ladybugs smiles that little smile of hers that she smiles sympathetically when I stuff up. I nod with the glimmer of a smile that I usually smile after receiving that sympathetic smile, wondering what difference this Vatican Two business had on practising exorcism. Brian seems to be inferring that practising exorcisms would have been a lot easier after Vatican Two. There must have been a relaxation of the rules.

Neither Pat nor Brian is inclined to divulge more about the exorcisms. It will be very interesting indeed to hear about this from Father Bob, if he decides to open up on the topic that is. Ronny is projecting all sorts of visions for my amusement now after this evocative information.

Brian, who hasn't spoken very much, tells us that he had an aneurism in the front part of his brain recently and remembering things is a bit difficult. "It doesn't help," he says grinning. Pat, who likes to talk, keeps quiet for a while giving Brian some thinking time.

He says that although they lived within walking distance of each other he and Bob never became friends until they went to primary school. They used to play cricket out in the street, marking a light post with chalk to use as the stumps and then they'd bowl across the road.

There were very few cars around then so they were able to kick the footy around the street during the winter.

Brian's memory isn't too bad if you ask me. He just takes a bit longer to haul up recollections from the deep: a bit like that fuzzy feeling I get on the morning after a party when the missus asks: "Did you have a good night?"

I nod and smile as Brian recounts his story; however Rene's worried about Vatican Two. He just hopes that neither Brian nor Pat ask me to comment on something pertaining to it. Ronny just chuckles and does a disrespectful impersonation of Brian: 'Ron, how have you and Ladybugs coped since Vatican Two and all the new rules on fornication.' Descartes says primly: 'It must have been a pretty big deal and someone who is writing a book about a priest should know all the ins and outs about it.'

Pat takes up the story and tells us that after they were ordained Bob and Paul went their separate way. 'All good things must come to an end,' was a favourite expression of my father's; it comes to mind now. I'm also glad that Bob had a good mate for all those years; he deserved him, especially after the hard times that he went through during his childhood.

Bob went to Ashburton, and Paul went to St Ambrose's at Brunswick, which Pat says was, "the most *dreadful* place." It must have been dreadful for the young assistant priest because the poor old parish priest had Alzheimer's. He used to keep the money in his wardrobe so Paul and the other curate had nothing to live on. Thinking that I might try to track down Paul Garland and ask him about this difficult time I ask Pat and Brian what became of Bob's mate. Pat says that Paul ended up being parish priest at Kilsyth for many years but suffered a mental illness and had to retire.

According to Pat, Bob's involvement with youth, keeping young kids off the streets, began when he became assistant priest at East Kew. She says that she remembers Bob cramming a VW full of kids and taking them to the football on a Saturday afternoon. He obviously followed in the footsteps of the priest who had taken an interest in him, Father McKew. Brian tells us that Father McKew used to take him and Bob to the football. According to Brian, McKew had a big influence on Bob and was instrumental in him becoming a priest. It came across like that when Bob told me about Father McKew, I suppose, although Bob never said that in so many words.

Not so long ago, Pat tells us, she discovered that her grandmother, who lived well beyond her mother and died at 96 in 1971, had been in the St Vincent's Girls Orphanage at South Melbourne from 1880 until 1891. She was not quite five years old when she went in and was sixteen when she left. One Sunday when they were visiting, Father Bob produced some old records from that orphanage and commented on "how terrible it must have been for people in those days: the dreadful poverty."

Pat looks at Brian and smiles before continuing. "Bob, in spite of all his swearing and carrying on is so compassionate. You go there and people ring the doorbell all the time. He says: "don't they know it's Sunday?" Pat laughs, "He sent Brian to the door once and there were two fellows on the verandah. They told Brian that they'd been kicked out of a boarding house. Bob had to ring up that place on the corner of Spencer and Flinders Street to see if they could accommodate them."

"The private hotel?" I ask.

"Yes, that joint," Pat replies, wrinkling her nose, and Ladybugs laughs appreciatively.

We stop talking about Bob for a while. The poor bugger's ears must be burning. Lunch is ready. As we eat, Pat asks Ladybugs and me about our family and then as we sip our tea she tells us a story about her ninety-seven year-old Uncle who is fond of a couple of homosexuals who live up the road. "Uncle Albert said: 'they are great blokes.' " Pat lets loose her infectious schoolgirl giggle and then gets straight back to the agenda, not giving Bob's ears a chance to cool down.

"It's very hard to get Bob to a plain social occasion, such as this, because he's the only priest I know who works seven days a week. He hardly ever leaves that awful mausoleum of a presbytery," says Pat sympathetically.

"He's all alone after hours too," I comment.

"Just him and the dog," agrees Pat.

"At least that dog's a lot better than his predecessor, the one that nipped me on the bum." Pat raises her eyebrows and says, "Oh?" and Brian laughs. Ladybugs merely smiles: she's heard it all before.

"I thought that he had a housekeeper," I tell them, "and when I mentioned that to him he said gruffly, 'There's no housekeeper here! There's nobody here but me. Just me, and the bloody microwave oven.' "

Brian tells us about the time when he and Bob were choirboys. I recall Father Bob showing me a photo of himself and Brian when they were choirboys. Brian says that he and Bob became part of the St Mary's Boy's Choir at East St Kilda. Bob had a deep voice, Brian tells us, and then when his own voice broke Brother Murtah put him alongside Bob to try to get him to go down low. "I could never get quite low enough," he laughs.

The St Mary's East St Kilda Boys Choir was, Brian tells us proudly, world famous at that time. Choirs came from all over Australia and overseas to various eisteddfods at the Melbourne Town Hall, but the St Mary's Boy's Choir used to knock them off. He says that they used to practise every day. "We even sang operas at the Princess Theatre. It was a fantastic choir and Bob was a big part of that."

"He was in Our Lady of Lourdes Choir too," chips in Pat as she pours another cup of tea.

Before we leave Pat compendiously sums up Father Bob: "I think that he is more of a priest of the people than any other priest we have ever, ever come across. Bob doesn't buck the system. He doesn't buck Jesus in any way. He has a great feeling for people, especially the poor. A lot of priests could learn a lot from him."

\We say our goodbyes. A firm handshake from Brian, and several warm wishes later we are back on the street. After we get into the car, Ladybugs turns to me, gently smiling and asks: "Vatican who?"

I laugh. "Buggered if I know, Bugsy. We'd better Google it when we get home."

# Chapter 7: The Wheel of Life

*"You wouldn't even wait for your mother, who was throwing up in the lake after a night out with the bridesmaids!"*

It is raining and cold as I turn the bike out of Ferrars Street into Dorcas Street, and head towards the church. The water is running off the brim of my felt hat and I pull the top of the bag closed to stop the mail from getting wet. I always leave the Disaster Centre wearing the mandatory bike helmet but as soon as I'm off the road and on the footpath at the start of the round I pull my comfortable felt hat out of the pannier and strap the helmet to the bike rack.

The drought, for all intents and purposes, has broken. Winter has arrived, or so it would seem. Cars squish by, a sound as welcome as the rain. Green parrots are screeching in the eucalypts along the centre of the busy road. According to Eric the parrots haven't always been in South Melbourne. He reckons they flew in from the bush during the drought of the 80's and never went back. They have become city parrots with plenty of tucker.

Eric who is now eighty-four is a quiet bloke who likes nothing better than to sit back with a beer and tell a few yarns. He originally came from a small logging town called Wards River, which is about seventy miles (Eric still talks in the 'old' scale: a bit like Father Bob) north of Newcastle in New South Wales. He left there about sixty years ago. "It'd be a ghost town now," says Eric. There were three sawmills close to the town and two further out in the bush that the town catered for. Eric worked with a mob of blokes cutting logs. They would camp out in the scrub from Monday through Friday and come home for the weekend. A truck would pick the men up and take them out of the bush but if it had been raining and a truck couldn't get in "then it was shanks's pony," says Eric, referring to his own legs and feet. The men would then have to trudge twelve miles back to town after working from dawn to dusk for the previous five days. He says that if it were still too boggy for a truck on the Monday morning they would have to walk back out carrying a week's supply of tucker. I have heard a lot of stories about those days.

"We used to take bully beef and big loaves of bread out with us. If they got mildewy, you'd cut the mildew orf. There was one old fella who used to bake damper in the ashes which was alright." He stops, thinks for a couple of moments and says: "We had a meat safe but the blowflies used to blow in it. I'd boil water and put the meat in and scoop the maggots orf the top."

I smile, thinking about that as I ride the bike up to Father Bob's front verandah for my next interview and have just finished shucking off my wet weather gear when Father Bob steps out onto the verandah.

"I'm going to bury the dead," he says without preamble, "You can't keep the dead waiting." He is dressed in a stylish black overcoat and is adjusting the rake of his pork-pie hat. He could be a punter going to the races. I arrange to meet him at 10.30 the following morning. (I will stick to my usual modus operandi whenever I have an appointment with Bob: work through my morning tea break and lunch break at the Disaster Centre, which gives me time for a session with Bob before delivering the rest of the mail.) Then I wriggle my way back into my cold, wet gear and ride away down Dorcas Street, smiling grimly as I go past a stationary council truck with two workers sheltering in the cabin.

By the time I have finished delivering to the houses in Nelson Road and turn back into Dorcas Street, my fingers are just starting to go numb. Ronny is enjoying riding through the puddles and is philosophical about my plight but Rene is urging me to go faster to improve my circulation. This has happened only once before. My fingers gradually froze up on that occasion last winter until there was no feeling left whatsoever. It is happening again and the drizzle doesn't look like easing. My fingers turn into wooden pegs that poke and probe and I am constantly trying to keep the mail covered, sometimes riding hunched over with my hand holding the letters against my chest like a card player. I never used to freeze up like this when I was younger and fatter and drank plenty of grog. By the time I turn into Smith Street, the last street on the round, I am so chilled that my teeth are chattering. According to St. Paul charity is the greatest virtue of all so you won't hear me saying that I'm as cold as charity! Even my mind is cold. The Cauliflower-twins are unusually quiet. I ram the soggy mail into the pissy little letterboxes that might have just been big enough back in the early 1900's.

Back at the Disaster Centre I run warm water over my hands until my fingers start to tingle. In the car I turn the heater on, run the motor for a few minutes and wait for bliss. I sigh as I pull out of the car park. I've got it easier than some though so I shouldn't whinge. Henri Ser, who works for the Maguire Foundation has started writing occasional 'Street Reports,' giving topical information about life on the streets. He sends them to Bob who posts them on his website in an attempt to bring the plight of the homeless into people's comfortable homes, especially now that the weather has turned cold.

Henri highlights the plight of homeless people in his reports. He is a compassionate man, just like Father Bob, Henry Nissen and *all* the other volunteer and paid workers; this is obvious when he writes about a lady whose defacto had been arrested by the police after he had assaulted her. She was in a desperate state, without food for her young son or herself. 'We gave her, food, money and cigarettes,' writes Henri. Cigarettes! It doesn't surprise me because Henri smokes too. 'It's cold out there,' adds Henri.

The fare that was listed on the **Hope**Mobile's menu on that particular night was: one hundred and eighty toasted cheese sandwiches, two huge pots of leek soup and Irish stew, and hundreds of slices of cake, all made by volunteers. Henri and his crew also handed out five blankets to people who were sleeping on the streets and helped a young family with a two-year-old son get emergency accommodation for the night. Henri again comments on the cold weather. 'Winter is biting and demand is at a record high for the basics: food!' Winter biting food.

It is not only in demand by homeless people either. Before leaving from Sts Peter and Paul's Church on this particular evening a family of four, the parents and two children under five, approached the **Hope**Mobile seeking food. They had just moved in to Park Towers, they said, and had no money. Park Towers sounds like it could be a fancy New York apartment building overlooking Central Park however it is actually a thirty-two storey Ministry of Housing block of flats. Most flats have magnificent views overlooking either the bay or the city. The problem is that because of the height of the windows the residents only get to see the view if they are standing up. It seems a cruel if unintended joke.

Henri says: 'We gave them food, milk, chocolates (non nutritional, but greatly appreciated by the kids) and some money, and told them about the supper tonight at the Church.' He says that at Park Towers and the Dorcas Street flats they were literally swamped by people trying to get the food that they had for distribution. 'It was chaotic,' Henri writes, 'and sad to see people who have accommodation but no food. After leaving South Melbourne the **Hope**Mobile headed down to St Kilda where Henri and his offsiders gave out food in Fitzroy and Barkly Streets, St Kilda. 'We also gave a blanket to a poor soul in Little Grey Street,' adds Henri.

And I'm bitching about having cold hands.

When Father Bob's secretary, Annette, admits me to his study the next morning, Bob is sitting in his chair at the desk wearing the overcoat that he wore to the funeral. It is as if he has just arrived home from the wake. Maybe he has. The electric heater is on too, making the study exceptionally cosy. I'm not going to want to leave here to finish the round I think as I settle into my usual chair.

"I met an old bloke at the funeral yesterday at Ferntree Gully who is ninety-two," begins Father Bob by way of greeting. "I used to deliver his newspapers in Pridham Street, Prahran, when I was a boy. Spencer was his name."

"It's amazing that he remembered you after all these years," I say. My mother's maiden name is Spencer but I don't mention it. Bob is keen to tell his story.

"Yes. It was a full house too. It's a lovely modern church in comparison to mine which is," Bob sits up straight and affects his Shakespearean voice, "bluestone, Neo Gothic, and dark and foreboding on the outside. It's alright on the inside though," he adds as an afterthought.

"This funeral yesterday recalled a few memories from the sixties," says Father Bob, "because a couple of blokes said: 'We used to play in your football team at Ashburton.' I recognised the face of one of them and said: 'Yes. How are you going, Lindsay?' He said, 'Good,' and then commented about the football team saying: 'It kept us orf the streets.' I asked him how many were dead and he mentioned the names of a couple. They would have died because of the grog, over the years. It took 'em a while. Not like nowadays with young people dying from hard drugs. I'm getting a plaque made to put up on that shrine outside. It will say: 'Forgive us our sins as we forgive you yours. We were only in our twenties and we died on your watch." The 'shrine outside' is a bluestone wall that Father Bob had erected in the Church's garden some years ago, as a memorial to those who had died in unfortunate circumstances.

"It's a tragic situation. It must be very hard on their families too."

"Yes! These blokes from Ashburton, though, lived into their forties or fifties and died from the grog. As children they would have only been smoking cigarettes, not dope. It's fascinating, when you've been around for a while, to see these people again. Then there was that bloke who I told you about: Mr. Spencer. His daughter said to me: 'My father says you used to deliver the newspaper to him.' That goes back to '44. I had an afternoon round delivering *The Herald* around East Prahran. The old bloke is still alive: he's ninety-two and I'm seventy-three. I would have been twelve and he would have only been thirty-two then," says Father, amazed.

"It's a good little yarn," I say and then tell Father Bob that I had a paper round once but found something much better when I was about twelve or thirteen: a job helping the milko deliver milk around the area where I now live. That was about forty-eight years ago, I tell him. I used to love sitting up on the cart behind the draught horse. He used to plod around with steam coming out of his nostrils, farting as he walked along and stopping at all the right places (a bit like Luvy, one of the posties, on his walk-round). Des Mitchell and I used to run backwards and forwards between the cart and the houses with either bottles of milk or empties between our fingers, sometimes with three bottles dangling from each hand. I came out of my house one New Year's Day to find Des flaked out on the nature strip with the horse contentedly picking grass nearby. "Deliveries were a little quieter that morning!" I add, noting the connection for the first time: papers, milk and letters.

"Yeah?" says Bob laughing. "Times were different then," and he steers the conversation back to his story: "I started out, as a priest, in the hills in 1960," he says with a faraway look in his eyes as if he is looking into the Dandenong Ranges. "I was at Belgrave which isn't all that far from Ferntree Gully. I remember the old priest from Ferntree Gully was on his last legs at that time. Flynn was his name. So after forty-seven years, I go back there to bury somebody whom I had met in the early sixties."

Bob started out as a priest out in the hills and I was running around the streets delivering milk. Somehow or other we've ended up here today talking to each other. I smile at the random nature of things.

"It is as if it were the completion of a circle," I say.

"The Wheel of Life," Bob says. He then picks up the pages of the Pat and Brian Harman interview that I had given him to comment on, waves them about, and says: "Now, this interview. I've never read such boring shit in my life."

I'm amazed to hear *both* the Cauliflower-twins laughing. "Well you could liven it up for a start by telling me about the exorcisms that you performed," I retort with a smirk on my face.

"I don't remember any bloody exorcisms," Bob growls as he leafs through the manuscript. That's that then. I can hardly pull out a rubber hose and interrogate the bugger.

"Anyhow, be that as it may," Bob says summarily dismissing the subject, "I don't know what you can do about this 'Life and Times of

Brer Rabbit.' You want murders and scams but there's none of that."

"If you are Brer Rabbit, I suppose I'm Brer Fox; I might have to make a tar baby"

Father Bob laughs before moving on to the subject of weddings. He says that he wants Thursday nights off from wedding rehearsals so that he can record his radio show with John Safran, which goes to air on Sunday nights.

"So for the first time in forty-seven years," announces Father, "I might stop taking wedding rehearsals on Thursday nights. I'll do the papers for the wedding, as required by the Commonwealth of Orstralia, *months beforehand*, and I'll do the wedding, but I might have to hand over to you, Ron, to take the wedding rehearsal."

I laugh and say: "As a mobile priest, I'm sure that will be acceptable to all concerned."

"Yes. You can do the wedding rehearsal, following the script that they have provided. It's easy. I can only offer you about fifty dollars for half an hour though," says Bob phlegmatically.

"That's not bad pay."

"Yes, but is it going to be worth the trouble? You'll have to go home first, wash your face and hands and come back at six pm."

"Wash my face and hands!" I splutter. It's an old saying that I haven't heard for years. Parents used to say to their kids: 'Go and wash your face and hands before tea.' "I'll do it for nothing, just for the experience."

"Alright," says Father Bob as if it is a done deal. "Up the aisle they come. You tell them where they have to sit. You should be good at this: you talk to the old sheilas at the front gates. 'You and your father can come up the aisle now dear.' Father Bob sings a few bars of 'Here Comes the Bride.' Up the aisle she comes with fourteen bridesmaids, and a small dog, Ron."

"A small dog!"

"With the rings in pouches," says Bob smiling.

"I take it that this actually happened."

"Yes," grins Father. "The rings were in a little coat with pockets in it."

"Jeeze."

"Now, up the aisle they come. You will say: 'I'm not the celebrant. I'm here tonight just to conduct the rehearsal.' Alright?"

'I'm not the celebrant. I'm the celebrant's postie,' cackles Ronny.

"Yes, that's OK with me," I agree.

"You say: 'Girls, you go there. Boys, you're over here. The dog can stay there.' " Father Bob dramatically raises his voice: "Oh, the dog has run away, out into the street!"

"With the rings!" I laugh.

"Yes, with the rings!"

" 'There's a space in the front seat behind you, Louise,' " said Bob to the bride. " 'Oh my God! Who's missing?' 'Your mother is missing.' We had just started, see," 'We are gathered here today.' What to do? Go on, because it's her wedding? The problem with going on without her mother present is that it could become a bone of contention later. 'You wouldn't even wait for your mother, who was throwing up in the lake after a night out with the bridesmaids!' "

"Did you wait?" I ask as I lean forward in my chair, thinking about bones of contention.

"We waited for forty minutes," says Bob remembering it all as if it happened last Saturday. "It started to get a bit spooky too," he says.

The intercom on Father Bob's desk rings. "That's the dog," he says, "Is that you Olivia?" he asks the machine.'

"Yes, Father," says a metallic voice. Father Bob presses a button.

"You've finally got that doovalacky working!" exclaims the dog-walker from 'Dogs Day Afternoon' as she enters the study. Strangely, Frank does not come bounding boisterously in as is his wont. Maybe the two of them have had a tiff.

Father Bob introduces us and tells Olivia about the biography."

"We are just up to the time when you, Olivia, first came into my life," says Bob who is thoroughly enjoying himself. "That should be an interesting chapter. Ron has got a friend who has just read the story to date and she told him that she has never read such boring tripe in her life."

"Oh dear." Olivia looks suitably concerned.

"So we are going to have to spice it up a bit," declares Bob. "We can let the readers know that Olivia wants to climb the church."

"Climb the church?" I repeat like a well trained cocky. Bob is in fine form this morning.

Olivia, who is slim and attractive, smiles fondly at Father Bob, then says to me: "I really *do* want to climb the church."

"Why?"

"Because it's there," says Bob, "Olivia is a rock climber."

"When would you like to do it?" I ask, as if I can arrange it for her.

"I'd like to do it in the summer as a charity show with a group of climbers," Olivia says looking pointedly at Father Bob who is reclining in his chair.

"Five years," says Bob, "We've been talking about this for five years."

"I've been trying to get Father to organise insurance for . . . " Olivia starts to explain.

"Bloody insurance!" Father Bob thrusts, "This is not . . ."

"Public Liability." Olivia parries and completes her sentence victoriously.

" . . . an intrepid bloody rock climber at all!" Father completes his.

"Well, I don't want you to get into trouble," Olivia says to Bob.

"Oh, isn't she lovely? Just listen to this," says Bob.

"I've picked out the spot. It's such an amazing building and to climb it would be awesome. It's just a matter of setting the project up," Olivia says to me.

"And the dog is also in training," says Father Bob. "Did you notice that he is a bit subdued this morning?"

"Yes, I was wondering why he hasn't come in," I reply.

"Because he got locked out last night by mistake," says Bob. "I dunno how he got out unless he got out through the bloody window. I locked the door and he was left out."

"Frank!" calls Olivia. The dog takes no notice and stays in the hall or one of the other rooms. If he's with Annette in her office she is not about to give him up.

"See?" asks Bob. "He didn't come in here to report like he always does. He says: 'You old bastard.' "

Olivia calls again but Frank doesn't respond.

"During the night," Bob continues, "I heard, 'woof, woof, woof.' I yelled at the dog, 'Frank! Shut up! Thinking that he was in his seat woofing, but the poor bugger was outside 'saying,' 'Hello, I've been left out.' "

"Frank, where have you gone?" calls Olivia.

"Where *has* he gone?" wonders Bob.

"Franklin!" Olivia calls again, giving the dog his 'official' title.

"He's sulking," says Father.

"He must be," I agree.

"It was cold last night too," says Bob adding a bit more atmosphere to the tale. "When I got up this morning I could see him sitting outside staring dolefully through the security door."

"Oh," says Olivia who is preparing to leave. Father Bob says, "Take this bottle of port for your lunch."

"Port! For my lunch!" There are two cockies in here.

"Two children who got married here last February gave me that," Bob says as he studies the label.

"I've never drunk port," says Olivia.

"Well you had better not start now. Wait 'til you get home," he instructs handing her the bottle

"I have to go," says Olivia, "I've got dogs to walk."

"Just have a look at Ron," says Bob. "He's supposed to be out delivering the letters and he's sitting there in the chair as if he's got no further obligation. Have a look at him!"

"'Bye," says Olivia as she leaves. We say goodbye and Bob turns to the subject of the biography.

"I'm saying, Rolando, that there will be a big difference between the biography that you are writing and the one Terry Monagle is writing. Terry will probably be writing a deep and meaningful spiritual odyssey. Now your story could possibly be categorised as light anecdotal entertainment."

'There he goes again with the light anecdotal entertainment bit,' sniffs Rene, 'he could be in for a shock.'

Frank wanders into the room with a rubber toy in his mouth and stops just inside the door.

"What's that he's got in his mouth? Come here, Frank."

"He's not going anywhere near you, Bob." Frank is standing with his head slightly lowered and is looking at Bob as if he were looking over the top of his glasses.

"No," laughs Bob, "he remembers the dark night, outside on his own. Oh, that's the new heavy duty toy that I bought him."

I call Frank over and he comes to me readily enough and proffers the toy which, when squeezed emits a squeak. Bob then returns to the subject of the Brian and Pat interview.

"Brian Harman points out that we used to play cricket in the street. It was only a narrow street so the pitch wouldn't have been very long. We used to play that other strange game of cricket too. Now what the hell was that called?"

"Tippety-runs." Thanks to Descartes I finally manage to answer one of Bob's rhetorical questions. I wonder if Bob knew the answer and was just testing me out.

"Yes, that's it. We had little homemade paper footies too. Brian and Pat have had more things to remember than I have. They've had children and grand children and parent's deaths later in their lives. All mine were gone. I haven't had to worry about parents dying because they both died years ago. Nothing much happened to me regarding family deaths between the age of twenty and fifty, whereas most people at about fifty years old have got daddies and mummies in their seventies who might be just about to shuffle off their mortal coils. Brian and Pat have been through that normal attrition."

"Do you remember all of the things that Brian and Pat talked about?" I ask, shuffling bones of contention with mortal coils and coming up with bones of mortals and contented coils. No wonder that I'm a bloody postie.

"I can remember some of the things they mentioned but not a lot," he says. "I sometimes think that when talking about that whole business about becoming a priest that I should remember some pious reason for going into the Priest Factory. One maybe should shut one's mouth, because one never really saw a burning light for God."

'Father McKew is your man,' says Rene. Ronny agrees: 'Become a priest Bobby, get yourself a big black car, go to the footy every Saturd'y, and forget about the bloody sheilas.'

"Pat says I wanted to be a priest because I liked looking after people. Maybe, in those days, you would have had to go to those lengths to look after people, non-professionally, whereas now there are lots of other ways of being a carer. In secular society there are lots of approved ways. I'm carrying a plastic card now that says I'm authorised by the State of Victoria to work with children. Back then you never had any of the limitations that are in effect now. However the secular needs a heart because it can, itself, be heartless. Do you understand?" Bob looks at me quizzically.

"No, not really," I admit (I didn't sleep too well last night).

'Wake up to yourself,' admonishes Descartes.

Bob then explains further: "It's not its fault. It's the nature of secular wisdom."

I nod sagely but at the same time think: 'I'll mull that over later whilst I'm riding around delivering the rest of the mail.' Rene gives one of his customary sniffs but makes no further comment. Father Bob continues talking. His words are interspersed with squeaks from Frank's rubber toy. It is as if he is making a parody of Bob's conversation whilst not going anywhere near him.

"I was thinking (squeak) about this (squeak squeak) last night. What have we got? There's Open (squeak) Family, Emerald Hill Mission, Spirituality Australia. We've got all of these (squeak) different things.

The truth be known, all of this is (squeak squeak) Catholicism as far as (squeak) I'm concerned. They say: 'Well, why don't you say it's the Parish working with (squeak)-kids?' I say: 'It's because the Parish doesn't want to work with Street-kids. *But* the Parish (squeak) doesn't prevent me from (squeak squeak) working with street-kids." The 'Old McDonald Had a Farm' song starts up in my head courtesy of one of the Cauliflower-twins: A squeak squeak here, a squeak squeak there, here a squeak, there a squeak, everywhere a squeak squeak, Old McDonald . . . "The Peter and Paul's Church parish could have done either one. It should be satisfied as being known as the heart of the neighbourhood." Frank interjects with another loud squeak. Bob smiles like an indulgent parent.

"I would then drag in all the other churches," he says as he watches Frank, "and say: 'we should all be a collective heart. That's a bit hard to do but I'll try it. I'll try to get other churches to admit to the fact that they've got resources that could be put at the disposal of the neighbourhood. Then we'll fall into a fight over theology I suppose. Some church might say: 'Excuse me, but we're not having any dealings with neighbourhood people.' I will then say: 'That's the end of that then.' We are not into that. They can all profess it in their little churches, but they won't share with others. I would have thought that by now we should be able to put a line through all of that and get going again. Together. Secular society needs a heart and we are in a position, after one hundred and fifty years, of being able to provide something in the way of a heart, but anybody who wants to provide a denominationally branded heart for the neighbourhood probably has to get thrown out. Now, you'd better get goin' or you'll get arrested." Father Bob growls.

"That sounds fair enough to me. Thanks, Bob." I draw in a deep breath and exhale as I unwind myself from my chair.

'Father Bob can certainly string the words together,' muses Rene as I walk up the garden path. 'I'd go so far as to call him a monologist,' he adds in one of Bob's fruity voices.

The cold, drizzly weather continues the next day with the Weather Bureau predicting more of the same for the whole week. I'm wearing fingerless gloves that Ladybugs has bought for me. I didn't think they'd make much difference but they seem to be working. My fingers are cold but so far haven't frozen. The gloves might make things a bit more bearable on rainy days and get me through another winter. I'm riding along the footpath in Nelson Road when I see a familiar presence walking towards me. He is walking briskly with his head held high, seemingly taking in all around him. A golden retriever is trotting along beside him. Four dogs bustle along behind them doing their best to keep up. One is a sausage dog, slightly overweight, which adds a comical air to the group. I greet Olivia, who is controlling the pack, and then say 'G'day' to Frank. He gives his tail a couple of perfunctory wags and forges on beside the retriever.

Around the corner, out the front of the flats in Emerald Street, where I deliver mail, a dapper old man in an English tweed suit with a scarf around his neck to ward off the cold wind appears to be talking to himself. As I ride up to the bank of letterboxes, my bike squeals to a stop. The old fella says to me: "I'm just talking to my dearly departed cat." He indicates the cat's bowl with his walking stick. He is a tall, slim gent, with a military-like straight back and a neatly clipped white moustache, the archetype of a retired Major. This block of Ministry of Housing flats is for elderly people who live alone. The old man's cat was his constant companion. I'm immediately reminded of Pepé and Matilda who were sitting on Father Bob's front verandah on the day I started as Father Bob's biographer.

The old fellow's younger brother lives nearby but they are not alike. Not for him the sartorial splendour. He prefers runners, tracky dacks, and worn out old jumpers. He can often be seen in the mornings with a cup of tea or a stubby sitting on a bench outside the flats and is happy with the way things are. 'I've got bugger-all,' he told me one day, 'but at least I'm not living on the streets.' I have nicknamed them the Antonym Brothers.

I say goodbye to the old fella and he salutes me with his walking stick as I ride away. I turn the corner into Bank Street to pick up another depot bag. An idyllic existence you might think but the life of a postie though is not all fresh air and exercise. Most of my working hours are spent inside the windowless Disaster Centre immersed in the fluorescently-lit banter of (mostly) long-serving posties engaged in the otherwise boring and repetitious monotony of poking letters into a green-metal grid. The Cauliflower-twins handle the tedium in different ways: Ronny dreams about getting the manuscript published; Rene sniggers and checks for accuracy as one letter follows another in an endless stream of mail. A natural human reaction to years of such monotony is to make light of it all: larger than life characters fill the vacuum created by the ennui. Ever present, a little madness lurks at the edges as people are up when they should be sleeping and corralled at close quarters when they'd rather not be.

# Chapter 8: Abbé Pierre

*"He had done the right dramatic thing to bring about a fair go for the poor people of Paris."*

"Bring your 'truck' in," says Bob. He is standing in the garden talking to an electrician. I nearly blow a fuse as I haul the heavy postie bike, with its yellow bag of mail, up over the high step in Dorcas Street that leads up the path to the rectory. The high step is the reason why I usually leave it leaning against the front fence.

Father Bob and I both seem to favour Fridays for our talks. When I say 'talks' it is mostly Bob who does the talking, and Rene Descartes is constantly niggling at me to ask some probing questions of Bob, but instead of providing me with the questions at the pertinent time he offers them up later when I am back on the round.

The electrician heads off towards his van. I lean the bike against a pillar of the front verandah, and then we wander inside to Father Bob's study. Frank quietly follows us into the room. I sit in my usual chair. Frank leaving aside the niceties of life comes over and sticks his elegant head into my crotch so that I can pat him. Ronny is wondering what it would be like if humans were so uninhibited and is flashing images onto the screen.

Father Bob is about to speak but I'm too quick this time and ask him about the French priest, Abbé Pierre, whom I'd turned up on Google the night before. I had thought immediately that the Frenchman had a lot in common with Father Bob who raises his eyebrows, smiles and nods his head. I ask him to tell me the significance of this Abbé Pierre bloke.

"Very interesting, Abbé Pierre: The Rag Picker, " intones Father Bob casually. "I read the bloody book and saw what he was doing and thought: 'that's the right thing to do.' It was 1959 or 1960. He had done the right dramatic thing to bring about a fair go for the poor people of Paris.

"Abbé Pierre said to them, flatten the model flatter than a pancake, because all the people living in rooming houses, out of sight and out of mind, are as much made in the image and likeness of Jesus Christ as the president of France or the Archbishop of Paris. He said to these poor buggers: 'On Good Friday all the Christians will be going to church and crying their bloody eyes out over crucified Jesus.' He said: 'It's no good going to church on Good Friday, praying to Jesus when in fact you don't even know what he looks like: your Jesus. I'll show them crucified Jesus!' So he blew a whistle and all the people living in Housing Ministry houses and all the people living under bridges came out in public into Paris. 'We'll show them crucified Jesus *because*, as often as you do it to the least of my brethren you do it to me.'"

Father Bob smiles again and says quietly: "I thought: 'that's nice; I like that.'" His voice rises dramatically now and he says: "Now that did me for another 40 years," and he slams a book down on the desk.

"Maybe you could pull a stunt like that."

"I could never do it in a thousand years," he says. "You've got to have a different bloody gift. I've never had anyone follow me in the last thirty-three years."

"I don't really believe that."

"Bullshit!" roars Bob, and then he almost whispers: "If there was a follower, my son, I wouldn't be sitting here talking to myself for most of the day. Anyway, I couldn't do it as well," he says in a normal voice, "because if you are French, you can do it poetically and symbolically. If you are Australian, it's got to be practical."

On a freezing cold day in 1954, in a desperate attempt to bring the plight of the homeless to the attention of the public, Abbé Pierre who had forged passports during the Second World War to help the Jews escape the clutches of the Nazis, broadcast the following message over the airwaves: *"My friends help me. A woman has just frozen to death at three this morning, on the pavement of the Boulevard Sebastopol, clutching the document by which she was expelled from her home the day before."*

As I trawled the Internet, reading snippets about this remarkable French priest Abbé Pierre, I suddenly saw him 'looking' directly at me with twinkling brown eyes. To me he looked oh-so-French with his wispy beard and his dark beret raked slightly back and to one side.

"Has Abbé Pierre had as big an influence on your life as God?"

"I'm not so much a God man or an Abbé Pierre man in this regard, except to read about things and then get on with it. I think the idea came from the womb, or a Scottish sense of repression of being badly dealt with by the English. I'm not much interested in redeeming the past. I'm more interested in the future. I know that you want the history for your book. Then you'll be after the dirt: 'he picked his nose in school' and things of that nature."

"I don't want dirt," I say smiling.

"There isn't any dirt anyway. I was immaculately conceived," says

Father Bob grinning.

"I don't think your mate Abbé Pierre was. He had a couple of mistresses." Ronny appreciates this; I can hear him chuckling.

Bob looks at me and wags his index finger, "*Late!* Late in life, *Ron!* That's enough of that. Enough of that thank you." I laugh and Ronny wonders why Bob thinks it was alright for him to have mistresses late in life. Maybe he thinks that Abbé Pierre was going senile at that stage of his life. In which case, senility can't be all that bad.

This brings out another story from the irrepressible priest.

"That reminds me of Archbishop Milingo who was here a number of years ago. The nun who lives over the road, Sister Eugenia, said: 'Can we have Archbishop Milingo visit us because he's good at driving out the devil?' So I said: 'Alright. He's in Australia at the moment. I'll invite him over.' He came and drove the devil out of here one Sunday. They all fell over, rolling around on the floor. It was good fun. I fed him in there." Bob indicates the dining room and I picture him carving the Sunday roast as Archbishop Milingo mops the sweat off his shiny black brow after his exertions in the church. "After he had gone I thought: 'That's nice, I know an Archbishop,' then lo and behold, it turns out that he gets excommunicated from the Romans because he falls in love with Mrs. Moon."

"Mrs. Moon?"

"Yes, the founder of the Moonies! He was the one. Now how could I end up with Archbishop Milingo in that room?" Bob bangs his hand down hard on the desk again and raises his voice a few decibels: "Santamaria sat there at that table and had lunch. He was supposed to be the arch-bloody-conspirator of anti-modern Catholicism."

"Was Milingo approved of by the Pope to perform exorcisms?" I ask, much more interested in the colourful Archbishop than Bob Santamaria, whose whingeing voice had always irritated me in the past.

"He didn't have to be approved of by the Pope," says Bob, "because he was a Bishop in his own diocese, which means he was the officer in command. The way they got rid of Milingo was by luring him into discussions in Rome where he probably put his foot in it. He should have just shut his mouth. They had evidence from people saying that he danced around in his own church and that he drove the devil out. The Africans have been driving the devil out since day one," Bob says dismissively with a wave of his hand like Milingo exorcising his devils.

Descartes is cynical. He tells me that someone like Archbishop Milingo would have been handy for Abbé Pierre. He could have driven the devil out late in life. Ronny chips in now; he has always had an interest in religion and was very interested in the articles that I Googled last night. He says that the Holy Father was furious when he learnt that the 71-year-old Archbishop had married a 43-year-old Korean acupuncturist named Maria Sung at a ceremony officiated by the Reverend Sun Myung Moon. Ronny says that the Pontiff summoned the old fellow to Rome and drove the devil out of h*im!* After all Archbishop Milingo was committing bigamy when he married Maria Sung, says Ronny, because he was already married to God. Pope John Paul II said that Milingo could keep his 'job' if he renounced his missus and went into retreat in Argentina. Interviewed at the Lusaka airport after this sobering episode he told reporters that the Maria Sung story was closed. He said that she should be satisfied with seeing him on television or in the newspapers. "I am not a common bread. I can't be consumed by one person," he said.

"The new churches in Africa are all driving the devil out," continues Father Bob. "There will be more churches and Christians in Africa soon than anywhere else in the world. It's the same in Latin America, but we white Anglo Saxons are not keen on demonstrably driving the devil out. We prefer alcohol. So instead of getting exorcised you go to the pub and get pissed; or go to the races and get fleeced."

'Some of us do both,' sniffs Descartes.

"The Greeks have drama: they get release through drama. It's called catharsis," says the erudite priest. "The Mediterranean people do it one way with their vocabulary, the Africans do it in their own inimitable way, and then the British say, (Bob sucks in his face) 'Oh, I don't like the sound of this.' How are they going to drive the devil out, Ron?"

Father Bob doesn't give me a chance to answer. "They'll do it with national hubris," he says. Then he quotes William Blake:

*And did those feet in ancient times,*
*Walk upon England's mountains green?*
*And was the holy Lamb of God*
*On England's pleasant pastures seen?*

"That's the way they drive the devil out," he says, "by saying that they were there in the beginning: the greatest chosen people on earth."

At this point, Father Bob Maguire decides that it is time to terminate the interview. "Come on, Ron, let's get out of here. It's nearly 12 o'clock. I've got to go to Mass." He then yells out to Chris Apostolidis waiting in the 'wings'. "Chris! Throw Ron out of here! Throw the bugger out!"

Chris comes into the study with a grin on his face. Bob sighs and says quietly: "I'm tiring myself out. I had a terrible dream last night." He becomes distracted as he looks out the window and watches someone walk up to the front door. Looking down he starts sorting through some papers on his big desk. Frank wanders into the room and comes over to me. I sit there patting him for a while. Seventeen years earlier his predecessor bit me on the arse, in the driveway, right outside this very room. It's funny the way some people stick to the same breed of dog, often all their lives. Why do builders like to drive around with blue heelers yapping excitedly in the back of their utes? Why does Bob like big black poodles? I look beyond the window, to where we had been that day, and see a gargantuan ginger cat with a bushy fox-like tail. He is lying near the tap where the birdbath used to be. A starling is sitting on the branch above the cat warning his mates. He is safe for the moment but a bird has only got a small brain and a cat has got the patience of an undertaker.

"The sheila in the coffin woke up during the funeral," says Bob suddenly.

"What?" I exclaim, aghast.

"In my dream."

I snort, say goodbye to Chris and Bob, and make my way to the door with Frank following me.

Easing the bike down the big step, I ride off down Dorcas Street and turn into Nelson Road. It's a glorious, sunny day, the mail is light, the bike creaks along and with the help of Ronny I'm soon in another fuzzy daydream.

## Chapter 9: Love and Best Wishes

*"I don't advertise on the street that I'm Jewish;*
*some of my clients are Muslims!"*

A warm northerly wind is blowing as I ride into the Disaster Centre, happy to be finished work for the day. It doesn't seem all that long ago that it was winter. After tethering my friend to the bike-shed fence I clock off, then slide into my car and drive down to the beach at Port Melbourne to meet Henry Nissen outside the kiosk in Beaconsfield Parade. When Henry arrives we sit on a seat outside the kiosk and talk as we watch the motley masses passing by. The Port Melbourne foreshore is a magnet for the weird and wonderful alike. The first subject is boxing. I sense Rene Descartes shaking his side of the brain but I remember watching Henry The Hustling Hebrew during the late sixties or early seventies on Channel Seven's 'TV Ringside' with the rotund Ron Casey calling the fights and Merv Williams commenting.

"We were only short-arsed little bastards," says Henry with a grin as he refers to himself and his brother Leon. Adept at the Marquis of Queensbury rules, the identical twins fought all comers. With Henry on one side of the amateur pyramid and Leon on another, they battled their way towards the peak. Comparisons were made; there was speculation and anticipation. Henry wouldn't let it happen. He left his brother to box scientifically and clinically on the left and split to the madness on the right, joining, the hungry, the vicious, and the bloody. As Leon became the amateur champ, Henry, fighting under the ring-name of Hammering-Henry-the-Hustling-Hebrew, battered his way to become the Commonwealth Fly weight champion and blames fight promoters for failing to get him into the ring for a promised world-championship bout. "The bastards let me down," says the little bloke bluntly.

Descartes becomes impatient with me: 'What's all this talk of boxing and fighting got to do with Father Bob? You are supposed to be interviewing this man about the role he played in the advent of Open Family with Father Bob.' Ronny chips in saying: 'It's got plenty to do with it! It's part of the panorama, from a champion boxer to a street worker, to Father Bob's most trusted disciple.'

Henry tells me that after he retired he was at a loose end so he started working the streets to help street kids whose own families, for one reason or another, had failed them. He heard word on the streets about a priest who had started a 'family' for street kids in South Melbourne. Henry says that he liked the concept so he teamed up with Father Bob and another of Bob's disciples: Brother Alex.

In 1978, after that early start in South Melbourne, Father Bob opened a youth hostel in a boarding house in Fitzroy Street St Kilda. Along with Brother Alex and the newly recruited Henry they moved to Grey Street St Kilda opposite the Salvation Army. "We ignored each other," says Henry of the Salvos as I study his battered nose. "We used to get into a lot of trouble when we first started. We were mavericks. The police were always hanging around the place. We were looking after kids, as we'd find them. If they had nowhere to live we'd take them back to the hostel. The proprietor usually had a few rooms to spare for the kids. For many years," says Henry, "we had a number of volunteers helping the Open Family and it worked well until it became such a big operation."

"Did it become unwieldy as it expanded?"

"Yes. Eventually they got their own Board of Management and the Board runs it more like a business now. Father Bob still does whatever he can though to help Open Family."

"You work for Emerald Hill Mission as I understand. Why did you leave Open Family, Henry?" I ask loudly as another wave of traffic passes. Fine grit is blown into the air.

"I left after nineteen years because the age limit of those we were working with was twelve to eighteen years, but these people were coming back to me for help in their twenties, thirties and forties. Poor old Father Bob was left holding the baby after that because Brother Alex had gone years before. After leaving I joined Emerald Hill Mission," Henry says, "which was set up by Father Bob about eight years ago, to help *anyone* who needed help in the area of Port Phillip. I was then able to continue working with these same people who kept contacting me for help. Father Bob has lived a selfless life for all these years," expounds Henry, "and he's done it through the vehicle that he loves: the Catholic Church, which has helped him set up and do what he wanted to do. Money is the biggest problem. The poor bastard is now trying to find money for three organisations," says Henry shaking his head, "Open Family, Emerald Hill Mission, and the Maguire Foundation. Maybe I should have become a Rabbi and done the same thing," Henry grins.

"The plight of the underprivileged seems to take up most of his time and thoughts," I say to Henry as I absently watch wind-surfers, being towed by colourful parachute-like kites, scud across the bay. Ronny is jabbering about boxing. I've also got Father Bob inside my head too. He groans characteristically and says: 'This is boring shit.'

"Yes," agrees Henry, "Father Bob has got this new thing going on the side now called 'Beyond Care' for people who are never going to make it. They are going to go in and out of gaol for the rest of their lives or they'll die of drug overdoses, and we've had our fair share of that happening over the years with the young as well as the old."

"God! Maybe Father Bob thinks that I'm never going to make it."

Henry laughs uproariously as another wave of traffic barrels toward us.

"Why do you say that?" he yells as we are lifted up by the roar and then dumped back into the trough between waves.

"A couple of years ago he gave me a cheque, drawn on the Bob Maguire Foundation, for Christmas. I mentioned it to a postie, Luke Madden, at work. His response was: 'You didn't cash it, did you?' 'Of course I cashed it,' I replied, 'Why wouldn't I?' 'You mongrel,' he said. He told me that they would have had to shut the soup kitchen down for a week because of me. I didn't know what the Bob Maguire Foundation was. I thought that it was an account where he kept his personal stash. I remember him sitting at his desk in the study and writing out the cheque and signing it with a magnificent flourish."

The Hustling Hebrew laughs again. With the kites in the background, I watch the wind tugging at his short beard and wonder about *his* cauliflower computer. During a fight there would have been more signals flashing than at the Battle of Trafalgar. With the left side controlling the right side and the right side controlling the left and Ron Casey in the background, "a left, a left and a left again by Nissen," describing the battle it must have been chaotic yet the Cauli' did it with aplomb. Henry has been fighting under a different name now for over thirty years working the streets helping the street kids: 'The Angel of the Street Kids' says drily: "I don't advertise on the street that I'm Jewish; some of my clients are Muslims!" His mobile phone rings for the second time and he shrugs in my direction as he responds to its persistent pinging. Terminating the call with what could well be a trademark phrase, he talks about the work that Open Family undertook: finding refuges for kids, fending off sleazy drug dealers, attempts at rehabilitation, and encouraging kids to take up sport through the RecLink Competition to keep them off the streets. "When the kids got into trouble with the law," he said, "we'd go to court and talk up for them, when they got locked up we'd go and visit them in the gaols or the youth detention centres. We used all our drive to help them in any way we could." Henry laughs. "Bob would say to me: 'Go out and get me some money, Henry.'"

"How did you manage that?" I ask, thinking that it certainly sounds like something Bob would say, typically blunt and to the point.

"Because of the popularity of TV Ringside I became fairly well known to boxing fans. I was invited to talk at sports clubs and other places; I would agree to do so, on the condition that they make a donation to Open Family," he says. "It was an arrangement that they were all happy with."

"It must have been thirty years of worry, doing this type of work."

"No, it wasn't stressful for me, Ron. I will do anything to help people in a positive way." Henry tells me that he does regret the impact all his late nights have had on his wife and kids though.

"I try to get home on time to help my wife but I'm a miserable failure," he says shaking his head. The strong wind buffets a group of lycra-clad cyclists and a car horn toots a warning.

"My poor wife is a wonderful person and an angel," Henry says as he watches one of the riders gesture at the driver. I look again at the magnificent profile of a nose that has made a fair bit of contact with leather.

"I'm sure she understands." I smile.

"Yes she does, but her usual response is: 'You bastard! When are you coming home to help.'" 'You bastard!' is said with feeling and I glance sideways at the passersby.

Henry answers his mobile phone again and talks to someone about a client who has re-offended and is now back in gaol. He terminates the call with his trademark signature and surreptitiously checks his watch.

"We'd better get going or you'll be late for dinner."

Henry laughs and we stand up. He leaves me with that same curious signature that he uses on the phone and then he strides purposefully away towards his car.

It all becomes too much sometimes.

'It's time to get up,' says Rene. Ronny is still dreaming about a late model Jag' and wondering how he can get the money to buy it. I'll ring up the Disaster Centre a few minutes before six and scratch myself from today's lineup, get up and have a leisurely breakfast and drive over to see Father Bob later this morning.

Not long after I arrive at Bob's another one of Bob's 'disciples,' Wayne Neilson, enters the study. Frank politely jumps down to offer him his chair as Father Bob announces him:

"Here's Wayne Neilson, one of Australia's best workers. Wayne is a street worker for Open Family."

Bob introduces us and tells Wayne about the biography that I am writing, "It's all bullshit, but here's the first chapter for you to read," says Bob. "It's a secret classified document. You can leak it if you like."

Fishing around in his desk drawer he produces a stamp and pad, then stamps the document CONFIDENTIAL in red ink and hands the pages to Wayne. He then picks up the mail from the desk, opens an envelope from City Link and drones out loud like a judge reading from a charge-sheet: "driving a vehicle in a toll zone when that vehicle is not registered in respect of that toll zone.' It's that bloody thing hanging under the rear vision mirror!" he exclaims, "One-hundred-dollars. The bugger fell off; it doesn't stick on properly; it slips off and then slides under the bloody seat."

"The miserable swine gave me a bloody parking ticket at 11 o'clock at night!" Wayne sounds as if he is talking to one of his mates in the pub. "I'm gonna go in and see them and say: 'is this the way you repay us for giving up our bloody Friday nights to help homeless people?'"

Rene gasps and Ronny laughs.

"You'll be arrested. Forget that," says the larrikin priest who has just paid a fine to Sergeant Ritchie for going seven kilometres an hour over the limit on the freeway "We want someone to drive the bus up and down Flinders Street. We were on the telly the other night. The next day we should have had the bus, with the face on it, travelling up and down Flinders Street." Bob's voice rises dramatically, *"or St- Kilda-bloody-Road!* Surely there are thugs out there who are safe enough to drive the bus up and down the street. If you want money you've gotta go out and get it."

The bus in question tows a trailer with a billboard attached depicting a giant beaming Father Bob on either side.

Wayne volunteers to take it out. "Where is the bus?" he asks.

"It's in the back-bloody-yard." Bob says in a high-pitched, mock, exasperated Aussie voice. "Don't take it under the bridge either," he orders. Bob is referring to the low Montague Street railway bridge where many a truck or van has come to grief. Vans have been turned into convertibles, with the tops peeling back like sardine tins, in a matter of a few grinding, splintering seconds when their hapless drivers have ignored, or not paid attention to, the flashing red lights and warning signs.

"I'm going to St Kilda now. Can I take it there?" asks Wayne, his shoulders jerking spasmodically.

"I don't care where you take it, darling," says Bob.

"I'm looking for that pregnant prostitute that I brought in. Do you know the one I mean?" Wayne's shoulders jerk involuntarily again.

"No, I don't look at prostitutes," says Bob quietly.

"You gave me the money to feed her and buy things for the baby. I went to her house the other day," says Wayne. "Her husband had her by the hair and was punching her in the face. I grabbed him, threw him down the bloody stairs and called the cops."

Frank looks at Wayne as he speaks. He turns with his head cocked to one side, looks at me, then turns and slowly walks out of the room. I grin and sit quietly. Descartes sniffs and tells me that I am supposed to be an interviewer and not a spectator at a show. 'Why don't you ask some appropriate questions?'

"If only the Board of Management of Open Family would work in with us," says Father before I can think of one. "Instead of organising worthwhile projects to help the poor, the Board is going to fart around until the wheels fall off and Open Family goes broke. Now the Board of Emerald Hill Mission has suspended Henry Nissen."

"Have they?" asks Wayne incredulously, his facial muscles twitching and one shoulder jerking.

"You know what he is like. He kisses and cuddles the sheilas," says Father Bob.

"He kisses and cuddles me!" Wayne exclaims, laughing.

The Cauliflower-twins are bickering. Ronny says that I should just sit back and enjoy myself as I take in the show. Rene says: 'Bullshit!' and asks me why I don't tell the others about the love and best wishes. Father Bob has launched into the next act:

"Mrs. Bloggs from Dandenong has lodged a complaint. After delivering a bed, Henry asked: 'would you like to try it out before I leave?' This is vintage Henry Nissen. He's saying it with a wry smile but everyone jumps to conclusions saying: 'We know what is going to happen next,' but with Henry Nissen it doesn't happen next, but who in the world would believe it? They won't. I believe it. That's the world in which the poor buggers live though. They'd get me if they could."

"I don't think they'd do that," I chip in.

*"Yes by God! Don't talk shit!"* Bob yells, venturing further into the milieu of posties and street workers. "They'd set me up in five minutes."

"Tell Ron about Henry's diary," laughs Wayne.

"Yes," Bob chuckles, "his big thick diary that keeps falling to pieces. If you ask for a number though he'll find it, despite being too scared to put it down for fear it'll fall to bits. He prefers to do things the old fashioned way."

"He's got the most famous of sayings too," says Wayne laughing.

Bob and Wayne chorus: "Love and Best Wishes." I raise my eyebrows and manage a chuckle.

"He hugs and kisses you and says: 'love and best wishes and then he takes off." says Wayne.

Bob adds: "And at the end of the day's play he always says: 'I must hurry home or my wife will throw my luggage out into the street. He's been saying it for thirty years. I used to believe him. Henry lives for drama: it's a film going on within a film in his head. He's gotta have drama. Now he's working on the wharf to feed the kiddies as well as working under cover for Emerald Hill Mission's clients without the ute. And without pay."

"After all the years he's put in," complains Wayne.

"Yes," Bob raises his voice again, probably hoping that Annette doesn't hear Wayne, "but you know as well as I do that some of us can become corrupt!"

"Too right!" exclaims Wayne.

"Now if Henry were a lesser person he would have had a nervous breakdown. He suffers though. I know he suffers, the poor bugger. They have negotiated his resignation. The Board wants a new man. None of this kissy kissy business. No more: 'excuse me would you like to play football against Odyssey House?' " Bob explains: "He runs around picking people up from, let's say, the middle of a bank robbery or somewhere saying: 'Can you drop that rifle? We've got to play footy in a few minutes.' 'Oh, alright says the young bloke as he pulls off his balaclava.' And off they go. This new boy, though, will do things in a different way. This new boy will not be able to 'learn' Port Melbourne, South Melbourne in twenty years," declares Bob emphatically. "Henry knows their children. He knows their fathers. And because he was a champion boxer he's got enormous collateral with them," he adds.

It's time to leave Father Bob because he's due in church for midday Mass. I shake hands with Wayne and invite him over to my place the following Sunday so he can tell me about his life as a street worker, working for Open Family.

A couple of days later, I see Henry crossing Montague St, heading towards the church to see Father Bob. I speed up on my bike and head him off. Still straddling my friend I shake his hand and tell him that I'm sorry to hear about him losing his job.

Henry shrugs. He doesn't actually mention Mrs. Bloggs from Dandenong of course. What he does say is that the members of the Emerald Hill Board disagreed, in some cases, with the way in which he carried out his duties.

"It was stressful for the people I worked with. I drove them crazy because I was on the go all the time," he tells me. "My boss was always saying do this, or don't do that, and of course I kept on *not* doing this and *doing* that."

I laugh as I dismount and lean my bike up against the brick fence. Henry would make a good postie.

"Eventually they asked me to resign, which I reluctantly did," says Henry. I still help people when they ring and ask for help. The only difference now is that I'm not getting paid for it. I'm still working on a voluntary basis for the RecLink Comp too but now I'm looking for a job." The ex-boxer says this with a courageous laugh.

"It sounds as if the Board has done the dirty on you," I say. What I actually *think* is that the Board took advantage of the minor indiscretion with Mrs. Bloggs to force Henry out. Wayne's words come back to me: 'After all the years he's put in.'

"No, they haven't done that," says Henry. "I respect both Open Family and Emerald Hill Mission and I've told them that I'm available to come back and work for them if they should ever want me."

I nod my head but I'd rather shake it. I'm with the indignant Wayne on this one. There's too much love, too many best wishes, and too much turning of the other cheek for my liking. Bring back Hammering-Henry-the-Hustling-Hebrew, I say. Henry smiles bravely. "I know that I have to pull me head in," he says, "because who's going to want to hire a fifty-nine year old has-been? I've got casual work on the docks and I'm thinking about getting a job in the mines in Western Australia."

I visualise Ron Casey sitting at ringside. Merv Williams says to him: 'Henry is like the boy with the pushcart: he's got the job in front of him.' I wish him luck and give him the mail for Father Bob before clambering back onto the sweat-wheel.

"Love and best wishes," he says with a grin as he walks up the path to the rectory.

# Chapter 10: The Peanut Farm

*"The paramedics gave him a jumpstart and he was back with us."*

Wayne and I are cruising the streets of St Kilda looking for young prostitutes. There are ladies working nearly every corner of the back streets of this bayside suburb where it's hard to get a good night's sleep. Cars slowly drive by doing laps. Their occupants are either in the market or just perving. I feel decidedly uncomfortable as Wayne slowly motors past a woman whose hair is as long as her skirt is short standing under a streetlight.

"Too old," he declares. I have a quick look. The lady looks to be in her early twenties. He's a fussy bugger. He's only interested in the youngies. I slide down further in the seat.

There's a full moon hanging over 'The Peanut Farm,' a nature reserve where boys and young men sell their bodies to the sleaziest scum of the city. Wayne eases the car into the kerb and turns off the motor. We sit quietly, not speaking, as if even the noise of the motor ticking will frighten the players in this drama. All is quiet down on the farm though. Not a soul to be seen. I sigh heavily, just wanting to get away from here. Wayne starts the car and we drive away.

We turn into a side street off the main drag. A young girl, maybe fifteen years old, stands nonchalantly on the corner. Across the street, in the shadows, a man is leaning on a wheelie bin watching. As Wayne drives past, the man shifts his weight from one foot to the other and makes a show of looking the other way. Wayne parks the car, gets out, and as he walks past the man he greets him. The man doesn't answer, just shuffles his feet and looks away. Wayne walks over to the girl, chats to her for a minute and then hands her one of his Open Family cards. He tells her that he is a street worker and that if she is ever in any trouble to give him a ring. "Even if it's two or three o'clock in the morning," he says. It's then that I remember that Wayne has an age limit to contend with. He's there to help street kids from the age of twelve to eighteen. I can't see why there has to be this age limit; it's a barrier. What if she had been nineteen? What would he have said then? 'Sorry sweetheart you're too old?'

We drive back into the bright lights and park near the Gatwick Private Hotel in Fitzroy Street. The Gat is an Art Deco rooming house with a marble staircase that dates back to the 1920's. There were over six hundred rooming houses in St Kilda fifty years ago, but the well to do have taken over these properties and turned them into trendy apartments. Middle class and wealthy people use the term 'gentrification' to justify this displacement of poorer people.

Three Kooris are sitting on the footpath out the front, drinking and making a lot of noise. Just around the corner is Father Bob's **Hope**Mobile, with a picture of his cheerful face on the side. In a sense this is Open Family Australia rendezvousing with the Maguire Foundation. Wayne is part of Open Family whereas the **Hope**Mobile is a part of the Maguire Foundation.

We are in the main street of St Kilda with a lot of traffic going by but a ringtail possum comes down the trunk of a small tree near the gutter and hops over to the Kooris, looking for something to eat. One of them feeds it a morsel and it turns and climbs back up the tree.

I've got a two day growth and I'm wearing an old pair of jeans and a windcheater with a bit of grease on the back, courtesy of the bonnet catch on my car; my elastic-sided boots are down at the heel and scuffed. Father Bob advised me to dress to suit the occasion. 'You will be entering the milieu of the street people so you should dress accordingly.' Henri Ser is the man in charge of the bus and there are a couple of other men helping him. It's quite a social occasion. There are about a dozen or so people around the food-van. The bloke at the window dishing out the tucker is a popular man and obviously well known to the regulars. His name is Jerry, and just like the Post Office Flea at work of the same name, is referred to as 'Geriatric.' There is a lot of banter amongst the homeless people; they remind me of posties. My appearance must be acceptable because one of the workers outside the van offers me a container of fruit-salad. I would like some but knock it back. It just doesn't seem right to take their food.

I hunker down next to a couple of blokes drinking coffee near the brick wall of the building. One of them, Snake, was released from gaol in New South Wales a few days ago, he tells me. His nose is tattooed, as are his cheeks and forehead. He is an epileptic and suffers from type-two diabetes, so the poor bugger hasn't got a lot going for him. A couple of days ago he had a seizure so his mate AJ, a skinny little bloke with a wispy beard, rang for an ambulance but by the time it arrived Snake was clinically dead, he tells me. AJ says: "The paramedics gave him a jumpstart and he was back with us."

Snake is wearing a hospital bracelet with his medical status on it. "Just in case," he says with a shrug.

Henri is handing out chocolates as we leave. "Courtesy of the wharfies," he grins.

"We were selling shitloads of drugs," says Wayne. We are heading west, not far from the Westgate Bridge and he is telling me about his early life before he became an outreach worker for Open Family a few years ago. "I was also smoking a fair bit of it and as well as getting ripped I was ripping off me stepfather too!" he says gleefully. "I ripped him off something bad, mate," he laughs. His face twitches and his shoulders jerk spasmodically as he talks giving an animated effect to his driving. He tells me that he was drunk, on speed, and on a motorbike when he slammed into a bus at Wollongong that shot through a stop sign. He was left with a forty percent loss of brain capacity and the spasmodic facial twitch and shoulder jerk. One night many years ago when he was about fourteen he was loitering in the streets of Albury, disillusioned and lonely, wondering where he could go for a sleep. For a while, after he left home, he used to go into the backyards of his friend's houses as it got dark and make enough noise for his mate's parents to hear him. He says that, without exception, they ignored his predicament.

Wayne can remember a man with a gruff voice, who was sitting in the shadows on his front verandah, calling out to him. The Koori invited him in and gave him a bed for the night. The next morning the Koori said to him: "We can't afford to keep ya full time but ya can live 'ere for a while then we'll send you to Auntie Myrtle. She'll look after ya for a while, and then send ya on to Uncle Albert. You'll be looked after." I smile involuntarily as I recall Pat Harman's Uncle Albert and the homosexuals.

In all, Wayne says, the Kooris kept him for a year but he got restless and took off for Sydney. Back on the streets he stayed at a church for some time before being picked up by the police. He had been told that the church doors close at 9pm and that if he were late returning he would effectively be locked out. It was Guy Fawkes Night and Wayne was at the Albury bonfire having the time of his life when he realised that he was locked out of the church. He 'borrowed' a banana-lounge from someone's back yard and took it back to the bonfire. The police found him snoozing peacefully on it in the early hours of the morning. They sent him to Albury, which is where his parents had been living when he last heard from them. Wayne ended up in a refuge and "that's when my drug dealing career took off," he says with a short laugh. There was a reconciliation of sorts with his stepfather. They teamed up and started dealing drugs from a caravan at the local caravan park. 'The family that works together stays together', sniffs Rene.

The following night the 15-year-old girl rings Wayne just before midnight. He agrees to meet her at the Southern Cross Station where he talks to her for a couple of hours. Most of the money that she has earnt, she tells him, has gone to buy drugs; she has nowhere to sleep. In desperation she has been ringing clients for help.

I ask Wayne why the clients would give her a contact number. He seems to think that it is probably because they want to keep up an association with a girl who is so young and desirable. Wayne takes the girl to McDonalds for a feed and discreetly makes a telephone call to the police. He wants them to pick her up and take her to a refuge. They initially refuse to do so, saying that Wayne should bring her in to the police station himself. He has to ring his manager at Open Family so that pressure can be brought to bear on the recalcitrant police. As the police are taking her away from McDonalds, she looks back at Wayne and smiles.

## Chapter 11: Brother Alex

*"The next thing you know he'll have the bloody Postmaster around here."*

It's a hard slog getting back on the bike after a month on holidays, especially when you are sixty years old. There it is, hitched to the bike-shed fence with a piece of chain, just waiting for me. Or maybe it is lying *in* wait for me. When I get to Father Bob's, I take the mail in and slump into 'my' chair in front of Bob's desk. Frank saunters in too and comes over for a pat.

When you go grey it's usually a subtle business. The grey sneaks up on you and takes you unawares. It's inconceivable I suppose that I hadn't noticed it before but the curly black hair is definitely turning grey. Frank is ageing. He jumps up into his favourite leather armchair in front of the bookcase, stretches his greying front legs out and rests his head on the armrest. We look at each other whilst Bob talks to someone on the telephone about his Collingwood Football Club membership ticket. Frank seems to be studying my features. Maybe *my* grey hair has captured his attention.

After Bob concludes his phone call, I say: "I'd like to write about this Brother Alex character. Henry tells me that Alex left Open Family because he fell in love and decided to get married."

"You'll get nothing out of me about Brother Alex. I haven't seen him for 20 years," Bob bristles. "All I will say is that he retired early due to ill health."

Ouch! "Henry says that he met Alex in the street one day and Alex said he'd never been happier in his life. Henry seems to be happy with his wife too," I add. "He said: 'I certainly couldn't live without a woman. That's why I got married in the first place.'"

Father Bob laughs loudly and says gruffly: "What do you want to know?"

"Did you know that Alex got married?"

"Yes, he married a Maltese woman and took her name as his surname."

Bob tells me that Alex Mc Donald was a Jesuit who was working with street kids from the early 1970's. He says that he saw the good work that Alex was doing on the streets and decided he wanted to help and, moreover, create an organisation in order to support the work. So in

1978 Bob founded what was originally called 'Open Family Foundation.' He says that he decided on 'Open Family' as the name because "family was in vogue even if you didn't have one." Bob and Alex often heard the street kids lamenting the loss of their families, he tells me, so Open Family would be open to all street kids and it would be a family whom they could turn to when no one else would have them. It came to be, as Bob explains, a part of the war-on-the-streets against corrupt police, drug traffickers, and pimps. The homeless kids flocked to St Kilda where they could be amongst their own.

"We decided against having the field workers wear uniforms," says Bob leaning back and yawning. "Because Australians aren't too keen on uniforms. Even the dog runs when he sees that uniform of yours. He says: 'He's part of the bureaucracy. The next thing you know he'll have the bloody Postmaster around here.'" I smile. It's been quite a while since they were called Postmasters. From a dog's perspective they are more like Fleas.

"For this story that you are telling in your book," says Bob, "an opportunity was lost in the early eighties when we began working with a police task force called Delta. We engineered it in that dining room through there and I thought it was fateful then."

A fair bit of business has been carried out in that magnificent formal dining room with its high ceilings, I think, as Archbishop Milingo and Bob Santamaria come to mind. There's a conference table in this study but the important decisions are made sitting on the hand-carved high-back chairs around the big mahogany table in the dining room. The table is long enough for a re-enactment of the Last Supper and the afternoon sun filters through the two stained-glass windows in the northern wall. A beautiful mahogany sideboard adorns the eastern wall but for Bob these trappings of wealthy Catholicism hardly exist. In fact I reckon that he'd sell the lot on Ebay if he couldn't get money for the poor from other sources.

"They said," and here Father Bob adopts a twanging Aussie accent for the role of the policeman: " 'Youse are going around saying that children are involved in prostitution and drugs in St Kilda and we are denying that.' But the publicity was so great that the police, as close to the Chief Commissioner as you can get, sat in the dining room and asked Brother Alex to give them any reason to believe that they were wrong and he was right. In the end they accepted Alex's story and they went away and formed the Delta Taskforce, which worked *with* street kids, not against them," he says with another yawn.

"Yes, I remember the name," I reply, suppressing a yawn of my own. "I read something about it in the letter you showed me from a former street kid. She was writing her memoirs which were tellingly called: 'Margie's Shitful Life To The End.'"

"Margie still keeps in touch," Bob sparks up, "whenever she is short of a quid mainly, but that doesn't worry me. She costs me a quid or two but not much." He rummages around in the desk drawer and comes up with the manuscript: 'Margie's Shitful Life to the End,' and passes it to me whilst he answers the phone.

Flicking through the pages, I re-read snippets of the tragic circumstances of this unfortunate woman's childhood and her tumultuous teenage years.

Margie says that she started taking smack not long after hitting the streets when she went to live in a boarding house. She describes her first hit: 'Another girl had just hit up and I was waiting for her to stick the needle in my arm. After she stuck it in, I felt queasy in my guts and then spewed everywhere. My face felt itchy. I still felt sick but it made me feel like I had never felt before. I felt as if no one could hurt me. How wrong I was. The only thing I didn't like was the sick feeling. I became very drowsy and found out later this is known as 'nodding off.' All my problems were gone.'

We are still for a few moments listening to the raucous wattlebirds in the eucalypts outside the study window whilst we think about Margie's shitful existence.

"I was looking at the dog a few minutes ago and I reckon he's turning grey. He's ageing," I declare authoritatively.

Bob grins, "No, he's not ageing. He's just had a haircut. He's silver and black. They call it blue."

"That makes sense," I laugh.

Frank jumps out of his chair and pads out of the room with his tail wagging.

The Open Family 'cart' trundled along with Bob and Alex working tirelessly but it "hit a ditch in the road that nearly crippled it" according to Bob. Brother Alex was accused of being an accessory after the fact of murder.

"What exactly happened?" I ask sitting up straighter. Frank walks back into the study and lies on the floor for a change.

"A street person allegedly murders her client. God knows what the chain of events was." I think of Margie: another Shitful Life. "Alex knew that she had done the murder and he allegedly gave her money so that she could run away. That was the way that Alex dealt with street people. He gave them leeway until he could convince them to give themselves up. The police were sick of him by then though and it was enough for them to charge him."

"How did he end up?" I ask.

"The coppers dropped the charges. It was too late for him though and it sullied the good name of Open Family. His name had been bandied around in the newspapers. So the charges were dropped and Alex disappeared off the scene and was never seen again," he says as if he has just written 'the end.'

"Why did the police drop the charges against Brother Alex?" I ask reopening the book

"That's the way they operate. If you are a source of trouble to them they charge you and then you are off the scene. Later, they drop the charges, but it's too late. Your reputation has been ruined." "Ruined just like Open Family's reputation," I say, carried along a little too easily on Father Bob's train of thought.

I look across at Frank and inspect his 'blue' coat. If you put your vivid imagination to work, you can see a bluish hue. In my estimation, then, he has gone from black, to grey, to blue: a Coat of Many Colours. Frank is developing a strong religious persona and his purple collar would suggest that he is reaching even great heights.

"With Delta we were actually digging around in the paedophile scene for the first time in my living memory," Father Bob continues, arresting my wandering mind, "because the information was straight from the street kids themselves. Unfortunately most of the cases that went to court were thrown out because the police case wasn't strong enough, so that was the end of that."

Father Bob sums up the stories of those earlier days: "Delta was a memorable experience though," he says glancing out the window as somebody steps onto the front verandah. There is a shrill warning from a mudlark that is strutting around on the front lawn. It flies off still giving out the alarm to all who will hear her. "And a high point that showed that you've got to form a strategic alliance at the street level. It was very impressive. I remember thinking at the time: 'I'm forty-five years of age and I've gone to heaven,' because the street kid could contact the street worker and say: 'my dealer is pressuring me into such and such. The street worker would talk to one of the Delta Taskforce and he or she would then follow it up. The dealer after a while says to self: 'What the . . . ? If I touch this child the policeman is going to come around and knock on my door.' That's the last thing he would want."

"Why on earth, then, was Delta disbanded?" I look Father Bob in the eye.

"The way it was explained to me was that they were recruiting people for the Delta Taskforce from suburban police stations. Now if you take the policeman from Sunshine, the sergeant jumps up and down and says: 'I'm sorry Mrs. Bloggs, I can't come down to the robbery at your house because I've just lost a policeman to the Delta Taskforce which is working with street kids. So after a while the Delta Taskforce was disbanded.

"From then on we deteriorated a bit," laments Bob, "because we'd got used to the support of the government departments, the public, and especially the police force. That wasn't maintained. Therefore we weren't able to perform as well. We had nowhere to go to ask for help. We were reduced to slugging it out in the street. Before long the propaganda turned against us. It was always a bit dicey because nobody loves street children. They are all bloody feral. But if the policeman says: 'Don't worry, this child has been badly abused and we are looking after him and he will be rehabilitated by the time he is thirty', the public will give you a go."

What I would like to know now is: what happened to Open Family after Brother Alex split? I'm not going to find out today though because suddenly Father Bob yells: "Get out! Get out of here! I've got to go to Mass."

A few minutes later, I'm back on the bloody bike in Nelson Road. From the parlour of the priest to the noisy street; now if only I owned that weatherboard house that I like, I could drop in and have a nice cup of tea. I could walk to work in the mornings, and casually stroll home in the afternoons. I'm a few hundred thousand short at the moment though. The other problem is that one third of the dream is missing. The boat has gone. It has been sitting out the front since I first started on this round and now it's gone. Who's nicked off with my boat?

# Chapter 12: You've Gotta Have Two Men

*"The members of the Board all cavorted around like monkeys."*

I now have to find the answer to two questions. The first should be easy enough. I'll simply ask Father Bob what happed to Open Family after the demise of Brother Alex. The answer to the other question will be harder to come by. I can hardly just knock on the door of the weatherboard and ask the owners what they did with their lovely boat: the old trailer-sailer that was a perfect match for the low-slung Citroen which still sits out the front of the house looking somewhat bereft without its mate.

Father Bob is sitting behind his desk waiting for me when Annette shows me into the study. Before he can wander off into the desert with the Jews or get onto one of his other favourite topics I pounce: "Good morning, Father. Can you tell me what happened to Open Family after Alex left?"

Bob fixes me with that 'hello, he's come prepared again' look and says: "Yes. There was only me and one street worker, who I installed over there in one of those white houses (Father Bob indicates the houses on the other side of Montague Street) as his office, left to continue the cause. We were effectively on pilot light because we were under a cloud. I kept it on pilot light because I knew Open Family to be a worthwhile endeavour. I didn't want to stop it because I knew there was a good thing in it, so we kept it going to the best of our ability."

Bob takes off his glasses and massages his head as he recalls the passage of events all those years ago. "I can't remember the exact stages but people came and went, came and went, and we kept using the name 'Open Family' to cover their projects. I was mucking around like that for about a year." Once again, Father Bob rubs a hand over his head and face.

"Then God sent Nathan Stirling from Canberra!" he says loudly and triumphantly. "He was a Christian Brother anxious to get out of school and to do good works with disadvantaged teenagers, so I said: 'Alright you can be Open Family Canberra. A year later he left the Brothers, came to Melbourne and said that he would now like to spend more time with disadvantaged teenagers. I said to him: 'You've been sent by God. You'd better run Open Family because we have hit a ditch in the road.'

He agreed to do so." Bob slams a book down hard on the desk and declares; 'Open Family Chief Executive Officer!'

"We got another lease of life after Nathan became CEO," says Bob "We got about fifteen years out of him. I encouraged him to go overseas a couple of times. We were invited to the United Nations as being experts in this field. Open Family was able to kick in and help pay for this. We got to the stage where we had a few quid. At that stage, we had workers in Queensland, Canberra, and Melbourne."

Father Bob is gradually building up a head of steam and Ronny is looking out the window just like he used to do when he was a kid in school. After my promising start, I still haven't uttered another word! The magnificent sounds of the raucous wattlebirds in the eucalypts make me wish I were in the garden. Rene coughs discreetly and I tune in to what Bob is saying.

"I encouraged Stirling to do a two year course in law, an accelerated course, so he did it and passed well. He was always passing courses and things of that nature, well," says Father Bob smiling. "Then he fell in love and got married. I talked him into taking six months off and copped a thrashing for my trouble. The members of the Board all cavorted around like monkeys. 'We can't have an absent CEO.' I said the other three will run the place. 'No, you can't do that. It's against the rules. You have to have *one person.*' I couldn't get a word in edgeways. 'Get out!' they said. Father Bob says that the Board took over Open Family and elected Ms Sue Renkin to replace Stirling, who went to the Supreme Court as an Associate of the Chief Justice. It's Bob's belief that Ms Renkin was on a $200,000 per annum package.

"So that was nice. They don't like me," Bob says matter-of-factly of the Board. "They eliminated me. Now you know all about Open Family," he says. "There's a fight ongoing."

'Phew!' says Rene Descartes, wiping the back of his hand across his side of the brain. But it's not over. Having a boiler full of steam now, Father Bob chuffs on like Puffing Billy going up a grade.

"The idea right from the start was to go out on the streets; go where they are. Now that's turned into buses that go out to Garden City, St Kilda, etc. but the buses don't go out enough. People don't like to go out. It's dangerous out there. You'll be found out on the street as being inadequate because you're out in their milieu. So instead of coming into your office and having to measure up to you and your culture, you have to go out there and measure up to theirs, like *you* do as the postman. If you start to stand over them out there you'll last five minutes. So you have to become an instructor in street methodology. If they ask me: 'who trains your street workers?' I'll say: 'Ron the postie.' Actually we've got a training manual around here somewhere, which you can peruse at your leisure."

Bob rummages around in the bookcase in amongst the books that are 'filed' higgledy piggledy. "Here it is!" He passes me a booklet titled *On The Road Again – a street workers handbook.* It's a small book with a black-and-white photograph depicting a city lane. The buildings on either side are close together. Although it is only a photograph, I get the feeling of actually walking down the lane towards some steps, like the pan and scan technique of Ken Burns. A pair of closed wrought iron gates awaits me at the bottom. The walkway is dirty and rubbish is scattered near the walls of the buildings. There is an old bicycle, under an old-fashioned coach light, leaning against the wall near a shadowy entrance. Ronny starts whistling 'The Third Man' in my head. I used to whistle it at work sometimes, over and over again, trying to get my mate Spooks to crack. All part of the morning's sledging.

"Does Willie Nelson know that you've called it *On The Road Again?*"

"Yeah, he knows," says Father Bob straight-faced.

I flick through the book. There is a close-up picture of the bicycle leaning against the wall on the inside page. It's an old trundler from a bygone era, with 28-inch wheels and white mudguards, not like the rugged-no-nonsense look of today's mudguard-less-mountain-bikes. At the foot of the page it notes: First Edition 2002. There are quotations in large letters, one per double page:

*People don't care what you know until they know that you care*
*We are not welcome until accepted. Above all expect people to be human*

I like the first one, but am puzzled about the second. 'Expect people to be human.' What else would you expect?

*God grant me the serenity to accept the things I cannot change; courage to change the things I can; and wisdom to know the difference*

I take this to be the street workers' prayer and like it very much.

*You must be perceived as an ally*

I love this next one:

*Don't perform surgery in the dark*

Then it's spoilt by the old cliché:

*Success comes from working as a team*

We hear this type of rhetorical bullshit from Australia Post. The only trouble is there aren't any bloody teams! We have team leaders in charge of groups of posties but they're more higgledy piggledy than Bob's books. All the mail is weighed, counted and calculated. Everyone is timed individually according to the amount of mail he or she has to process and deliver. Unless a postie takes pity on a fellow sufferer and gives him a hand, there *is* no teamwork. It's every postie for himself and bugger the rest.

The last one is a beauty:
*When all is said and done, be sure more is done than said*
There is a rider after this one that I like too:
*(for the benefit of the clients)*
The back cover shows the wall opposite where the bike is parked, with the walkway down to the wrought iron gates. I walk through the gates and back into Bob's study.

Barnabus then enters and a strange conversation takes place:
Bob: "Do you want to get out of here or what?"
Barnabus: "Has that man finished here?"
Bob: "I haven't seen anyone here."
Barnabus: "Hasn't he come yet?"
Bob: "No. My man?"
Barnabus: "Yes."
Bob: "No, he said he'd ring up at half past eleven."
Barnabus: "I thought he would have come here first; the same man who came to my house."
Bob: "No, the story is building up in your 'ead. You've gotta have two men."
Barnabus: "Two men?"
Bob: "One here and one there."
Barnabus: "Oh, yeah."
Bob: "But common sense would say the one who's here would go there."
Barnabus: "No, maybe not, Father. If he's not here then that's not the case."
Father Bob turns to me and gives an explanation of sorts.
Bob: "Here's a man, deprived for the first time in his life of television. On demand. He's hanging out. They turned it orf. There's a notice in the paper here that says: 'Don't panic; we're gonna turn it orf at midnight. He (Bob indicates Barnabus) gets up and turns it on."

Barnabus: "It was on this morning. It went off about 9.30."

Bob: "Oh Jesus! That's been off for 2 hours; I dunno how you've managed."

Me: "He's having a go at you, Barney."

Barnabus shrugs and grins in a placid good-natured way.

Bob: "Why don't you turn the other one on and have a dose of that?"

Barnabus: "No, I don't want a dose of that."

Bob: "Maybe that one's orf too."

Barnabus: "Do you reckon?"

Bob: "Go and have a look, coz I reckon they turn 'em orf when they're on the way."

Barnabus: "Yeah, I think so too."

Barnabus exits stage right.

Father Bob smiles and resumes 'normal' conversation, continuing the story of Open Family. "That was the origin of that map on the wall," he explains, indicating a map of Australia on the wall of the study. There are about a dozen blue stick-on dots, mostly along the eastern seaboard and a myriad of red dots over inland areas. The blue dots are stuck on the areas where Open Family Australia actually operates. The red dots were Father Bob's plan for expansion until:

"In 2002 I said to them: 'This is too slow. We've been around for twenty years. Let's go all over the bloody place like a dog's breakfast. We should have an exponential growth, an explosion of street workers, not desk squires, street workers.' 'No we can't do that. We haven't got enough money,' they said. 'Well, just form alliances.' 'No we can't do that, we don't want to, and we're not going to do it your way.' So one thing led to another and bang! They politically bumped me."

Father Bob's mobile buzzes and whilst he is talking I take out my notebook and try to shape the Open Family fiasco.

My interpretation of events would be, first, that Bob, who founded Open Family, made all the decisions and worked tirelessly on its behalf, suddenly finds that the Family has been inadvertently undermined and its name besmirched by Brother Alex. Secondly, with the help of his street worker, who he installs in the white house in Montague Street, Bob sets about rebuilding the Family and restoring its good name. Thirdly, as this gradually happens, he finds that it grows to such an extent that it is too much for him to run alone so he sets up a Board and hires Nathan Stirling to run the thing but then finds that he is no longer the lynchpin. Fourthly, there is the fight with the Board: Bob wants to expand further.

He wants 'exponential growth' as he puts it. The other members of the Board say that there is not enough money for further expansion and despite Bob's dogged insistence refuses to consider it further, so the Board votes Father Bob out and elects Sue Renkin as CEO. It's Bob's perception that Ms Renkin is on a package of $200,000 per annum to do what Nathan Stirling was doing for an unknown sum and Bob was doing for the love of it. The crux of the crumpet is the honey: the disdain that the one who-does-it-for-love feels towards the one who-does-it-for-honey and who by accepting this honey, in the opinion of the love-of-it man, diminishes the resources available for helping the Family.

I put an asterisk against my fourth point. This does not seem reason enough to sack Father Bob. Maybe there is more to it.

Bob concludes his phone call and I say: "It's a crying shame that after all these years that it has come to this." I close my note pad. "You started Open Family and the Board seems to have ruthlessly taken over without regard to your feelings." Thinking about what I've just said I decide that I'm probably naive: this is the way business operates. 'Business is business and love is bullshit' is an old saying. "It would be good to hear what the Board members think about this injustice," I say, wondering how in the world I would be able to get them to talk to me.

"I'm getting sick and tired of them. I'm seventy-three now and they're all fighting with me. I wouldn't have minded them taking over if they had known what they were taking over. I invented the bloody thing and the inventor's advice should be heeded." Bob sounds like a schoolboy throwing a conniption because the rules of the game have been changed.

"Be that as it may though," says Bob, "I want to make sure before I'm dead, or incontinent, that all of this is tied up so that the Board cleans up the relationship with Open Family and with Emerald Hill Mission."

"That was five years ago. Now that you are no longer a part of the executive of Open Family are you still having trouble with the members of the Board?" I ask.

"Yes. Open Family Australia is now being run like a business," says Father Bob as he takes off his glasses and massages his face, "and the Board and I are currently at loggerheads. They are still farting around in the same way and they've changed the administrative staff to get rid of anyone who was infected by my ideas, and now they've got people who are so bloody businesslike that you can't tell the difference between them and McDonalds. I've told them that they are full of shit. I said that they spend too much money on administration. I'm still doing Open Family work though," Bob adds defiantly, "but I have to call it something else, so I call it the Father Bob Maguire Foundation."

A few days earlier, I sent Bob a précis from the manuscript, called 'A Brief and Colourful History of Open Family', which I intend to send to the Chief Executive Officer of Open Family, along with a letter asking for an interview. Bob has now got the précis in front of him and wants to talk.

"What are we depicting in this précis of yours?" he asks.

"That there is animosity between you and the Board of Open Family," I state firmly.

"Yes, that's true," Bob says,

"But do we have to speak so crudely?"

"I don't think that we have spoken crudely."

"You haven't, but I have. It's me that's doing the talking,'" Bob retorts.

"You've spoken honestly, I would say."

Father Bob smiles. "What about a pious Roman Catholic priest saying nice things, like: 'Father, forgive them for they know not what they do,' instead of 'They give me the shits,' or 'I don't give a rat's arse,' says Bob, as I sit there chuckling. I suppose a lot of people would feel uncomfortable when reading their earlier words transcribed verbatim. I'll give him credit though: he is not asking me to change them. Somehow, I think, I wouldn't enjoy writing this book if Father Bob were pious. Frank looks up at me, then wanders casually over to his armchair and springs up into it. He settles down with his long legs hanging over the front of the seat and his head, with its tongue hanging out, resting on the armrest, looking like a worn out postie who has just arrived home from work.

"After the publication of the manuscript, there will be questions," says Bob, affecting a plummy accent, " 'Excuse me, Father Maguire, but was it really necessary for you to express yourself in such a crude manner when you were talking to that nasty postman?' " His mobile phone is buzzing in his pocket again so this line of thought is interrupted. His humorous mood remains intact though because he talks to someone on the phone about needing "fifteen thousand tins of SPC Baked Beans and Spaghetti to feed the hungry little human be-ans." He concludes his phone call with, "Alright, Your Grace. Goodnight."

We arrange another session for the following Friday. As Frank walks me to the door, he farts. There is no noise but it's enough to make me hold my breath until I get out the door and walk towards my bike. Maybe he's been eating Bob's baked beans. I think of Harry as I mount my bike and head out through the gate and back into the South Melbourne sunshine. Harry was a golden retriever that belonged to the picture-framer in Bank Street. I used to take him on the round with me; with his lead tied to the seat post, he would trot along behind me or run alongside the bike but he was a brainless bugger. I would get off the bike to go into a house to get a signature for a registered letter and he would pull the bike over scattering mail all over the road as he tried to chase after a cat whilst still tied to the bike, or simply got restless and tried to join me on the front verandah. I had no choice but to retire him but for months after people would call out to me: "Where's your dog?"

# Chapter 13: Nathan Stirling

*"Bob's got a charity and I've got a charity."*

Next course of action in the biographical quest is to find out more about Open Family and Bob's involvement there. Nathan Stirling, ex-CEO, agrees to meet to talk about his take on Father Bob and Open Family. To facilitate matters, I send him a chapter from the manuscript that specifically deals with the early days of Open Family and the alliance of Father Bob and Brother Alex.

We arrange to meet outside the Melbourne Town Hall on a blustery afternoon. I had earlier reconnoitered the area and found a coffee shop in an arcade across the road in Swanston St where it would not be too crowded or noisy to record our conversation.

Our order is taken and with the aromatic smell of coffee in the air we get down to business. Nathan makes it quite clear that he has to be careful about divulging confidential information. However he says: "there are things that are just a matter of public record."

I ask Nathan Stirling to talk about his experiences with Open Family from the beginning of his involvement. I ask if he could begin by explaining the structure of the organisation, which I have always found confusing.

"Yes." the solicitor nods. "From a structural point of view, Open Family was founded in 1978 and was set up as Open Family Foundation, which was an incorporated association under the Victorian legislation. As you point out, I came in later," he says. "I set up Open Family in Canberra and with the help of others, set up Open Family ACT Incorporated in 1989. Soon after, Open Family Foundation in Victoria changed its name to Open Family Victoria Incorporated. In 1992, we set up a new entity: Open Family Australia Incorporated and the other two entities ceased to be." Rene is satisfied with this talk of structure and order; he is quietly taking it all in. Ronny, on the other hand, is beginning to fidget; he's wondering about how often the family sits down to dinner together.

Nathan sums up his description with: "It was at that point that I became the CEO." He indicates a sheaf of papers which is the chapter that I posted to him and says: "As a matter of accuracy, where you write about Open Family being open to kids from twelve to eighteen, they were in fact more flexible about it in the beginning and were probably dealing with young adults as well.

"For most of the time that I was the CEO, we used the terminology 'street children' which I suppose parallels how it is often spoken of in the European context where the legal definition of children is under eighteen, so we focused on under eighteen. That's not to say that you don't work with them once they turn eighteen, but I think some of the earlier projects had a broader definition than that. It's quite consistent with what Bob's trying to do now with the Father Bob Foundation, so it's not just restricted to street children," explains Nathan.

"Who was the CEO before you?"

"There wasn't one. Historically," he says, after sipping his coffee, "if we pick up the story . . ." he glances at the sheaf of papers. "Bob says the thing was trundling along on pilot-light after Alex left in '85." I get the distinct impression that Nathan does not agree with Father Bob's pilot-light metaphor. He asks me if I know Chris Apostolidis. Readers will remember meeting Chris in an earlier chapter in Father Bob's study on the day that I was ordained as a Mobile Priest.

"Chris was an important figure, more than merely keeping the pilot-light going," says Nathan. "He put a lot of his time and energy into it. He would remember a lot of the early part of Open Family. That was around about 1985 to 1987. It started back then more as a movement. Bob often talked of it as being more a movement than an organisation. And as you can see, it's historically sort of a quasi-Catholic left wing organisation. Even though it's not formally associated with the Catholic Church, it's obvious that its founding values are very much in accord with the Catholic social justice movement."

Open Family does come across as being left wing I suppose but I don't think the Micks have a monopoly on social justice. I keep these thoughts to myself however as Descartes demands that I tune in to what Nathan Stirling has to say.

"When Open Family first started, there was quite a lot of activity. Alex McDonald was in the public spotlight quite a lot, highlighting the issues. But soon after he left, Chris Apostolidis became effectively the CEO although I don't think they used that term. They might have used Manager, or General Manager or Director. At that time, Open Family had an office in South Melbourne and Chris Apostolidis was running the organisational side of the operation."

"I didn't know that Chris had been involved with Open Family."

"Chris is also a director of the Father Bob Maguire Foundation," Nathan says, "so there are still connections. I was the CEO for quite a long time: 1992 to 2004. Nathan describes how in 2002 he decided to pursue a law degree: "I put it to Bob and the Board in 2002 and the Board agreed; so there was no animosity."

"There was plenty of animosity toward Bob though," I interject. "The members of the Board have definitely dealt him a raw deal." I immediately pick Bob's side of the argument as if I'm the solicitor for the defence. "They politically bumped him, as Bob puts it," I state unequivocally.

"This is more recent times," says the prosecutor calmly.

"Since you left?"

"Yes, that's right, since I left. I resigned in July 2004."

"Were you politically bumped?" I ask.

"No, not at all! And I don't like some of the implications in a couple of places in here," he says indicating his copy of my chapter. I wasn't bumped at all."

"Oh." I compress my lips and hold my own council.

"If they'd said: 'We can't have you going off for two years,' I would have considered my options, but there was no animosity. So I did it," he says simply. "In the first year, 2003, I was still working the equivalent of one day a week for Open Family and, I think you alluded to it in your chapter, there was a group of directory, like the group of operations and administration and so forth. They formed a triumvirate, as it were, and ran the organisation. I think it worked quite alright really."

The use of the word 'triumvirate' is interesting, especially when describing the running of an organisation involving Father Bob, because of its Roman connections. The first triumvirs were Pompey, Julius Caesar, and Crassus (60 B.C). More importantly, it is worth noting too that the idea of a triumvirate running Open Family was Bob's. He described the Board's reaction when he suggested it:

*The members of the Board all jumped up and down. 'We can't have an absent CEO.' I said the other three will run the place. 'No you can't do that; it's against the rules. You have to have one person.'*

Nathan considers for a few moments. "Now come 2004, maybe it wasn't working well. I honestly can't remember all the ins and outs of it. I then moved back to working three or four days a week whilst still doing the law degree. It was just a matter of working around the hours," he says without rancour.

Nathan notes that later that year he left Open Family to take up a position with the Chief Justice of Victoria. When I ask what happened between Bob and the Board and the new CEO, Sue Renkin, Nathan steers clear of the topic.

"They've gone down their own path now, but that's another story I suppose. When I gave notice that I was resigning, we discussed it at length and Bob and I initiated a process for a succession plan. In the end, the Board did their own thing. I don't want to speculate on what they've done."

What happened was that the Board sacked Father Bob and elected a new chairman after Nathan left. Bob was 'boned', as former Channel Nine CEO and Collingwood Football Club Chairman Eddie Maguire (no relation to Bob) might have colourfully expressed it.

"They've subsequently appointed Sue Renkin, as you've noted," says Nathan glancing at the chapter. "She commenced in early 2005 so she's been there just over three years. I've been away from there for four years and don't wish to get into discussing Open Family's performance. The public can judge that. Their financial accounts for the last couple of years are public information so they can make up their own minds," he says. Until Nathan mentioned this, I hadn't thought of investigating their performance.

"Bob is the actual owner of the Open Family trademark," states Nathan. "It's a more recent development. Part of the basis for him registering as the owner, as I understand it, is that he was actually the founder of Open Family. He came up with the concept."

Descartes agrees. He says that it was a brilliant tactical move too.

It is a bit noisier than I thought it would be in the arcade because the voices are echoing and there are the constant sounds of cups, saucers and spoons rattling so I nudge the voice recorder a bit closer to Nathan's side of the table. I'm still mulling over the idea of investigating Open Family's performance since Nathan's resignation.

"Did you remain on the Board after you resigned as CEO?" I ask.

"No, I haven't been a member for four years."

"Bob says he wanted Open Family to have exponential growth and they said to him: 'No we can't afford to do that.' Are their finances fairly limited?"

'That's a *great* question' enthuses Rene. He seems to be amazed.

"When I left, they had significant amount of financial reserves and significant amount of outreach workers." Nathan spells it out: "If you compare what their financial reserves are now, people can make their own assessment in terms of how they are growing or otherwise."

"Yes," I say, looking at Nathan expectantly and hoping for just a little bit more. I reckon that he wants to tell me too, so maybe Open

Family's performance has slipped since he left.

"After I left in 2004, Bob was not elected as chairman at the annual general meeting. Terry Higgins, the Canberra based Chief Justice, was elected as chairman at the end of 2004. He stayed in that role for a year and then in 2005 Phil Ruthven was elected and is still there." I nod and sip my coffee as I listen to Nathan against the background noises which seem to be getting louder.

"Open Family is certainly an interesting phenomenon," he says. "Bob often speaks about it, and he is completely right in my opinion, that it is more of a movement than an organisation. Once you start losing that sense of it, it becomes a slippery slope."

'Maybe that is what is happening,' says Rene. 'And Bob has perceived that it's now on the slide'

"Bob's opinion is that it has become too businesslike," I say to Nathan but Rene is not impressed with this line. He thinks that it could be perceived that I am blindly championing Father Bob's cause. 'You're supposed to be his biographer, not the Counsel for his Defence,' he chides.

"What do you think?" I ask Nathan.

"It depends what you mean by businesslike. In the time I was the CEO we ran it quite professionally," he gives a little laugh. "It wasn't a business in the commercial sense. It was a non-profit organisation and provided great service to hundreds of young people and had very dedicated street outreach workers and was run financially in a very responsible way. When I left, it had significant reserves and a dedicated bunch of people."

"Do they still have significant reserves?"

Nathan laughs uproariously at my blunt approach. He might be more accustomed to the subtle questioning of the legal sector; perhaps he does not expect this kind of question from a postie. Or maybe this is just the question he has been hoping for. I am startled; his raucous belly laugh seems out of character, but is infectious and I find myself laughing along with him. A few people at other tables look our way.

"Do you want me to turn the recorder off while you answer? I ask jocularly.

Nathan is still bubbling with laughter. "You would have to look at annual reports," he says, shaking his head. Then more seriously: "They are public documents. Last year, the current Board must have obviously made a decision to incorporate it as a company so it is now Open Family

Australia as a company limited by guarantee, so they've changed from being an incorporated association to a company. I'd only be speculating why they've done that. There could be a raft of good reasons. Either way, whether you're an incorporated association or a company, you have to provide your annual reports to the appropriate authority and then they're published," he explains, obviously realising that this is not my field of expertise.

"It should be a simple matter for me then to make comparisons between what it was like before you left and what it is like now," I say, hoping that Nathan will make it even simpler.

"It's a matter of public record that they've had financial deficits for the financial years ending 05, 06, and 07," says Nathan, deciding to give me the little bit that I was fishing for. "Last year, 06/07 they had a financial deficit of four hundred thousand and the year before that two hundred thousand." Obviously Nathan continues to follow the fortunes of Open Family in the transition from 'movement' to incorporated association and finally to company.

"Why do you think this has happened after you left them with significant funds?"

"I am not going to speculate on the reasons for that," he says. His legal training breeds cautious responses despite his earlier appreciation of the humorous side of things.

"Father Bob believes that too much money is being spent on administration which obviously takes in the CEO's salary."

"I've seen no evidence of what the current CEO is on," says the wary lawyer, "but, obviously if a CEO is on that amount of money for a non profit company that's got a turnover of two or three million, that's quite interesting," he says with a little laugh. "But that's for the Board and others to say. They are not required to disclose. There's no public requirement to disclose what the CEO is on. And as I say," Nathan qualifies, "I don't know if that is the amount she is on. Most non-profit companies do salary packaging so you'd have to look at how that's packaged. You'd have to ask her that question and she might not want to disclose," he says with another raucous laugh. I join in really appreciating this other side of Nathan's rather dour character. I'm satisfied with what I've found out about Open Family from Nathan; the annual report for 2008-2009 will show whether Ms Renkin has been able to stop the company from continuing its slide.\*

After working in the legal sector for several years, Nathan describes how he realised that his passion was in the non-profit area so he established a new charity.

"You've actually started up your own charity?" I ask incredulously.

Nathan laughs at my amazement, "Yes, Bob's got a charity and I've got a charity."

"What's yours called?" It's a bit liking asking him the name of his dog.

"I'll give you a card," Nathan digs a card out of his wallet and says: "People often misspell it. 'Kids Off the Kerb' it's called. "Initially we are focusing on training and employment opportunities using the environmental and recycling platform."

"That's an interesting slant on things," I say. Quite a different approach to Bob's I think to myself where the emphasis is on giving rather than training.

"It's only been going a few months," says Nathan, "We are looking at doing a few joint ventures with the Father Bob Maguire Foundation. I've had discussions with Bob about that."

We wind up our talk, drink up our almost cold coffee, and go our separate ways. As usual, I am impressed with the help that yet another complete stranger has provided in my quest for information.

As I rock from side to side in the tram, I am swayed into a surrealist reverie: You'd have to dig a big hole to bury a tram I think to myself. The Rock Farmer, one of the posties who was around during The Wombat's reign, used to have a small farm at Rockbank. He bought a tram when they were being sold off to make way for new model stock. He had it trucked up to Rockbank and left in a paddock near his house. The council was not impressed. He should have applied for a building permit, they said. He applied. They knocked him back. The Rock Farmer dug a hole amongst the rocks and buried his tram. "It was the cheapest way out," he explained to us.

*The Annual Report for Open Family for 2008-2009 does indeed show whether Ms Renkin has been able to stop the slide. It would appear that Bob has been a bit harsh in terms of the impact of the Open Family CEO. In the 2008-2009 financial year, when revenue fell by more than $300.000 the organisation reduced its deficit from $125,000 in 2008 to $43,000: an improvement of more than $80,000. However, in that same period "Donations, gifts, legacies and bequests" fell by $500,000. Could this drop reflect Bob's diminished role in Open Family or are there other factors at play? (These figures have been drawn from the 2008-9 Open Family Annual Report.)

## Chapter 14: Betrayal

*"I don't know what I could say to some sheila who's pocketing thousands a year, whilst I've got to try to find money to help people."*

I'm somewhat preoccupied as I deliver the early part of the round. My preoccupation is centred on my recent interview with Nathan Stirling. I have been mulling over contacting someone from Open Family to discuss the rift between Open Family and Father Bob, but I don't want to do it behind his back. 'Betray' is a word I've heard him use a fair bit. It's probably tied up with the Jesus thing. After getting off my bike and shambling down a laneway off Park Street (houses have now been built in the lanes that were once the domain of the night-carts), I stumble on the cobblestones and fall, wrenching my knee.

I sigh as I dismount outside Bob's and then try not to hobble as I walk up the path. When I get into the study I wince inwardly as I sink into my chair. Bob and I make small-talk for a few moments, which is unusual and then as I gently rub my knee I say: "I've been thinking about this business of the Board taking over Open Family from you after you've done all the hard slog to get it going."

"You are obsessed with this, Ron! I don't worry about it anymore. There's nothing I can do."

Obsessed, maybe. I just think that there is more to the story and wonder why Father Bob won't divulge it.

"It's the same with Emerald Hill Mission," says Bob. "I've got cars sitting out in the car park ready to go out to see the poor but I can't get 'em out because 'they' want logbooks and this and that. So the cars just sit out the back tied up with red tape. As the Area Commander I'd like to know how many of the tanks are available to go out into the street."

Father Bob sounds like Rommel gearing up for a big offensive against the Rats of Tobruk.

"If we used all the resources that we had in Open Family and Emerald Hill Mission I wouldn't have needed the bloody Father Bob Maguire Foundation," he growls.

"I'd like to know how this all came about. Who instigated this? Why did the Board take over from you?"

"Because, as I've already mentioned, I threatened them," says Bob. "I told the Board that I was into exponential growth, but they said: 'We can't possibly expand further because we haven't got the money.' I then said that we would have to go out and make the money so that we can do it because that was the spirit of Open Family in the beginning. They all panicked and before long I'm edged out. I waited for about 18 months until such time as I had this foundation going (the Father Bob Maguire Foundation), my third child, and by then I was getting a bit snaky and people were encouraging me to get it going."

I've still got this niggling feeling though. It is as if I've got one more number to get in a game of Bingo. As Bob just said, he has mentioned the disagreement about exponential growth before. I had the same niggling feeling then. There has to be one more number.

"I owned the Open Family trademark," Bob says, like a company director, "but they countered with: 'You may think you own it but you don't own it because we have been using . . .'" Father Bob sighs and doesn't complete the sentence. "Away we go. So I said: 'I'm not going to court over it, I'm telling you that right now.'"

"No, that could have got pretty messy for a man in your position." Ronny has started a film in my head now. I am the prosecutor this time, instead of the defence, in the case of The Crown v Father Bob Maguire, who is sitting in the witness box. He really *does* look like Edward G. Robinson: a stocky man with thick rubbery lips. I've got him dressed in a light grey double-breasted suit. I am wearing a solicitor's gown and a horsehair wig.

"Father!" I bluster, "you have sworn on the Holy Bible to tell the truth, the whole truth and nothing but the truth."

Father Bob is indignant. "I *am* telling the truth."

"Yes. But what we want is the *whole* truth. There is something that you haven't told us."

"Yes. The stalemate lasted from last year sometime until the present," says Father bringing *me* back to the present. "I told them that they could use the Open Family name under licence. I don't want to go around bragging that I was the founder all the time, although I did so at a talk that I gave last week. I said to the audience: 'I was the founder but I have been bumped by the Board of Open Family.'

"It would be nice," Father Bob says wistfully, "if the Archangel Gabriel were to appear before the Boards of Open Family and Emerald Hill Mission and say: 'Do whatever Bob says.' I'd like a strong, global, regional, local, personal operation . . . and I'd like to run it. But, I think that's a fairy tale."

"You as Beatrix Potter," I smile congenially.

"If it were the old days and I was younger, I'd go around there and say to the sheila: 'What's wrong? Let's get this thing going.' Then again, I don't know what I could say to some sheila who's pocketing thousands of dollars a year, whilst I've got to try to find money to help people."

Rene is listening intently. He says: 'Bob has been willing to compromise to some extent. The 'sheila' should now reciprocate. Maybe offer him his job back on the Board.'

To put 'the sheila's' salary into perspective though let's look at the CEO of Australia Post: Graeme John. A union organiser told me: 'that bastard is on nearly three million a year while he chips away at the posties' pay packets." He explained that new employees were now starting at 6.30am instead of 6am thus cutting out their 15% penalty rate for starting early and putting them in the untenable position of working beside, and doing the same work as, posties who are taking home $200 per fortnight more than they are.

'Four 'n' Twenty. Sauce. White maggots. The centre bounce. He's marked the ball at centre half back and roosts it forward with a thumping dropkick. Strong in defence for the Bloods. The people's champion. Then he sticks it to us,' wails the romantic on the right.

'How about this for perspective,' says Rene, dismissing Ronny's theatrics. 'Ladybugs recently completed twenty years service working at Highpoint Post Office. The big-hearted Fleas gave her a voucher for $120 and a muffin for her morning tea as a big thankyou for twenty years services.'

"That's a lot of money," I say, "She's on around $4000 a week."

"It's a sin!" says Bob indignantly.

'Isn't that the way a do-it-for-love man *would* feel towards a sheila whom he believes is doing-it-for-the-honey?' asks Descartes.

"Go and take some photos of her," says Bob.

"Alright," I enthuse, willing to do it for either love, money or honey.

"Hide in the lavatory or somewhere, like the paparazzi," he says with a grin. And then becoming serious he warns: "Make an appointment. Don't stir her up. Tell her that you are writing a book about Maguire. Then I'd say, *if* you are granted an interview, that right from the beginning, she'll start paying out on me."

"I'll send her a letter first to see what sort of reaction I get."

"She probably won't even answer it," declares Bob firmly.

Later, as I ride gingerly along Tribe Street, I greet Flo who is pushing an old shopping jeep heavily laden with newspapers that she is delivering. There are plastic shopping bags full of flattened aluminium drink cans tied to the sides and to the handles. Flo, who has been delivering local newspapers around South Melbourne for forty years, has to travel home to Dandenong on the train with her laden jeep during the peak hour but like an interstate truckie knows the value of a backload. At least the newspapers are gone by then. As we talk she takes out a pouch of *Drum*, pinches some tobacco from the wad with fingers that are black from the newsprint and, with the expertise of a shearer, begins to roll a 'greyhound' between her thumbs, index, and middle fingers. Her pointy tongue darts out like a bluetongue lizard; she runs it along the rice paper sealing the skinny cylinder and then nips a few stray strands of tobacco from one end. After delicately wetting this end she lights up with a bright red *Bic* lighter. Then she sucks in the smoke, turns her head away from me and blows it out in a long luxurious stream.

When smoko is over, Flo sighs and says: "See you later love." With a grunt she pushes the old jeep, with its wobbly wheels, on its way towards the next house. As I pull out another bundle of mail, I sit on the bike and watch her go. She is wearing a Carlton football beanie, a tattered old cardigan, a three quarter length pleated skirt and a pair of scruffy runners. When describing someone as thin as Flo, my mother used to hold up an index finger and say: 'She's like that.' A South Melbourne icon, I decide, as I watch her wedge a folded newspaper between a gate and a fence post. As iconic as Father Bob I further decide as I ride towards the next house.

A few days later, with some trepidation because of Father Bob's words, I write a letter to Ms Sue Renkin, the CEO Open Family Australia, and someone I imagine being anything but an Aussie battler.

*Dear Ms Renkin,*

*I am currently writing a biography about Father Bob Maguire. Bob has spoken at some length about his role in the founding of Open Family, and his dealings and relationship with the Board. I wonder if you would like to contribute to Bob's story by telling me about your involvement with him and with Open Family.*

*Towards that end, I have compiled a précis of my writing about the history of Open Family as told by Bob. It is incomplete without your side of the story and I hope that after reading the précis you might feel like contributing.*

*I can make myself available at any time and place you choose, should you be agreeable. I don't envisage taking up too much of your time: certainly less than an hour.*

*Yours faithfully,*
*Ron Burrows.*

As it turns out, I don't take up any of her time because Ms Renkin does not acknowledge my letter. Mulling it over some time later, I change places with her. She was last seen riding up Nelson Road, the bags on her bike bulging with mail. Meanwhile, the Board of Open Family has just sacked Father Bob Maguire and appointed me as CEO.

'About time you got out of this postie caper too,' sniffs Rene.

The Board has set my package at $200,000 per year. I am happy but Father Bob is ropable. It's a corporate takeover of the movement that he started is the way he sees it. We argue constantly; he is strong-willed and not prepared to alter his perspective on how the organisation should be run. This is not conducive to a healthy blood pressure so in the end we break off relations altogether. One morning, a letter arrives from Father Bob's biographer: a postie named Ron Burrows. He's probably one of Maguire's disciples; I've got nothing to gain by being interviewed by him and much to lose so I don't answer his letter. A reasonable response in hindsight.

After dropping off Father Bob's mail and walking off the front verandah of the rectory the following day, I meet Les Twentyman, a prominent Melbourne social worker, on his way in. We stop to chat and because Les works for Open Family I ask him to reflect on the sacking of Bob from the organisation that he (Bob) founded. I also tell him about my futile attempt to gain an interview with Ms Sue Renkin, the CEO.

"Bob was abruptly and rudely pushed out of Open Family through political manoeuvering by the new administration. They just threw him out!" he says with a shake of his head as if, after all this time, he can still hardly believe the injustice. "There are quite a few workers who . . ." Les shrugs apologetically, deciding on discretion. "It's been very disappointing," he laments. "The senior workers were dedicated to Bob and believed in his cause. It can be a bit disheartening at times too. I might be talking about Open Family at a gathering and someone will say: 'Oh, Father Bob. How's he going?' and I have to say that Bob's no longer a part of Open Family."

'Open Family is not so open you might say,' quips Rene as Les and I part.

# Chapter 15: Chuck A Buck

*"Dancing had real control over me. I had a passion for it and I kept dancing towards my passion."*

"I punched holes through the wall. My blood was pumping through my body. I could have knocked *down* walls that day."

'Holy shit!' exclaims Ronny, his side of the cauliflower working hard.

I'm sitting in an armchair in a modern garret with cathedral ceiling and two skylights set into either side of a gable roof. Chris Apostolidis is sitting opposite me on a two-seater couch, talking. The only other piece of furniture in this remarkable light-filled room is a coffee table. A door from this room leads to a new recording studio.

" 'Bugger youse!' I said to the Board." Chris sighs as he reins himself in and then takes us back to when he was twelve years old and hanging out at Father Bob's gym with his mates. He tells me that he and his mates were a bit on the wild side and used to get into trouble with the police. There was a clash of cultures with migrant parents clinging to the cultures of the old countries and their kids embracing the Australian culture where kids had more freedom.

"How did your association with Father Bob start?" I ask, looking at the large framed Dance World logo on the wall behind Chris. Dance World won an award for the highest selling single at the ARIA awards in 1999.

"A couple of the fellas had met Father Bob because of the circumstances that they were in: they were from broken families and in trouble with the law. I met him through them, in particular my friend Mehmet Kochen, when we were hanging out at the tennis courts and gym, break-dancing and boxing. This area didn't have a lot of things going for young people. Kids had nothing to belong to and that's what Father Bob provided in his presbytery. We were all finally becoming Australians and he helped us to fit in. He was the kind of figure that represented my own dad after he died. One was Scottish and the other was Greek but I saw the same values. He spoke in the same manner, with the same energy. Bob was a cool man for youngsters like me. He was always willing to engage in conversation with you. He made you feel that you mattered."

"Did you get into much strife on the streets?" I ask.

"Yeah, I suppose you could say that. Mehmet and I were borderline cases. I took off from home for weeks at a time and did a few things that I shouldn't have done."

"Did you get into drugs?"

'Where's your badge?' asks Descartes. 'You're starting to sound like a bloody copper.'

"I did, a little bit," Chris admits, "we all did, but I never ended up in a situation where I lost control. A lot of the friends I had died from abusing drugs."

"What do you think held you back?

"Dancing," he states simply. "Dancing had real control over me. I had a passion for it and I kept dancing towards my passion"

"I didn't know that you were a dancer. I thought that you were a builder. You and your mates built this place bit by bit over the years." Chris and a few of his mates *have* been building this place for years. I often used to think as I saw them mixing concrete or lifting timber into place: 'these builders are the slowest I've ever seen. This project is dragging on interminably.' Now I understand why. Chris and his mates are dance teachers not builders. Chris tells me that people who have watched the project develop sometimes ask: 'Do you guys know what you are doing?'

"Yeah, we did all the work ourselves," says Chris. "I'm not a builder. I started off as a break-dancer. At the time when all my mates were becoming drug addicts I had just won the *Countdown* Australian Championship."

"Gee, that's impressive."

"That was a national competition that started after the new trend of break- dancing came out. My crew and I won the Australian Championship and we got to go to the United States."

After arriving home from the United States, Chris says that he talked Mehmet into going to Asia. "I had heard that there was no one doing break dancing in Asia and I wanted to see the world, so at fifteen years of age I convinced Mehmet who was seventeen, to come along with me. We took off and travelled around Asia for nearly two years."

"Were you and Mehmet instrumental in making break-dancing popular over there?"

"Yes. When we first started we were like Martians to them. They'd never seen anything like it but, just as it did in Australia, it all came to an end."

"How did you come to be a part of Open Family?"

"When I got back from Asia my objective was to start an Arts Education Centre, predominantly for Dance. I was looking for a space to rent. Mehmet got a job through Father Bob managing the old World Vision warehouse in Dodds Street for Open Family. I rented an office off him and when I had classes, rented the bigger spaces by the hour. That's where I was introduced to Open Family."

"Is this about the time that Brother Alex took off?"

"Brother Alex had taken off before that. Towards the end, his objectives were completely different to Father Bob's. They had similarities but he had almost become a street kid."

I recall Father Bob describing Brother Alex in similar terms.

"He became the victim," says Chris. "He was there to help the victims and he became one of them."

"That's a good way of expressing it," I offer, somewhat redundantly.

"He went a bit nutty towards the end. His whole philosophy about street kids became a bit," Chris' words trail off as he re-jigs his answer. "He began to *enjoy* the spot that they were in instead of working towards giving these kids a life of their own. The whole idea is: you go *onto* the street to help *them* get *off* the street." That could almost be Father Bob speaking. Chris has the ability to draw his listener into the story in a similar way.

'As long as the listener isn't stargazing at the architecture,' says Rene Descartes.

"But it became a culture," Chris continues. "I think he enjoyed the suffering. It might have had something to do with him being a Brother and that whole suffering process. He was a very clever man just the same but in the end it all became too much and got the better of him."

"That would have been about the time that he was charged by the police."

"Yes. That caused the split between Alex, the Board, and Father Bob."

'Bingo!' exclaims Ronny loudly as he waves his card. At last, thanks to Chris, the whole Open Family saga is becoming clearer.

"What happened then?" I ask feeling pleased with myself.

"Everyone left!" Chris exclaims. "Father Bob was in trouble because the Board and administrators had all bolted. At that time, Open Family still had volunteer street workers and the only one who was being paid would have been Henry Nissen. There was no one left to do any administrative work. Father Bob came into the warehouse one day and dumped a big bag of receipts onto my desk. He explained the situation and asked if I knew anyone who could help him with this paperwork. My wife, Pamela, had worked for an accountant and was working with me at the time so we, in a short space of time, without anyone appointing us, or without much being said, became voluntary administrators. Pamela and I were the only ones there." Chris laughs. "There was my wife doing the accounting and me thinking: "Shit! How do we raise some money for this guy? I can't remember the exact amount but I think Open Family was in the red to the tune of about a hundred G's. Nathan says that I was in control but that's not strictly correct. Father Bob was doing his thing and I was desperately trying to create some kind of capital to get it going. My mind was continually ticking over trying to work out a way to pull him out. I was talking to him and throwing ideas around and a few of them worked to some degree and we ever so gradually got Open Family going again. It then needed people like Nathan who were engaged in the politics of the welfare business. I was only twenty-five and I had no idea. I came from a completely different background. For me it was like: why are you giving money away? This is silly. You can't help people this way. It made no sense to me half the time. You're giving them this money to go to accommodation where all the drug addicts live. Why would you do that?"

"I agree. Why *would* you do that? Did you ask Bob why?"

"Of course. He said: 'They've got nowhere else to go.' I became a street worker then and I think that deep down, Father Bob liked the fact that I was challenging the ideals of Open Family and the way people like Henry Nissen did things. 'Why do you do that?' I'd ask Henry. 'You've got to give them legs. You can't just *give* it all to them. What happens then? How far do you go?' I was talking to kids under the age of eighteen, who were in dangerous situations, because I didn't want them to go to these refuges where Open Family was sending them. I knew, having hung around on the streets as a youngster, that that was where all the drug dealers hung out." Chris, a la Father Bob, launches into a scenario: "This kid has left home thinking that he wants to be free and independent. 'Screw you, Mum and Dad,' he says, because Mum found a joint in his sock drawer or a porno magazine under his mattress and has had a go at him. He leaves home at sixteen, ends up in one of these places and a year later this kid is selling his body at the Peanut Farm. What I used to do was talk to these kids, ask them why they were leaving home. They would give me their stories, and I used to say to them: 'I can tell you where you will be in six months to a year from now." Chris balls his right fist, little finger down and slaps it up and down several times in a piston like motion against the palm of his left hand. "'Do you want that?' I'd say, looking at the kid. I remember one kid: he started crying. 'Call my granddad,' he pleaded. Granddad came and picked him up and took him home. I used to scare the living daylights out of them." We both laugh.

"The way I saw it," Chris says, "it was better to get these kids back with their families rather than place them in the welfare system, hopping from refuge to refuge, where the disease lives. The kids who live in those places are on everything going and they are going to introduce that to any new kid, and in six months," Chris shakes his head and repeats his earlier actions. "The system that was in place just didn't make sense to me."

"What was it that you actually *did* to get Open Family going again? Where did the money come from?" I ask.

"Between us we had a lot of fundraising ideas but where it really hit off was when we got those Lucky Envelope machines. Ken Morgan, the Toyota salesman, was instrumental in getting them into pubs, which was legal as long as there was a charitable interest. We were one of those charitable interests."

"Yes, they had one of those machines in the Railway Hotel across the road. I remember taking mail in and often seeing one old bloke who used to treat the Lucky Envelope machine like a poker machine. Whenever he got a winner he'd buy more envelopes."

"Yeah," Chris laughs. "Money started flowing in then and I was gaining in confidence. I read about a forthcoming tour by Phil Collins in TV Week. He had written a song about street kids called 'Another Day in Paradise.'" Chris picks up a sheet of paper off the coffee table and hands it to me. "When you said you were coming to interview me, Ron I downloaded the words for you." I read Phil Collins's lyrics:

*ANOTHER DAY IN PARADISE*
*She calls out to the man on the street*
*Sir, can you help me?*
*Its cold and I've nowhere to sleep,*
*Is there somewhere you can tell me?*
*He walks on, doesn't look back*
*He pretends he can't hear her*
*Starts to whistle as he crosses the street*
*Seems embarrassed to be there*
*Oh think twice, it's another day for*

*You and me in paradise*
*Oh think twice, it's just another day for you,*
*You and me in paradise*
*She calls out to the man on the street*
*He can see she's been crying*
*She's got blisters on the soles of her feet*
*Can't walk but she's trying*
*Oh think twice...*
*Oh Lord, is there nothing more anybody can do*
*Oh Lord, there must be something you can say*
*You can tell from the lines on her face*
*You can see that she's been there*
*Probably been moved on from every place*
*cos she didn't fit in there*
*Oh think twice...*

"Thanks a lot, Chris. They're moving words," I say after reading the lyrics to the song. "I'm intrigued now. What happened next?"

"I decided to get in touch with Phil Collins. I contacted his touring company and asked if they would be interested in doing something to help the homeless kids of Melbourne. I was playing the executive director without having been appointed. The day Phil Collins arrived for his concert, his manager rang me saying that Phil had agreed to help. This guy asked what we wanted to do. I told them about this idea I had. I said: 'We'll have our people at every entrance with a big bucket and a sign saying: 'Chuck a Buck for the Homeless of Melbourne' and all Phil has to do before he sings 'Another Day in Paradise' is give us a good plug.' Phil Collins did just that and we raised two hundred thousand dollars over four concerts. We gathered up the money after the bins were full. One by one we took them back to the cars, drove back to the old warehouse, and then with everyone there we started counting."

Ronny loves it. He is laughing and says it sounds like a gang going back to its hideout to split up the loot after a big heist.

"I was overseeing the whole thing," says Chris laughing. "I could have been a con artist and a great thief. We had two hundred thousand dollars worth of coins in front of us. We could have pocketed that!" I laugh too, thinking that you'd need a good strong belt to hold your trousers up. "Five hours later," he says, "when the counting was done people were hungry. I never had any money so I took some of the money and bought pizzas and drinks."

"That sounds fair enough to me," I comment. Chris nods but his eyes are glittering; I sense that he has got more to tell about this.

He splutters with laugher as he recalls the events: "Chuck a Buck was more successful than I imagined it would be. Then lo and behold, the members of the Board came running back!" I start laughing too. "Before you knew it there was a full Board. Nathan established Open Family Canberra and then later he was elected CEO. He did a great job of taking Open Family into the future. He took it from where we left it to a National operation with lots of funds. He made it work."

Chris is quiet for a few seconds and then goes back to the story about the pizzas and drinks. "But what pissed me off," he says, his face darkening, "was when we took those buckets of money to the Board and said: 'Here's the money that we've raised.' There we were, a bunch of street kids and street workers with buckets and buckets of money for Open Family." Suddenly they no longer trusted me, or the others. They said: 'Armaguard should be in charge of the money: not you guys.'"

"Jeeze. Miserable buggers!" I say, imagining the scene.

"Yeah, it was devastating. They told me off for spending five hundred dollars on food and drink."

"You told them about that?" I ask in amazement.

"Yes, I had nothing to hide. I gave them the receipts for the pizzas and drinks. I think there were about eighteen of us. They got angry with me and that's when I lost it. I said: 'Bugger youse! I'll take youse and break youse in half." He sounds just like Jeff Fenech at a weigh-in. Chris angrily picks up his black beanie from the couch and stretches it over his shaven head. He's been wearing black beanies ever since I've known him. I then realise that I am now under the spotlight. The sun's rays are slanting through the northern skylight and picking me out. Ronny says that it feels as if we are about to be beamed up to the Mother ship.

"There were millionaires on that Board who were blasting me for feeding these helpers," continues Chris. "All of a sudden what we had done wasn't good enough." He looks at me and sighs. Then he says philosophically: "When people's hearts are *in* the right place everything falls *into* place, but when there are different motives and there is no trust, it all collapses. Father Bob trusted us youngsters. When I explained the concept of Chuck a Buck to him he said: 'Right, go and do it.' I went and bought a stack of big buckets, and got official tags and signs made; we were all very proud to be official members representing Open Family. But, the moment the Board saw this much cash, it was a bit like the story of Jesus and Judas. The reaction wasn't: 'Fantastic! You guys have done a great job,' which is what we expected. Oh, no! It went the opposite way. I was shocked and indignant. And that's when I gave it to them."

I nod in sympathy. "What happened after your conniption, Chris?"

"I left. I had by this time spent two years in this Open Family. Their lease at World Vision was up and the place was going to be knocked down. Two years of my life had gone by and I thought: 'What for? *For this!* I'd better go and do what I love.' So I started looking for somewhere else to establish my dance school."

Chris tells me that Father Bob came to see him and said that he had a place in mind for him and asked if he'd like to go and have a look. Chris says that he was still angry, even with Father Bob. "My way of thinking at the time was: 'You're all the same,' " he says laughing. "It was like: 'As much as you are trying to help me, mate, I see it this way: I was helping you guys and you kicked me in the guts. I don't need your help!' I have never felt as if I needed anyone's help in this life, but God's. I said to him: 'Nah, I don't trust any of you.' 'Come and have a look,' Father Bob insisted. So I jumped in his car and went and had a look. That was next door to where we are now, and as you know, it's where we started. Maybe Father was thinking: 'This young man's done a lot for us; I'd better help him out. He was very generous too, so I was grateful at the same time."

Father Bob has stayed indirectly involved with Chris and Dance World; he is their patron. "He is a member of this place forever, because I say so," says Chris grinning. "I'm the founder and I recognise his genuine desire to help me, whether it's because I helped him to start with or not."

I nod and smile and thank Chris for his time.

"I reckon that I've seen you more times than I've seen my mother," says Chris as we walk to the door.

More times than his mother! "That makes me sound pretty old. I'm probably nearly as old as your mother."

"No, I wouldn't say that. My mother is in her seventies."

"I'm sixty-one."

"You don't look it," he says.

"I'd say you are about forty-eight," I say after doing an on-the-spot appraisal.

"I'm forty-two," he says. Whoops.

# Chapter 16: Father Smooch

*"He was a good storyteller, a tall Hungarian, a good-looking man and therefore a bloody good marketer."*

A couple of days later, Luke, my 'Advisor on Catholicism,' walks over and says to me as we are setting up our rounds at the Disaster Centre: "Ask Father Bob about the events concerning Father Smooch. Your story will be a bit tame without that."

I laugh, "Father Who?"

"Vince Kiss. He embezzled a lot of money from Open Family and buggered a few boys while he was at it. Surely you've heard about him?"

"Isn't he the one they dubbed The Society Priest several years ago? I knew it was in South Melbourne but I didn't know that he had anything to do with Father Bob and Open Family," I respond as I snap rubber bands around a large bundle of mail. We've both got another three hundred bloody householders to deliver as well as our normal mail today.

"How many Catholic Parishes do you reckon there are in South Melbourne, you idiot?" says Luke laughing as he walks back to his frame.

'Bloody Catholics!' exclaims Rene, curling his lip like Elvis Presley.

"Keep your hands moving," growls Luvy who works beside me. I grin as I pick up a label to tie around a depot bag, and get on with the job.

There are not many of the original characters left: the posties who were here during The Wombat's time. The Wombat is gone, of course, along with Spooks. Luvy has hardly changed a bit over the years though. He's a lifer; been a postie for forty years, poor bastard. He has only recently lost his title of 'gun.' A young bloke, The Machine, stripped him of it. The Machine doesn't even feel like saying good morning to anyone. In fact he doesn't unless somebody greets him. He steps up to his frame as soon as he arrives a few minutes before six o'clock and goes like last week's pay. Then there are the 'new' posties who hate the place right from the time that they find out that they've been conned. The insolent Fleas hire them and start them at 6.30am instead of 6am to cut out the fifteen percent penalty allowance that they would otherwise be entitled to. They then have to work beside, and do the same work as, posties who are paid fifteen percent more. I'm starting to feel depressed this morning just thinking about this. I'm set up and ready to go. I have to get out of here. Once I get away from this conditioned air and get some fresh air into my lungs, I always come good. Why don't you come along for the first part of the round? I'm going to get a haircut so I'll be able to introduce you to the barber. He's been around for twenty years too. There's a spare bike right at the end of the bike-shed. Don't go looking for gears though; there's only one. We turn left at the round-a-bout into Cecil Street and ride past the South Melbourne Market. There's a bike lane along here but the van drivers use that to double-park so you have to be careful. That long queue of people on the footpath is waiting to buy some of the famous South Melbourne Market dim sims. They're alright if you like plenty of cabbage and salt. I'll have to ride harder, get the blood pumping, and lose these blues. We ride along Cecil Street and then turn right into Bank Street, go past Park Towers and along to Ferrars Street. There's the barbershop on the corner with the Railway Hotel opposite. Up until three or four years ago, it was quite common to see a battered old wheelchair, with the stuffing poking through the vinyl upholstery, parked outside the Railway Hotel. You might have seen an old fellow, who was slightly unsteady on his feet, step out of the door holding a carton of stubbies, place the carton in the wheelchair, then push it across Ferrars Street and up Bank Street towards Park Towers where he lived.

Aziz Habib's shop is not a fancy up market barbershop; he hasn't even got an adjustable barber's chair. Hell, he hasn't even got a steriliser to put his clippers and combs into after each customer. I've been going there for nineteen years though and I've never had a problem. Aziz never gets the blues, at least not in public. He never stops talking but you don't have to listen for long: he is a prestidigitator like Luvy and the Machine; you're only in the chair for five minutes. I asked him once if he used to be a shearer when he was in Egypt. "Too dry for sheep in Egypt," he said. In between customers, he can be seen sitting at the most untidy desk in the world writing in Egyptian into an exercise book. A black covered Bible, sitting on a pile of papers, magazines and other detritus, will be open beside his book. He copies passages from the Bible into it. There is a little porcelain statue of the Last Supper sitting on the shelf below the mirror in front of the barber's chairs. On the wall above the front window hang two framed certificates from Melbourne University. Aziz has got a degree in engineering. Years ago, I asked him (I have to ask him things whilst he is snip, snip, snipping otherwise he doesn't stop talking and cuts off too much hair) why he is barbering when he could be engineering. He said that his father was a barber in Egypt and that he wanted his son to become an engineer. Aziz became an engineer just like his father had dreamed about then he became a barber. This simple

Christian said: "My father was a (snip) barber, now I am a (snip, snip) barber. I like (snip, snip) being a barber."

After another day at the Disaster Centre, I do some research on the Internet. *The Age* newspaper reported that in 2002 the seventy year old Father Vincent Kieran Kiss had pleaded guilty to ten charges of indecent assault and three of 'the abominable act of buggery' on four youths aged thirteen to seventeen and would be going back to gaol. He was released from Ararat gaol in July 1999 after serving seven years for stealing $1.8 million from a charitable trust that he was employed to administer.

As I ride out of Queen Street into Dorcas Street, I slow down. Bob might not be too keen to discuss the paedophile priest considering that the Catholic Church has been in the news so much of late so I'm dawdling as I draw closer to the rectory.

After settling into my chair, I turn on my voice recorder and broach the subject. Without any qualms, Father Bob gives me a rundown on the lowdown priest:

"Kiss was a Roman Catholic Priest who ended up working for the ANZ Trustees." Father Bob effects a high-falutin' voice, "We were encouraged to go into the World and spread the Gospel to every creature." (Bob rolls the r's in creature.)

*"Frank! Get out!"* yells Bob. Frank has just bounded into the room with a hamburger-with-the-lot clamped in his jaws. He vigorously tosses his head from side to side and then lets the hamburger fly: it whizzes across the room, with the dog in hot pursuit.

"Somebody had said to him," says Father, unfazed now by the hyperactivity, "Geez Vince, you're a good seller of The Cause. How would you like to work as the fundraiser for the ANZ trustees? It was an unusual kind of situation, whereby he was a priest in good standing with the Wagga diocese but he was on leave as the head of the Charitable Trusts part of the ANZ Trustees.

"This is not a Roman Catholic area of expertise. All these type of trusts were set up a hundred years ago by the Protestants to be charitable trusts. In other words, the rich knew that they were expected to look after the poor. That was a British tradition. It was called: what the hell was it called? There was a phrase that was used." Father Bob's voice increases a few decibels: "Noblesse Oblige: if you've got it, you are obliged. The trust itself wasn't looking after the poor, but it funded people who *were* looking after them. Most of those would have been Protestant and Anglican agencies, like the Brotherhood of St Lawrence and the Salvation Army and the Mission of the Streets and the Lanes.

"Vince Kiss was seen, at about forty years of age, as having talent at selling Catholicism. He was very good. He was a good storyteller, a tall Hungarian, a good-looking man and therefore a bloody good marketer. Now somewhere along the line he decided to go for the ANZ Trustees job. It might have been offered to him. He thus became an employee of the ANZ Trustees and ceased to practice as a Roaming Catholic Priest, although he was still on the List.

"I think it was in the eighties; all the priests were gone. The lines were thinning," says Bob. Ronny projects a picture of a line of priests in a trench at Gallipoli being picked off by the Turks. "I had three priests here but they took 'em away and employed them elsewhere. I was in church one day, worn out, no assistance, and there's a bloke, sitting on a pew in the church, who I knew. I'd met him once before at a youth forum where I was performing like a trained monkey. That was the only time I had met him. Then he turns up on a seat in the church.

"I said: 'What are you doing?' I thought that he must have left the priesthood and become a layman. 'No, I'm in good standing with the diocese of Wagga,' he said. I then asked: 'Well, what are you sitting there for? Why don't you come up and give me a hand? You can have half the Masses.' So one thing led to another and he agreed to do Saturday nights and Sunday mornings. He said that he was living in Cecil Street and was not in need of accommodation."

"I know the house that Kiss used to live in, in Cecil Street. It is like a Spanish Villa. Just the house for a flamboyant priest," I say.

Father Bob nods curtly. "It all seemed a bit unusual to me," he says. "I rang Wagga and unfortunately the Bishop of Wagga was dead so that put the chain-of-command out of whack a bit. I wanted to know whether Vince Kiss was in good standing or not."

"Do you mean that you actually suspected otherwise?" I ask.

"I suspected nothing: just old Army. Is this man, who is wearing a uniform, an officer or a fraud? It wouldn't matter whether it was Vince Kiss, or you, who turned up and said: 'I'm Ron Burrows. I used to be a priest in Sydney. Remember me? If I then dealt with you on your word only I'd be a bloody idiot. So I checked with the senior officer at Wagga, in lieu of a Bishop, who said: 'Yeah, he's on the List. That was the start of about a year's free service from Kiss. He knew, just by being here, that I was part of Open Family Orstralia. He said: 'We might be able to help you.' I said: 'Who's we?' I didn't know anything about the ANZ

Trustees. Kiss told me all about it and said: 'All you have to do is apply and I will make sure the application is attended to. *Who's chasing the bloody dog?"* Father Bob snaps. Ronny guffaws as Frank snatches up the hamburger-with-the-lot again and flings it, with a toss of his head, from the study to the hall, then from the hall back into the study. "Frank!" I call. He bounds over, wagging his stumpy tail, and stands in front of me, the hamburger-with-the-lot in his mouth. He looks expectantly at me and then bites into the burger, which emits a mouse-like squeak, before slinging it across the room.

"I applied for something," continues Father Bob with a chuckle as he mellows towards the dog's antics, "street worker assistance or something. Money, money, money, and it came through. He ended up helping us considerably. Then he revealed that he had a special interest in South Pacific youth: young people of Vanuatu and the Philippines, which I thought was nice, whereby he helped people set up courses for people at RMIT. Early days in computer technology too: the eighties. Then they'd go back to their own countries to work. I thought: 'what a lovely idea.' Time passes, about a year later or so, and Vince Kiss becomes much loved of the Pratts and other members of high society. Much loved."

In the article from *The Age*, one of the arts patrons, Sheila Scotter, had described Kiss as 'an utterly charming man,' whilst Jeanne Pratt described him as being 'like Jesus Christ. He is not priestly, he is saintly,' Pratt is reported as saying in the same article.

"One of his jobs," continues Father Bob, " for the ANZ Trustees, may well have been to try to encourage high society to contribute to the ANZ Trustees, to invest money with them, which was a fair and reasonable part of his job."

Frank is enjoying his hamburger-with-the-lot, long threads of drool dripping from the sides of his jaw, which means that Bob is speaking against the background of a squeak, squeak here, and a squeak, squeak, there, as well as panting and thumping as the dog cavorts around the room.

"One thing led to another and before long I had a visit from a policeman, who said: 'Vince Kiss has been charged with fraud.' I could never work it out because everything was above board with bits and pieces of paper and God knows what, to cover all monetary transactions. Somewhere, though, in the murky depths, I suspect an intra ANZ jealousy of Kiss, who earnt millions for the ANZ Trustees by his flash style. I don't think there is any argument about that. It was the distribution that was being questioned: that he was distributing funds to his Vanuatu Development Project, which was supposedly his vehicle for funding the Vanuatuans and the Filipinos both here in Australia and over there.

"What I was being alerted to was my dealings with Kiss, and thank God I had good books. Thank God! They proceeded against Kiss and he went to gaol for fraud. But I was more interested in the moral side of things: did he in fact use money that he had raised, and applied to projects of his own choice, which I couldn't see as being wrong if the ANZ Trustees, in fact, approved of those projects, which were offshore? That was the crux of the matter. Kiss apparently didn't do that."

From what I read in *The Age,* there was no 'apparently' about it. Kiss pleaded guilty.

"Frank Little called me in and asked: (Bob puts on a high-pitched voice to imitate the Archbishop) 'Do you know anything about this?' I said: 'Well, he says Mass at South Melbourne and he is in good standing and sometimes, through his good services, we've received a few thousand quid from the ANZ Trustees. We've got all the receipts and appropriate paperwork.'

"Poor old Frank Little was a bit nervous, thinking that the Church was going to be tarred with the brush. It was a bit unfortunate that, in fact, Kiss was a priest and working for the ANZ Trustees. He was working with me as a priest first and then as an ANZ Trustee distributor of funds. It was typical Maguire where nothing is simple. It's all gotta be a bit of this and a bit of that."

I nod, not interrupting, allowing Bob to continues his story.

"He was also dealing in this way with two other groups, one of which was the Lions' Club and the other the Fitzroy Community Youth Centre. All bloody good projects and the beneficiaries got a few quid, but at the same time, I think the three of us were probably acting as sponsors of the Vanuatu Development Project, so he might say: 'Here's a hundred thousand dollars: there's fifty thousand for Open Family. Give me a cheque for fifty thousand for the Vanuatu Development Project,' because we had accepted that we could be sponsors. He may well have been doing the right thing by these people but the suggestion that the ANZ Trustee levelled was that he was living orf it.

"He was living a very high lifestyle and there was a further suggestion," says Father Bob in a serious tone of voice, "that he was taking advantage of the students, but I know nothing about that. It was sleazy enough though, to create enough smoke, for anyone who wanted to have a go at me, or Open Family, to do so. It got them nowhere though because most people accepted . . ." Frank interrupts Father Bob's train of thought with his exuberant antics with the hamburger-with-the-lot.

"Working with young people seems to have its occupational hazards where Catholic priests are concerned," I comment. "It must have been difficult for you at the time knowing that you and Open Family were going to be smeared because of this deviate."

Father Bob simply smiles sadly.

"It must have taken a long time to get your operation back on track," I probe.

"Yes, it took a number of years to reassure people at the top level, because they hate the thought of having their reputation and good standing being tarnished. The Pratts (the richest family in Australia) were very good. They took Open Family on board and eventually, after a couple of years, the ANZ Trustees accepted applications from us. They knew that it was Vince Kiss, the conman, who had duped both them and us. Thank God. We all had to accept that we had been conned. It wasn't just us, the charities, which had been conned; it was also the ANZ Trustees high command. We were equally conned and we accepted that we were equally stupid or gullible, *but* at the hands of an expert fraud."

It's quiet now except for the sound of Frank and his burger.

"It was a pain in the arse to me that Kiss was a Roaming Catholic priest to boot," complains Bob, "because once they charged him he disappeared from the scene here, which was a disappointment to the locals who all liked him. He was personable. Kiss went to gaol and I've never seen him since."

Bob was right enough about it being the distribution that was being questioned. *The Age* article stated that Kiss had defrauded four charities of $2.5 million: the Fitzroy Community Youth Centre, Lions International, International Social Services, and the Open Family Foundation. The name of his non-existent charity was the Vanuatu Development Project, with Kiss being the only member.

"They probably wouldn't have liked him after they read all about it," I comment.

"I dunno," says Bob casually. Rene is astounded. "The Micks are a bit like that," says Father, "sin is one thing and crime is another. Most of the Micks, early days, would have had members of their families who were criminals, but not sinners."

"Can you be a criminal and not be a sinner?"

"Oh, yes," says Father Bob, "you can be a sinner without being a criminal."

"No. Can you be a criminal without being a sinner?"

"Yes!" Bob says exasperatedly. "The Irish were brought up on that: the penal laws. In other words, if you get caught you have to do time and if you don't get caught you've got no further obligation to society because, you see, it was them and us."

'Ned Kelly's outlook on life,' says Descartes.

"But morally, you would have, wouldn't you?" I argue, laughing.

"No. Morally you wouldn't have. If in fact you are that poor," he says, "your first moral obligation is looking after your family. If you are to be arrested for stealing a loaf of bread and transported to Orstralia, then you would be a criminal and not a sinner. There are other things. The list goes on. The Jews are much better at this than we are because they tend to want to cover every eventuality in everybody's life, ever."

"You've got a high opinion of the Jews, haven't you?"

"Yes. I like the Jews because they are so fixed on their own destiny and past that they become exclusive. I keep asking the Jews: 'When are you going to come and save us?' Because they think that I'm part of the Messiah push that says the Messiah will come and save us, but I'm saying: 'when are *you* going to come and save us? You've been around for 5,000 years and learnt a few tricks, what about making the tricks available to the rest of us?' "

"You're definitely right when you say they are exclusive."

"Yes, and the Roaming Catholic Church, too, will always be tempted to exclusion. Always."

"What about you, personally? You're not tempted to exclusion. You've got a lot of Jews who are friends. Good friends."

"Friends, friends," says Father considering, "Friends is not the word I'd use, Ron."

"Colleagues, then?"

"Well, whatever you say. I've never had friends. Once you are born an orphan, I don't know that you can have friends."

"You're not an orphan."

"Yeah, I'm an orphan. No mother, no father. What are you talking about? That's an orphan."

"You had a mother and father."

"No; they were only there five minutes."

"They were around a bit longer than that."

"No, they weren't. Five minutes!" He asserts with more than a hint of frustration and bluster.

"You've probably got a lot of repressed memories."

"What do you mean repressed memories?" he says bluster becoming anger.

I'm about to remind Father Bob of what he said during one of our earliest sessions. I decide not to push it. Talking about his early life was unsettling for Bob. I want to know more but I am worried that he might kick me out. Bob quickly shifts direction.

"I haven't got repressed memories," he says, "I'm one of God's Frozen People."

"God's Frozen People? Who are they?"

'Wake up, Ron,' says Rene.

"I was born into God's Frozen People, not God's Chosen People."

I shake my head and laugh. Frank shakes the hamburger-with-the-lot and then launches it across the room with as much gusto as he showed when he first started. I watch as a tiny spider darts across Bob's desk and takes cover under a sheaf of papers.

Bob grins and says, "We've done very well, considering."

The spider breaks cover, races across no-man's land, and runs off the end of the desk.

"Yes," I agree, "you have, considering the adversity you've struck along the way." I miss the opportunity to question Bob further about God's Frozen People and I am left to wonder about Bob's thoughts on Father Smooch's other shenanigans. A spider of another type, maybe? It's time for me to break cover too and get the bloody round finished.

As we are saying our goodbyes, I glance at the whiteboard. It's unlikely that Father Bob will ever be part of the Open Family executive again but it's not completely out of the question. After all he is still the owner of the Open Family trademark and his map depicting the existing Open Family centres with his stick-on-dots showing the exponential growth that he would like *is* still on the wall.

## Chapter 17: The Cause

*"They all look as if they've just found half a rat in their salad rolls."*

One of the best things about this job is the prospect of an early day. When I walk in the door and see that the volume of mail is light, I fairly rejoice. Today I'm on the road just after 8am. Father Bob won't be down from upstairs when I reach there so I decide to keep going for about another hour and then double back for the interview.

Don't look now, but there's a bloke who I have to dodge hanging over the front fence at number ## on the other side of Mountain Street. Spooks warned me about blokes like him when I first started in the job: "The old bastards have got nothing to do all bloody day so they wait out the front until the postie comes along and then hold him up. Keep on riding, mate," he advised with a laugh that day. It's an ideal time to double back.

"We daren't have the poor whingeing," says Father Bob getting right into it as soon as I sit down, "which we have, because we encourage it. We go out and say: 'Oh, you poor bastard. You need this or that,' and they take the bait. They want whatever we've got to offer them. Then they start whingeing. Now when you put that on the television or in a magazine the Aussies are not impressed at all. 'Get off your arse and get a job,' Prime Minister Keating said to that boy, 'Get a job!'"

Father Bob sifts casually through his mail and then turns to look out the window before continuing. "We're all saying 'get a job.' I'm saying it under my breath, *but* I realise that there are mitigating circumstances, because I've known these people since 1970 when they were twelve. They're now forty-five. I know what they were like when they were twelve because they never had a hope. They had no access to finding a way out or finding a way up, so we've produced twelve-year-old welfare dependents. The males of them have all been in gaol because you can't have twenty year-old, or fifteen-year-old even, males, wandering around the neighbourhood with nothing to do.

"How long ago was it that they took away the football club; they took away the management of Albert Park and handed it over to the Grand Pricks; they took away the bloody council, and they also pulled down all the factories? Now where are the young males going to go to learn to fit in which all young males have to do? If they don't *learn* to fit in then they are never *going* to fit in. Then they become resentful," he continues. "They become anti-social. They knock down Mrs. McGillicutty in the Street, because unfortunately it's as if they have been taken hostage and buried in a cellar. They're still carrying on like fourteen-year-olds. Football can help that; cricket can help that; bastardball can help that, but you are pushing ice cream uphill with a stick when they are forty-five." (Ice cream surprises me). "I don't know what we are going to do because we are warehousing all these people; they are all round the place in new prisons and they all come out aged fifteen with worse habits, as well as addictions to chemicals."

Because of the monological nature of this explanation, I haven't been able to join the conversations since Father Bob said: 'We daren't have the poor whingeing.'

"What do we do?" Bob adopts his Aussie nasally accent, "We say: 'Ah well, don't worry, we'll look after you. Here's a flat to live in.' On your own! He's fifteen. They're no good living on their own. 'Nah, he's not fifteen, he's forty-five.' But, get that scanner out and run it over him and you'll find that he's only fifteen. Now who the hell wants fifteen-year-old males living on their own?"

I am just about to respond but too late! Bob forges on: "I want," his voice shakes slightly, reminiscent of another Bob, whose voice also trembled as he announced on national television in 1987 that: 'By 1990 no child in Australia will be living in poverty' "every man woman, and child," says Father Bob uninterrupted by my thoughts, "to accept responsibility for somebody other than themselves. And better still, not only somebody other than himself or herself, because they might take the easy option, that is, their own family and friends, but somebody, other than themselves, who is a stranger."

It is as if Bob suddenly finds himself at the pulpit because he delivers what feels like a sermon to me; perhaps he is rehearsing or straightening out his thoughts for tomorrow's homily.

'It wouldn't be a bad idea if you straightened yours out,' sniffs Descartes. Bloody smartarse.

"Take an interest in the stranger, Ron, has always been a part of Jewish, Islam and Christian teachings. Don't ask me why. It's in the book. 'Take care of the stranger,' it says, 'don't forget you were strangers in Egypt. So if a stranger staggers into your camp, and if he staggers in, he is strange, the natural instinct is to chop the head off the bloody stranger because he's strange and he may cause harm. The Jewish God, Adonai, and the Islamic God, Allah, say a stranger is a very special factor in your life, probably because it will make you change your behaviour and routine, which may well be what we are all in need of." It reminds me of Wayne Neilson's story about the Koori who took him in and then passed him on to yet another stranger in Uncle Albert and how these encounters changed Wayne's life.

In 2007, Bob Hawke said that he regretted declaring that no child would be living in poverty by 1990 and wished that he had stuck to the written speech. He said that his government had, indeed, increased payments to parents but, 'a lot of them pissed it up against the wall.' If the Prime Minister can't make a dent in child poverty, what hope has a parish priest? Realising the dream of the two Bobs will be like winning the lottery, perhaps just fanciful hope.

The doorbell rings. The monologist looks out the window and says: "Now make a note of this, Ron. Here's a sheila ringing the doorbell coz she wants a handout. The Roman Catholics pretend to man the place to hand out groceries to the poor. They don't give a bugger. They've gone away for a month. That's a sin. Now if I start yelling and screaming about it they'll report me to headquarters."

Father Bob, friend of the poor, gets up out of his chair and comes around the desk. "We'd better give her some money," he says, pulling his wallet from his back pocket as he walks out to the door. When he comes back into the room he says: "She's got three kids with her and the bloody Roman Catholics with their pretend Mission." Father Bob doesn't finish his sentence. "It's worse than not having one at all. It's contempt," he declares. "Now it doesn't matter if she's a fraud, cheat and liar. That's not the point. We pretend to be in a different category to her. Someone else is floating around the place pretending to organise this but it's gone off, off, off, until it's a pain in the arse." Bob bangs his hand down on the desk.

"They all drive me mad in this place," he says angrily. "They look as if they've just found half a rat in their salad rolls. Now the only way to take control of the situation is to throw your weight around and then you're the worst in the world. Anyhow, God's good. Get on with it," he says as if I've been holding him up. "What do you want to know?"

"If God is good then what is the meaning of 'The Glory of God'?" I ask off the top of my head not knowing where this thought came from or how it relates to finding rats in salad rolls or easing the pain in one's arse. Maybe Ronny instigated it; he's a bit of a philosopher and is interested in religion. I listen quietly as Father Bob slowly enunciates his reply.

"Glory is the success story publicly acknowledged by all. It's not *just* the success story. It has to be publicly acknowledged by everybody.

You've got to have a gathering, and that is, allegedly, 'The Glory.' It's like an ovation by ten thousand people clapping their hands and cheering loudly. Now take that tennis match last night: Federer beat Sanchez. Now that's glory. Everyone acknowledges that this man has done magnificently. Now If Sanchez had won it would have been even more glorious because he was the underdog. Harking back to the days of Peter's Pals when the birthday kids' names were flashed up on the screen, that's glory for a small child. Each person will be exhilarated by the public recognition of your contribution to the human race."

From the Glory of God to the Great Depression is merely a twist of the tongue for Father Bob who doesn't need my help to shift from one seemingly unrelated topic to another.

"The memory of the Great Depression has indelibly marked this place, South Melbourne," says Father Bob. "I think it's almost stamped on their faces. When I came here in 1973, I said of the older ones: 'What happened to your faces?' They didn't seem to know how to smile or laugh. They had been through the Depression. That's what happened to their faces.

"Kids would come home from school during the Depression to sit down to a feed of bread and dripping. There's the story of the man who left home with his Gladstone bag. My God, how many times have we heard that story? He never had a job but he went out at the same time every morning with his Gladstone bag, as if he did. And he came home at night at the same time 'after work'. Nobody said: 'Bullshit! That's bullshit:' because they knew. A lot of people were proud, too, that they had lived through the Depression because they learnt all sorts of survival techniques."

Father Bob had to learn how to survive when he was younger too. Maybe he identifies with the poor because of the hardship he suffered as a boy. He doesn't own now. The Catholic Church supplies his living quarters and provides him with a car to drive; it also pays him a nominal salary but he gives most of it away to the poor, and lives a Spartan lifestyle.

"Because I'm poor," he says, "all I can do is rely on books. I've never been anywhere, seen anything, and done anything, as a child. Book characters mean more to me than real life people, because I've had a limited experience. If I see a film or read a book I resonate. I am a sponge. I learn by osmosis. As soon as the basic characteristics stick out like a dog's ears I identify with one of the goodies."

I think about his statement: *Book characters mean more to me than real life people, because I've had a limited experience.* Surely this can't be. An advisor reading an early draft of this chapter commented: 'It's no surprise then that he is willing to *become* a book character.' Perhaps Bob's observation also suggests that he is fundamentally a solitary figure more comfortable with make believe characters than with those of flesh and blood. This might also help to explain Bob's religious calling. Perhaps he was won over by the larger than life stories and characters of the Bible. His comments also substantiate the feeling that I've had for some time that beneath the actor's rouge, Father Bob is a lonely man. For all his giving to others, there doesn't seem to be much being returned, at least not in this life.

On the round a few days, later it's early when I reach the Church so I cruise along delivering. As I'm delivering the 'odd side' of Mountain Street and slotting a couple of letters into number twenty-one one of the two resident Dalmatians greets me with a short bark as the other comes to the gate to be patted too. Number 21 is my second-favourite house on the round. I ride on, turn left into noisy Pickles Street and down Tribe Street after which I double back to the rectory for my talk with Father Bob.

Minutes later, I am sitting in Bob's study and yet again he is talking about The Cause. "We have to raise awareness of The Cause," he says. "Your church doesn't give a rat's arse about The Cause. The Archbishop doesn't give a rat's arse about The Cause. Your State of Victoria may, but can't express itself in money. That was chiefly why I started the Maguire Foundation. 'You'd better do it yourself darling,' I said to myself. The Maguire Foundation has currently got forty people housed in ten houses, ten Public Housing kids are on full scholarships. I won't go on, but you get the gist of it."

"Yes, I get the gist of it." I'm impressed with Bob's belligerent dedication.

"If somebody who everyone admires, a real celebrity, was backing us we would have a show. They try to make me into a celebrity but I'm not a bloody celebrity," Bob growls wearily.

"They've developed a high profile for you though," I add.

Rene agrees but says that Bob has been the principal architect and promoter of this profile.

"Yes, but it's not enough. To actually compel the upper class to give you their support in goods, services or cash, we have to do better than this." Bob's voice drops a few decibels and he repeats himself: "We have to do better than this." He sighs and then says: "I haven't got the strength or the energy now." He almost slumps in his chair like an actor in a play. "We need that exponential growth, in which case it would grab people's attention. If I were kidnapped or shot dead I would become a martyr for The Cause. It would be easier to do the job from the grave than it is from here."

"We might have to orchestrate a kidnapping then," I say, grinning.

"Yes!" Father Bob exclaims loudly. He then comes out with a beauty: "The personification of the personalisation of the thing: the establishment of the brand."

I look across at Frank and shake my head; he lifts *his* head from the armrest of his chair and looks at me quizzically with his doe-like brown eyes. If only he could talk. Mikhail Bulgakov managed to get a dog to talk in *Heart of a Dog* with hilarious consequences. I don't suppose you could do it in a biography; the Cauliflower-twins are unconventional enough. Maybe a postie could get away with it, I muse idly to myself.

"Yes, but how are you going to bring all this about?" I am quizzical.

"I'm buggered if I know," Bob says raising his voice. "Hopefully through the bloody Maguire Foundation. Someone from the Town Hall says: 'Please come down to the Port Philip's launch of something-or-other and talk.' So, I say: 'Alright, I'll talk at it again.' They are gradually deciding that there must be an asset: me." The asset grins and takes off his glasses so that he can rub his eyes.

"They've encouraged me to speak beautifully but that doesn't pay the rent for people. The trouble is I'm not an actor; I'm an activist, but I'm only one person," Bob offers belying the many voices and characters he temporarily takes on.

"If only more priests would get involved." I say sympathetically. At the same time I ask myself, feeling somewhat guilty, why I don't get involved?

"Yes," he says patiently, "But I've explained this to you before, Ron. Not all priests are the same. Some just want to be priests. They don't want to be doing neighbourhood things like helping the poor. What they offer, through their church, is a spiritual oasis. They are the sit-on-your-arse Catholics." He finishes in a typically acerbic way.

I laugh appreciatively. It's been a particularly easy morning at work and I'm looking forward to having an early beer with Eric. "Then maybe you need someone to take charge of marketing so that you've got more free time," I say, whilst wondering if the job would pay enough to allow me to quit work as a postie.

"What will he do?" asks Bob, "Dress me up in a tutu and shove a magic wand into my hand. I know what I need, but at the moment I'm doin' it myself. You're right though," he concedes, "If I had someone to do the marketing I could go and do other things, as I've said in my whingeing Parish Newsletter and my Blog."

Father Bob picks up a page with his handwriting on it and passes it to me. "This is a copy of my next blog," he says.

It's about time that I got moving but another couple of minutes is neither here nor there I think, as I lounge back in my chair, take the page from Bob and begin reading.

In his article, Father Bob makes the point that newspaper reports of life on the streets are often glamourised. He writes that maybe 'street workers should have a camera at the ready like war correspondents to record what it's really like sleeping on the footpath or in the park.' According to Bob: 'Real street people are environmentally friendly. They usually keep a low profile and do all in their power to avoid attracting attention from law enforcement officers.' He says: 'they cringe at the goings on of drunken, disorderly ravers and ragers.' These people are, he says, 'moths' attracted to the seedier side of life. To these people, 'street people's clothes have become chic. It's not the poor who shop at the many opportunity shops run by charities.' Bob poses the question in this piece: 'Do clothes make the woman or man?' He cites his own lack of sartorial splendour. 'Brought up to wear a black suit, dog collar (as the clerical collar was called by irreverent Aussies!), and black hat. Then, following Vatican Two, thrust into the public eye without comfort of that black uniform and forced to dress somehow to fit into the secular society.'

Reading the words 'Vatican Two' reminds me to ask Bob to give me a description of Vatican Two. I've already Googled it but I want a description in Father Bob's own words for the manuscript. I ask Rene to include it on the agenda for the next session.

I read on: Arguing that because of the lavish amount of money spent on high fashion a balance should be struck, Bob states that 'high fashion leaves a toxic imprint which should be offset by a contribution, monetary or otherwise, to civil society.' He writes: 'we can all accept responsibility for the global freezing of the minds and fears of those few with more, by becoming one of the more with less.' He proposes a way for Christians to go about doing this by way of an Islamic example. 'Ramadan challenges Islamics, annually, to choose a path.' Father Bob writes: 'I'm recommending Lent as practiced annually by Catholics, and some other

Christians, as a forty day/night exercise in choosing to join either the 'few with more' or the 'more with less.' '

"That's a well though-out proposal, Father," I say as I hand back the page. It's all a dream though really and I wonder if Bob has got a name for the right side of his brain. Father Bob's mobile phone buzzes again. I often use these interruptions in the way I'd use an alarm clock.

"Why don't they leave me alone?" Bob asks shaking his head and screwing up his face.

"I'll leave you alone, Father," I say, giving him a sympathetic smile as movement out in the garden catches our attention; we notice a man, with WATER PATROL emblazoned across the back of his shirt, snooping around the garden. "I wonder what he's up to," mutters Father Bob as I leave the study.

Back on the round as I work my way along Glover Street, I see a man striding jauntily along the footpath towards me. As he draws closer I hear that he is whistling. I've heard the tune before but just can't place it. That isn't what intrigues me though. It is the act itself. It's a pastime that has died out and I feel unnerved as if transported back in time. I look to see if he is carrying a Gladstone bag as he whistles his way past.

'I reckon he's just had sex,' says Ronny.

After Glover Street, I round the corner into Pickles Street, tug my hat down and ride for the border. Then I turn left into peaceful Henderson Street. On the corner of Pickles and Henderson stands the old Albert Park Infant School the product of a division that took place in 1914 at the Albert Park State School. The school just wasn't large enough to accommodate the latest influx; children were being taught in the corridors, so a line was ruled under grade three and the grades below were subtracted. It was seventy years before the second-graders, first-graders, and bubs crossed the divide and rejoined the school at Albert Park.

Just outside the school, a tow-truck driver is driving a wrecked car off his tilt-tray truck. The wreck shudders to rest in the gutter beneath the huge overhanging boughs of a eucalypt that stands guard in the little quadrangle. Faded bulls-eyes on the brick walls look out through the high cyclone fence.

Some of the residents of Henderson Street South Melbourne are living just this side of heaven. Only a few metres away is St Vincent Street, and St Vincent Street is in Albert Park. The residents at # and # Henderson Street know that within a few tantalising metres the

Chardonnay flows from the taps in the front gardens. I hum a few bars of a Ry Cooder Song as I stuff mail into letterboxes on my way to the corner:

> There's a place where I've been told
> Every street is paved with gold
> And it's just across the borderline.

They even try to will themselves across this borderline by having their mail addressed to # Henderson Street Albert Park. I've got this little stamp in my drawer at the Disaster Centre: 'Please advise the sender of your correct address.' It's a nice little stamp with a maroon handle. The tow-truck starts up and the driver waves as he drives past heading towards St Vincent Street.

Well I'll go hopping to buggery! Here's one of those 'Henderson Street Albert Park' letters now. Moments later, I turn hard left out of Henderson Street without crossing the divide into the Promised Land. Smiling, I hum a few more bars of *Borderline* as I turn the bike hard left into Iffla Street South Melbourne with St Vincent Street off at a forty-five degree tangent.

> You've paid the price to come so far
> Just to wind up where you are
> And you're still just across the borderline.

The tune fades as I turn into Smith Street, the last street on the round. The last house, number 38, has caused me headaches in the past. There are people named Smith in 38 Mountain Street.

# Chapter 18: Father Bob: Star of the Wireless . .

*"You're going to send over your little Catholic boys in their balaclavas to see her and there's gonna be a reprisal."*

A few days later, Bob tells me that someone from the water company has rung to say that a neighbour has lodged a complaint. Apparently the automatic timer for the sprinkler system has not been turned off in accordance with the current water restrictions. This dobbing-in rankles Bob; he tells me that he is going to air his grievances on the wireless, as he still prefers to call the radio: wireless is a bit like his preference for pounds over dollars and the poor (or pooah) over the currently politically correct disadvantaged. Father Bob goes to air every week on Triple J's 'Sunday Night Safran,' a show that is intended to appeal to listeners between 18 and 30. He is an accomplished radio presenter and the show serves to highlight another facet of this talented priest.

Before meeting the celebrated comedian John Safran, I watch a few episodes from his shows on YouTube where he confronts people and uses subterfuge, all in the name of black humour. He has won four Australian Film Institute awards for 'John Safran's Music Jamboree,' and 'John Safran vs. God.' Talking to him before the recording of the show, he tells me that he met Father Bob before he began filming 'John Safran Versus God' in 2002. He says that his manager, who was a parishioner at Sts Peter and Paul's, knew that he was researching for his religious show; he said to John: 'You should check out this guy: he's pretty funny. "I came to one of the midday Masses," says John who is Jewish, "and sat politely up the back: low-key. But Bob spotted me and started doing shtick right at me."

John's radio presenter persona is a much calmer one than the one he presents on his television show: 'John Safran Versus God.' He frankly admits that he is obsessed with religion and I'm tempted to ask him about a confession he made related to a childhood experience with another priest. I toss up a mental penny and go for tails to see whether I should ask him or not. The coin spins through the air; I catch it and turn it over on the back of my imaginary hand: tails.

"I read a promotional bit associated with one of your shows: a confession." This could be a bit awkward, I think, because I've only just met the man and I hesitate momentarily.

"Yes?" he asks expectantly.

I look directly at him. "You claimed to have masturbated in a priest's bed," I say softly and somewhat hesitantly.

"Ah, yes," John calmly acknowledges without embarrassment and only a flicker of a smile. He has discarded that television persona that I had familiarised myself with: his cloak that allows him to ask embarrassing questions and manipulate people. This is the self-assured, away-from-the-cameras John Safran whom Bob likes so much. The radio personality is much closer to his 'real' personality I decide for no other reason than I prefer this version of the man.

"It said that the priest subsequently forgave you."

"Yes." There is another glimmer of a smile.

This predicted bombshell has fallen as flat as a shitcarter's hat so I pick up John's cloak and pull it on over my shoulders and ask bluntly: "What were you doing in the priest's bed?"

"I was just staying over," he says in that matter-of-fact voice of his, as if we are discussing an everyday experience. "It was like, accommodation. I wasn't like, in the bed with the priest." We snicker like fifth graders, Michael Jackson nowhere to be seen.

"You actually told him that you had masturbated in his bed?" I smile, recalling a line from John Updike's *Henry Bech:* 'as stiff with Elmer's glue as a masturbator's bed sheet.' The cloak doesn't seem to fit me as well as it does John though because I'm unable to get a rise out of ,him so I decide to discard both the cloak and the bed sheet.

"Ah, yes: for the TV show," he adds with a gentle smile.

"Poetic licence?"

"Yes."

John tells me that he and Bob have been together on Triple J for five years. "We've got three writers to interview this week," he says. "I haven't read all of the books either so I'll have to consult my cheat notes." He says that although Bob always reads the books, "I'm a bit selfish; I have trouble reading something if I'm not liking it so depend heavily on Bob during the interviews. I'm very grateful to Bob for coming on the show every week. I think that he definitely makes it. I'm not good at just talking to the listening audience alone in front of a microphone."

Safran is not like Bob, who only requires someone else breathing in the same room to crank out stories, homilies and anecdotes like a human Wurlitzer.

"Yes. I'm going to let him talk more and me talk less."

That wouldn't be hard I think to myself.

"I always plan that but it doesn't work out because I start worrying when he rambles on, and wonder if people will understand what he is getting at. He should be the main guy and I should be his sidekick," he says, sounding like the Cisco Kid promoting his paunchy Pancho.

I jokingly say to John that it's just as well Bob isn't married because, if he were, his wife would have trouble breaking in to the 'conversation.'

"I'm not married either," he confides, "but I will get married just for dignity's sake. So people don't think I'm a loser who never got married. I really want to get married for that benefit."

"Then you can get rid of her." I prompt provocatively.

"No, I don't want to get rid of her," he says as if he's already got her. "I'll get married by Bob, unless it's like, a Jewish wedding I guess. If she's Jewish, then I might as well get married by a rabbi."

"Would you enjoy getting Bob to marry you?"

"I reckon it'd be good. Craig Melville, the bloke who directs my show, is getting married by Bob in November. A guy from *The Chaser* got married by Bob. Everyone's getting married by Bob," says Safran, marking Bob's papers as the celebrity's celebrant.

"He's got a good affinity, not only with Jews but with just about anybody who is not a Catholic. Personally I think that he prefers to keep company with non-Catholics," I prod with a laugh. "Why do you think that might be?"

"With Bob I think that it's because he grew up in the Catholic community and sees more of the negative things with them. With the Jewish community or the Muslim community or the Hindu community, on the other hand, it's easy for him to be positive about them. I've tried to tell him that: to just stop bagging the Catholics because all the other communities are just as flawed as the Catholics."

It's a cool summer night. In the studio, John Safran, a slim man with headphones over his neatly cut curly brown hair, sits behind his wraparound desk. He is wearing a red and black striped jumper with his sleeves pushed up; like a man with a pen behind each ear he obviously means business. On the wall behind him is a poster featuring and promoting Safran and Maguire with the bold caption: 'Everyone Offended Equally.' A potplant on a ledge below the poster looks incongruous in the midst of slide-controlled mixers, bright coloured lights, important-looking knobs and dials, and the ubiquitous mouse sitting patiently near John's right hand. The monitor sits, glaring, watching John and waiting for the mouse to move.

Father Bob, wearing his oft worn black jacket, sits with his notes in front of him; a large plastic ID badge is hanging around his neck on a thick red cord. He looks the part in his headphones, with a black microphone on an adjustable neck a few inches from his mouth.

A signal is given and Father Bob leans forward slightly and talks into the mike: "During the middle of the night a neighbour was wandering around the block, doing nothing, when he noticed a leak in the front garden. Now I put it to you . . ."

John Safran interrupts to tell listeners in the Ukraine about, "Our, like, big drought" and about the so-called Water Police.

"This is probably what Stalin did. This is how it begins: with the tiny persecutions," says Bob indignantly.

Safran interprets: "For our East German listeners: They're like, the Stazi."

"Exactly," says Bob, "and they've got files on people who have got slow leaks in their front gardens. There was this trickle of water coming out of the church's front garden and your more-than-conscientious neighbour spies this, doesn't leap to the conclusion that some drunk has happened to stand up against a tree and is relieving himself, (voice rises) but immediately, through some inherited bias, says the Roman Catholics are breaking the law."

"That's like, sectarianism."

"What does she do?" asks Bob righteously.

"Dobs? For our East German and Ukraine listeners, to dob is like, to tell."

"To betray," Bob corrects theatrically. "Yes, she rings East West Water."

"You were like, dobbed. It could have been like, anything. It could have been like, the Virgin Mary crying," says Safran in his idiosyncratic manner.

"Well, there is a statue of the Virgin Mary in the front garden and if I had written back and said: 'Dear Sir or Madam of East West Water, that statue regularly weeps; now you do a DNA test on the water and see if it is not lachrymose.' Now, Sylvie, the commissar of East West Water rings up and says: 'Listen, Sir, you are under arrest."

"What was like, your punishment?"

"I haven't been punished yet, just warned. I asked for the identity of the person who did this because that person deserves a medal."

"You're going to send over your little Catholic boys in their balaclavas to see her and there's gonna be a reprisal," says Safran relishing his Jewishness.

"No; I'm going to send her a medal that makes her a member of the Order of St Peter and St Paul and immediately qualifies her for eternal life."

During a break in recording before the first interviewee arrives, I slip into the interviewee's chair, glancing at the headphones as I sit down. Father Bob slips out the side door his hand dipping into his pocket for a cigar. Silence. John and I sit still for a few moments and look across the desk at each other without speaking. We nod at one another. Neither of us speaks. John picks up a pen and starts doodling in a red notebook that is lying on the table. I watch him. He stops and looks up. We look directly at each other for a couple of seconds. He smiles, almost secretively, shuts the book which is entitled 'Zapbook.' Strangely enough as the silence continues I do not feel panicky. There is an aura about John Safran that is comforting. If I were a talent scout searching for someone to play Jesus, I'd pick him.

I sit and watch the duo in action as they interview three writers. Before, and in between each interview they banter or simply discuss everyday matters that are of interest. The camaraderie is obvious and it's easy to see why Father Bob is willing to spend hours every Thursday night recording the show. 'Sunday Night Safran,' is an enjoyable programme and you can make the music disappear simply by downloading the podcast.

Father Bob takes off his headphones and escorts an interviewee out of the studio. As John divests his ear-warmers I ask him about this friendship between him and Bob: after all Bob says that he hasn't got any friends.

"I'm happy to call him my friend except he would probably spit it back in my face and say: 'We are not friends; we are colleagues or acquaintances,'" he says doing a not-very-good impersonation of Maguire but I smile at his role-playing: a definite Maguireism. "Have you ever mentioned to him that he might be your friend?"

"Yeah; I've brought it up on the show. I always like saying awkward things to him on the show." They're a fair bit alike these two intellectual men, I think, with their black humour and penchant for shocking people and the multiple personas that they employ.

"He says that he doesn't have friends in the conventional sense and that characters in books mean more to him than real life people."

"I guess we've just got to put up with all his eccentricities because of his positive attributes," says this even more eccentric man. After all I can't see Father Bob going to Manila to be crucified at Easter, or for that matter heading off to London to con the local Imam into taking out a fatwa on his television rival, Rove. In Bob's case it wouldn't be Rove of course, more likely the Archbishop.

"Yes." I laugh. "Bob is a significant figure in your life and vice versa, wouldn't you agree?"

"Yes. He always talks in code with me. I think he's always a bit worried that he is putting me out. Unless I'm fully concentrating . . . I'm always trying to work out what the hell he's getting at."

That sounds like Bob, metaphors and analogies at every turn. "That must make life interesting for you. It would stop you getting complacent." I say.

"Definitely. I'm getting older and more confused. I'm becoming like Bob. I'm turning into Bob!" he declares. "Sometimes I'm confused when I'm in the moment with him but when I listen back to it I realise he wasn't an idiot after all." He considers for a moment and then asks: "What secret things have you found out about Bob that people wouldn't know?"

After the next interview with a Brazilian physicist the banter continues:

"This is the last I'll talk to you about you," says John Safran, meaning Bob.

"Yeah."

"Because we should talk about bigger issues than just you. Your biographer, Ron . . ."

"He's listening," whispers Bob.

"He told me that you used to have a rifle around the church."

"When I got there, there was an air rifle . . . kiddies if you don't know what an air rifle is I can't help you. A long thin barrel . . . anyway you put bb's in one end. It belonged to the previous parish priest. Our house is two storeys high and because the pigeons used to gather on top of St Peter and Paul's Church, lots and lots of pigeons doing pigeon poo, monsignor would fire shots at them from the presbytery balcony. When I got there I wasn't keen on shooting pigeons anyway."

"No."

"Enter Mr Martin Bryant down in Hobart who shoots lots of people. An amnesty on weapons follows."

"So you turned up at the police station with your rifle."

"I got someone else to take it to the police station. Even a bb rifle is prohibited but I didn't know. The old bloke used to shoot 'em. I think a lot of people had what we called bb rifles in those days. They weren't bullets but they could do damage to you if somebody shot at you for

God's sake. Has Ronny got that in the biography?"

"No; he said 'cutting room floor.' "

"But you bring it up."

"Yes. How come nobody who works at your Church, except for your assistant, is really normal?" Safran asks Bob with a grin. "I keep on seeing people walking around your place who at first glance look normal and then I think: 'Oh something's wrong,' and I look back and it's something like they're not wearing pants."

"Yes, something like that: something minor; there's something missing isn't there?"

"Like, for example I'll walk up the driveway and there'll be a guy raking the leaves and…"

"He's not wearing any pants."

"What about the other guy who's always a bit like, on edge and possibly a bit threatening: younger guy."

"Barnabus. He's been around me for thirty years."

"Yeah, he started screaming at me."

"He thought that you were from *A Current Affair*."

"He thought I was Henry Roth from 'Project Runway'. People do confuse me with Henry Roth. It's quite insulting." I had never heard of 'Project Runway' and discovered later that it is a reality TV show about fashion design and Roth is one of its stars.

"Yeah, I know. But these are the kind of people who hang around my place."

"What about the PR guy" interrupts Safran, "who works in the office, he seems like, normal. And then he walks in on stilts."

"He does; that's Tim, he's a circus person. I got him in the off-circus-season for six months."

"He's your PR."

"PR and FR."

"What's FR?"

"Fund Raising." Bob rattles back before continuing with his story, multiplying the mayhem by adding another Tim to the mix, the circus strongman.

"What!" exclaims John.

"Yep."

"These are the *normal* people at your church?"

"Yes, these are normal people: real clowns. They might think I'm the resident clown but these blokes swallow hot coals." Bob on the other hand would be more likely to spit hot coals than swallow them, I think to myself.

"I don't know how good it is for you. When you compare yourself with all these mad people who hang around the church do you think you're normal?"

"Yeah. I'm not a clown. I'm not a complete and permanent clown." The banter fades out as music takes over.

# Chapter 19: . . . and Television

*"If you do good, you do God."*

Frank is lying behind the desk, stretched out on the floor, as still as an animal rug. The cameraman is practising his yoga, camera in hand for this shot: down at dog level in the corner of the room with the lens focused on Father Bob who is sitting behind his desk. We are seeing this from Bob's side of the desk. It's been a busy day for Father, the camera lens tells us; he has got his shirtsleeves rolled up and the wastepaper bin that is on the floor beside him is overflowing with balled up paper. The ones that have missed the bin are lying on the floor around the chair. I don't have to see the top of the desk to know that it is covered in books, papers, pens, paperclips, batteries and other odds and sods. This is a scene from 'Talking Heads' compèred by Peter Thompson. The commercial channels are always keen to have Father Bob on too; he has appeared on many of their current affairs programmes and morning breakfast television timeslots because he's pugnacious, funny and irreverent and he pulls in the ratings. Australia wide! There's not another priest in Australia with such a high profile or who is as popular with so many Australians; he is Father Bob the battlers' benefactor. You could say then that he is a star of the wireless and television.

I know most of the information that Bob tells Peter Thompson about his life: most but not all. He tells him that he never set out to be a priest (which is what he had told me) *but* he didn't tell me that he had a mate who had in fact made up his mind to become a priest and who said to him: 'Let us go down and have a look at this Roman Catholic Priest Training Factory.' Bob says that he tagged along. Peter doesn't ask who this mate was but of course it was Paul Garland.

One of the black-and-white photos that flashes up onto the screen shows a starkly different scene in the study from the modern one described above. There's the optimistic new priest unaware of the pot-holed path ahead, sitting behind his small, *tidy* desk in 1973. There is an In and Out tray on each corner, a bunch-of-dates calendar, a desk lamp and a couple of sheets of paper. Behind him is a very small bookcase with a cross sitting on the top. Decades later he will say "it's been hell in this place: hell. But then again the feeling persists: it might be hell but it's home." Thoughts of hell are far from his mind on this day in '73 however. Bob, black hair slightly receding, hands clasped on his little desktop like a schoolboy, is smiling proudly. He is dressed in the priests' uniform of the day: 'dog-collar,' black shirt and trousers. We can't see under the desk but he won't be wearing thongs.

The director crosses back to Bob sitting behind big untidy desk in the present day talking to someone who is not in the frame. It's almost as if the desk size is commensurate with the workload. Bob has his raised right arm, slightly bent, stretched forward in that customary way of his when he is explaining something. I feel as if he is talking to me. In another shot, his head tilted back, he is looking through his bifocals at the computer screen. This really is déjà vu.

The director, producers, and film crew follow the **Hope**Mobile, Father incongruously at the wheel, to St Kilda where it parks outside the Gatwick Hotel. Bob is seen on the street with Henri helping to feed the pooah. "Hello, Your Grace," says Bob as he hands a homeless man a sausage in bread.

"If you do good, you do God, but The Romans hate the idea of the **Hope**Mobile because it's open to all; they can't command and control," Bob explains to his Talking Heads host.

It's interesting listening to Father Bob tell his story to Peter Thompson because always there is the knack that he has with language and storytelling. When Peter mentions the troubles that ensued after his organisations (Open Family and Emerald Hill Mission) were taken over by Boards of Directors, Bob's expression becomes serious. Peter points out that it was because of convergent philosophies. Bob explains that those two charities chose to be business-like first. He says: "My argument is: if you've got ten heads and nine hats you've got a choice: it's either cut off a head and you'll have enough hats, or find another hat."

Peter asks him: "How can you find another hat?"

Bob replies with just a hint of exasperation: "You can because you become creative, innovative and fund-raising." Exactly what Bob has been doing all along; the hardest of the three has been the fund-raising because the big corporations, and even small ones, don't really care about the poor. Australia Post sponsors horseracing, harness racing and the Stawell Gift but couldn't give a rat's arse about the pooah. The question is: which race should you sponsor: human or horse?

The compères of this type of show invariably play for a happy ending; it's Bob's philosophy too: leave 'em laughing.

"What happens next after you die?" asks Peter.

"Well, I presume more of the same (long theatrical pause) but digitally enhanced," says deadpan Bob, one eye gleaming.

Thompson is delighted.

"See, I don't know," says Bob. "The ancient religion says maybe we will go around in circles or maybe we'll come back as something else. I don't mind that. Maybe there are other experiences waiting for us and maybe we'll experience them before we arrive. It's bigger than these petty explanations about what happens after death." Bob seems to be suggesting reincarnation but perhaps it's just his slantwise view of heaven and the hereafter.

"Perhaps after we get there we'll have a chance to talk about it."

"I'm sure we will but, you see, it won't be Talking Heads," quips Father Bob.

## Chapter 20: The Mad Micks

*"A woman, who recognises me, comes up to me in the supermarket, this thin sheila, and says that she is a bit short of money and would I pay her grocery bill."*

What we've got at the Disaster Centre is a bike-shed which is full of bloody motorbikes, cigarette butts, and other flotsam. The pushies are chained to racks and to the bike-shed fence shoved aside like the poor bastards who ride them. They stand among the detritus. As I mount up and ride out, I think to myself: if posties want to smoke and go early then maybe they should tune in to JJJ next Sunday night and find out how easily it can be done: No racking coughing fits, no gasping for breath.

Just as if it were written into the script, Father Bob's mobile phone rings as I walk into the study. He talks to Liz Trevaskis from radio station JJJ about a forthcoming interview with Doctor David Nietchke, or Doctor Death, as he is commonly known.

"I like Dr Death," Bob tells me after he terminates the call. "I wonder if he is going to bring his pills with him? Maybe I can make an arrangement for myself. I'm getting close," he jokes. "He went overseas with that doctor and his wife. They all had drinks, then the doctor drank the cocktail and he was dead within five minutes. That's good fun. I like all that."

"What's the Church's position on euthanasia?" I ask as Ronny imagines a Catholic priest, decked out in his Sunday-best alb, standing at his altar knocking back the deadly concoction.

"The Catholic Church was very smart in the early days," says Bob. "They said: 'You are not bound to take extraordinary means to survive.' You can then argue until midnight what exactly constitutes extraordinary means. That will be a fun afternoon talking to Dr Death."

"Doctor Nitschke takes extraordinary means so that people can *die* when they want to, rather than survive in agony," I say, giving away my own views on the good doctor.

"Yes," agrees Father. "I don't understand all this. If you want to go, I know that you can't just go because you feel like it. You might feel as if you have blown your engine and ought to go. The fuss comes at the end when people try to ascertain whether you should be allowed to go, or about who's going to disconnect the battery. The Catholics have always used that word 'extraordinary', even to the point of view of money. I'll give you an example," he says. "If you had to spend a million dollars to save your mother, and the consequences of this would be that your children would starve to death and your wife would be sent into prostitution, then presumably that would be considered to be extraordinary. Now you might say: 'I want my mother to live,' and pay the million dollars. Bugger the wife and children. The Catholics would probably say it's the wrong decision because you owe something to your wife and children. We have two thousand years, or if you throw the Jews in, four thousand years of accumulated wisdom about morality and it tends to say that there's a principle of double effect. In other words to keep your mother alive kills your children and wife, so it would not be immoral to terminate your mother. Well, not if she's sitting up in bed drinking and smoking and reading the *Women's Weekly* and saying, 'Good on you, Ron, I'm going to live for another fifty years doing sweet f.a.' Now you might say: 'I've got news for you, Mrs.' But if you want to get into the finer details, I find it very difficult."

"It certainly gets involved," I say, glancing out the window. It seems almost surreal that part way through my round I should be sitting around discussing euthanasia, philosophy and morality with the local priest. It's almost bloody bizarre. Posties just don't do this sort of thing. Pulling myself back from my reverie, I listen to what Bob is saying.

"That's where Safran's got an advantage because he's Jewish and the Jews have been arguing about what's right and what's wrong for the last four thousand years," he says. "They've got books, and books, and Rabbis, and Rabbis. Are you allowed to eat an egg that a chook lays on Saturday? I remember when I was a chaplain at Prince Henry's Hospital, if a Jewish person came in on a Saturday he or she would not be allowed to ring the bell or press the button on the lift. Thou shall keep holy the Sabbath day."

"It sounds a bit drastic to me," I say.

"The Jews take all of these things so deadly seriously that you end up with a Jewish lifestyle," explains Father Bob. "The ones who take things to extremes are the Orthodox Jews. The Reform Jews say: 'We are going to observe the Sabbath meal and things of that nature but we are not going to take things to extremes.' The two groups have a different lifestyle. At Caulfield you've got the beards and the Russian coats and they walk everywhere."

"They're doing their bit to help stop global warming," I add limply. Rene Descartes groans so loudly that it's a wonder Bob doesn't hear him.

"Yes," Father Bob smiles indulgently as I sink lower into my chair, "they keep away from Gentiles so they don't get corrupted. In other parts of Melbourne, you've got Jewish people who drive their cars to the synagogue. So when it comes to things like deciding whether you should turn off Mum's life support system, if there's an extraordinary need for Mum to be kept alive on life support, a Jewish person would be better at that because he would have to go through it in great detail. *Great detail.* Whereas we get a bit lazy and say 'how much is it all going to cost?' "

"How does Catholicism stand with the hanging of Saddam Hussein?" I ask. Bob considers for a moment, then theatrically comes forth with:

"Love Saddam Hussein and love Osama Bin Laden. 'How will I love those swine that blew my mother up in Bali?' you ask. You can do that by flogging and hanging if you want to but you can't enjoy it, like the naughty boys and girls jumping up and down on the scaffold at Saddam's execution. If you can't work out some other way of dealing with bad people, because you're too lazy or it's too difficult, then flog and hang 'em."

This is enlightening and nothing like the answer I expected. I thought that there would be something about forgiveness: turning the other cheek. Then again, maybe I should have expected something different after what Bob said about the Micks not being too concerned about Father Smooch's criminality, although of course he would only have been alluding to the embezzlement, not the paedophilia.

"If you got into a confessional with a bloody orthodox priest," says Father, "and you confessed, then you might be forgiven your sins."

I strongly doubt that I'll ever get into a confessional with a bloody orthodox priest or any other kind but nod my head.

"It was not immoral," intones Bob, "because you knew that you didn't really want to be there and that if you didn't do it then the general would shoot you." He raises his eyebrows and says succinctly, "Now, get a Jew."

Catholicism, then, says there is nothing wrong with exacting revenge as long as you don't enjoy it. They are good, these Catholics, at forgiving one another horrific deeds as long as they are not intimately involved. Given involvement they can dish out retribution safe in the knowledge that they will be forgiven. This could probably be debated at length and I'm about to probe further when Father Bob picks up a magazine from his desktop and changes the subject. We never get bogged down in the complexity of things at these sessions.

"According to this article," Bob passes me a publication called *The*

*Tablet* with a photograph of its correspondent, Margaret Hebblethwaite, on it, 'giving to those who beg solves nothing except very temporarily, and often creates more problems than it solves. If people can earn more by begging than by working, they will not work.'

"One of the main 'rules' to the pragmatic approach to poverty," says Father Bob, "is don't give money to individuals. But is it practical? Imagine this: a woman, who recognises me, comes up to me in the supermarket, this thin sheila, and says that she is a bit short of money and would I pay her grocery bill. I look in her basket and see that she only has a few things. She looks in my basket and sees a bottle of red wine, amongst other things."

I picture Father Bob with a basket hanging off his arm digging into his wallet to give money to 'this thin sheila' in the supermarket, and can't help smiling. It *is* what he would do. Most of us, myself included, would fob her off, probably annoyed, too, rather than sympathetic. The Phil Collins song 'Another Day in Paradise' that prompted Chris to launch his Chuck a Buck for the Homeless People of Melbourne plan comes to mind.

Father Bob ponders the situation and then says: "Not giving money to individuals is the exact opposite to what I do. I'm driving myself insane. I'm sending myself broke so that I can give money to individuals."

We can faintly hear voices. 'Open House,' the feeding of those who are hungry, is still in progress around the side of the rectory. A derelict person is as welcome to eat at the Open House table as a single mother and her children. Everybody is made to feel welcome. Once again I hear the man who had just left the table after breakfast singing gloriously on the day that I was talking to 'Pepi.'

"Instead of 'Open House,' " says Father Bob, "I'd like to call it 'House of Hospitality' and model it along the lines of an organisation of that name run by a lay preacher in America named Dorothy Day. Now make sure you get this right, Ron. It's Dorothy Day, not Doris Day or Dorothy Dix." A few days earlier, I had confused Vinnie Pierce with Victor when writing about the funeral of a criminal and so had the wrong man in the coffin.

"Somebody put me on her mailing list years ago and I can't get off it," Bob says as he tears the wrapper off the latest edition of *The Catholic Worker*. He is quiet for a few moments and his voice becomes serious.

"I want to get this done before I die and I dunno if I'll succeed. This will be, for South Melbourne, the equivalent of what Abbé Pierre did for Paris because Day is his equivalent in the American model.

"There are two points to the way this is run and none of 'mine' can see it," he says. "I can talk until I'm black in the face, write it on the bloody wall in texta. They can't see it. The first point is helping the poor. The second one is educating the rich. Day, or in fact, the organisation that she founded, attempts to do both. They let anybody in; a lunatic is welcome. The team will fuss about this person without even mentioning Jesus, Joseph or Abraham. If this person wants to move in he or she can do so. That's why it's called 'House of Hospitality.'

"I want to do a similar thing here. It's more than social welfare. It's much more than anything else we've had here in South Melbourne. The *Sisters of Mother Theresa* in Gore Street Fitzroy is run along these lines. A derelict person can go there, eat and be fussed over. The nuns will kiss his feet as though he is Jesus, but they won't let him move in to the convent."

You could hardly blame them for that, I think, as I listen to Bob.

"Other places start out heroically, saying: 'We all love each other. We all love Jesus who died for us,' " says Father, "but then they discover how difficult it all is. They start lamenting: 'Oh Christ, only one or two have got the gift to do this work. The rest of us will have to knock off doing this otherwise we will go bloody mad.' "

I hear what sounds like a postie tooting his horn as he rides his Honda past the Church along Dorcas Street. Maybe he noticed my bike leaning against the fence.

"We, on the other hand," continues Bob, "could have two houses next door to each other, one where the poor can live or come and go as they please, and one where Brother Bloggs and the other Brothers can live. Bloggs can serve the poor in the 'House of Hospitality' and then return to his own house when it suits. He has to be able to get away from the madness so that he doesn't become a lunatic himself. All the risks in the universe are associated with this. I accept that. The people who live here should be able to cope with the occasional lunatic though."

I can't help laughing when Bob says this but he is not finished with the subject of lunatics yet.

"I also believe," he says, "that there are one or two in the world who have got the gift to live with the lunatics without going mad."

Yes, I think to myself, they're posties like me who have to work in confined spaces cheek by jowl with the unloved and the unwashed amid a cacophony of transistor radios tuned to different stations and the relentless mad-banter of posties teasing or taunting each other. The banter can be funny and witty but it is also delicately balanced on the knife-edge of sarcasm. In hot weather, when everyone is tired and resentful of the hours of poking meaningless paper into thankless slots, things can shift from good-humoured niggling to irritated and angry and sometimes to push and shove. The protagonists are like prisoners, trying to send one another mad. It all takes place in a climate where the workers aren't trusted. The Post Office Fleas, instead of doing something productive, are busy counting letters, weighing mail or timing posties as they sort: transferring every scrawled number to an all-knowing computer. 'How many letters are you sorting per minute? According to the figures you should have been set up and ready to go twenty minutes ago. What's the hold up?' Is it any wonder that sometimes an inmate goes postal? Neither should it be assumed that this attitude of power and mistrust is confined to the Aussie Post Fleas. In 1984 in his story 'At Auxonne' John Berger wrote:

*The post office was large and I suspect that its director was either inefficient or vicious; there was something demoralised about the staff behind the counter, as if unnecessary absurdities had been added to their burden of overwork.*

"Now I'm saying in Orstralia," says Bob interrupting my musing with a heavy Aussie accent, "especially down here, in the badlands, someone should be setting up a model along these lines." Bob raises his voice: "That's what I want but I can't get them to see it. Thirty-three bloody years!"

Bob stops talking and watches Frank as he gets disdainfully out of the armchair and ambles out of the room with his nose in the air. We sit quietly for a while listening to the wattlebirds trumpeting to each other in the big eucalypts outside the study.

Father Bob resumes his soliloquy: "We were called the Mad Micks in the early days. Much of that was to do with socio-economics. There was the Great Depression, Irish loyalties, and bigotry to name a few contributing factors."

"My grandparents arrived from England," I say, "together with my Mum who was only four years old, in 1927. They lived in rundown terrace houses in the slums of North Melbourne, doing 'moonlight flits' just like your parents when they couldn't pay the rent during the Depression."

"Yeah?" says Bob.

"Yeah. Pa forbade any member of the family to patronise the milk bar on the corner because the shopkeeper was a Catholic. I remember him referring to Catholics as Mad Micks. He hated you buggers."

Father Bob laughs, our roles now reversed as I continue: "Pa knew a bloke who worked for the Victorian Railways. This bloke knew of a job going and he told Pa that the job was as good as his as long as he said he was a Catholic. My Mum told me, that at this time she was going to school with bare feet and Nanna had a hole in her heart and was often sick. A job would have been handy but Pa knocked it back!"

Father Bob smiles sympathetically. "We had some bigoted Catholics and some pig-headed Protestants," he says, apportioning blame equally. "The main difference is that the Proddies will burn in hell."

We both laugh. Maybe Bob could become *my* biographer. "Now where was I?" asks Bob, although I think he knows exactly where he was. "We get to the fifties. We've done all the right stuff for the Catholics. Some of 'em become upwardly mobile, they move out into suburbia and they become part of 'The Great Australian Dream' but there was a rump that stayed behind". I like that bit. "People who moved into public housing with no connections to South Melbourne: ex bush, old people, single people or people from other public housing areas. We started a new village. Roman Catholicism better start shaping up, show them the way, as we did amongst ourselves."

"You'll have to get them into church if you want to show 'em the way, won't you?"

"No!" Bob exclaims loudly. "We daren't mention the bloody Bible because of the Aussies' allergy to Bible-bashers. Never mind the Mary, Jesus or Joseph. We can *be* Mary, Jesus or Joseph if we want to be, but you're not allowed to talk about Mary, Jesus or Joseph."

I nod a couple of times because this rings true. Until I started writing the biography I can't recall Bob ever talking about Mary, Jesus, or Joseph unless he was blaspheming. "What about God?" I ask.

Frank, seemingly bored, wanders back into the room again, cocks his head to one side, and looks quizzically at Bob.

"I'm not going to argue with people about God, Frank," Father Bob says. "I don't mind being God, but I'm not going to argue with anybody. People start talking about the existence of God, but I'm not interested in debating it. 'Oh,' they say: 'we like you because you're so funny.' I say: 'Alright then I'm going to reveal my true identity: I'm God.' "

A few days later the message on the notice board outside the church reads:

*Let's meet here before the game.* It is signed: *God.*

"They don't want to fight about Jesus but they don't mind fighting

God. Everybody is comfortable with Jesus," says Father.

"The Yanks love talking about God," I say.

"I'm amazed with the Americans talking about God and religion, breathing fire. It's hardly ever Jesus; it's usually God and it's usually Old Testament God; they're a bit nervous once they get to Jesus. They like to wheel out the evangelists though. Jesus said this, and Jesus said that, but I don't want to know what *they* think He said because the bloody writers could have made it all up. There are no cross-references. You daren't use it as a reference book as the clowns do."

"Writers love making things up," I say with a smile.

Bob grins, "I don't care what you write. If the Religious Police come knocking on the door, I'll simply deny I ever said it."

"I'd better go and deliver the rest of the mail," I say. I've been talking to Bob for some time and I can picture my bike with a bag of mail sitting in it, leaning against the front fence.

Bob nods absently and then continues! He looks across the room at his wall map and says: "I wanted to have all of this online; all of those red dots, and more, on line. You could have a street worker in Meekathara. The trouble is if you are identified as a street worker, bureaucracy wants to deal with you. 'Excuse me have you been registered as having qualifications to care for kids? Have you got . . .' " Bob stops mid sentence and swears softly. Pick your own word. "Now you either have to go through all that or you're a volunteer. Even then it's open to abuse because, I suppose, there are lunatics in Meekathara the same as there are here."

"I'm sure there are one or two people in Meekathara who would go along with that sentiment," I add wondering what it's like being a postie at Meekathara. I'm not even sure where bloody Meekathara is.

Father Bob laughs and goes on with his story. "So if somebody gets onto the network, what am I going to do? Fly around bloody Australia checking them out. I had hoped to involve my colleagues, the Roman Catholic Clergy, around Orstralia. I could have communicated with them and said every Catholic Parish in Australia is in fact a sub-agency for Open Family."

"That sounds like an excellent idea to me, but I don't know anything about Catholic Parishes or priests. Have any of them taken up the idea and actually become agencies for Open Family? You'd tend to think that they would jump at the chance to get involved."

"No."

"Why not?"

"Because they are priests! Not all priests are the same, just as not all posties are the same. I think that this is the *third time* I've told you this."

Rene tells me that Bob is right. 'This *is* the third time,' he says exasperatedly.

"They've all got a different perspective," says Bob. "They want to go to church. They want to assure the Roman Catholics that everything is alright."

This seems to be a big part of Bob's take on Catholicism. The sit-on-your-arse priests, through confession, want to assure even the wrongdoers that everything is alright.

"Even if they didn't want to start their own charity or have soup kitchens in their backyard," he says, "they could at least be a kind of a franchise so that anybody could . . . " he peters out again, yawns and then tells another little story about Meekathara. Maybe he's got a key in the middle of his back that his secretary winds up every morning. I really will have to get going soon.

"It's 100 degrees in the shade at Meekathara and someone comes up and rings the bloody doorbell. The priest thinks: 'Oh Christ! Go to buggery; I don't want to have anything to do with you.' "

I laugh. Bugger the letters. This is a lot more stimulating.

"The woman at the door says: 'I believe that you are an agency for Open Family Orstralia.' The priest says: 'Yes,' and gives her a card, which might say: 'The nearest Open Family worker, or Father Bob Foundationer is, happily enough, in Meekathara at 48 Smith Street, and there's a phone number beneath the name. He can get rid of her for a start. 'Thank God,' he says, 'she's gone.' But at least she has gone with some piece (voice gradually rises) of empowering information." The word 'empowering' is drawn out.

Bob says: "I'd like a GPS in place." He thinks for a few moments. Frank looks at him and starts panting loudly, his tongue dripping saliva. Bob shakes his head at the sight and says: "If people are looking for a refuge there's a mob now called Info-express that says they'll give you up to date information in five seconds, for anywhere in Orstralia. Then they'll upgrade it twice a day, so the only thing that I have to supply to my agent in Meekathara is a Blackberry or Blueberry, or whatever you call it, that will do everything for her apart from cut her toenails."

Bob is fully wound up now and there's no chance of me getting out of here in a hurry.

"I'm getting stalled by Open Family though when I ask the simple question," Father Bob lowers his voice and shakes his head, 'what the *hell* are you doing?'

'What the hell *are* they doing?' asks Rene Descartes. 'They are not doing a very good job if they are trying to run it like McDonalds. Oddly enough, McDonalds practises what Father Bob preaches: exponential growth. Their outlets are all over the place like Frank's hamburger-with-the-lot,' he sniffs.

"I read books and do all the right things by Mother Church but Mother Church is at her best, I think, when she gets away from holding the fort and runs the risk. We've got a history of that. We went to China. Then you've got the problem: do you turn Chinese?"

I smile. It's a long way from Meekathara to China. This is now getting very involved and I've got to get out of here!

"You can't change the world," says Father Bob, "but you can change the patch for which you are responsible. We can try to make up for the lost opportunities of the last thirty-three years."

His sentiments and ideas make a lot of sense to me. If we had a few politicians who thought like he does, then there would be a chance for the poor and if we had a few Fleas who thought like that there would be harmony in the workplace.

"Tomorrow night," he says getting back into stride, "we will have the inaugural Maguire Foundation Art Auction. We'll have these wealthy people, I suppose, whose drug is art. They'll all be swanning around in the church inspecting the Blackman's and the Drysdale's. It may set them thinking as they wander around: 'Geez, this is a lovely building. I wonder what goes on in here?' My two food buses will be parked out the front in a prominent position. They'll say: 'What are these?'

'They feed people, your Majesty.'

'What people?'

'Other people.'

'Oh, I didn't know there were other people, Father Maguire. I thought they were all at Portsea with me.'"

Laughing, I tell Father Bob that I must take my leave: the letters await.

"Goodbye, Your Grace," says Father.

As I ride off, I wonder whether Bob has ever been to Meekathara.

## Chapter 21: God is Good

*"Can you imagine it? A priest sitting there, on the shore,
taking pot-shots at Mary and Baby Jesus!"*

The next night, the inaugural art auction (or 'orktion' as the orktioneer calls it) for the Father Bob Maguire Foundation does indeed take place. When he gives his introductory speech, the orktioneer praises the Father Bob Maguire Foundation saying that it is one of South Melbourne's honest charities. It would be enlightening to hear his opinions of any other charities in the area, perhaps the ones that aren't so honest.

The orktion is held incongruously in Sts Peter and Paul's magnificent bluestone Church. Could this be the first time a church in Australia has been used as an auction house? As we wander around looking at the paintings, sipping red wine and eating pâté on biscuits, (no, not *that* red wine or *those* biscuits) Father Bob tells us a little story as he is wont to do. My daughter, Penny, comments on one of the religious statues and the story unfolds from there. It seems that the priest in a small country Victorian parish (I've decided to withhold the name but Father Bob will attest to the veracity of this tale) wanted to get rid of some religious statues because there were so many that the church was looking cluttered. The town in question is situated on the banks of a large lake in Victoria (there's a nice little clue for you) so the priest loaded the unwanted statues into his boat, rowed out into the lake, and threw them overboard. Unfortunately for the poor bugger the statues came to the surface and could be seen bobbing around in the water. Undeterred, the quick thinking priest rowed back to shore, went home and got his rifle, came back to the scene of the crime and shot the statues full of holes until they submerged.

"Can you imagine it?" says Father with a horrified look on his face, "A priest sitting there, on the shore, taking pot-shots at Mary and Baby Jesus!"

'A priest with a rifle!' exclaims Ronny.

The following day, I duck into Father Bob's for a couple of minutes to ask him if his Foundation made much out of the auction. 'Nosey bloody postie,' sniffs Descartes.

"No, we never sold enough." he says. "We had hoped to make a hundred thousand dollars out of that like they did for a similar auction they held at Scotch College. It wasn't God's will," he adds.

As I am about to leave, he pulls a bag from under the desk. "Do you ever get presents?" asks Father Bob.

"Only at Christmas," I say, looking at the bag.

"What about whisky?"

"No, I don't normally get bottles of whisky."

"No, do you drink whisky?" asks Father.

"Ah, well, the occasional drop."

"Here take this home," says Bob pulling a bottle of 15-year-old Dimple from the fancy bag to show me. "I don't drink it. It's a nice bottle isn't it?" he asks as he appraises the bottle.

"Yes, it's a lovely bottle," I agree, my eyes widening as *I* appraise it.

"Can you carry it on the bike? You don't want to smash it."

"Don't worry, I'll look after it. I'll put it in the pannier."

Father Bob reads the card that came with the bottle. It was from a couple, he says, who he had "married off nicely." He puts the bottle back into the bag and hands it to me smiling. "God is good," he says.

"Thanks very much Bob."

"Now don't drop it or they'll be talking about you. 'He was drunk out in the street after leaving the Church.'"

"Goodbye, Father," I say as I head for the door.

"Goodbye, my son."

Anyhow, I think as I stash the bottle in the pannier and ride off down Dorcas Street: God is Good. I am conscious of its presence as I ride along delivering and I reflect on Bob's generous nature. I vividly remember the first year that he gave me what was to become the yearly Christmas tip. I set my round up differently then and I used to deliver to the rectory via the Montague Street entrance. Bob was out on the front verandah when I rode up and handed him a bundle of mail. He pulled his wallet from his back pocket and opened it. He took out a twenty-dollar note and I remember thinking: 'Gee, that's alright, a twenty-dollar tip.' Bob slipped out another twenty, glanced at me, and then removed the remaining ten dollar note, leaving himself broke. I was astounded. I remember blaspheming. "Jesus!" I breathed as he handed me the money.

"Good on ya, mate," said Bob. We shook hands and I rode away like a bushranger with the priest's money in my pocket.

Father Bob had been cleaned out before I got there the following year.

"You're too late!" he said loudly as I rode up the drive from Montague Street. "The garbos got here first." Sure enough, the garbage truck, with sullage dripping out the back, was heading up Montague

Street and about to turn into Bank Street. We both laughed about it, shook hands, and I rode off empty handed, but smiling broadly. Other years come to mind too: one Christmas eve, late in the afternoon, I was down the end of Gladstone Grove (a lane in reality) when I heard a car pounding over the cobblestones behind me. Father Bob was at the wheel with Barnabus beside him with a big grin on his face. The giving of the yearly gratuity had now become so entrenched that Bob was not about to let it slip. I don't know how long they had been driving around looking for me but they now had me trapped at the end of the lane like a rabbit in the spotlight. The money was in an envelope with a card endorsed: 'Merry Christmas from Bob and the parishioners.'

## Chapter 22: Shiny Suburban Catholics

*"Let's open the windows of this stinking church
because it has become foul."*

"Good morning," I say to a customer as I hand him his mail. He is standing just inside the front gate with his four children. They are all dressed in their finery. Maybe the man is about to take his boys on an outing despite it being a school day.

The man smiles and replies: "Morning."

The eldest son follows suit: "Morning."

Followed by the next in line: "Morning."

The third boy quickly follows the second: "Morning."

The youngest, who is all of four years of age, follows like the imitator that he is: "Morning," he peeps seriously in his little-boy voice.

The voices are pitched from low to high. It's like a scene out of a child's book. The melodious sounds of the voices are still playing in my head as I approach the church. Morning, Morning, Morning, Morning.

Father Bob is alighting from his car with a plaque tucked under his arm as I approach on my bike.

"Morning, Bob," I say with a grin as I dismount.

A neighbour is out walking his four little black-and-white dogs, which scamper across the lawn behind the memorial wall where the plaque is to be displayed.

"They come in here for their daily constitution," remarks Bob shaking his head as we walk along the footpath toward the rectory. The last word on the plaque, I see, is *RESPECT*. The dog walker could do with a dose of that.

In the study I look at the plaque that Bob places in Frank's leather armchair. The gold writing proclaims:

*Forgive us our sins as we forgive you yours. We were only in our 20's and we died on your watch.*

Beneath these words there is a list of names, Christian, or first names, followed by an initial for the surname. There are about thirty names of people, from the South Melbourne and surrounding area, who have died because of drug abuse over the last thirty years or so.

There would have been another name on the list but for the sheer dedication and determination of Father Bob. Barnabus is still alive.

It was whilst Bob was telling me a story about a Mass for the deceased writer Niall Brennan that I first hear about this man who I often see at the rectory or in the church grounds.

"I did the Mass up in the hills at Gladysdale," said Father that day. "I got involved with the Brennans because Mrs Brennan was the woman who said to me: 'Bob,' 'Yes', 'Look after Barnabus; he's fifteen years old; he has terrible migrant family issues.' I said: 'No, no, no. I don't want to take one person on; I don't believe in it; the books say don't do it;' She said: 'Bob, Bob, Bob.' I said: 'At your request I will break the rules.' So I took Barnabus on. That was because she recommended it. She was a thoughtful and intelligent woman as well as a social worker at the Prahran Multicultural Centre where she came across Barnabus' mother."

Father Bob has been mentoring Barnabus, who has become a big part of The Cause, now for over thirty years. I think that it would be right to say that Father Bob is Barnabus' surrogate father. Whenever he has been in strife with the police or has had to front the courts Barnabus has turned to Father Bob and Bob has stuck by him despite criticism from some members of the parish.

Life was still tough at home for Barnabus despite Father Bob's mentoring. As he got older, he turned to drugs just like his two brothers and a lot of his peers, but he was not to die whilst Bob was around. Both of his brothers died though which is why Father Bob stuck by him through the desperate times when he was trying to kick the heroin habit.

'Barnabus: not Father Bob' quips Rene with a laugh.

I 'see' him now, running along Dorcas Street towards Pickles Street, with the big black poodle loping along at his heels. Frightened pedestrians move aside as they steam past rounding the corner into Pickles Street, the man and his dog as one.

Until a few years ago, Pickles Street was Port Melbourne territory but local government boundary changes saw a cleavage and Port Melbourne residents living in houses on the even-numbered side of the street suddenly found themselves living in South Melbourne. If only it were that easy for the Henderson Street unfortunates! At the time of the changes I was reading R. D. Laing's *The Divided Self* and made a human analogy, with the street becoming schizophrenic: the 'true self' on one side of the divide and the 'false self' on the other.

Barnabus shouts, angrily into the wind: 'Carn the Pies.' His voice is deep and loud and attracts a lot of attention. Cars slow down, heads twist, eyes widen and jaws unhinge.

"Bugger youse!" he booms, waving his arms about. His face is contorted with pain and there are droplets of perspiration on his brow. His T-shirt is soaked. The rangy dog stays hard on his heels, looking around, his bright red, dripping tongue lolling out the side of his mouth like one of Father Bob's lunatics.

The schizophrenic street analogy seems appropriate somehow I think as Frank wanders into the study. He is definitely not unique. If I didn't know otherwise I'd swear he was the original arse-biter. He looks at the plaque sitting on his chair then wanders over to Bob.

There is a further inscription on the plaque after the list of names: *24/7 Anzac Walk.*

"What do you mean by "24/7 Anzac Walk? I ask.

"That means," says Bob, "If you want to talk the Anzac Talk you can do so until the bloody cows come home, but if you want to walk the Anzac Walk, you'd better start putting in". He rubs his hand over his face like a face-washer, looks at me grimly and says quietly: "I knew all these young people because they were in and out of this house. This was the first wave of deaths from drugs." No doubt some were Chris' mates, I think; they used to visit the rectory.

My mission today is to find out about Father Bob's time at the Werribee Seminary so after a respectful silence I broach the subject.

"What can you tell me about your time at the Seminary?"

Father Bob screws up his face and groans. "It was boring!" he says loudly. "It was like going into a bloody Boys' Home." He gets out of his chair and goes over to the bookcase. Selecting a book, entitled *Young Stalin* by Simon Sebeg Montefiore, he hands it to me.

"The author of this book went into the Seminary in Georgia," says Bob as I read the blurb inside the cover. "Lots of boys, especially the children of the rich, were sent to the Priest Factory," he says describing the story. "A lot of young men went into Seminaries, both Anglican and Roman Catholic, for various reasons. It's not like going into a monastery. Once you are in a monastery, you're buggered."

I smile.

"It's similar to a convent," he continues, "in that it feels as if you'll never get out."

I know of a place like that.

"In comparison to a monastery, the Seminary was more of a general practitioner's training centre. The length of the course was arbitrarily set in the middle ages. They decided that it would be *eight bloody years!*" he says with much stress on the last three words. "That takes you from eighteen to twenty-six, so that's the end of your youth. I suspect that what happens after that is that when you get to twenty-six and you are commissioned by the Bishop to go out into the World, I think that you go out almost a permanent adolescent. You've had no youth and you are going out to captive audiences. There was a Catholic revolution whilst I was still in the semetery."

I think that if I had to spend eight years of my life in a seminary where I was bored to death, 'semetery' would be an appropriate epithet for the place. "Tell me about the revolution, Father," I say. The opening has come at last and perhaps Father Bob will now relate the story of Vatican Two.

"It was called Vatican Two," says Bob, as if following a script. "That said: 'Let's open the windows of this stinking church because it has become foul.' I am mentally appeased, thinking that's exactly what I want: colourful language about Vatican Two, but even now when I should be concentrating I can hear Jelly Roll Morton singing mournfully in my head:

'I thought I heard Buddy Bolden shout:
Open up that winda and let that bad air out.
Open up that winda and let the foul air out.'

I have been looking forward to hearing about Vatican Two so decide to keep the song to myself. I resolve to concentrate but now Father Bob is distracted! His bloody mobile phone rings before we've had time to open up them windas. The author of 'Margie's Shitful Life to the End' is on the line trying to get Bob to give her some money.

After the call ends, Bob says: "People of this nature are feral and smart. They are emotional blackmailers. That's all they've got. *They* are total and permanent adolescents too. They've been robbed of their youth by drugs. They think that they are smart. Some of them have killed people and done all kinds of criminal things over forty years so they've got the false feeling of being in charge. If they look at their daily lives though," Bob continues, "whether they know it or not, their lives are wrecked. They're all totally and permanently confused. I'll have to go down to the bank and put a dollar in her account." Bob smiles. "It's the only way to appease her." He has been appeasing Margie in this way, perhaps making her life a bit less shitful, for nigh on forty years.

"Back to the Seminary!" Father Bob declares emphatically. "We come out and are posted to Roman Catholic parishes. We are not monks therefore we are not part of a team. When I came out I was posted to a place and worked in a parish with another priest. In those days you had a housekeeper, and in some cases a parish secretary. That was it. You were the ruling Junta. You could be posted to the bush, not because you were suited to the bush, but because you were next in line. Alternately you could be sent to one of the poor inner-city parishes. These were rough areas then: Fitzroy, Footscray, Richmond. You had to adapt."

I look across at Frank lounging on the floor next to his armchair. He blinks and looks at me. The unusual circumstance of these sessions still astounds me. What would the Post Office Fleas have to say if they knew this was going on whilst my every move was being timed to the nth degree. Bob probably wonders why I'm smiling. The whole scenario is outlandish; I feel as if I am acting a part in one of Bob's plays.

"The Vietnam War coincided with the arrival of the drug culture," says Bob. "There was more dope being smoked and heroin being used by the Americans in Vietnam than you can shake a stick at. The Aussies probably learnt it from them and introduced it here. That was when the big cultural change happened."

Hang on a minute, I think, what happened to Vatican Two?

"The preferred drug of the alienated clergyman would have been the grog, I would have thought," says Father Bob. "That was the predicament. You were sent into a place with a captive audience: the parish. Then, because you were ordained in the sixties like I was, you had a bit of the old style clergyman on you, which meant you were treated with the utmost respect as if you were the personal representative of Jesus. That's the old theology: another Christ." Father Bob says 'another Christ' in a humorous way stretching his lips across his teeth. "You were also tarred with the brush of Vatican Two," says Bob. I sigh inwardly with relief and fervently hope that Bob's mobile phone doesn't ring for a while. He says: "Vatican Two said: 'Hey, don't get tickets on yourself because you are one of many.' In other words, all the people in your parish have to be priests. You are the clergyman. You are the public servant of the other priests. Vatican Two said: 'Listen, something awful has happened. We've designated some of you as priests, whereas if you look at the scriptures, the Bible for the Christians of the first hundred years, it looks as though the ideal is that every man and woman believer is in fact a priest.'"

'Even the bloody postie.' Rene Descartes is as quick as Spooks sometimes.

"The ideal," says Bob, "even in the Jewish scriptures, was: 'I wish,' says God, 'all of you were priests.' It was the same with Jesus who said: 'You *are* all priests.' Now that slips through to the keeper and is not seen again for a thousand years until Vatican Two."

I find Bob's words 'even in the Jewish scriptures' interesting. He places the Jews in an exalted position. "That must have been a big shakeup," I say, thinking of the enormity of the changes that must have been sparked by this reinterpretation.

"It *was* a big shakeup," Bob agrees. "I was thinking earlier that I'd love to have enough money to commission a medal with a campaign ribbon. I'd get a medal struck and award it to all those clergymen who were involved in the campaign called Vatican Two. Those who fought that campaign and . . ." Father Bob's voice fades. "It looks as though we've lost because the Church authorities and their public servants have reverted to pre-Vatican Two Catholicism. This is guerrilla warfare because you daren't attract their attention or they'll eliminate you, so you've got to run with the fox and hunt with the hounds. It's better for a parish to be cashed up because the main reason for attracting attention from headquarters is if you are broke and start asking them for money."

"Do they blame you personally if the parish is broke?" I ask incredulously.

"Oh, yes!"

"But the Roman Catholics have got oodles of money."

"It doesn't matter. If you were to say: 'Can I see the figures please, Your Grace?' he would say: 'No; I'm terribly sorry but it's confidential to me and my council members.' "

"What would they say if you asked them for a housekeeper? You should be entitled to one."

"They'd have none of that. You don't ask 'em for anything. That's why we are sitting here on the corner of Dorcarse and Montague," Bob delights in mispronouncing Dorcas, "in an empty house, unserviced and, mind you, these days you don't want housekeepers and people here either because of the accusations that have been levelled against us: that we are a pack of drunks and sexual deviants."

I nod sympathetically. The toxic cloud left by Smooch and his ilk will hang low over the heads of the priesthood for a long time to come. "The best way to do it," says Bob, "is the way we do it here: people come in and perform their tasks then leave, such as the ones who come in to feed the poor. They're all gone by 4 o'clock and I'm left on me own. Ah, if you had a house-creeper there would be innuendo: unmarried man was observed with…"

"You could have a male house-creeper."

"No! You'd be labelled homosexual. If you had a child running around feeding you they'd say you were a paedophile; if a teenager was running around you'd be a hebaphile or something."

"This has all been brought about by the actions of people like Smooch," I comment.

"Well, yes. The revelations of that nature have also uncovered a source of infection because of the inability of churches to provide leadership. This came up on Denton's television show: 'Enough Rope.' He was on about celibacy. I said: 'Look I'm . . .' Oh, Christ! Here they come," groans Father Bob as he looks out the study window.

A group of well-dressed people has just stepped onto the verandah. Bob continues the conversation where he left off.

"I said to Denton: 'I'm married to the Parish of South Melbourne. You've got to be married to the parish or the neighbourhood or both.' Bring 'em in," Father yells out to Annette, like a farmer ordering his dog to bring the cows in for milking.

Ronny projects a picture of Bob running around a muddy paddock in a pair of gumboots with a couple of blue-heelers yapping excitedly as they muster the cattle.

"Have a look at them," says Bob quietly. "They're all shiny. They're all shiny these suburban Catholics. They're all bloody shiny."

Bob's repetitive sentences remind me of Spooks. The difference is that Spooks talks like that continually.

"They've come here from St Albans South," says Father Bob, "to learn about practical Catholicism. I dunno what it's supposed to be about meself: feeding the poor and kicking the arse of the rich, maybe." This is the sort of language that epitomises Father Bob Maguire the larrikin priest. It also puts a Peter Costello smirk on my face.

I haven't found out anything about life in the Seminary so I'll have to take up the theme next time. I thank Father Bob, turn off my voice recorder and take my leave so that he can entertain the Shiny Suburban Catholics who are trooping into the study like a class of school kids on an excursion. He will treat them with respect. He will entertain them, impress them with his knowledge, and leave them laughing, but pandering to Shiny Suburban Catholics interrupts his work on behalf of the pooah. He prefers the stubble on the chin and the worn-out runners or work-boots.

'There's a stubble on your chin this morning and your boots are a bit scuffed. You're getting a bit lazy in your old age,' says Rene Descartes as I pull a bundle of mail from the bag before riding off down the street.

# Chapter 23: You're in the Army Now

*"The Mick priest would have been smoking and drinking and gambling, which to the ordinary soldier would have been a bonus."*

What do they think, these locals, when they see this old postie larruping his heavy old bike around the streets? I ride hard, making sure though that I don't end up with someone on the handlebars as I round a corner. The idea is to get as much of the round delivered before my talk with Father Bob so that when I return to the round there's not much mail left to deliver. After all, it is Friday. Heading south in Montague Street I turn left into Patterson Place but I'm going too fast and as I turn from the road onto the footpath the handlebars clip the fence and I go down, still in the riding position flat out on the footpath like a cartoon character who has been run over by a steamroller. I gash my shin on some part of the bike on my way down. Scrambling to my feet, red-faced, I shovel the mixed up mail into the bag, looking around to see if anyone is watching. I remount and ride halfway down the street where I sit on the footpath, leaning up against a fence, and re-sequence the mail. My shin is badly gashed and already swelling up. I should start riding around at a pace more appropriate to my age I suppose. The trouble is on the inside I'm still about thirty!

"You were in the Army Reserve for twenty-five years," I declare as I settle into my chair, turn on my recorder, and make myself at home. Frank wasn't at the door to greet me when I arrived but he wanders into the study and pads over to me. I pat him still feeling a bit shaken from my fall but glad to see his trusting look. He then trots over to his chair and sits down as if ready to take part in the discussion.

"Was I? That could be right. I'm buggered if I know," says Reverend Father Robert John Maguire, AM, RFD. The AM stands for Member of the Order of Australia. He was awarded this in 1989. In 2003, he was awarded a Centenary Medal and named Entrepreneur of the Year for the Southern Region of Australia for a Social, Community, or Not-For-Profit Organisation. The initials RFD (Reserve Forces Decoration) recognise twenty-five years service in the Army Reserve. During his school days at Christian Brothers' College St Kilda, Bob was the Senior Army Cadet. \*

\*Since this was written, the Liberal State Government awarded the

Victorian of the Year to Father Bob in 2011.

"I started in the Army Reserve in the sixties when I was in my thirties," says Bob after I ask him to tell me about his time in the army. "The Army was looking for replacements for the Army Reserve chaplains who had served with distinction in the Second World War and the Korean War, and who were now retiring. Chaplains were given a lot of respect back then because they did a lot of good during the war. The Army said: 'What about some of you young blokes taking it on?' I considered it and thought: 'Aussie soldiers don't mind chaplains,' so I agreed to become one," he concludes.

"Was the one chaplain used for all denominations?" I ask, thinking that that would have simplified matters.

"No. We followed the English model, although we modified it a bit. We ended up with a Chaplaincy Department that was a secular department within the Defence Department. We had rank, so you went in as a captain, the same as the dentists and doctors or other professionals went in. As your position became more responsible you rose in rank, the next one being major."

"What rank did you attain?" I have a vague recollection of seeing Father Bob in his army uniform not long after I started to deliver his mail. It was a day or two before Anzac Day I think and I remember him coming to the front door wearing the uniform of an officer in readiness for a memorial that he was to attend. I remember being surprised at seeing him in this garb because I had no inkling that he had been in the army.

"I only went up to a Half Colonel," says Father modestly. "This was depicted by a star and a crown. I was only full time duties as a Reserve Army Chaplain whereas the *real* chaplains were Regular Army."

Yes, I remember the red (I think it was) crown on one of the epaulets on Father Bob's uniform. If I could get my short-term memory back to this level I'd be right for another sixty years.

"Did you live in the barracks?" I ask, wondering if the chaplains did it tough.

"Yes, I lived in the bloody barracks at Puckapunyal for four years. My first posting was to the Royal Australian Artillery. We used to run around the hills at Jamieson."

"You trooped around with the soldiers then?" I try not to grin.

"We had to. That's the job of the bloody chaplain," Bob takes off his glasses and stifles a yawn.

"I thought that the chaplains would have stayed in an office and then just been on hand when required."

"No!" Bob bellows. "The good chaplains were out in the field. They were never in their bloody offices. Of course you got some who were attracted to the cushy job, which is the same in any profession. The only place you could find Chaplain Bloggs was in his office."

Ronny, who is always interested in the broad perspective, wonders if Chaplain Bloggs bore any relationship to Mrs. Bloggs from Dandenong who got Henry into trouble, and indeed if Mrs. Bloggs from Dandenong is related to Mrs. Bloggs who rang the Sunshine police station after her house was robbed only to be told that no one could attend the robbery because the station had just lost an officer to the Delta Taskforce. Ronny says: 'I know that Bloggs is a common name *but* could Mrs. Bloggs from Dandenong, Mrs. Bloggs from Sunshine, and Brother Bloggs from the House of Hospitality all be related to the good Chaplain Bloggs from the Army?'

I now find that, like a schoolboy daydreaming during class, I've lost track of what Father Bob is talking about. I pick up on the words 'secular society.'

"The secular society was fairly broadminded and provided facilities for the chaplain," says Father Bob. "It was divided up into Church of England, which allegedly was the biggest, Roaming Catholic, and Protestant Denominations. Then you might have the odd Jew or two. These days I would expect you would have to have a Muslim chaplain, although the Aussies are a bit inclined to say: 'It's all too much for us. Chuck 'em all into the Protestant Denominations.' " Father Bob grins and raises his eyebrows.

What exactly did these chaplains do? I wonder as I glance out the window. I hear the resident wattlebird trumpeting in one of the trees.

'Why don't you ask him?' sneers Descartes who can be bloody sarcastic at times. Before I can ask Bob he tells me just that.

"The Australian Defence Force developed a model called 'Character Training,' with the ideal of injecting the strongest characteristics into a young man of twenty years of age, which the conscripts were."

"I was under the impression that the course was only for the young officers," I read this in Bob's cousin Francis Maguire's history of the family and realise that I did in fact know what occupied the chaplains.

"No, it was for the whole Army, Navy and Air Force," says Bob. "I was asked to come into the Army, full time, whilst I was stationed as a priest at Seymour. They probably thought that I was a bit of a clown and would entertain the troops."

I laugh. It's easy to see Bob in this role. Posties are a bit like the troops too, I think. They troop into the Disaster Centre every morning, step up to their frames, and perform the task of throwing off their rounds at twenty-three letters to the minute like some sort of automatons. The Fleas, in a similar role to Army officers, make things as difficult for the troops as they can, by timing how long things take, counting tubs of mail, and holding meetings on a Friday morning.

"So, off I went as a professional bloody spruiker to huts full of twenty-year-olds for four years," Bob says. "They were divided into denominations, as I've said, and each denomination would have a Character Training Team. I became the Southern Command, which meant Victoria and Tasmania. It also meant an advance in rank. I became a major, strutting around like a bloody joker.

"Interestingly enough rank did protect you from the obstructionism that naturally comes from sergeants, corporals, or any junior officers," says Bob. "The Character Training Course lasted about five days during their basic training."

"Why did the sergeants and officers want to obstruct you?" I ask, puzzled.

"Because this is sceptical Orstralia. They would question the course: 'Four and a half days! What the bloody hell's the use of this? People are going overseas, possibly to get shot, and you're stuffing their heads with bullshit!' I found it exhilarating because one had to argue one's position."

Father Bob puts his glasses back on as he recalls it all: "I remember an old commander, Colonel Kirkland, who was a Vietnam War Veteran asking: 'What the hell are you doing? You're arguing with these bloody soldiers' trainers, some of whom have been overseas and know the dangers these boys will be facing. They're trying to get these people into shape, for God's sake!'" barks Bob. "I said to Kirkland: 'They're questioning the value of Character Training. This is not my doing. This is not the Pope! This is not the Archbishop of Canterbury! This is Army, man! Have a look in the Instruction Manual and you'll find it's *their* course. It's not mine. It's *theirs*!'" he says passionately. "Kirkland then said to me: 'Well, you'll have to explain it to the whole bloody battalion.'" Father Bob slams his hand down on the desk.

"So everybody from that training wing trouped into the bloody Puckapunyal picture theatre: all the officers, all the instructors, from himself down. He then made me get up on stage and present a case for Character Training so that nobody could say: 'I'm not going to listen to this bullshit from the chaplain,' because his immediate superior was there." Bob groans as the door buzzer squawks from the box on his desk. "Oh, go away! Send 'em away, will you?" he says knitting his eyebrows together.

"Who, me?" I ask raising mine. "You want me to answer the door?"

"Yes! There's nobody here yet to answer the door. That's the problem. Say I'm interviewing some bloke, or something," says Bob.

This is my first official assignment as The Mobile Priest. I walk to the front door with Frank padding along behind me, like the Phantom with his dog, Devil. Next to a verandah post, sits a young woman in a wheelchair with another woman standing behind the chair. They are both surprised to see, instead of a priest, a postie in a luminous safety-vest answering the door. I manage to answer their questions satisfactorily and 'Devil' and I go back inside.

"What did they want?" asks Bob.

I am about to answer Bob's question when someone else presses the front door buzzer.

"Everyone's pressing these bloody buttons," complains Bob, "and if I don't jump up like a jack-in-the-box and see to them straight away, they get upset."

"Is there anyone to answer the door at all today?"

"Yes, there's a woman volunteer coming in at 11 o'clock."

The person on the front verandah walks off and Father smiles.

"It must have been a big change when you left the army and came back to normal parish priest duties," I prompt.

"My mob won't do as they're told. That's the difference between the Army and this place," say Bob frowning again.

"Yes, in the Army you have to do what you are told whether you like it or not," I agree.

"For better or worse it was presumed that the officer in charge was no better than you but was there to help the unit work at its best. Now, at this place you've got a bunch of people who've lost any sense of what the Church is about," says Father Bob. "In the early days, the church was supposed to be a fighting unit: not to convert people and bring them to Jesus, Mary and Joseph, but simply to get the bloody job done. A big part of the job was not the huddle. The huddle was the prayers, the bread and wine, oil and water. The main thing was looking after those who had less."

Ronny joins in again: 'Father Bob, then, is true to The Cause, as he is fond of calling it. He is the shepherd of his local huddle, as well as the spearhead of the fighting unit that fights for those who have less.'

"What was the message you wanted to get across as a Character Trainer?" I ask, trying to bring us back to the topic.

"It was that, to be a soldier, an Australian soldier in particular, you had to have a strong character. Discussing this now is appropriate because this is the anniversary of Woodstock, marijuana and all that goes with it. I can see 'em now over at Batman Avenue, which was the assembly point for those whose marble had come out of the barrel. They're all twenty years old and they've all got long hair." Bob swivels his chair and looks out the study window as if he can actually see them. I can see them too. My number never came out of the barrel but my best mate, More, was conscripted (I'm looking at a crew cut though instead of long hair). The twenty-year-old ended up in Vietnam where the local friendly prostitutes loved him long time and loved him short time. More wrote to me and said that he thought that he was in heaven here on earth but the poor bugger fell down some steps coming out of a bar, broke his leg in three places and was repatriated. With his leg in plaster nearly up to his crotch he sat morosely on his front verandah drinking beer all day and watching the traffic go by along Anderson Road, Sunshine. All he wanted was for some girl to love him – long time or short time.

"The first Character Training session was about 'Who am I?' or something of that nature," explains Father Bob. "We had small discussion groups of about ten. You could lead the discussion or you could, and this is where I developed a technique that stood me in good stead over the years, have an open-ended discussion. In other words don't try to guide it. Chaplains are so used to preaching. There goes that bloody door buzzer *again*!"

Frank is off like a greyhound jumping out of the boxes. I laugh as his back legs nearly slide out from under him when he goes out the door of the study.

"There's a little woman who'll stagger up at 11 o'clock," says Bob, "to answer the door and help with the breakfast for the homeless. Some of these people coming to the door get aggressive if you can't attend to their problem immediately, saying: 'Excuse me, you are supposed to help people. Help people. Help people. Help people. Now, what answer have you got to that?"

I haven't got an answer to that. My time is up anyway because Bob moves briskly on.

"Your lot was in the paper yesterday: Australia Post. There is a dispute about the division of labour. It said that there would be fifty percent working in the sorting room and fifty percent working in the street."

"Yes. The management wants to gradually sack the full time workers, like me, and replace each one with two part-time workers."

"How the bloody hell will that work?" asks Bob puzzled as Frank returns from his mission. The interloper can be seen through the window talking to the gardener who has just arrived.

"The indoor workers will street sort the mail and set up the round. They will be called 'Slotters' because their job will include sorting the mail into vertical slots arranged on a frame. A slot is allotted to individual houses. The outdoor workers will be called Dodos."

"Are the poor buggers to become extinct then?" asks Bob with a look of mock horror on his face.

"The acronym stands for: 'Dedicated Out Door Delivery Only.' It's hard to believe that the Fleas didn't work on that one too. We've also got Dildos," I add.

"The mind boggles," says Bob grinning.

"That's for those who have injured themselves in the line of duty and are put on light duties: 'Dedicated Indoor Light Duties Only.'"

"We'd better get back to the bloody Army," says Bob laughing but it doesn't last for long. "Whoever keeps these places or expects them to stay open . . ." His voice trails off. "They won't provide infrastructure. That's the bloody problem."

"Is this to do with Emerald Hill Mission?" I ask. Emerald Hill Mission is the church side of business.

"Well, it's your Roaming Catholic Church or your City of South Melbourne or somebody who is bigger than me. It's not the Aussie way to stick a poor old bloke up the front where the fighting is."

"That's right. You're in the front line. You should be able to direct operations from the study and have an underling to attend to mundane business," I answer, inflaming the matter.

"Where are they? Where's the rest of the bloody world?" Bob asks as he looks out the window. "There are two blokes over there in lycra, riding down the street on their bloody bikes. Why can't they come over here and answer the door for us?"

We splutter with laughter at life's absurdities.

"It's obvious that you need more help around here," I sympathise.

"Yes, but us Aussies are so casual. You've got to have volunteers manning these places." Bob sighs. "What I'm hoping for, if I can survive this next ten minutes until the volunteer arrives to answer the door is, " Father Bob breathes momentously and starts his sentence again. "Emerald Hill Mission or the Roaming Catholic Church shouldn't be leaving me here for one hundred and sixty eight hours a week whilst *they*, as volunteers, turn up for two hours a week then squeal like stuck pigs when there's some glitch in the running of the show."

I shake my head.

"I had hope," says Bob, "when I came here: hope that the Military model, at its best, could be applied to a church with a mission, perhaps even using Character Training."

Bob hears a noise out the back and cocks his head to one side like Frank does. The lady volunteer has just arrived.

"Thank God!" he sighs as Frank wanders out to greet her.

"How well was Character Training received by the troops?" I ask Bob as he looks at his watch.

"Sometimes very well. It depended. I learnt to carry on like a bloody galah. It was infotainment. Infotainment in the 60's and that was palatable to these twenty year olds. Other chaplains had trouble but learnt a bit as they went on. The Catholic chaplains who had the most trouble were the ones who were more redneck, hardliners. For example: 'Abortion is a sin and a crime.' My approach to that was to broaden the discussion. It was called 'Respect for Life,' so you'd end up saying: 'Life from the womb to the tomb. What about you and the Viet Cong, who is your enemy? Are you going to bayonet him and shoot him? That doesn't seem to have much respect for human life. Are you going to take captives? What about the child who we know runs up to your personnel carrier with a land mine and sticks it underneath? What are you going to do about that? Are you going to shoot the kid first and ask questions second?' "

"That's a conundrum, sure enough." It gets me thinking hard: what should soldiers do under desperate circumstances such as these.

"If you hit these boys over the head with one issue they're not going to take it well. Toss it all up in the air and hope to God they get something out of it, that all human beings deserve a fair go. If you take prisoners, they deserve a fair go."

"Did the Character Training teach you anything?"

Bob leans slightly forward and says: "What I learnt from the Character Training was that the twenty year old Australian male was perfectly capable of, indeed good at, cutting through the bullshit."

Just like somebody whom I know. "In hindsight do you think that the Character Training course was much benefit?"

"The boys were asked to fill out an assessment at the end of the course: 'what did you think of the course and the instructors?' I wish they had kept those records because it could have given us an indication of how to go about tackling the problems of twenty year-olds in the post-war churches. The assessments, in general, were heartening for us, the Micks. I don't know about the others. The Mick priest would have been smoking and drinking and gambling, which to the ordinary soldier would have been a bonus."

More told me the other day that he went into Bob's group despite not being a Catholic. Until he got to Vietnam, smoking, drinking and gambling were his favourite pastimes.

"The Orstralian soldier anecdotally is a larrikin. He wears the uniform with pride and salutes Sir, but as soon as Sir is gone he tends to get on with what he considers to be the best way of doing things: after Sir is gone." Father Bob reiterates with a grin.

I should have left long ago but Father Bob is enjoying himself immensely and I haven't got the heart to pull out. I'll just have to ride like Breaker Morant when I re-start the round. So much for riding around like an old man!

"Then the poor buggers were shipped off to Vietnam," I declare, not even bothering to check my watch.

"Yes, when the Vietnam War crept up on them," says Father Bob, "the Australians followed the Americans. We were told 'the Chinese are coming, the Chinese are coming,' " Father Bob chants like a Gregorian monk. "The Yanks, as usual - and they're using similar tactics in Iraq - will frighten the tripe out of you and say: 'The Chinese are coming to take the Pacific Islands and *you*. So, the Aussies were 'All the Way with LBJ' which was coined by the Australian Prime Minister, Harold Holt. So off we went to war."

More went back to war too after his leg healed. The girls were still there but he spent most of his time out in the scrub cooking for the troops.

Outside the study window, the gardener is waltzing his motor mower around the lawn. The motor is revving hard and a murder of crows in the eucalypts is cawing mournfully in what seems to me to be a protest at the racket.

Frank wanders back into the study with what could be the jawbone of an ass clenched between his teeth. This is not a rubber toy, but the real thing. There are still a few sinews attached to one knobby end. He stretches out on the carpet at my feet, with the enormous bone between his paws, and begins crunching. Bob grins, collects his thoughts, and returns to his tale.

"After their bad experience in Korea against the Marxist Chinese, they said: 'Sweet Mother of Pearl! We are up against people who have got tunnel-vision.' In other words," exclaims Father Bob, "they were fighting people who had an ideology! The Yanks ideology is money, and a pious thought that they are destined to be the rulers of the Universe."

Father Bob stops once again, this time chuckling, "For the benefit of Ron's voice recorder, and any listener," he says, "that loud crunching is not me chewing a bone. That's the dog. You should interview the dog, Ron," Bob says to me, "He's seen a lot around here."

"Yeah, if only he could talk," I reply pensively.

"Off we trotted, the Aussies, following the American model with helicopters, and napalm."

Suddenly there is a helluva roar from outside the window as the gardener adds a raucous soundtrack to the helicopters and napalm.

"We thought we were going there to defend democracy against the Communist ideology," yells Father Bob. "The Russians, meanwhile, were arming the Viet Cong." Bob continues his tale but like that kid in school again listening to Ronny my mind wanders. The gardener's noisy blower, with its long, black barrel looks a bit like a bazooka. The vicious looking crows flying between the branches of the eucalypts are shiny black helicopters circling menacingly. The gardener wanders down the path blowing the grass clippings back onto the lawn. I wonder if he will spray the weeds. Agent Orange was the Americans' weed-killer of choice during the Vietnam War.

"We were more humanitarian, so to speak, in our aggression." Bob smiles, perhaps recognising an oxymoron but humans and aggression are inseparable.

"The Aussies did well," he goes on. "The North Vietnamese won the day and they seem to have respected the Orstralian soldier. I don't know that they had much time for the American soldier because the Americans did it the American way, which is: throw hundreds of thousands of soldiers into the fray, soldiers who are also young, and who unfortunately became chemically addicted over the years because they were in one of the easiest spots in the world to get heroin and cannabis. Your Aussies on the other hand were more like Bushmen," says Father Bob proudly.

"When the Americans fought," he says, "they had to fight with aeroplanes and bloody helicopters and they wouldn't get near the enemy. Whereas the Aussies, who weren't afraid to physically combat the enemy, were more defensive than aggressive. The Yanks had an ideology that said: 'We've got to stop the Red Peril,' so they were more aggressive, bombing North Vietnam and denuding the land with their napalm. And they were being embarrassed, as they are now in Iraq, because the North Vietnamese simply dug trenches and lived in the ground. They also ran a thing that really must have embarrassed the Yanks: The Ho Chi Minh Trail, which went from North Vietnam right down to South Vietnam under the bloody ground and conveyed their personnel and munitions *under the ground*," Bob emphasises.

I remember that after the Viet Cong had beaten the allies and the Aussies flew home from Saigon, they were shunned by a large section of the populace. It was as if *they* were the warmongers rather than the Liberal government who sent them to war. The Diggers came home to silence and found it hard to fit back into normal society. After the danger and excitement of war, many of them found it hard to hold down a mundane job so they drank, just like Father Bob's father James did after he got home from the war. I recall that when he got home, More was very aggressive and took a long time to settle down to civilian life. He used to refer to himself as a 'trained killer.'

Outside, the gardener and his partner have finished their waltz and have glided to a standstill. The little petrol motor on his blower splutters then cuts out. The battle is over. All is peaceful in the garden for a couple of minutes as Father Bob marches on with the history of Australia's involvement in the Vietnam War.

"There were terrible examples in the Vietnam War of what they call 'fragging' in the US Army. Occasionally a soldier would go berserk and throw a hand-grenade into the officers mess or something."

"Like a postal worker going 'postal' and running amok."

"Is that what they call it?" asks Bob.

"Yes, I think the phrase was coined after the Queen Street Massacre," I add.

"A priest then would go 'clerical'," laughs Bob.

We glance at our watches simultaneously. Before rising, I rub my hand over my shin feeling the huge lump.

# Chapter 24: The Moon, the Morgue and the Man

*"You can eat for a whole day with $8."*

 Isn't it annoying when you get something inside your head that keeps replaying over and over again like one of those vinyl records of long ago, where the stylus gets stuck in a groove? It's those Bloggs characters from this morning's sessions. The name Bloggs has invaded my head and Ronny is wrapping it around the neurons like amyloidal plaque. I'm about to check Father Bob's Blog when I'm struck by the similarity of the words: Bloggs, Blog and Bob. I decide to apply another strange word, Google, to check up on Bloggs. Yes, here they are. Mention is made in the *law GAZETTE* of a certain Mr. and Mrs. Bloggs being at a disadvantage in the big-money cases.

 Father Bob's Blog hasn't got anything to do with Bloggs in this instance but the name of his article is intriguing: *The Moon, the Morgue, and the Man,* and is two little stories with the well-publicised lunar eclipse as a backdrop: stories that set my mind to work.

 Bob writes:

*Just before the lunar eclipse, I was called to the morgue, an old fashioned name for the Coroner's Court facility where dead bodies are kept waiting for a coronial enquiry into the cause of death.*

*The body was that of a 46 year-old man. He had suffered from MS for years and died of a chest infection that afternoon.*

*Was this the total eclipse of that man or had he just faded from the sight of his family and friends?*

 Bob's evocative prose about the body in the morgue brings forth a memory. Many years ago an autopsy was performed on my father's body. I had to go to the morgue, which was then situated near the Seaman's Mission in West Melbourne, to formally identify him. The attendant on duty that morning was a brusque, burly man with piercing blue eyes. He had big yellow teeth like a camel with the breath to match. After he rolled out the drawer I looked at my father for a few moments, then fixed my eyes on the attendant and said solemnly and without blinking: 'This is my father.' I managed to hold eye contact and remain composed in the presence of this unsympathetic man.

 Father Bob's words set me to wondering: was that the total eclipse of my father or had he just faded from sight? I can still hear his voice inside my head.

Bob's second story is a poignant one about the living. He writes:

> *Just after my visit to the morgue, I was locking the parish church. I pocketed about $9 from the poor box.*
>
> *There was a man in church quietly sitting and contemplating, as he often does.*
>
> *Let's use another old-fashioned word to describe this man – 'swaggie.' He's a man of the road, a non-conformist. He's a street poet and philosopher, a graduate of the university of hard knocks.*
>
> *He's a man of few words, talks only when he has to. I offered him the $9. He took $8. "I only need $8", he said. "You can eat for a whole day with $8." He left the church building but I think the 'church' left with him, instead of staying with me.*
>
> *The lunar eclipse followed.*

At the end of his article, Father Bob poses a question for the readers, followed by his own opinion:

> *Which of the three events was the most spectacular?*
> *Each in its own way, I'd say.*

Father Bob's title: *The Moon, the Morgue, and the Man*, was the catalyst for both of my stories. The second one combines both the moon and the man until they merge and become one.

When my son Geoffrey was about two years old, I used to sit him on my shoulders and take him out into the back yard to look at the moon. I did this on many a night if it was visible. As he learnt to talk I would point to the moon and say: 'There's A Man in the Moon.' He became fascinated with the moon and was soon saying: 'Man-in-the-Moon' as he pointed at it.

Recently *The Age* cartoonist, Leunig, penned a marvellous little poem as a caption for one of his cartoons. The drawing depicts a father, standing outside with his young son, pointing at the moon. Both are smiling at The Man-in-the-Moon who is looking down at them with a crooked little smile on *his* face. The caption reads:

> All my father left me was the moon
> "When I'm dead, it's yours" he said

And all too soon his will was read
But he continued speaking from the grave:
"It will not save you this moon I gave you
From sadness, human madness, life and death.
But step outside into the night and take a breath,
And while you do, for what it's worth,
That happy man up there who got away from earth
Will smile at you".

Thinking about The Man in conjunction with The Moon, I think that this meeting in the church could be the manifestation of Father Bob's vocation here on earth because many poor and homeless people revolve around him like the moon revolves around the earth. Many of Bob's Blogs tell stories about the poorer Mr. and Mrs. Bloggs of this world and in one such story he mentions other Bloggs who themselves are "feeling the pinch" but who still share what they have with those less fortunate. "We know and honour you who give glory to God in the lowest," writes Father Bob.

There are many dimensions to Father Bob and like the Man in the Moon he is always there. When Margie's life becomes too shitful she blows away the dark clouds by writing to Bob. When the bloody postie decides that he wants to write a biography he waits for a full moon and then pesters Bob. When the media wants to portray a human-angle story in a different light whom do they ring up? It must be tiring.

'He has to learn when to duck in behind a cloud,' says Rene. Sometime I wish that he'd duck behind a bloody cloud. I try to elucidate these dimensions. Sitting in my chair at home I envisage Bob sitting at his desk behind his old computer in his study. The timber desktop is barely visible and the bookshelves are just as cluttered. This is the bunker where *Bob Maguire* runs his money-making-for-the-pooah business. *Father Bob* can be found at noon in Church every weekday, at weddings on Saturdays and at the pulpit on Sundays. Of course it's not quite as straight-cut as that but he tends to run two distinct operations. He is a bit like a well-respected businessman, say Frank Hardy's John West, who runs an SP business on the side, the only difference being that instead of ripping the punters off Bob Maguire is there to fight for them and if the Maguire Foundation is floundering, why then, he simply sells off one of the Church's properties and gives the money to the pooah – much to the chagrin of the Archbishop.

I'm trying to think of other facets of Bob's character but it's a hopeless case. Ronny has got shady looking characters slipping into the side door of the church to put on their bets. Bob, a cigar clamped in his teeth, is behind the altar writing out tickets for the clamouring punters. On a whiteboard behind him, the horses' names have odds marked beside them and thick lines drawn through the scratchings.

Geoffrey, who is now a part-time photographer as well as a postie at the Richmond Delivery Centre, enjoys hearing about the progress of the biography and reading Bob's Blogs; he says that he is looking forward to meeting the renowned Father Bob. A few days later, I meet Bob outside the rectory as I am delivering the mail. He says that he is glad that someone reads his Blogs and agrees to make time next Wednesday afternoon for a photo shoot at the rectory.

## Chapter 25: The Grin

*"We have put so much lead in God's saddlebags
that he can hardly run at all."*

Father Bob's IT assistant Michaela, says: "Try to smile, Bob," as she indicates the camera.

"I don't wanna smile," grumbles Father Bob. Meanwhile Geoffrey has started taking photos.

"I'd like to have a photo of Frank lounging in his favourite chair," I say to Bob.

"Why do we have to have a photo of the bloody dog?" asks Bob grumpily.

"Because he is in the book," I state simply.

"Oh," says Bob, *"Frank!"* Then; 'phweeeeee!: an incredibly loud high-pitched whistle, which the dog also ignores. "We'd better leave the poor bugger alone. He's got a bucket on his head," Father Bob says matter-of-factly.

"The dog?" I ask stupidly.

"Yes, one of the other dogs took a piece out of his ear while they were out walking," says Father.

"What happened exactly?" I ask. "Frank's not a street-fighter. He's an aristocrat."

"The dogs were walking together on their respective leashes when a dog jumped out of a builder's utility. Frank reacted to it and another dog beside him reacted to him and I think accidentally tore his ear."

Father Bob pointedly looks at his watch. "How do you want to conduct this photo-shoot, Uncle?" he then asks Geoff in a business-like manner.

"Just do what you usually do when Dad comes in to see you," says Geoff who hasn't stopped taking photos since he walked into the room.

"Nothing!" growls Bob. "I abuse him."

"That's OK then," laughs Geoff, "Just do that."

"He wants you in your natural habitat," explains Michaela catching on fast.

"I'll set the ball rolling then," I say. "Would you like to give me a definition of The Power?"

"What power?" asks Bob looking momentarily perplexed. "The Power and the Glory?"

"Yes."

"It was written by four blokes," he says without even having to think about it. "It probably means the Fight Club. You've got all these records of fights between people who allegedly believe in God, don't believe in God, believe in a bunch of Gods, however," declares Bob in a louder voice, "using your Jesus as a model, power is powerlessness. It's a contradiction. It means: more power if you haven't got any."

"Hmm," I manage weakly.

"Like a mother," continues Bob, "The father is the silly side. He thinks he's got the power because he can knock the kids' teeth out." We all laugh. "The mother, on the other hand, doesn't usually knock the kids' teeth out. She . . . what's the word: comforts."

"Soothes," adds Michaela.

"Sues?" asks Bob.

"No, soothes."

"God, I could have sworn you said sues," says Bob and then shifts into his thespian voice. "What an impossible child. I'll take you to the civil court, you swine! You're driving me mad! That's The Power," he adds emphatically.

I had been expecting a definitive answer that would sit snugly beside his definition of The Glory, which he had composed during one of our earlier talks but this is a bit different.

Father Bob continues his story as Geoffrey moves freely about with his camera. "Now a way of explaining this powerlessness: this whole situation is so ridiculous that God decides to start again. So he uses the crucifixion of Jesus and then the resurrection as a way of starting again."

I nod my head. Geoff takes another photo as Father takes off his glasses. Michaela, who is sitting at the conference table, starts working on her laptop.

"Your Jesus," continues Bob, "was the starting again by God, because God was nobbled by the human beings who used God in the religion industry, whether from Confucianism or Buddhism, Hinduism, Judaism, we have put so much lead in God's saddlebags that he can hardly run at all."

Geoff grins widely.

"Then after God started again," says Bob, "he had to strip away aaaaall the stuff that had built up over the centuries and He ended up with an innocent human being on a cross, executed and looking powerless. But two thousand years after that new start, it is once again showing signs of being nobbled. The disciples then turned themselves into another religious industry known as Christianity.

"There was what I call the 'Peter' kind of Catholicism," says Father, "which is institutional and do as you are told. The other form is the Paul side of things," says Father, "which is innovative, creative, pro-active and inventive. Catholicism has got to have both of those elements."

This symbiotic relationship is instantly familiar. It's all in me 'ead. All I have to do is substitute the names Peter and Paul for Rene and Ronny.

"Sts Peter and Paul's Church South Melbourne is a stable and institutional heavy-duty church compared to a lot of the others in the Melbourne suburbs," continues Father Bob as I marvel at my insight. "For one hundred and fifty years it had a big school system. It had everything that a settled church would want: Convent, Christian Brothers, Orphanage: the whole bloody lot," he says. "There is no argument then. This place has got its Peter ingredient. The Paul ingredient had to wait until I turned up in 1973." This is the nearest thing to bragging that I have ever heard from Bob; he sounds a bit like Ronny. Bob says: "We became creative, innovative, and went into the neighbourhood. We got mixed up with the locals. We had to help the outsiders."

Bob seems as pleased with his explanation as I am with my insight and he applies it further. "I'm becoming more and more convinced, as the years go by, that it's time for me to start again too."

"Who better to take guidance from?" I ask glibly as Geoff moves in closer for another shot.

Father Bob chuckles, "Well, all I'm trying to do is start again right here on the corner of Dorcas and Montague Streets. Start again. Nobody knows I've started again. People just say things like: 'He's unconventional,' or 'He's different.' That suits me. They can say what they bloodywell like."

The word 'bloodywell' always reminds me of the now deceased Henry Bolte, a past premier of Victoria, who when told that the unionists were going to march through the city, said: "They can march 'til they're bloodywell footsore." It's hard to get the bloody posties to march. They are so apathetic, allowing the Fleas to do as they please.

"They might even say: 'The poor bugger's mad,' " says Father Bob who is still talking about himself, "but as far as I'm concerned I'm starting again." Having said that, Bob folds his arms and leans back in his comfy chair with Geoffrey leaning forward, zooming in on him.

"It sounds to me like you're trying to get the power," I say cheekily.

Bob laughs. "Outside is the plaque that I showed you a couple of weeks ago, Ron. Geoffrey will take a picture of that later. Next Friday is the 34$^{th}$ anniversary of my arrival. I'm going to throw water and smoke at the plaque which commemorates the young people who died of drugs on the streets in the 1970's".

"What time is that on?" I ask, wondering if I can fit it into my round.

"Half past twelve. I'll stagger out of church after the midday Mass. Not that I want to make too much of a fuss," he says mildly, "but I'd like the people to know that it's there. There were 40 young people who died from drugs during the 70's and 80's."

Geoff indicates that he has taken enough indoor shots so Father suggests that we go outdoors.

"Geoff and I both liked that story about The Man, The Morgue and The Moon that you posted on your Blog," I say, making small talk as we prepare to go out into the garden.

"I'm glad you enjoyed it," says Bob graciously as we amble out of the rectory and into the garden chatting away like guests at a tea party.

"Yes, Geoff and I are both 'into' the moon."

"You probably both come from the moon," laughs Bob. He shows Geoff the plaque, which is erected on the bluestone wall, and explains the sentiments expressed on it.

"This is a bit garbled and in code; I'm having a bit of a go at the parish." He shrugs and says: "It's all deep and meaningful bullshit."

"I notice that someone's been putting flowers next to the plaque, Father," says Geoff.

"Yes, I've been putting bloody flowers there," says Bob grimly as he looks at the posy sitting on the bluestone wall.

"Have any of the relatives put flowers there?" asks Geoffrey.

"Nah! Nobody does anything. They bloodywell forget." He sighs. "Worn out, I am. I oughta go and have a lie down. I'm sick of it."

"Can we get a photo of you in front of the church first?" I ask Bob.

"No, I want to be alone. We are running out of time. It's 3 o'clock."

"Don't worry about it then, we can do it another day," I reply.

"No, I'll do it," he says with resignation. "It's all too much for me though."

Despite the traffic noise, it's pleasant in the garden with the birds tweeting in the trees and a cool breeze on our faces. A cup of tea would be nice.

"It's probably all true," Father says enigmatically to me as we casually stroll to the front of the church, the postie and the priest.

"What's all true?"

"The whole bloody story. What I'm doing here. What *am* I doing here?" he asks frowning.

"What are we all doing here?" I ask. "You've done well over the years," I tell Bob. A lot better than I have, I think, as my life as a bloody postie flashes before me.

"I haven't done well at all. If I were a woman I'd do better because I'd be braver. You have to be brave," he concludes.

This is the second time that Bob has made a comment of this nature. Rene wonders if he subscribes to the *Journal of Medieval History* because he says that in Volume 29 issue 3 there is an article entitled: *'Stronger than men and braver than knights': women and the pilgrimages to Jerusalem and Rome in the later middle ages.* The pilgrimages referred to in the article were long and arduous; women such as Margery Kempe and Felix Fabri who took part were confronted with social barriers because of the strong resistance to women's pilgrimages.

After this exchange about the profundity of life we stop in front of the church. Bob asks Geoff: "Is that a real camera?"

"No," says Geoff, "It's digital. It just looks real." They both laugh.

"He's very good at this photography caper," I say to Bob.

"You should be carrying his bag for him then," he replies with a grin, "You might have a future."

Father Bob stands in front of the steps leading up to the church door in what will be a posed shot. He starts to ham it up though: "Smiling, ha, ha, ha, ha, the laughing priest! Ha, ha, hu, hu, ha ha!" Having exhausted this he grins wickedly like Jack Nicholson as The Joker. The grin is fleeting but the photographer is fast and I hear a click; whether it was in time or not I don't know.

"Can you take a photo and make it look like I'm up in that niche at the top of the church?"

"Well," says Geoff.

"I'd like to be in the niche," says Bob.

"I could take a photo of the niche and then put you in later," says Geoff.

"Yes, that'll do," says Bob, "put me in later. This is where Father Maguire is dying to go. After death he will be stuffed. By putting me in later you're saying that in virtual reality lovely things can be done that we can't do in real life," says Bob eloquently.

"That's *right*," agrees Geoff.

"We could . . ." says Bob, and then interrupts himself: "Hello, comrade!" he yells to an old man slowly creaking past on a bike that is nearly as old as he is. It is a nondescript rust colour with twenty-eight inch wheels, mudguards that rattle, and what were once chrome racing-bike handlebars turned upwards like goat horns. The chain is as rusty as the frame and there is a build up of dirt and grease around the sprockets. A cardboard box of groceries is tied to a rack on the back of the bike with a piece of twine. "See the old man?" Bob asks us, his eyes shining excitedly. "Look at 'im."

"Yes," I reply watching the old bloke, "I often see him inching his way along Smith Street when I'm on my round. He gets around a bit on that old relic."

"By God he does," agrees Bob. "When I used to ride my bike he'd stop me in the street and hand over $2. How are you, Uncle?" he says to a middle-aged man coming out of the church. "Here's one of Collingwood's finest," Bob tells us. "Did you light a few candles?" he asks the man.

"If I thought it'd work, I would," the Collingwood supporter says.

"Just light 18 candles. C'mon," Bob encourages.

The man merely laughs as he moves on, walking down the path towards the school. "Who do you reckon tomorra?" Bob asks his retreating back.

"Maybe the Pies," the supporter says over his shoulder. "They haven't been playing well but they tend to find another leg when they play the Swans."

"Righto," says Bob, "I'll put me wages on 'em."

"Yeah," the football supporter calls back. "I'm a rough judge though, Bob." He shoves his hands into the pockets of his tracksuit pants and strides away.

"That's where the kiddies were tortured for a hundred years," says Bob indicating the school. "The Catholic Detention Centre. I dunno whether we used to beat them or what."

"From hearsay it seems that the Brothers were the worst," comments Geoff.

"Allegedly," says Bob, "It's hard to know. The nuns here used to comment that as long as they could get you to the stage of being able to read and write and count they'd be doing the right thing by you, and if they couldn't get you to pay attention then they wouldn't be doing the right thing by you and your future. Now, I've got to stop talking or I'll have a stroke."

"That's looking on the bright side," I say with a snort.

"Well, I could. I could have a stroke and drop dead. How many more?" he asks Geoff who has been busy clicking away.

"That'll do for the front of the church," Geoffrey replies.

Michaela, who is ready to go home, comes out onto the path.

"Are you off?" Bob asks,

"Yes. I'll see you next Friday."

"Well, we 'ope so," says Father. His answer reminds me of a customer who used to come into our shop when Ladybugs and I ran a small news agency in Middle Footscray. A poor old lady who was nearly bent double and whose false teeth were ill fitting used to come into the shop at dawn every day and buy twenty-three newspapers for the nursing home where she lived. Bent over a stack of newspapers on the low stand and dribbling all the while she would plonk down a big heap of shrapnel. "See you tomorrow," I always said cheerily as she left, leaving me to clean up the mess. "We 'ope so," she always disconsolately replied.

Michaela gives Bob an affectionate peck on the check.

"Don't take a picture of that," he instructs Geoff. "None of that."

Pedestrians use the path that runs diagonally from Dorcas St to Montague St as a shortcut. Bob cheerfully greets each and every one of them. Many are regulars whom he has come to know over the years but if he doesn't know them, his response is along the lines of: 'Good afternoon, Father.'

A small Vietnamese man walks by and Bob greets him: "G'day, Your Grace,"

The 'Bishop' responds with a big grin, which displays a magnificent row of teeth with a sliver of gold top-dead-centre, "Good afternoon, Father," he replies.

On the Montague St side of the garden there is a fork in the path. A narrower path with the shape of the cross, displayed by the paving stones, leads to the white statue of The Holy Mother, which the birds have stained. As we walk up the little path Father Bob points out the plaques which are mounted on rocks on both sides of the path.

"Here are the dead," he says. "This bloke died in prison. This woman hanged herself from a tree. This poor bugger accidentally shot himself." Bob stops beside one of the markers. "This boy died in a motorcar accident. He had a hard upbringing and was eventually taken away from poverty by his grandparents and was living a happy life until he was killed. It was bad luck. He was just about to start a good job. Who else is there?" says Bob as he checks the plaques. "This next one alongside Jesus in the crib, is a baby, only days old. There are no ashes there. The poor little bugger actually died in prison. Further along are the memorial plaques for stillborn babies and on the other side, facing the main path is my Lest We Forget plaque." Bob's voice rises slightly as a few green parrots start squabbling in the gum-trees. He rattles a wind chime hanging from a branch and there is a tintinnabulation that immediately gives the feeling of tranquility despite the traffic noise.

"This could be magical, Ron," says Bob. "We could be Buddhists here."

"There are little frogs in the chimes. I quite like frogs," I reply.

Father Bob suddenly remembers something important that he thinks he should immediately impart and the frogs are instantly dismissed.

"The statue of your Mary," he says loudly as he leads the way up to it, "came from the grounds of the Vincent De Paul's Girls Orphanage down in Napier Street." Geoff takes a photo of Bob standing next to Mary. "I pinched that when the government closed it down and cordoned off the building. I asked: 'Can I have that statue? Otherwise it will be lost forever.' You can just see the writing on the plaque beneath it telling of its origin."

He reads the words inscribed in gold on the plaque:

*This statue is from the grounds of St Vincent De Paul's Girls' Orphanage in memory of DENISE GANGELL and all those who passed through St Vincent De Paul's Boys' and Girls' Orphanage.*

"Who was Denise Gangell?" I ask.

"Denise Gangell used to work here. She was one of the earliest volunteers here. She had emphysema. I remember her getting out of her car over there and hanging on to that church there, then she'd gradually make her way to the door."

"Was she a heavy smoker?" I ask.

"I think she must have been. She was an old girl who never had a bad thing to say about this place, because this is where she learnt all her personal and professional skills that got her a good job. I think she was a secretary at HSV7. If we don't get that statue refurbished nobody will remember the Boys' and Girls' Orphanage. And that's very sad, very sad," says Bob as he stands looking at Mary. I hear the click of Geoff's camera as I watch two boys on mountain bikes ride past along Montague Street. Knowing Geoffrey as I do I'm sure that the photo will show Father Bob talking to Mary.

I concur with Bob. "Yes, it would be a crying shame. It's not only Catholic history. It's also part of South Melbourne's history."

"Oh Christ! exclaims Bob grimacing. "Here's 'Mad So-and-So. Do you see him around the traps, Ron?" asks Bob.

"Mad So-and-So," I laugh. "No, I can't say I've had the pleasure, Bob."

Mad So-and-So stops and whispers in Bob's ear for a minute then moves on.

"All the best," says Father. Then he roars, "Have you got enough yet, Geoff?" as an aeroplane flies over.

"Yes, thank you, Father. All done," Geoff yells back, laughing at the risible situation.

"What about you, Ron. Have you finished delivering your letters?"

"Yes, I told the Post Office Fleas that I had to finish early."

"Ah," says Bob, "the Post Office Fleas!" and he laughs. "Hello, Sir, how are you?" he greets a young bloke walking past. "He can't hear me, the child, because he's got those earplugs in his ears," says Bob to Geoff and me, "but he knows I'm talking to him because my lips are moving. In the old days you ran the risk if you spoke to strangers. These days it's not so bad."

It's time to leave.

"Get out!" says Bob. He notices me turning off the voice recorder and says to Geoff, "That's been on the whole time. He's like that."

"Sneaky," says Geoff.

"Cunning bastard," says Bob, his eyes crinkling around the corners. Geoffrey and I look at each other and laugh as the old Character Trainer walks back inside.

After dinner, I check my emails. Geoff has sent me an image of that ephemeral Maguire grin. He says that he 'captured the devil in the priest.'

When I see Father Bob the next day he tells me that Geoff sent him an email of 'The Grin,' which is what he captioned it. Bob says that he was amazed that Geoff captured the shot because the grin was only fleeting. He shows me Geoff's email, which says:

*Father Bob,*
*'You were quick, but I was quicker - $500^{th}$ of a second.'*
*Regards,*
*Geoff.*

Father Bob doesn't show me his reply but Geoff forwards it to me later:

*Geoff,*
*Yes, but . . . reptilian?*
*Respect,*
*Bob Maguire*

## Chapter 26: They Died on our Watch

*"This little memorial, insignificant as it might be, shows what I have been about all my life."*

The flock is emerging from the church after the noon Mass. It is wending its way to where the plaque sits on the memorial wall in the garden. I bring up the rear, riding my red Aussie Post bike, with a yellow bag of mail, along the path behind the stragglers. I'm like an old sheepdog whipping them in. Two Board members of the Father Bob Maguire Foundation standing at the back of the gathering look conspicuous in their dark suits, like a pair of task force detectives. The 'shepherd,' standing in front of the plaque, which sits on the bluestone wall, begins without further ado:

"We are here representing the Maguire Foundation. Come on 'girls', get in a bit closer," says Father Bob to some stragglers at the rear.

Mandy, a survivor of the urban drug war, hands out booklets.

"This is magic stuff," says Bob, sounding like a hippie from the sixties, as he gets the thurible smoking. "Barnabus is here to represent all those who were on the street in the 1970's. Were you there?" he asks.

"Yes, I was there," confirms Barnabus softly. His head is slightly bowed and his shoulders hunched but he lifts his big brown eyes and looks around shyly. It's hard to believe that this is the same person who used to charge down Dorcas Street, with Bob's dog at his heels, abusing pedestrians and nosy drivers alike.

"His brothers aren't here though," Father Bob states emphatically. He reads the names of two people off the plaque. "Two dead brothers!"

Barnabus nods and then bows his head further.

"These people listed on the plaque never made it," says Bob. "Interestingly enough we maintain that a lot of them died because they weren't well treated by the public service." I take it that he is referring to the police. "We are not arguing about whether it was malicious, or whether it happened through ignorance, but the fact remains that a lot of them would have lived longer had they been dealt with in a respectful way." Then he adds with a grin, "Even though they were a pain in the arse." There is a smattering of laughter from the gathering.

"We are grateful to the Aboriginal people for the land on which we are gathered, because they were the original owners. Sts Peter and Paul's Church started here, on this very patch, in 1854. We had a tent pitched here where we gathered to say our prayers." "I didn't think Bob was that old," says Ronny. Cheeky bastard.

Bob opens a small container and says: "We also thank the early settlers. So here is some soil from Eureka, which also took place in 1854." He sprinkles some of the fine soil around and about. "We are acknowledging the connections."

Swinging the smoking thurible around, Father Bob says: "It's not Roman Catholic smoke. It's just smoking gum leaves and a bit of rosemary to make it smell aromatic. If we were Aborigines we could have a smoking ceremony. I'm sure that the people named on this plaque would appreciate this, wouldn't they?"

"Yes they would," vehemently responds Mandy.

"Now we have the water," says Bob as he sprinkles it lightly on the people gathered around him. "It's not special Roman Catholic water: it's just water."

Father Bob asks Barnabus to step forward and say a few words, which he does in a gentle, respectful voice. Unfortunately the wind whips the softly spoken words from his mouth.

"Can I step up, Bob?" Mandy interrupts brashly.

"No, you can't. Yet." There is a fair amount of laughter and the odd snigger.

"What would they say if they were able to speak?" Bob asks Barnabus instead.

"Live on," says Barnabus emphatically.

"Alright, you can go now," says Father kindly. Barnabus, his shoulders slouched, head low, puts his hands in his pockets and slowly walks away alone like a sheep that has been banished from the flock.

Bob asks Mandy if she would now like to speak. Mandy is waiflike with a face like a road map but she steps forward confidently as if she does this sort of thing regularly and stands in front of the plaque.

"I just want to say to everyone here that I knew most of these people. Some were family, some were very good friends and I'm sure that they will be looking down and seeing us here today. Others who knew them and helped them are here. Henri Ser, Henry Nissen, and Les Twentyman. They are here to say that we believed in them. Regardless."

"Beautiful," says Bob. "Give her a round of applause." Everyone claps and there are a few encouraging comments.

Bob then asks Les Twentyman to say a few words. "I apologise if you can't hear him," says Bob, "but I can't do much about the wind."

Les looks at the names on the plaque, selects one, and steps up to speak. "I looked after Liz Shaw for three or four years when she was a ward of the state. In the book, *The Patriarch*, it tells how Liz was given a hotshot because she had been talking to the police: informing on a notorious drug dealer of the time. Both her parents died of drug overdoses when she was just thirteen years old. She then became a ward of the State. Although Liz lived with a relative for a short period of time she was virtually on the street from that time on until the day she died, just before she was eighteen. I remember a particular incident when she was living in the State run hostel in Carlton."

Les's voice is nearly drowned out now by the droning of a light aeroplane directly overhead. That, combined with the wind, and the traffic going past in Dorcas Street causes the gathering to crane its collective neck towards the speaker. The droning seems to add a funereal effect to the ceremony, becoming a part of it: normal everyday life going on as the living reminisces about the dead.

"I remember a poignant story about her sixteenth birthday," continues Les. "It was a long-weekend and I was a bit annoyed because she could have gone away for the weekend with a few of the others but she wouldn't go. As a consequence I had to work because the other Social Workers all had the long-weekend off; I had to come all the way back to Melbourne from Albury to look after her.

"When I got back she said: 'Let's go to the pub; I've got no one to share my sixteenth birthday with.' I felt guilty then because of my selfish feelings and decided to spend some time with her to celebrate her birthday. I had no money on me either, which is nothing unusual, so she leant me $20 so I could go and have a few drinks with her. I told her that on payday I'd leave the $20 in an envelope on her bed, which I did. When I came in to finish the late shift the next day she said: 'The others found the envelope with the $20 in. They think that you were getting sexual favours off me for $20.' " Les looks around and smiles grimly.

"I vividly remember one time when she ran away to work in a brothel in Fitzroy. I found out about it and had to go and get her. I knocked on the door and a woman came to greet me. I said: 'Have you got any other girls working here?' She got a bit upset and walked off in a huff."

There are a few smiles and a couple of chuckles.

"Lizzie came out then and panicked. She knew that being a youth worker I had the power to put her back in Winlaton. I had a chat to her instead and said: 'You're in a fair bit of strife. You could end up being locked up again. You'd better come back to the hostel tomorrow.'

The wind is whipping Mandy's long hair across her face and around her throat but she is oblivious, hanging off Les's every word.

"She agreed to this," says Les, "then went off to the kitchen to get a cigarette. When she came back she said to me: 'Be careful as you go out, Les. Two blokes were going to shoot you but I told them you were a copper.' As I walked back out, sure enough, when I looked back over my shoulder, there were a couple of sleazy blokes near the corner of the building. That's the type of kid Liz was: larger than life. It's just so sad that her life was terminated at such a young age."

The gathering shuffles in a bit closer as Les' voice softens ever so slightly.

"Some time after that I tried to find her grave. After searching for eight months, I found out that she was buried near Tullamarine. There was no headstone so we arranged to have one made for her. There are quite a number of street kids who are buried two or three to a grave in some instances. During their lives they are in the care of the State but yet when they die no one seems to give a damn."

One of the ladies near me wipes a tear from her eye; others look down or shuffle their feet.

"The erection of this plaque," says Les indicating the plaque, "is yet another heart-warming thing that Bob has done on behalf of the street kids."

Loud Jazz music interrupts proceedings. I've heard that tune before and there is a vibration in my trouser pocket as I fumble desperately, trying to silence the infernal thing.

"It's a touching moment," continues Les, "and I'm honoured to be asked to speak."

Eventually I pull my mobile phone out and the music grows even louder before I can switch it off. Father Bob is not perturbed though; he thanks Les and continues. As he talks a commercial plane roars overhead.

". . . had this strategic relationship," I eventually hear Bob say, "between us, the churchgoers that is, and the street kids for thirty years. In a sense it was a curse because sometimes the churchgoers got frightened and upset. In the main, however, they understood. They saw through it all; still it was disturbing. I had coppers coming to the bloody door, bashing on it insistently trying to find out whether we were hiding a street kid who they happened to be after. We knew that most of the trouble was brought about by the interfering public servants. According to them, as church-goers we are supposed to be…"

"Idiots!" interjects Mandy coming in a tad late.

" . . . on the side of society in general," continues Bob without faltering. "Whereas we tended to be on the *side of the kids*".

"This little memorial, insignificant as it might be, shows what I have been about all my life. If anybody wants to know what I have been about, and what I'm going to be about for the rest of my *natural* life, they will have to come and talk to me here. It's no good coming to talk to me in there," he says, indicating the church. "Come and talk to me here! That's what the Maguire Foundation is all about, and it would be nice, in fact, if we could make the call, from here, to the local population to come and join us in this, I was nearly going to say 'crusade.' What is the word I'm looking for?"

Mandy comes up with one but the wind plucks it from her mouth and a tip-truck belching black smoke carts it away along Dorcas Street.

"Continuing struggle against the odds." Father Bob triumphantly adds.

Then, lo and behold, there's that Jazz band again! *Beat me Daddy, Eight to the Bar.* I must have pressed the cancel button instead of turning it off completely. The caller is insistent. I don't suppose it will look too good if I throw it on the path and jump on it. Someone grumbles. Father Bob is unflappable though; he turns to his disciple: Henri Ser.

"Will you say something Jewish please, Henri? We need something Jewish because they've been around for four thousand years," says Bob.

The Jazz band in my pocket is loud and I'm having trouble turning it off. I can hardly believe that this is happening. Finally I shut it down, head down, tail between my legs.

"How long?" asks Mandy incredulously.

Henri Ser produces the Torah and reads a verse of the Mourners' Kaddish in Hebrew then translates the prayer into English.

"Enough?" asks Bob when Henri stops. Henri shakes his head and reads the last verse in Hebrew.

"And say, Amen." (Henri prompts in English).

"Amen," we all conclude.

Henri closes the Torah and says in English: "We hope that you all have eternal life and look down upon us in happiness."

We all say 'Amen,' to that too.

"Thank you, Henri," says Bob. "Would anybody else like to speak?"

"Henry Nissen! Please stand up!" calls out Mandy. "He knew every one of these people," she adds for the benefit of those around her. "Every one of 'em! Henry, please stand here and have a say."

"Thank you," says Henry graciously as he moves forward.

"The names on Father Bob's plaque bring back a lot of memories. Either the Open Family, or Emerald Hill Mission helped them all to some extent. Now we've got the Maguire Foundation that Bob is running along the same lines."

"It's never ending," says Father Bob.

Henry agrees and then says: "God bless all the people who have come and gone. We loved them and helped them to the best of our ability."

"We loved 'em," agrees Mandy wholeheartedly.

"You chased them and they chased you," adds Bob.

"Sometimes armed with a knife," Henry says with a laugh. Everybody listens as Henry elaborates:

"I remember one kid saying later: 'I didn't really want to catch you, Henry, because I didn't want to stab you. I just wanted to make you understand that you should be careful what you say in future'."

"We could never tell if it was love or hate," says Bob, "but when you delved further into it you could tell the difference I suppose. In the main it was love, even if it was violent. Anyone else like to speak?" asks Bob smiling. Violent love.

A lady who has been to the midday Mass which preceded this ceremony steps forward and says quietly: "I hope that as many young lives have been lost here, can be saved."

"We've definitely saved many more," Henry assures her kindly.

"Anybody else?" asks Bob.

There are no more takers. People stand around talking to each other for a while. Henry mentions a name from the plaque to Mandy who says fondly, "Yeah, he was me boyfriend."

"I remember when I first met him," says Henry, "he was a skinny little bugger. Then I ran into him a few years later and he was built like a brick shithouse. He was a good comrade."

"Yeah, a good comrade, Henry." Mascara runs down Route 1.

"Some of them only lived for twenty years," says Bob, "but twenty years is a long time if you consider tragedies that happen around the world: kiddies dying in diamond mines, children's armies, brothels in Thailand."

A tiny bird in the tree above Bob whistles noisily.

"This is the last word," says Bob as he raises his voice dramatically and reads a prayer:

> *When I'm gone, release me*
> *You've got so many things to see and do you mustn't tie yourself to me with tears*
> *Be happy that we had so many years*
> *I gave you my love and you can only guess how much you gave me in happiness*
> *I thank you for the love you all have shown*
> *But now it's time I travelled on alone*
> *So grieve a while for me if you must*
> *Then let your grief be comforted by trust*
> *It's only for a while but we must part*
> *So bless the memories within your heart*
> *I won't be far away for life goes on*
> *So if you need me call and I will come*
> *Though you can't see or touch me I'll be near*
> *And if you listen with your heart you will hear*
> *All of my love around you soft and clear*
> *Then when you must come this way alone*
> *I will greet you with a smile and a 'welcome home'*

"Very nice," someone says and we all agree. It was too.

"Now, if you're not careful," says Father, "it becomes religious." There are quite a few chuckles. "As it is," he continues, "it's Aussie."

"Keep it that way," declares Mandy impudently.

"Alright," says Bob, "Goodbye and Good Luck."

The little bird continues merrily, giving his own 'sermon' amongst the branches.

"Happy birthday, Father!" Henri Ser smiles at Bob. A chorus of 'Happy Birthday, Father!' follows this!"

"Oh, forget about birthdays! I declare this to be the Memorial Day. And the Board of Open Family and Emerald Hill Mission might like to remember it and keep this in mind every year. They *might*. Every year."

The crowd breaks up, some staying to talk. Les Twentyman gives Father Bob a Cuban cigar housed in a cylinder for his birthday and it disappears quickly into Bob's top pocket.

I give Bob his mail and shake his hand. As I ride off I marvel at how he has given the occasion dignity despite minor irritations such as the wind, traffic, and my mobile phone. He started at Sts Peter and Paul's Church South Melbourne on his birthday in 1973. It is 14$^{th}$ September 2007 and Father Bob is seventy-three today.

## Chapter 27: Christmas Eve

*"The bloody **Hope**Mobile was stolen yesterday from out the back of the church."*

It's Christmas Eve, 2007. Christmas Eve is not nearly as big a day for posties as it was years ago. There is still plenty of mail to sort and deliver but nowadays we get help with the delivery. There is usually a team leader, or two, running around the area on a motorbike delivering parts of rounds. Some of the posties don't like it because it cuts out some of their overtime but it suits me. Back in The Wombat's era I can remember wobbling away on my bike from Eric's well after 6pm at Christmas time. Leaving the bike leaning in its usual position I walk up the path and step up onto the verandah at Father Bob's, where there is a Father Christmas statue with blinking red lights in the window. I ring the 'bell-from-hell,' as Bob calls it. A lot of things seem to come from hell these days: neighbours-from-hell, the patient-from-hell; Google comes up with the bastard-operator-from-hell, and rotten-tomatoes-from-hell. "You can't turn the bloody thing off,' Bob growled one day. 'Even when the visitor takes his finger off the button the bloody thing keeps ringing until it's answered."

Bob's relieving secretary, a young Goth, dressed in black with contrasting shocking-pink hair answers the door. She is very efficient and businesslike. As I walk in she hands me a red envelope with gold Chinese writing on it: one of those envelopes known as 'Red Packets' or 'Ang Pow' that are for Chinese New Year, weddings, or special occasions.

Frank comes out of the study to greet me. He is stately, not exuberant, like some sort of canine butler. He precedes me into the room to announce my arrival. Father Bob is sitting behind his desk as I enter holding the bright red envelope. There is a row of coloured candles for Advent on the mantle-piece next to the photo of Kathleen.

"I don't want any money, Bob. Keep this to feed the pooah," I say by way of greeting, a copied Maguire mannerism: just start talking, brushing aside formalities such as polite signs of recognition.

"Bullshit!" exclaims Bob. That's not a bad greeting either! The Cauliflower-twins are amused. "That cheque is drawn on the Church account, not the Maguire Foundation." Bob must have been reading my mail. "It's from the parishioners," he says.

Frank jumps nimbly into his armchair and rests his head on the armrest and looks devotedly at Bob.

"Give it to Henri Ser. He can buy a couple of slabs of beer for the street people for Christmas," I protest.

But Bob won't change his mind. Predictable. I've been worrying about this all week. I don't want the Christmas tip this year. Our relationship has changed subtly since I've been writing the biography this past 11 months. Before that he was a friendly customer. Now he is a friend. Although Bob reckons that he hasn't got any friends.

"The bloody **Hope**Mobile was stolen yesterday," says Bob, "from out the back of the church."

"What!"

"I was sitting here, dozing off in the chair. I can't recall hearing anything but I felt a presence glide past the open door. A minute or so later I heard a noise upstairs. I was here on my own so buggered if I was going up to investigate. This was followed later by the sound of the bloody van being driven out of the yard. When I checked I found that a back window had been forced open, despite the fact that the back door was unlocked. The van keys were missing from the peg on the wall in the back room. Later in the afternoon a bloke rang saying that he had found the van out on the highway. He was noncommittal about which highway but said he would return it. I asked him to try to get it back by 9pm because it was due on the road," and here Bob's voice rises, "to feed the pooah!

"True to his word the caller drove into the drive about 9.30pm. He wanted his photo taken with me beside the van. It was a bit bizarre but Henri took the photo for him. I've got it here on the computer," says Bob.

"What happened after the photo was taken?" I ask Bob after looking at the blurred image that he brings up on the screen.

"He said that he needed some money to get to Adelaide for Christmas, so I gave him a hundred quid," says Bob.

"A hundred dollar ransom for the van, do you think?"

"I dunno. Why would he want his photo taken if that's the case?"

"Stupidity, probably." I marvel at Bob's generosity towards the bloke returning the van, thief or Samaritan it did not seem to matter to him, *and* to me with the red envelope. It's astounding. If some bastard knocked off my car I certainly wouldn't give him a hundred dollars and send him away smiling.

Father Bob picks up the mail: a couple of bills and four or five Christmas cards. He reads the messages, makes the odd comment and then like a solitaire card-player flicks the cards towards a wastepaper basket in the corner. Ronny is appalled but Rene says astutely that it's business as usual: Bob is looking for money to help the poor. The last one says 'card only' on the front.

"No money in this one then," says Father Bob laughing, "Unless it's from a lying Catholic." He shrugs resignedly as he opens it. "We've had more exposure for The Cause this year than any other and yet we've received less money. I can't work it out."

"You've got to make some money so that you can go to Glasgow."

"I've got to get to Scotland to find my roots and you've got to find a bloody publisher for the manuscript. That won't be easy."

"Don't worry. I'll find one."

Father Bob and I shake hands, and wish each other a Merry Christmas. Frank shows me out.

It's time to resume my round. I get a bit worried about my bike leaning against the front fence sometimes. The Post Office Fleas won't be too impressed if another bike of mine gets pinched. My bike was stolen last Christmas from the Disaster Centre because I hadn't locked it to the bike-shed fence. Perhaps some teenager found an odd red bike under the Christmas tree next morning.

## Chapter 28: A Priest for all Religions

> *"It's very trendy to look after the young and just forget about the older ones."*

Early in the New Year when I arrive at Father Bob's with the mail, I am surprised to find Henri Ser in charge of the rectory. He says: "I'm home alone," and invites me in for a cup of coffee. We sit in the airy, light-filled kitchen at the back of the rectory. Classical music emanating from Father Bob's hi-fi is playing softly. Sunlight glints off the diamond stud in Henri's left earlobe whenever he moves his head. I ask him about his association with Bob. "My first impression of Father Bob is a vivid one," says Henri Ser laughing. "It must have been the brightly coloured Hawaiian shirt that he was wearing."

Henri tells me that about twelve years ago he applied to become an Open Family bus volunteer. There was a four-week training course after which the group was to be introduced to Father Bob. He says that they were all sitting in a room, awaiting Father Bob's arrival with some expectancy. "At 8.20, I remember precisely, he came in wearing this outrageous Hawaiian shirt and started yelling at us." Henri chuckles at the recollection. "He said that it's very trendy to look after the young and just forget about the older ones. Then he said that we should be caring for everyone and not just be bleeding hearts for a certain group. At 8.26, I remember that too! He looked at his watch and said: 'It's nearly 8.30. *Law and Order* is on. I'm going. Goodbye.'"

Henri and I laugh. It must have been Bob playing Mr. Grumpy in his Vatican Two outfit, perhaps gliding on the edge of overwork or over commitment. By 8.20pm, he would have been buggered and cranky, hardly the charismatic leader inspiring his flock.

"That was it!" says Henri. "We just sat there looking at each other dumbfounded. I remember thinking: 'what a cantankerous old fool this guy is.' He was so rude! But over the years I've come to realise that he builds a defensive wall around himself so that people don't take advantage of him. He is an easy touch unfortunately. People hear that he gives out money and they're all lining up, jostling and harassing him."

According to Henri, Father Bob is a priest for *all* religions. He says that he and Henry Nissen were doing a TV interview once. Whilst the crew was filming, Bob walked by saying: 'Don't worry about me, I'm the undercover Rabbi.'

"He is never judgmental," says Henri. "He has had a big impact on my life in the way I work and think. I started out on the Open Family bus and Henry Nissen approached me one day to line up a meeting with Father Bob. We had a chat and next thing you know I'm working for Bob. I've been working for him full time for the last five years. I work on the food bus. I go to court and to the prisons to support our clients. Henry Nissen and I are spreading ourselves pretty thinly. We need more volunteers." Henri must not have heard about Henry losing his job but it's not really my business to tell him.

We talk about Bob's association with Open Family. In many instances, says Henri, Open Family gets the money that is intended for the Maguire Foundation because people don't know that there is a difference between the two.

The name Open Family has always been synonymous with Father Bob. Knowing what I know, I think that this must rankle with Bob.

Henri says that Bob is fiercely loyal to the people who work for him. "Even if they are in the wrong," says Henri, "he will always go into battle for them. He'll try 'til the last gasp of breath to do what he can. That's reflected in the good results that he gets too. Not many people know that his Foundation pays to send kids to Christian Brothers' College, and other schools. He pays for books, and he also pays for housing for quite a few people, which is not well known." Yes, I reflect, Bob *is* loyal to his mates. He would have bitterly fought the sacking of Henry Nissen, probably the only man in Henry's corner. Then there was the split with the Board of Open Family. I've got no doubt that he would have fiercely gone into battle against the members of the Board on Chris' behalf too.

Like the bell announcing the start of the next round of a boxing match, the phone rings loudly interrupting my reverie. Henri tells the caller that Bob will be back later. The irony of the situation strikes me. Here we have a Jewish man acting in the role of secretary to a Catholic priest. The postie in his ludicrous fluoro uniform is lounging back in his chair as if he owns the place whilst they talk about the absent abbot.

We talk about the camaraderie amongst the homeless people when they gather outside the **Hope**Mobile in St Kilda.

"It's a social gathering," says Henri, "and our being there makes them feel wanted because they are being waited on. They like the attention that we give them."

This is the impression that I formed too when Wayne and I visited the food van outside the Gatwick. Most of those present were homeless but you wouldn't have known it to listen to them.

"We don't push any religion down their throats," says Henri, "unlike some of the other groups. I'm sure they feel more at ease with us." He chuckles again. "I'm there outside the Gatwick Hotel every Thursday and a lot of them call me Bob. They think I'm Father Bob."

"You don't look much like the picture on the side of the van," I comment. With his curly brown hair, big white teeth, two-day stubble, and that diamond stud Henri has a rogue-ish appearance, more gypsy than clergy.

"No. They're either too busy eating or gossiping to notice that. Some of them call me Father. Bob's got a good name in the street. He loves helping people," continues Henri, "although he gets a bit tired of people who've always got their hands out, especially when they turn up two days in a row. He has to deal with ticklish situations too. A woman came to him one day complaining that her husband was having an affair. Bob said, 'Get real, madam; it's 2006: everyone's having affairs. Why ask me about it? What would I know? I'm a priest; I've never been married.'"

"The **Hope**Mobile must be a popular bus on the streets of St Kilda," I say to Henri.

"Yes, the bus with all its exposure means a lot to Bob. People in the street identify with the bus. They see it coming and it's not just food that people get from the bus. I'm often there for quite a while listening to people unload their problems. I've taken a few confessions in the street too."

"A bit like being a barman listening to the woes of a drunk", says Rene. "That's incredible!"

"Yeah," he says grinning, "I rang up Bob and asked him what I should do. He said: 'Just listen to the person, and then say something in Hebrew.' I say the prayer for wine or the prayer for bread and they go away happy. It's all confidential."

"You might say it's all Kosher," I add smiling. I groan inwardly at my corny comment. I'd better watch what I say or this will end up sounding like some schmaltzy American sit com. Henri smiles and says:

"We were worried when the **Hope**Mobile went missing just before Christmas. Peter Thomas, a real estate agent of Stockdale and Lego bought us the bus and is going to buy us a second one."

"That's heartening to hear. You don't hear a lot of good things about real estate agents," I comment. "They're a bit like used car salesmen: a much maligned breed. I know an agent named Mario in Sunshine who even refers to himself as a sleazy real estate agent."

Henri laughs. "Peter's one of the few good ones and a second bus will be a Godsend. Bob and I have started something rather unique with that bus. I have trained people from the Synagogue to take the bus out one day a week."

"You've got the Catholics and the Jews working in harness then." I am suitably impressed and wonder what Eggs Benedict would think of the arrangement.

"They pay for their own food and cover other expenses of the Mobile, which is ideal. It's not a burden on Bob. We now want to get onto an Islamic or Sudanese group to train them so that they can do the same thing."

"That's good thinking. Some Sudanese people are having trouble settling in to the Aussie way of life according to the newspapers. What is the Aussie way of life anyway? It used to be drinking beer and eating pies."

Henri laughs. "Yes, that's why we want another bus. It'll probably take a few months to get it organised but that's what we are working towards. We would look at them taking it down to Noble Park, where there is a large Sudanese community with many in need of help. Brunswick is another suburb where the Islamic community is having problems. We've got no intention of interfering. They can run it as they see fit. I can show them what we do and then all they have to do is vary the menu according to their dietary laws."

Henri grins then and says: "We've got one guy who comes every week and wants vegetarian sausages. We buy two especially for him."

"That's very kind of you."

"We like to cater to people's needs. Nobody complains about the food."

"On the night that I was there with Wayne Neilson I was astonished by the camaraderie among the street people. They were obviously enjoying the occasion."

"Yeah, we like to get there early," says Henri, "around 6.30 and leave about 9 o'clock. There is another welfare group who goes there on Wednesdays. They don't get there until about 9 o'clock and are there until midnight, by which time there is usually chaos in the streets. The street people get into fights and throw their rubbish everywhere. The neighbours complain and the police turn up. We know that if you are hungry you'll be there at 7 o'clock. We had extra food last night and it was all eaten. We drove off at a quarter to nine. I came back about 9.30

just to make sure the area was clean and that no one was hanging around. We've got a good system and it works well."

Henri tells me that his mobile phone means that he is on call twenty-four hours a day. "Sometimes our clients want us to help them sort out their matrimonial disputes. We keep out of that. They split up but always get back together. Then the cycle starts again. The woman has got a black eye the next time you see her. Or the man has got a black eye! Some of these women are tough."

We sit listening to Father Bob's hi-fi for a few moments then Henri asks: "Were you here for the blessing of the dogs about eighteen months ago?"

"No, I didn't hear about that. It would have been a lot of fun."

"It took place on a Sunday. People brought their dogs along and Father Bob sprinkled Holy water on them. I spoke from the Torah, blessing all the animals that God created. I then realised that Franklin was missing so I asked Bob where he was. He growled: 'I'm not letting Frank mix with this riff raff.'"

I laugh. "You also read from the Torah on the day that Bob blessed the plaque."

"Yes, I said a Jewish prayer for the dead called the Kaddish. That was a touching ceremony. A lot of people who are on drugs seem to die in their forties, either from a drug overdose or from suicide. They just give up on life. It's very hard to break the cycle once you are hooked. I've got a couple of clients who have managed to do it though. The thing they've all had to do is move far away from their friends. It's very hard for them. They have to make new friends and they are reluctant to tell *them* about their past."

"Father Bob seems to understand and relate to the problems faced by drug addicts, doesn't he?"

"That's right. He's never had the habit, yet he is able to empathise with them."

Maybe watching someone who is close to him played a big part in that. Father Bob had to watch as heroin ravaged Barnabus who he has now been mentoring for forty years.

"Being religious yourself and employed full time are you still able to observe the Sabbath on Fridays?" I ask Henri.

"I am religious but not as devout as I once was. We have a Sabbath dinner every Friday at home. I go to the synagogue, mainly over the High Holidays, but occasionally at other times. I do work on Fridays though. There was a Friday, for instance, not so long ago when I was called out at 10am and never got home until 5am the next morning."

"What happened?" I ask, my curiosity piqued.

"The police picked up this Aboriginal lady with her two-and-a-half year old child. They said that the child was in danger by being in Fitzroy Street, St Kilda at 9.30 at night. Then a worker from the Department of Human Services came to the police station and the police wanted to give the child over to her. I objected saying: 'You can't do that. You'll have to get a Justice of the Peace.' So they called one in. By the time he arrived and I had finished arguing her case the four hours that she would have been held was up. I said: 'She's not drunk anymore. I give you my word that she will be in court tomorrow.' They wanted her to front the court to see whether the child should be taken from her. The JP said: 'I wouldn't normally allow this, *but* I'll allow it this once as long as you take her home and make sure that she is in court in the morning.'" Henri doesn't say whether he took her home or not but says that he had her in court in the morning and the matter was dealt with in her favour. "Since that time she has, allegedly, not had one drink. Now both the daughter and her are flourishing," he says.

"Part of that story was in one of your *Street Report*s. It's gratifying to hear a success story like that."

"I'm glad to know that someone actually reads them," says Henri. "We had an incident last night that will I will write up as a *Street Report*. We had a young student from the Australian Catholic University. He volunteered to come along in the **Hope**Mobile to help out. A fight broke out between two ladies. He just stood still, petrified. He couldn't move. We had to drag him away because he was close to the fighting. I was scared that he would get hit. The poor chap was just scared out of his wits. He said: 'It's not what I expected. I never thought it would be like this. Can I work *inside* the bus next time?' Everyone split their sides laughing. All he was doing at the time the fight broke out was handing out chocolates." Henri and I laugh.

"We don't mix in if there's a fight, and we never call the police. Just as we never call for an ambulance, even if someone is dying. We always get someone else to ring. When I was on the Open Family bus one of our workers called the police to report that someone had broken into a car. That woman was subsequently harassed and belted by street people. We make it a rule to always get someone else to ring for help."

The way people work for Bob's various causes, such as Open Family and the **Hope**Mobile, reflect Bob himself and the unconventional ways that he works. They're not quite 'according to Hoyle.' Like Bob they work on the fringe, which I suppose is pretty appropriate because that's where the people who Bob helps live. They're all fringe dwellers. When Hoyle gets involved in things, as seems to be the case with Open Family, Bob's bottom up movement becomes a top down bureaucracy, Bob gets the arse and the bureaucrats rule the day. The problem is that bureaucracy stuffs up the things that make Bob's work possible. You can't help people on the fringe with rules and meetings, the CEO getting about in a fancy car. No wonder Bob gets so frustrated and cantankerous.

Then you have to wonder about what motivates the **Hope**Mobile volunteers to do what they do. It couldn't be the cranky clergyman in a Hawaiian shirt 'It's nearly 8.30. *Law and Order* is on. I'm going. Goodbye.' No, I reckon that what keeps them coming back has something to do with how things are run and I think this is down to Bob. With Bob out of the picture I reckon Open Family is shickered.

Henri answers Father Bob's phone again and then we shake hands. He looks quite at home, this Jewish man, in his temporary role as the Catholic Priest's secretary. It's been an interesting interlude. Henri is a genuinely good bloke and I have enjoyed talking with him but it's time to get back on the bike and finish the round.

Later as I trundle along Glover Street poking letters into slots Rene says that my next step should be to get some bloody religion into the book.

'Even you can't have a biography about a priest without a modicum of religion,' he says. I grin and give a little snort at the thought. I'm worried though because I'm just about an ignoramus when it comes to religion.

## Chapter 29: The Three Flags

*"One of them symbolises the workers, one St Patrick's Day, and the other the Aboriginal people."*

As I ride up to the church on the following Wednesday 13th February 2008, there is a flag fluttering from Father Bob's first story window. It is half black and half red with a big yellow circle in the middle.

It is Sorry Day: the day that the Australian Prime Minister, Kevin Rudd, says 'sorry' to the Stolen Generations. He simply stands before the parliament and says what stubbornness and lack of empathy prevented his predecessor, John Howard, from doing.

After hearing him apologise on behalf of the government and the parliament I cannot help but reflect on the plight of the Aboriginal mother and child in Henri's story. Although the mother had not been in trouble before, the DHS worker wanted to remove the two-and-a-half year old child from her mother, at least until the next day when her case would come before the courts. Thank God for Henri Ser.

Father Bob succinctly sums up Sorry Day in his Blog:

*Let's all be sorry, not just sorry for past losses but also for present unwillingness/inability to do something about present inequalities, right here, right now.*

Bob is on the front verandah when I arrive a few days later to deliver the mail. He is dressed in purple. This is not the usual purple robe that priests wear to signify the crucifixion of Jesus. According to the Bible, after Pilate ordered that Jesus be flogged and crucified:

*'They stripped off his clothes, flogged him, and cast a purple robe around his shoulders. They twisted the branches of a thorn bush into the form of a crown and jammed it on his head. They shoved a stick into his right hand as a mock sceptre and began to make fun of him, kneeling in front of him and chanting "Hail! King of the Jews!"*

(I warned you that I was going to put some religion into the book.)

Father Bob is not wearing the crown of thorns either. No, this is not a robe that Bob is wearing but a more modern garment: a bomber-jacket in fact. It's silky with a Melbourne Storm emblem on the breast. It is his purple Rugby League jacket.

"Mr. Burrows!"

"Father Bob."

"Do you think he might be dead?" Bob asks.

"Who, Jesus?" (I'm still thinking about Pilate, Jesus and the purple robe.)

Father Bob looks at me queerly, and then gives one of his short laughs, "No! Terry Monagle."

When I last talked to Bob he said that the cancer that was afflicting Terry had attacked again. This followed a period of time where he was stable and able to write. Terry knew that it was only a respite though and that the cancer was merely lying doggo.

"Why, haven't you heard from him lately?" I ask.

"No, not for a while. This is not good, Ron," he says as he flicks through the mail, "No money here. I'll have to go on the streets. What else is happening?"

"I'd like to get a bit more religion into the book," I say looking Father Bob in the eye.

Bob nods sagely, his eyes twinkling. "Yes," he says, waiting to hear what I've got in mind.

"I'd like to come to Mass on Good Friday," I declare.

"Yes, that will be alright, three o'clock in the afternoon," he says casually. "The Protestants will have an Ecumenical gathering at the Gasworks Park and do the Stations of the Cross. I'll be in here carrying on with bloody Roman Catholicism."

Sometimes I wonder whether he's really 'into' this Roman Catholicism business, the way he talks. Maybe he's just tired of it all. I smile. I've heard him say often enough that he is sick and tired. A bit like me with the Fleas, I suppose.

"Are you up to anything in particular at the moment?" I ask.

"Yes. An idea I've had would be to commemorate key days. I'd like three flags. I've got one: the Aboriginal flag."

"Speaking of the Aboriginal flag," I cut in, "I dropped in to the rectory on the Sunday after Sorry Day to take a photo of the Aboriginal flag fluttering from your balcony but it was . . ."

"Gone!" exclaims Bob loudly. "I'll try to get these three up before St Patrick's Day. I don't know if I'll have time to do it, but if I manage it I'll leak it to the press, just to get a bit of publicity."

"Are these flags to be a permanent fixture?"

"Yes. For St Patrick's Day I'd like the green flag with the harp on it."

"Oh."

"Yeah, I know," says Bob grinning, "that'll stir up the Protestants." He ponders, and then says meekly: "I don't really want to be seen as a Nationalist though so I'd better fly the orange, white and green."

A little bit of research reveals that the gold harp on a green background was an early, unofficial Irish flag and served from 1798 until the early twentieth century as a symbol of nationalism. As the revolutionary James Connelly wrote, just weeks before he participated in the quixotic Easter Rebellion (1916) that led to his execution by firing squad:

*For centuries the green flag of Ireland was a thing accurst and hated by the English garrison in Ireland, as it is still in their inmost hearts.*
*The green flag of Ireland will be solemnly hoisted over Liberty Hall as a symbol of our faith in freedom, and as a token to all the world that the working class of Dublin stands for the cause of Ireland, and the cause of Ireland is the cause of a separate and distinct nationality.*
—Worker's Republic, April 8, 1916

"I only have to walk around this parish house," says Father Bob, "work in it, and sleep in it, to feel the presence of all the church people who've used this as a base since the 1850's, blokes who left Ireland to spend their lives at this end of the earth, never to return home. I want an Irish flag flying from this parish house in memory of them. These original settlements by Catholics were called "missions." Where we are right now was "Emerald Hill Mission." It was from here that Sandridge, now Port Melbourne, was begun. We were busy even then," he says.

"Lots of loneliness was the norm for ex convicts and free settlers alike," Bob tells me. "All were far from home but they made the best of it by forming a community, the only sure cure for aloneness. The other flag would be Eureka!" proclaims Father Bob, who is all for the workers.

"I'm sure the Builders' Workers Union would lend you one of theirs."

"Yes," he replies, "but I want it for good. I'll have to buy one. If I get time to arrange all of this, I'll have three flagpoles with the flags flying proudly. I don't know whether to have them over there, or over that way further." Bob indicates a couple of places in the garden with a pontifical wave of a hand. "People might ask: 'Why has he got those three flags flying?' Then: 'Oh, I see, one of them symbolises the workers, one St Patrick's Day, and the other the Aboriginal people.' "

There is a screech of brakes as a mechanical monster comes to a halt behind a four-wheel drive vehicle at the traffic lights. The monster, with sludge leaking from the back, stinks like buggery, but despite his close proximity to the 'fourby', that has probably just dropped the kids off at school, he is benign. The black rhinoceros-like horns that he employs to lift the *Dumpmasters* up for unloading are folded back on either side of his windscreen. It's often noisy in the garden, yet somehow the underlying feeling of peace remains. Perhaps it has something to do with the sanctity of the grounds.

"It's of no earthly use for fundraising," continues Father Bob unaware of my zoological/mechanical analogy. "It's for awareness raising: until the penny drops. They might say: 'this bloke is either a lunatic or a bloody genius.' How are you, sir?" he asks cheerily as a man walks up carrying a large bag of bread rolls and other goodies for the homeless people.

Father Bob introduces me as: "Ron, Australia's leading postman."

"There must be a large number of posties in Australia," states the visitor doubtfully.

"Yeah, but there's none like Ron," says Father drily as our man takes the rolls into the rectory.

"I think Henri's in the kitchen," Bob calls after him, "Just say you've been sent from heaven."

"He's from La Firma, the bread shop in Clarendon Street," explains Bob.

"That's generous of him to spare the time to bring the food around."

"Yes, he's trying to find his soul."

The man from La Firma comes back out and says: "There was no one in there but I've left the rolls on the table."

"Thank you, La Firma," says Bob, rolling the 'r' magnificently, in the Italian.

"La Firma is Italian meaning 'The Signature,' explains our man who can't pronounce it anywhere near as well.

"Not 'The Firm'?" asks Bob who spies Henri coming around the corner of the rectory. "This man's just bought a nice bag of rolls and sandwiches," he yells to Henri. The monster on the road lets out a roar as the traffic lights turn green.

Henri and I shake hands as the man from La firma leaves.

"Bob's ready to go to Scotland as soon as he can find the funds," I say to Henri.

Father Bob comes in fast. "I'm not going near bloody Scotland until such time as there is lazy money." He drags out the word 'lazy.'

"Anything else to tell me, Ron?"

"Geoffrey is going to enter the photograph of 'The Grin' in a competition and donate the winnings to the Foundation."

"Let Geoffrey know that it's quite OK for him to keep the money. What we want is the awareness raising. 'Who is this person with the mad grin?'"

"I'll let him know. I'd better be on my way. I'll see you on Friday at 10.30am then, Father?"

"Yeah," he drawls, "10.30 is alright by me, but make it Thursday. Do you want to discuss religion then?"

"Yes, thanks.'

"Alright. I believe in God the Father Almighty and all that stuff. The Pope says: 'If you baptise the baby, other than in the name of the Father, the Son and the Holy Spirit, (some of 'the boys' like Peter Kennedy from St Mary's in South Brisbane were saying 'in the name of the Creator and of the Redeemer and of the Sanctifier') it's not valid!'" Father Bob yells as he walks back inside. In his purple bomber jacket he looks as if he has just come home from a rugby match.

"It sounds as if he's got problems to me," I retort just as loudly.

"He's a ..."

The screen door slams and the traffic drowns out Bob's reply, though it might have been 'fine fellow' that he said.

As I pedal my way back to the Disaster Centre later, it suddenly dawns on me: 'three flags: the Aboriginal, Irish and Eureka banners, but no Australian flag'. Meanwhile Ronny is practising mad grins as I ride down Cecil Street past the market.

A few weeks later, a large framed black and white photo of 'The Grin' hangs from a wall in a photographic competition at a gallery in Collingwood. A throng of people attends the opening night and it is not until we are leaving that we see Father Bob. He has just hopped into his car and is about to drive off. How he managed to get a parking spot right outside the venue is astonishing. It must have been divine intervention although he is parked in a driveway. Bob winds down his window to talk to us. His smiling countenance is mirrored by the picture of a kindly looking Father Bob on the driver's door which is captioned: 'In Bob We Trust.' Father Bob might be a resident priest but he is not a reticent one.

# Chapter 30: Back to the Desert

*"Jeez, you can even kill His son and the bastard still loves ya."*

It's Thursday and the head Flea has called a general meeting! This is unusual: he prefers to hold us up on Fridays. We all troop up the stairs to the windowless lunchroom to listen to a lot of bloody tommyrot. Spooks is cautioned gruffly by Luvy on the way up: "Keep your mouth shut, ya big lug. We don't wanna be hanging around here all bloody day."

My sentiments exactly: I've got religious instructions this morning.

Father Bob doesn't muck around when I next walk into his study; he picks his glasses up off the desk, puts them on and announces: "History of Religion up to Jesus of Nazareth." It sounds like the title of some paper that he has just written and is about to read to an audience. I asked for religion and Bob is about to oblige. I am sure we will be in the desert soon.

"You've got God far, far away, atop of mountains, in the river, up a tree trunk. You might have to go out in the desert to find him," says Father Bob looking off into the distance like Burke or Wills. I smile; he is becoming predictable.

"A change of tactic: away in a manger now. So he's not away at all. He's in the maternity ward of the Nazareth pub or somewhere. God now becomes human. Other human beings get frightened. 'What do you mean when you say you are the Son of God? Excuse us, but we know your mother,' "says Bob in an indignant voice. "One thing leads to another. Thirty-three years later, human beings sick of all of this, nail him up. That's the end of it. No it's not! Because now, bugger it! God doesn't take offence. If He had taken offence we would have been happy because we would have had the old God back throwing thunderbolts and all that. He would never have come back to life. As it turns out you end up with the Great Atonement."

"Forgiveness and turning the other cheek?" I ask.

"Yes. We've seen a recent example of that when José Ramos-Horta was shot by Alfredo Reinaldo. He said: 'I forgive the one who shot me and I ask the East Timorese people to take care of his family.' This is the voice of God," declares Bob explicitly.

I nod my head, mulling this over.

"If this happened to Burrows," Father Bob says, "Burrows would say: 'If I get my hands on that bloke who shot my son I'll rip his eyes out. Then I'll go around and massacre his family.' "

Strewth! Bob must have a high opinion of me. "That's a bit gory," I say. "I don't know whether I'd go that far. Massacring his family, I mean."

"That's human at our most natural," says Father Bob, "because we are animals. If you take the point of God at His most *supernatural*, the Jesus story says," and here Bob turns on his Aussie twang, " 'Jeez, you can even kill His son and the bastard still loves ya.' "

Bob looks at me intently. "It's too much for the human mind," he states. "Therefore we will install a body corporate that will personify and personalise this from now on. Enter Church. Da, dah." He gestures, maestro and magician, as he makes the sound effects.

"They would have needed some way of explaining it all," I say.

"But," says Bob strongly, "you can't trust the bloody church, because all of a sudden, what happened to forgiveness? The Old Testament God has made a reappearance in the Church. Burn the heretic."

Father tells me that the Catholics were good in the first two hundred years. "We even helped people who were suffering the effects of the plague which wiped out the Roman Empire," he says. "People weren't looking after themselves whereas the Christians were part of a set whose lifestyle *was* to look after themselves. They would also look after others if the people would let them. "We were pains-in-the-arse when it came to ideology." says Bob.

"Most ideologists are." I counter cheekily. Bob laughs.

"But when it came to practice," he says, "they liked the results of our lifestyle."

Father Bob's phone buzzes in his pocket and he slips it out and starts talking. If he's not talking to me he's talking on the phone. He must have been thinking whilst he was talking though because when he terminates the call he says: "The Amish in Pennsylvania have a level of forgiveness that is unbelievable. The man comes and shoots their children at school. They then go to the bloke's funeral to comfort the widow. Following that they invite her to come to the funeral of the kids, and once again assure her that everything is alright between her, her family, the deceased gunman, and themselves as a community. That is divine."

"Can you think of any example of that sort of behaviour in Australia?"

"Weary Dunlop, is one," Father Bob answers immediately as he takes off his glasses, throws them onto the desk and begins massaging his face as he is often wont to do. "He came home from the prison camps hating the Japs. Then he said: 'We've got to put others first and I'm putting good relations with the Japanese atop of my things to do.'"

"He must have been close to divine to be able to do that after what the Aussies endured over there. I'm sure his men must have thought that he was too. They loved him," I say to Bob as Frank wanders into the room, walks over and sticks his head in my crotch.

"Yeah!" exclaims Bob. "That's why I like his statue in the Botanic Gardens. I almost had to bite my tongue off last Saturday. I was walking the dog through the gardens and saw a bloke doing his stretching exercises using the base of Weary Dunlop's statue as a pressure place for his feet. I thought: 'Mate, couldn't you do it somewhere else. We haven't got many icons in Australia.' He had just seen the base of the statue as a convenient place to do his exercises. It could have been the statue of Mary, Jesus and Joseph, or Buddha. I don't think the boy would have noticed."

"It probably wouldn't have worried Weary anyway."

"I agree. Weary, who is looking down at the boy, may well have said: 'This is what we had to do in Changi, make use of whatever was available to stay alive. This boy has decided to use my statue, so good on you, mate.'"

Father Bob then covers his bets. "Maybe this is desecration, but then again it mightn't be," he says laughing. John Safran would say: 'that's Bobbywaffle. You can't make up your mind.' The Jews have got to make up their minds." Father Bob now moves onto the fundamental difference between the Jews and the Christians. "Whereas a Christian doesn't have to. That's why he is valuable to us." Safran in particular, or the Jews in general I wonder? "But at the same time an advisory goes with that: Beware, because when you are *that decisive* there may be ramifications that are not helpful."

'The Jews in general,' says Descartes.

Bob talks of the Jew's assertiveness as opposed to the Christian's procrastination. He gives an example of the Jew's cut-and-dried attitude in the Gaza Strip. "'We want the Gaza Strip back! God gave it to us and we're gonna get it back and we don't give a rat's arse about who gets hurt in the process because it's *ours!*' Now that is Jewish decisiveness. See what I mean, Ron?"

"Yes, you've spoken of the Jew's decision-making before. That's a straight forward example if ever there was one."

"Jewish decisiveness," Bob states flatly. "Occasionally the body corporate, the dog, wakes up and says: 'Excuse me,' to the tail, 'you're wagging me. Thirty years ago I had a nice experience of reconciliation with the Palestinians. Thank you very much. What happened to that?' "

"But the Palestinians have been firing rockets indiscriminately at them," I say, trying to be fair.

"Yes, Hamas and Fatah have to get their acts together," says Father, "there's no question about that. But it's no use attacking, attacking and attacking. You end up in a cleft stick. When a Jewish person gets into a cleft stick he becomes determined not to let the holocaust happen again. He didn't defend himself on that occasion."

'The abused has now become the abuser,' observes Descartes.

"What do *you* think they should do then?"

"I'm not advising one way or the other," says Bob putting up his hands as if someone has stuck a gun in his back. Given his age and the fact that he looks like Edward G Robinson it could be James Cagney. "I'm simply saying that the Jesus principle is that if you are going to seek revenge you should dig two graves."

"One for yourself?"

'You're brilliant!' quips Rene. Bloody mongrel.

"Yeah!" Bob exclaims. "One for the victim and one for yourself, because as soon as you've taken your revenge, you're buggered and Jewish people know that. An eye for and eye and a tooth for a tooth," he says like some American evangelist, "but don't take any more than the eye for the eye, or a tooth for a tooth. So the Jew says to the Palestinian: 'You have killed three people in one of our villages just over the border. We will now retaliate and blow up what? Twenty-seven people?' "

Frank moves away, picks up a chicken neck that is lying on the carpet and crunches it noisily.

"It's a vexed question which is why we are talking about it four thousand years after the origin of the Hebrews who developed into the Jews."

"It's a fascinating conundrum."

"It *is* fascinating," agrees Father Bob. "That is how John Safran has made a name for himself with his programmes: *John Safran versus God,* and *Speaking in Tongues*, just to name a couple, because he drags the eccentricities out into the open. To the secular humanist these are eccentricities."

Frank stops crunching and hops up into his armchair, looking first at Bob and then at me like a spectator at a show.

"You would have a whole new lifestyle if you take this digging of two graves on board," says Bob as I look back at Frank.

"Jesus never actually said that," he explains, "but it was something similar, one of his wise sayings. You would have to change your retributive system of justice, which we have in Australia. If you are found guilty of a crime, you are punished in a prescribed manner. It's done in a sanitised place where there is no reminder of reality: a courtroom."

Father Bob then launches into a detailed description of how our court system works! Frank settles lower into his chair. He looks as if he is preparing for a long session.

"The judge is dressed up. He sits up on a high place," Bob says, setting the scene for his next little play. "You (he makes extended eye contact with me like the archetype detective interrogating a suspect) are in custody. You're brought out. There is a jury, a magistrate or a judge who is going to make a decision. He will say: 'I find Mr. Burrows,' which means, 'I don't know at all Mr. Burrows, but I *find* on the evidence' which means the game of barristers versus each other. It's up to them to then present his Honour or his Worship with a whole smorgasbord of evidence. Mr. Burrows will be sentenced if found guilty. It depends on the skills of the barristers and on whether their evidence is better presented than the other sides." Bob's voice rises, "Now that's cynical I know. The other form of justice is restorative justice."

For scene two, Bob clutches his cardigan in each hand with his thumbs pointing upward. "This didn't happen in a vacuum, ladies and gentlemen of the jury. It happened on a train between the city and Footascray.'"

The crime is now described by Bob in short grabs,: "Mr. Smith was travelling . . . The boy was . . . He stabbed . . . This was . . . 'Oh Jeez, what happened? *He* stabbed that man!'"

Father Bob picks up his glasses from the desk, rubs his eyes before putting them on, and says: "No, you didn't just stab that man because if you stab the man it means that you stab the man's wife, his children, his mother, his neighbourhood. 'Hello! No I didn't.' Yes you did. That's the implication."

The magnetic pull of the desert drags Father Bob back from the courtroom. He says that as far as he's concerned, Jesus introduced or reinforced an already existing system of justice, which was tribal. Bob tells me that this is where a lot of Islamic justice comes from because it's based on the tribes. Muhammad was a tribal man. Keeping the tribes in balance was the only way to have harmony in the desert, "and to live happily ever after," says Bob. "There were horrendous punishments: stoning people to death and cutting a thief's hand off. That's all tribal," says Bob.

"It was practical too," I add.

"That's right. They never had any other way. They would have had a drop of mercy though because Muhammad introduced drops of mercy into tribalism. There's no question about that. He'd give somebody a fair go. Unless he knew, for instance, that the person concerned was an absolute swine and had betrayed the Muslims to the other infidel Arabs, he'd let him go. 'Let him go,' says Mr. Muhammad."

As Father Bob talks, I marvel at his theatrical storytelling and find that I too enjoy being in the desert with all these Biblical characters whom Bob is bringing to life. Since the very first interview I have found these sessions to be therapeutic and I derive a vicarious pleasure as I listen to the stories. Time seems to stand still and yet when I check my watch it has actually flown by. It reminds me of when I used to play cards when I was younger: the Friday night card session with the boys, drinking and playing poker or pontoon when sleepless nights were just a part of youth. We'd start about 8.30pm and then the clock would seem to stop. I'd look at the clock in what seemed about two hours later and it would be 3.30 in the morning and I would have to start work a few hours later.

"It's the same with Jesus," says Bob recounting yet another story as I evoke memories of those long ago card nights. "The woman caught in adultery," he says loudly "about to be stoned to death. Off we go back to the desert. Jesus bends down and writes in the sand. The old men who had brought her to Jesus said: 'What would you do with this sheila?' Jesus says: 'Nothin'.' He bends and writes in the sand and allegedly the blokes all leave, one by one. He then says to the woman: 'They've all gone away, luv. Why don't you go away too?' Jesus has introduced a mysterious ingredient which is presumably called . . . I don't know whether you'd call it justice."

"Mercy," I put in.

"Mercy," agrees Father Bob, "A fair go, because the boys themselves should have been dragged before the court. They would have been the ones taking advantage of the woman allegedly caught in adultery, and it takes two to tango."

I nod my head in agreement.

"It's happening today as we speak, Ron."

"Things haven't changed much in some parts of the world."

"There are villages around the world where women are *still* being stoned to death for adultery: pack raped in punishment for crimes not committed by *her* but by her brothers. Restorative justice means that you are supposed to involve more persons than the accused person."

"Does this happen anywhere?" I ask.

"The South Africans tried it," Father Bob says. "The Truth and Reconciliation Commissions."

"Yes, I remember reading about those Commissions. I remember thinking at the time how strange they were."

"Extraordinary things happened," says Bob and launches back into his improvised play. " 'Yes, he's the man who killed my husband and children,' in that terrible slaughter where a million people were killed. 'Oh, yeah,' they said. 'But,' she said, 'I'd like ya to take me over to him. I'm not very good on me feet.' 'Oh, yeah, what do you want to do?' She says, 'I'd like to tell him he's forgiven, and I'd like to invite him back to my home where I will treat him as my son.' Well what the? You can't have that going on in a British system of justice."

"Definitely not." I declare smiling.

"We've only got the adversarial system. Ron Burrows is dragged before the court."

Hang on. Not again. We've had this one. Father Bob hauls me before the courts yet again.

"It's the job of one party to depict you to the public as an absolute bloody monster. Alright?" asks Bob.

"Yeah alright," I laugh. We might have had it but it's the way he tells 'em.

"Your defence barrister will have to catch up and it's hard to do. The prosecutor is the one who starts orf. The first thing the public reads in the paper will be: 'Mr. McGillicutty's QC says Ron Burrows is a monster.' That's the first shot fired. Your boy has to stand up and catch up."

'Could Mr. McGillicutty be the husband of Mrs. McGillicutty who got knocked down in the street?' wonders Ronny.

"Show the jury that I'm as pure as a choir boy," I join in.

"Yeah, but also try to convince the public, because the public reads in the paper . . . " Bob allows the sentence to drop out and court has been adjourned.

"That to me is religion," he says summing up my religious instructions for the day. "Take nothing for granted. Your Jesus is the character who is responsible for that: take nothing for granted. Whereas your church has co-opted your Jesus as if he was the rule maker and the law maker, and he was anything but!" he says, the decibels rising towards the end. "If people want to argue with me about religion, the Bobbywaffle would always be: trying to restore the balance between Jesus, as depicted by the Church, and the Jesus, not only that we could read about in the Gospels," he says Gospels to rhyme with decibels, "but I'm saying there's this X factor called the Spirit who in fact will wake you up to the real presence of Jesus in society in the least likely ways. Like you might see on your round as a postie."

"Ye-es."

"Of the beauty of the human race, or something."

"Occasionally," I allow, trying desperately to think up some such occurrence.

"Yeah! You're not gonna get it all the time."

Father Bob trudges back into the desert. He talks about the desert dwellers being blessed because they are getting the stars by night, the desert by day and the occasional oasis. Against those blessings, he says, is the fact that "it is bloody hard yakka." He wanders back out of the desert to paint a picture of city life "where people have got the bloody electric lights going day and night in office buildings and the towers, and we can't see the stars." He's bloodywell right.

Bob treks through the city and takes on the urban sprawl where "we're gonna have houses going for miles and miles and miles and children will miss out on experiencing the natural high of seeing the moon and stars in all their glory." He says that we would be well advised to "go back to the book of nature, which is what the green revolution is supposed to be all about. As long as we haven't been stooged by some of the technocrats of the world," he says, "who have decided that we all need desalination plants, and we need this, and we need that, so that the rich can live better. What about the pooah?" he asks. Father Bob claims, and it has been said by others too, that we are going to end up with a few people with more of everything and more people with less. "The main religions say that that is not good enough," says Father Bob emphatically.

"Thanks, Bob." I say. "That's a good start to getting a bit of religion into the book. Maybe we should have a bit about the Bible just to round off the morning's work."

"I was thinking this morning about that *bloody* book: the Bible. It fascinates large groups. The Jew is fascinated by the book; the Muslim is fascinated by the book; and the fundamentalist Christian is fascinated by the book. I'm saying the book will kill you," Bob says prosaically.

Here am I thinking that the 'bloody book' is what religious people base their philosophy on. Not so, at least in Father Bob's case.

"Your Jesus said: 'I will send you the Spirit and the Spirit will teach you *everything* you need to know.' Now that means get away from the bloody book. The book is not going to teach you. The fools go to the book, turn the pages and say: 'What does this tell us for today? It's like going to this thing here," says Bob picking up a slim volume of verse from the desk and flourishing it: "What does this book tell me for today?"

I laugh and Frank gets down out of his armchair, arches his back like a Yogi and then lies down on the floor.

"The Bible is not meant to tell you for today. It's meant to give you a general outline. Don't get lost in the book. The fundamentalists get lost in the book. They go on and on, woof, woof, woof," Bob barks. Frank lifts his head and cocks his ears. "They talk all day and night about the bloody book." He sticks his nose in the air and parodies a fundamentalist, spouting in a fruity voice: 'In Chapter fourteen, page such-and-such He says . . . ' Put the bloody thing away!" Bob exclaims loudly and bangs his hand on the desk.

"The guideline is…" he pauses to think of an example. " 'Stone all homosexuals.' People fascinated by the book take that literally," he says. "According to them it means exactly that: 'Stone all homosexuals.' " Bob shakes his head in disgust. "No it doesn't, you fool. Work out where and when it was said. That might have been said in the jungle in Vietnam when you had to have a tight fighting combat unit and you found that some of the boys were playing hanky panky, which put the rest of the platoon in danger because that particular spot was unguarded because the boys were indulging themselves in their hanky panky. 'Stone these homosexuals,' says General Bloggs." I chuckle at the mention of *that* name. General Bloggs is giving the Bloggs clan a bad name with his homophobic attitude.

"He means stone them *here* in Vietnam because they've let the side down. 'Oh no,' these fools claim, 'we're gonna extend that now back to Californ-IA.' "

Father Bob tells me that the things written in the Bible are advisories. Naturally I ask him about the Ten Commandments. Surely they are intended to be commandments, not advisories. Bob says that they certainly sound like commandments but he is not sure if that's true. He plucks an example from his stock.

"If you say to the kid: 'Don't put your hand on the hot plate,' it sounds like a commandment whereas in fact it's only advice. How are you going to enforce it? 'If you put your hand on the hot plate I will cut it orf.' You are *advising* the poor soul. I think the relationship between God and your human beings . . . " Father Bob taps a couple of keys on the computer keyboard as if summoning up further information, leans back, takes off his glasses and massages his eyes. "I wrote something strange for the Newsletter yesterday," he says. "Part of God becomes human. Other humans kill the human part of God. God forgives them for killing the human part, and becomes human himself."

"Succinctly put, Bob." Maybe, merely by chance, I was instrumental in Father Bob nutting this out when I asked him for a definition of 'The Power' during the photo shoot with Geoffrey. On that occasion he said: 'This whole situation is so ridiculous that God decides to start again. So he uses the crucifixion of Jesus and then the resurrection as a way of starting again.' It's been over two thousand years now and the poor buggers are still trying to explain it.

I check my watch. I've got to go. Father Bob says that he can spare time for a short session tomorrow morning so I agree because I would like to get him talking about the Pope before Good Friday, which is next week. We say goodbye and Frank, as usual, escorts me to the door.

## Chapter 31: The Tail Wags the Dog

*"Jesus of Nazareth said: 'Girls! Don't carry on as though youse are the dog, the main item, because youse are the tail.'"*

This is a Friday with a difference, apart from the fact that we haven't got a meeting. It's warm and drizzling lightly as I *drive* to the church. The windscreen wipers slap back and forward smearing the glass. The heat over the past weeks has dried out the rubber blades. As I pull into the kerb I hear the parrots before I actually see them. They are flying flat-out into the eucalypts and stopping suddenly like jets landing on an aircraft carrier. Wattlebirds are trumpeting as they too fly between the trees in dogfights, their beaks snapping. They all seem to be rejoicing in the rain.

I finished my round early today and had time to take the bike back and clock off before coming to see Father Bob. This is my first 'legitimate' session. As I step up onto the verandah he calls out, through the security door: "Is that you, Your Grace?"

"None other, Father," I reply cheerily.

Frank pads up to greet me as Father Bob opens the door to let me in. Bob tells me that he has got a wedding later this afternoon, which could well be in the rain. That would be a novelty. I sink into my chair and, as soon as Bob is seated, I open my notebook.

"Henri Ser says that he thinks you are a priest for all religions." I read, somewhat woodenly and self-consciously. "What do you think about that?" Father Bob says that it is a typical Jewish comment. He tells me that he read an article yesterday where someone allegedly complained to God in the desert. I smile.

The story goes that God asked all the wise Jews to assemble and listen to Him so that a few decisions could be made. After the assembly, one of the Jews was overheard complaining to God. According to Father Bob, the complainant said: 'We've had the assembly of wise Jews, God, but there's a couple of blokes who stayed out. They're down there in a tent beside the river and *they* are starting to say wise things.' As was typical of the times, the complainant asked God whether these two blokes should be eliminated. And God says, through the prophet: 'No, leave 'em alone. I wish that everyone was a prophetic person.' Father Bob declares: "That's the whole bloody point."

I read from my notebook again: "I think the Pope's dogged attitude in regard to the Good Friday Liturgy, where the Jews are denigrated, is casting Catholicism in a bad light,"

"Yes. He's wrong," declares Father Bob bluntly as he picks up a letter from his desk and abruptly changes the subject. I glance at my notes.

'Holy shit!' laughs Descartes. 'The Pope was going to be the main topic!'

The letter is from an English visitor who says he has been 'converted and saved.' Before coming to Mass last Christmas Eve, he said, he had been disillusioned with Catholicism and was a member of the Society of Lapsed Catholics. I'm tickled by the name and a search later will reveal that there is a website called CatholicBlogs.com. There's that name again, Blogs not Bloggs.

I swat at a fly that is taking shelter from the rain. It lands on top of Bob's computer and seems to like the warmth beneath its tiny feet because it keeps walking around like a homeless person sheltering from the cold in a shopping centre.

Bob affects his fruity Frank Thring voice as he reads the letter to me. In it, the man seems to be glowing, saying that he 'felt the goodness in the air in the church.' For the first time in his sixty years, he claims, he did not want the Mass to end.

'Poor bastard,' sniffs Descartes. Ronny takes exception, 'Bloody cynical Darwinian,' he says, and they start bickering.

Bob looks up at me when he finishes reading and raises his eyebrows. It is then that he produces another letter that he just happens to have at hand. This one contains a cheque for the Maguire Foundation "for five hundred quid from a local," says Father offhandedly. I watch the insignificant fly strutting around the mall of Bob's ancient computer monitor and then tell him that I'm most impressed with the lady's generosity. I glance at my notes and steer the conversation back to the Pope. I make the point that he doesn't agree with the Pope on a lot of matters.

"I don't give a bugger about agreeing with the Pope," he blusters. "I don't have to agree with him on most things. It's a matter of opinion." He tells about an edict from Rome forbidding the celebration of St Patrick's Day this year because it falls in Holy Week. He declares with conviction: "This is a classic case of the tail wagging the dog. The hierarchy in the Roman Catholic Church believes that *it* is the dog, and that the rank and file is the tail, whereas Jesus of Nazareth said: 'Girls! Don't carry on as though youse are the dog, the main item, because youse are the tail,' "says Bob in his Aussie drawl.

Frank picks just the right time to stand up and walk regally over to Bob wagging *his* tail. We snicker, and Bob pats the dog and continues the analogy: "The dog should wag its tail, like Frank, not the bloody tail wag the dog. The leadership is the *tail*," he insists ruefully and leans further back in his chair.

Frank walks back and hops up into his chair and looks at Bob as though he understands the argument. His soft brown eyes focus on his master and I almost expect him to nod his head in agreement. I'm sure that he knows the word 'dog' and thinks we are talking about him. I lounge back in my chair, especially relaxed today. Father Bob explains that occasionally in the history of the Roman Catholic Church the tail wags the dog. "That stopped in the sixties with Vatican Two," he tells me. "but it's now reasserted itself and the Tail has taken over again."

Oddly enough, if you substitute the words 'Roman Catholic Church' with the words 'Australia Post' and 'Vatican Two' with 'Industrial Participation' you'll find that a similar revolution (on a much smaller scale) took place in that organisation too. In the 1980s, Australia Post revolutionised the mail centres by installing sorting machines that sorted by postcode. The workforce was worried about the resultant loss of jobs and work bans were put in place by the Union. In 1989 with the Fleas fighting a losing battle against the well-organised unionists, especially at the Redfern and Clayton South Mail Centres, they had no choice but to enter into an agreement with the Union. A Joint Statement of Understanding on Industrial Participation was signed. Both parties agreed that there should be consultation before decisions were made at a local level; in particular Australia Post agreed to consult the workforce before making major changes to work practices in the future. This agreement was so successful that a national Industrial Participation Training programme was implemented and feelings between managers and staff improved dramatically. But as with the Tail in the Catholic Church, the minority, longing for the power that it had lost, gradually reasserted itself.

Both were worthwhile undertakings, both were successful in their own rights and both suffered the same fate at the hands of a powerful minority. As with Vatican Two, Industrial Participation was so popular with the workers that it is still talked about today. 'Whatever happened to Industrial Participation?' one hears one of the older workers ask after yet another unreasonable directive from management where the workers have had no input.

'Whatever happened to Vatican Two?,' the priests wail. Ratzinger is dragging the Catholic Church down . . .' I've got to stop Ronny from bringing forth all this nonsense because I'm losing concentration. I hurriedly consult my notes again as the images that he is projecting fade. There is a gleam in Bob's eye as he scrutinises me. He must wonder about me.

"Do you think the Pope . . . ?" I begin.

"The Pope!" expostulates Father. "The Pope should have behaved himself from day one. Some of them did and some of them didn't. It's this continuing struggle between the dog and the tail," he insists.

Ronny is hard at it now and I can't shunt him aside. I picture a dachshund: the long body is chock-a-block with a myriad of tiny parishioners and parish priests dressed in ragged white albs. The tail is covered with flea-like Archbishops, Bishops and Cardinals all dressed in ermine; purple clad Monsignors are vying for attention. On the very tip is a flea dressed in an Armani suit and wearing bright red shoes.

Bob, somehow or other, is managing to work on his computer as he talks. I look out the window: it's still drizzling and the birds sound as if they are enjoying it. A fat sparrow lands on the windowsill and peeks in. Maybe he's trying to tell me that it's time to go. I check my watch; I wouldn't like Bob to be late for Mass.

Frank is out of the chair again attacking the remains of another chicken neck with gusto. They must be his favourite fare. Father Bob comments that the background noise that anyone listening to the recorder might hear "is the sound of the dog eating meat on Friday, not the priest eating the dog."

I ask Father if he feeds meat to the dog on Good Friday and he says: " 'Oh we just let the hundred flowers bloom and a thousand thoughts contend,' which as you know Ron, comes from Mao Zedong. He went around opening everyone's minds and closing their mouths." Rene Descartes nods his head as Ronny conjures up hordes of Chinese people being dragged off to prison where they are systematically tortured.

That sounds like a good note on which to end. Bob says that he has to go to the bank before Mass so we wander out into Dorcas Street, which is a long way from the desert, to where our cars are parked side by side.

"That's a nice old thing, Ron," exclaims Father Bob loudly as a truck whistles past his ear. Despite having driven this Jag since I was a boy it's the first time that Bob has seen it. His old Ford van that he sometimes drives is parked beside it.

"What year is that?" he asks.

"1970."

"I had a Statesman which was a similar colour. It was pinched from outside a café. The boot was full of women's dresses," he adds with a cheeky grin. Even Ronny has trouble trying to conjure up an image of Bob as a transvestite.

"What were all the women's dresses doing in the boot?" I laugh.

"A man who had a store said that they were seconds. 'Do what you bloodywell like with them,' he said. There were hundreds of them in there."

"Your car was probably stolen by a cross-dresser."

"He might be still wandering around in them," yells Bob as he climbs into his van.

Cross-dressers are far from my mind as I surf the net, reading about Vatican Two, Eggs Benedict, and matters related to St Patrick's Day and Good Friday.

It becomes apparent from what I read that The Holy See, the tail of the body of the Catholic Church, the dog, has started wagging, moving the animal back from Vatican Two. The Jews have been insulted by Pope Benedict XVI's new version of the Good Friday Prayer, which they claim is anti-Semitic. Catholics who celebrate the Mass in Latin will now hear: 'Let us also pray for the Jews: That our God and Lord may illuminate their hearts, that they acknowledge that Jesus Christ is the Saviour of all men.'

The new version is merely a watered-down rendering of the original pre Vatican Two prayer, which read: "Let us pray also for the faithless Jews: that almighty God may remove the veil from their hearts so that they too may acknowledge Jesus Christ our Lord."

The prayer was made more palatable to the Jews at the Second Vatican Council. It was amended to: "Let us pray for the Jewish people, the first to hear the word of God, that they may continue to grow in the love of his name and in faithfulness to his covenant."

Eggs Benedict is obviously not in accord with the Second Vatican Council. The tail is indeed wagging the dog.

Father Bob comments on the Pope's decision in his Blog. He says that: "someone in Rome insists the Jews need a special mention in the ritual prayers. I thought we'd got over all that 40 years ago. The majority of Aussie Catholics won't have a bar of anti-any-race or religion infiltrating parish churches."

I'm glad to see that Bob is willing to speak out against the Pope when he believes that he, the Pope, is wrong. I'm thrilled that he is also willing to stand up for the Jews especially in print. I'm sure it will give great heart to his friends, Henri and Henry.

The tail has also decreed that because St Patrick's Day falls on the Monday of Holy Week this year it will have to be celebrated on the 14$^{th}$ instead of the 17$^{th}$ so as not to compromise the holiness of the week. Father Bob writes: "Tell that to the Irish, who will no doubt say: 'Let the Roman Catholics do what they like but no Irishman will celebrate St Patrick except on the 17$^{th}$.'" Father Bob says that he admits that there is plenty of grog around on St Pat's day but he says that doesn't defile the meaning of the day itself.

Bob's intention all along has been to celebrate the Irish-ness of the Parish by flying the Irish flag beside the Eureka and Aboriginal flags from the balcony of the Parish House. Perhaps not coincidentally, each of these banners represents resistance to a ruling order, a resistance founded on the solidarity of the oppressed. After reading the papal edict nothing will stop me from attending the St Patrick's Day Mass on Monday. I wonder whether Bob will toe the official line set down by the tail in Rome, or whether in fact the dog will bite its own tail.

# Chapter 32: Hot in the City

*"Have you sent the hundred pounds to The Frog?"*

It is a hot, noisy Friday morning in South Melbourne with the temperature tipped to peak at forty degrees. Formula One cars are screaming around Albert Park Lake and helicopters are clattering overhead ferrying the well-heeled to the track the fast and easy way. Father Bob is in the garden with a film crew when I arrive. He is wearing a straw boater and looks relaxed.

"This is Ron Burrows," says Father to the crew. "Ron is writing my life story. You should interview him."

They laugh obviously thinking that Bob is joking.

"Yeah!" he exclaims indignantly. "We are going to sell it around the world."

Maybe if I had walked up wearing a suit instead of a luminous shirt and was carrying a brief case, instead of a bundle of letters for the priest, the film crew would have given me some credibility. They start talking quietly amongst themselves dismissing the subject. Father Bob then begins talking to me so that we've now got two distinct conversations going simultaneously.

"Have you sent the hundred pounds to The Frog?" asks Bob. The others are conversing in the background.

Bob's question is in relation to a deal that we have been negotiating with the Frenchman, Monsieur Van Den Bosch, for the rights to publish his drawing of Abbé Pierre.

"No, the deal has fallen through," I answer, glancing sideways at the film crew.

Skillful conversationalist that he is, Father Bob then turns to one of the film crew to include us all in the one conversation. Flourishing a letter that he is holding he says: "Here's a woman from the Ivory Coast who says she will give us a donation."

"Oh, yes?" the interviewer says as his mates set up the tripod for the camera.

"That's what I presume this interview is about," says Bob, deadpan.

"Ah, no." laughs the interviewer uncertainly, "but we could probably do it if you like." He now seems to be a much more agreeable character.

"Well, it's either I invest in the Ivory Coast sheila who says, by the way: 'I've got 5.5 million dollars for youse.' "

"Youse!" laughs one of the cameramen."

"Or," continues Bob, "I go prostituting myself to South Melbourne business and end up with sweet f.a."

"That much?" asks the interviewer.

"Like last year," adds Bob.

"Like last year," parrots the interviewer as one of the cameramen motions that Father Bob should now be seated. The camera is in place.

"I'll see you later, Father. Nice to have met you all," I say as I walk away towards my bike.

"Yes, Ron. Drink copious amounts of water," instructs Bob.

I move out from under the shady trees and ride away along Dorcas Street delivering mail in the tar-melting heat. On Monday I will be going to Mass to see Father Bob in his element. Hopefully it won't be this bloody hot.

# Chapter 33: St Patrick's Day

*"The Roman Catholics have been told by the Pope not to celebrate St Patrick's Day this year."*

It's three minutes before noon as I pedal up the driveway to the church. The forecast is for another forty-degree day and it feels as if it is nudging that mark already. I've been riding hard, despite the intense heat, to get here in time and I'm in a muck lather. Just to the right of the entrance, around the side of the church, there is a shady cranny. It's important to leave your bike in the shade on a hot day if you are going to leave it for a while.

Spooks was teaching me the round many years ago. It was only my third or fourth day on the job and the searing heat was knocking me around. The heat radiating off the bitumen footpaths was shimmering before our eyes as we rode along. The streets were deserted and I distinctly remember seeing a tiny bird with its mouth open sitting on the rim of an empty birdbath. We stopped and I filled the birdbath using next-door's hose. I was feeling as wrung out as that bird and a bit sorry for myself too. An old bloke in Morris St popped his head out the front door of his house and yelled out to Spooks. He invited us in for a beer so I dismounted and leant my bike against the front fence.

"Ronny! Put your bike under the tree. Under the tree, put your bike under the tree, mate," said Spooks casually leaning back as he sat astride his bike, his wide brimmed hat shading his face and his big flat feet splayed at right angles. That was nearly twenty years ago so we were both about forty then.

"What's the difference?" I asked. "The bloody bike is not going to feel the heat." The perspiration was running down my face and I had a sore arse. I'd been listening to the silly bugger prattle on since 6am.

"A bloke asked me in for a beer many years ago," Spooks said. "It was nearly Christmas just like now and stinking hot. 'Have another one. Another one. Have another one,' he kept saying. It was bloody hot outside. Bloody hot. I think we had about four cans. Four cans," said Spooks. I remember him pushing his hat to the back of his head as he spoke. "When I came out I had two bloody flat tyres. Two flat tyres, mate."

"What did you do?" I asked, wishing that we could get into the old bloke's house out of the heat.

"I rang up the nongs at work and said: 'I've got two flat tyres, two flats, send out another bike in the van.' The nong on the phone asked me how I got *two* flat tyres. 'How the hell would I know, you idiot,' I said, and then I went back inside and had another beer."

Smiling at the recollection I push the bike in to the cranny so that it is not too obvious. This, after all, is close to where the **Hope**Mobile was stolen. I can remember in years gone by trying to make my bike look inconspicuous outside a pub but this is the first time I've had to take these precautions outside a church. I take my camera from where it has burrowed itself between bundles of mail in the yellow bag and enter the church.

There are only seven worshippers, all scattered within the first four or five rows of pews, a small turnout for such a large church. It reminds me of a night that I went to the greyhound races at Sandown Park where the crowd barely outnumbered the two bookies and the dog handlers.

The hot weather has probably kept the faithful away. It's fairly cool inside the church, although the side door to the left of the altar is wide open letting the heat in.

After taking a prayer book off the pile on the front pew, I sit in the second row so that I can position my voice recorder on the vacant pew in front of me. As we sit and wait for Father Bob I decide to take the camera from the bag. It's got a wide flap sealed with Velcro and it's impossible to open quietly. Do I open it slowly thus prolonging the noise? Or do I rip it open fast like you do when you take a band-aid off a hairy forearm? I choose the latter. The other members of the congregation are all behind me and I can only imagine the start that they get when I suddenly wrench it open.

An old nun, Sister Eugenia, who lives across the road in Dorcas Street, fusses around preparing for the Mass. She checks to make sure that the lectionary on the lectern is open at the right page and then straightens up the little stack of prayer books. Sister Eugenia is dressed in a traditional blue habit. I have known her for twenty years and have never seen her wearing civilian clothing.

Maria Orlando, another one of my customers, is also on hand to help with the Mass. She probably arranged the two vases of white lilies. Both vases are a bit unusual in that there are small Irish flags amongst the arrangements.

Father Bob, dressed in a simple white alb, enters by the open side door and starts talking to me without preamble as he walks in. "There are the Irish flags, Ron," he says as if he has put them there especially for my benefit. "We won't be able to have too much Irish content because St Patrick's Day has fallen in Holy Week, the week preceding Easter," he explains to the small congregation and me. "The Roman Catholics have been told by the Pope not to celebrate St Patrick's Day this year. We have the place dressed in red cloth instead of the green we normally use on St Patrick's Day. We'll show a bit of form though," grins Bob. I'll wear green *and* red." He puts a green stole around his neck with a red emblem on it.

"He's Irish, aren't you, sir?" he asks a man sitting behind me. "Have a look at 'im, Ron. The poor man feels alienated." I nod but don't turn around. The Irishman replies in a quiet Irish brogue but I can't hear what he says.

"You're Irish, aren't you, girls?" Bob asks two ladies whom I saw on my way in. I've seen them around South Melbourne on numerous occasions; I think that they are sisters and are just about inseparable.

"They'll make us use 147, the Monday of 'oly week, won't they?" Father Bob asks the congregation. This is the number of the page in the prayer book for this particular day. If we were celebrating St Patrick we would be using 141. "What do you want to do then?" he asks the congregation. Silence.

Bob answers for them. Loudly. "Monday!"

'Has the 'dog' capitulated?' asks Rene.

"The liturgy, then, will be number 147 'Monday of Holy Week,'" says Father Bob. I shift about on the hard pew.

'Well he *is* under the Pope's orders.' Ronny defends Bob but his voice is weak unlike Father Bob who reads from 'the script' in a strong, confident voice that reverberates in the church.

"Defend me, Oh Lord, from all me enemies," he says sounding as only an Aussie priest can sound. The Lord be with you. Coming together as God's people let's remember that we need salvation ourselves. *You raise the dead to life including all the Irish ancestors who built this church. Lord, have mercy,*" he intones

'The dog has given the tail a nip to ease the irritation,' says Ronny who is paying close attention to this religious ritual.

"You are the Son of God, the Son of Mary. Christ, have mercy," Father continues and then in his every-day voice says: "The Germans sank the *Sydney* in 1941. They've now found her off the coast of Western Australia along with the German ship, *Kormoran.*" He then continues chanting the liturgy: "You are the Son of God, the Son of Mary. Christ, have mercy. May Almighty God have mercy on us, forgive us our sins, bring us into everlasting life, 147, Ron." All in a singsong voice.

"Yes, Father," I smile.

Father Bob then asks: "Who's reading? Ma'am? Sir?" He looks around and then says: "Ron, you are the only one wearing glasses. You'll have to read."

"You want *me* to read?"

"You'll have to," states Bob. "All the other girls have left their glasses at home."

"Alright," I say after a couple of moments. I walk up the step onto the chancel, stand at the ambo and glance at the book. I'm now on stage with Father Bob: the postie and the priest.

"The first one you see there," instructs Father. "Oh, Jesus help us," he prays as I pretend to turn the page.

I snort at Bob's antics and then read the Sacred Scripture, pausing at the appropriate time for the other seven members of the congregation to respond. Standing before the congregation in my luminous safety shirt, I conclude confidently with the words: "This is the word of the Lord." This has got to be a first for a postie and I wish that Spooks could see this. He'd talk about it for a week. No. He'd probably still be talking about it.

"Thanks be to God," says Bob seriously. "Now you've got to read the psalm. What's the verse, girls?" he asks the Irish ladies.

"The Lord is my Light and my Salvation," the Irish duet responds in unison.

I read the psalm with the ladies responding and the grinning spectre of Spooks looking over my shoulder. This breaks my concentration and the Mass goes on without me until Bob's voice rises dramatically and I'm back in the bluestone Church again.

"Judas said this, not because he cared for the pooah, but because he was a crook." As Bob tells the rest of the story I reflect on how a lot of these teachings could have impacted on his decision to become a champion for the poor. Combined, of course, with the enduring impression that Abbé Pierre's story had on him. I also wonder how many of the old Italians in the congregation now say 'pooah' because of Bob's influence. He says something about a large number of Jews trotting up to see Jesus and Lazarus who had been raised from the dead. He says: "the church authorities decided to kill both of 'em, Lazarus and Jesus, since it was on account of Lazarus that a lot of people started to trust Jesus. See what I mean?" Father asks the gathering whilst looking at me. I nod slightly but I'm fading out again. Ronny is projecting a picture of a large field of Jews in chariots, their horses kicking up a cloud of dust as they rein in beside Jesus and Lazarus.

"It's like when we muck around with Monday and Holy Week and what's the other one?"

"St Patrick's Day!" the Irish duo responds. Strewth!

Someone behind me says something softly about "Freddie from Gosford."

"Your brother Freddie from Gosford. He's alive! He's alive!" exclaims Father Bob raising his arms, or was that the old TV evangelist Billy Graham? "This is the Gospel according to the Lord. Have a seat, girls and boys," he directs. "What's the other bloke's name?" he asks the congregation. No answer. Bob turns to me. "The man with one arm, Ron. Did you ever see him?"

"No, Father," I reply. The question conjures up an image though of *The Fugitive,* a television series from about 40 years ago. An innocent one-armed man is on the run, hunted relentlessly for the murder of his wife. The poor bastard is hounded from one episode to the next for about five years.

"I can't think of his name," says Bob. "I've only just received the missive." He chants in a singsong voice: "Through your goodness we have the bread; earth gave it to us; human hands made it for us; nevertheless the bread becomes the bread of life."

I used to deliver the bread of life when I was a bread carter back in the sixties. Every time I hear the screeching of tyres on the road it evokes memories of the time that I was driving for *Tip Top* delivering bread to houses and shops around Deer Park. I became friends with a bloke who delivered for a rival company called *Bakerboy.* We used to have drag races around Millbank Drive, which wends its way around the Kororoit Creek. It was the policy of both companies that the drivers check the tyres on the vans every week. We were both lazy buggers and never bothered about checking them too often. We would drag around the creek with tyres squealing and the vans, full of bread, leaning at alarming angles. His van was older but lighter and faster so I never ever caught him. I mentally chalk up 'bread' on my mind's earlier list of delivery occupations: papers, milk, bread and letters. I've been a bloody delivery boy all my life.

"The prayer is for the glory of his name. Pray over the bread and wine." Bob starts chanting again, "For Freddie of Gosford, the man from Port Melbourne. He had a lot of friends down in Port Melbourne." Father then amends that. "Has. Pray for all the posties of the world. Ron's a postie," he tells the congregation.

'Oh, no!' I mutter. There's that music again. In church this time no less. Father Bob doesn't skip a beat but his voice rises dramatically. I fumble with my mobile phone and throttle it quickly this time crushing the life out of the bloody thing. Father chants: "By the power of the word of the Eucharist, and our being together as a local church, toughen up our love and strengthen our faith as we celebrate the feast of Patrick in Holy Week, and tie us up more and more to each other in unity and peace. We ask for this through Christ the Lord," he says and then begins chanting again. "The Lord be with you. Lift up your hearts. Let's give thanks to the Lord our God." Normal voice once again: "It is right always and everywhere to thank You through Jesus for men and women *like Patrick*, adventurous, *like Patrick*.

Father Bob then prays over the bread and wine. He looks at the assembly before chanting about supper being ended and disciples drinking cups of blood, "the Everlasting Covenant shed for you for all so that sin may be forgiven." The congregation then joins with Father Bob to proclaim the mystery of faith. He begins chanting, the sound of his voice echoing in the sparsely populated church. Lord, have mercy on us all. Make us worthy to share eternal life with Mary, Peter and Paul and all the others. *Patrick*. They did your will in their own day-and-age may we do it in this day-and-age giving you the Glory through your son, Jesus."

The small congregation joins with Father Bob in prayer again after which he declares: "Now we will eat. Our Father who art in Heaven . . ." He concludes the Lord's Prayer with, "May the peace of the Lord be always with you."

The prayer continues with the congregation and Father alternately reading lines. Sister Eugenia and Maria Orlando prepare the altar for Holy Communion as Father takes up the paten with the Hosts arranged on it.

*And down there at the end you can see the cocktail bar waiting for the barman to shake a drink – the specialty of the bar is a cocktail of red wine taken with wafer biscuits*
Graham Greene
'Monsignor Quixote'

After the consecration of the bread and the wine, the communicants move from the pews and slowly file past the priest who intones: 'The

Body of Christ' as he takes a 'wafer biscuit' from the paten and hands it to each communicant.

"Grazie, grazie di Mio," Father Bob says to the two Italian ladies, Sister Eugenia and Maria Orlando, who have prepared the bread and the wine. We could be in an old stone church in a little village in Italy on a hot summer's day two hundred years ago.

The churchgoers now file past Senora Orlando for a sip of wine from a silver chalice. Maria wipes the rim of the chalice with a white cloth after each person has drunk from it.

"Grazie, grazie, Senoras," repeats Bob after the last person has drunk from the chalice. Then he says: "Oh, my Jesus, help us through the day," and sighs. We all have to suffer like Jesus when we leave the sanctuary of the church.

Then Maria, carrying the chalice in both hands, walks from the altar, stands humbly before me, and proffers the wine. Ronny reckons that I am like some sort of god sitting there with his tongue hanging out. At the same time I feel a rivulet of perspiration trickle down my back.

"Have a drink," Maria whispers after wiping the rim of the chalice.

I have a drink and roll the wine around the palate. It's a strong full-bodied wine. I thank Maria and start to hand back the chalice but she shakes her head and whispers: "Finish it off." I've never been known to refuse a drink so I do as she bids. It's not a bad drop and I could quite easily get the taste. This is no piddley-pale weak-kneed altar wine.

"Now you'll probably fall orf your bike," laughs Bob.

We sit quietly for a few minutes. Father Bob breaks the silence.

"Tomorrow night we have the Reconciliation, with some of the school kids having their first Reconciliation. God knows how many the rest of us have had. We are here at 7.30pm on Thursday and then 3 o'clock on Good Friday." Father Bob prays: "Almighty and ever-living God, be close to us. Watch over those who receive the words of the Eucharist and being together as a local phenomenon and keep us in your kind of Love. We ask for this through Christ our Lord. *And look after the Irish!* And look after *your* colleagues, Ron, who are riding around delivering mail and suffering from the effects of the heat. Thank you all," says Father Bob as the small congregation gets to its feet to leave after celebrating St Patrick's Day during Holy Week.

"Thank you, Father," the congregation choruses.

There is a furnace-like blast of heat as I walk from the church, down the steps and into the sun: from Heaven's sanctuary in South Melbourne into a withering blast from hell in the north. The back half of the bike is now in the full sun but thankfully the back tyre is still up. I sigh as I mount the bike and then reach down and take the plastic water bottle from its frame. It's too hot to drink. I dismount again, tip the water out and refill the bottle at the garden tap. Then I stick my head under and let the water sluice over me for about a minute. Bugger the water restrictions! There is an empty saucer lying on the ground, which I fill up for the birds. As I ride down Dorcas Street I think back on those days with Spooks, who has now retired; it's not too far off for me either. Looking across the road I can 'see' Spooks ahead of me on the other side, a lanky, sun-tanned, middle-aged bloke who looks as if he should be on a horse.

"I'm allergic to horses, break out in a rash if I go near the bastards," he said to me when I first went out on the round with him. "I've certainly lost plenty of money on the bastards though," he said with a grin that day. "The bush would be no good to me Ronny. I've gotta be near a pub and a racetrack: a racetrack and a pub, mate. I went to Hawaii for a holiday once but I was bored shitless. I came home again after three days. Three days. They haven't even got a bloody racetrack there."

Today is just like that one when we stopped at the old bloke's place for a beer. We only had the one. I could have stayed there all day but Spooks was anxious to keep moving. I remember him saying: "We've got a fair way to go yet, and there's a big Christmas break-up at a truck works in Thistlewaite Street. They knock off early for Christmas. We don't want to be pissed when we get there. Johnny, the boss, always puts on a good spread: crays, prawns, oodles of grog, and plenty of meat for the barbie." We thanked the old fella for his kindness and rode off down Morris Street with the northerly blasting us.

Thistlewaite Street was a place full of industry: mechanical workshops, panel-beating shops, radiator repairers, glaziers, plumbing and electrical suppliers and engineering shops, to name a few. When we turned out of Montague Street into Thistlewaite Street though, it was like a ghost town. A lot of the places had already closed for the Christmas break but according to Spooks most of the workers would be at the truck works further down the street.

"They would have started hoeing in by now. They'll be all half pissed. Johnny the Turk puts on this spread every year; most of Thistlewaite Street will be there by now," he said.

We had to start without you." The Turk greeted us with outstretched arms.

"Johnny! Meet the new postie Ronny."

The Turk shook my hand then shoved a stubby into it. I remember him saying: "You are most welcome, my friend."

The large gathering welcomed Spooks as if he were shouting the free grog. He was beaming as he upended his stubby, then turned to attack the prawns, cracking the shells off the backs, chewing vigorously, sucking the heads, talking, spraying bits of food in all directions as he did so, wiping his greasy hands on his shorts, laughing loudly then washing down another mouthful, yelling out to another free-loader on the other side of the shed, long arms outstretched, sausage-fingers wagging.

"Have some prawns, Ronny, some prawns, try some prawns, mate," he sprayed. The shells were littered all about him on the concrete floor. There was grease all around his grinning mouth, with little pieces of shell stuck to his stubble, his faded shirt with the frayed collar was looking somewhat the worse for wear, and his greasy shorts which came down to his knobby knees, would have earned points from a motor mechanic.

Amid the hubbub, Johnny's brother-in-law Pete was trying to keep some order by cleaning up, throwing paper plates and leftover food into one bin and empty bottles into another. He crunched over the broken shells, pieces of bread and empty stubbies around Spooks, shook his head and said: "You've been coming here every year for over 20 years now, and the best thing I can say about you is that you are consistent."

"Thank you, Big Boy," said Spooks.

The BBQ was outside the back door of the shed in a small back yard that backed onto a lane. The fire had been lit earlier, the large hot plate well greased then covered with big T-bone steaks fitted together heads to tails and tails to heads with a curved band of white fat on each one contrasting with the red meat, but the cook had neglected his duties and wandered off to drink with his mates.

"Bugger me dead!" said Spooks in disgust, "have a look at this. We better get this fire going' Ronny, we can't stay here all day. The bastards will be sending out a search party for us." He guzzled more beer from his stubby, and looked around for suitable fuel to fire up the Barbie. The back fence looked as if it were just about knackered anyway so Spooks ripped off a couple of palings, broke them into pieces and fed them into the fire, which was just about out. He picked up the tongs, turned the steaks over and moved them around: heads to tails now tails to heads, and tails to heads now heads to tails. Tendrils of white smoke curled up around the plate. He broke up some more palings and shoved them under the plate, belted some more beer down his throat, shifted the steaks around again. The smoke got thicker. He was still moving the meat around, talking to people, laughing uproariously. He stuffed a couple of more pieces of wood under the plate but soon stopped talking when he heard the fire crackle, looked around to see the flames licking up around the hot plate. He started turning and moving the steaks around faster with no time to fit them nicely together. The fire had started to take hold now. The flames got higher, singing the hair on his arms. The tongs got hotter. The stark white fat on the meat caught fire. Pete, who was nearby, became concerned and hastened to Spooks' side. The flames were now about three feet above the plate and the meat was beyond salvation. Spooks handed Pete the tongs and yelled out: "Hey, Johnny! Have a look at your brother-in-law. He's burnt the bloody meat!"

## Chapter 34: The Last Supper

*"Prior to Vatican Two we won a reputation around the universe as being obsessively compulsively engaged in religious practices."*

It's Thursday, the weather is milder and I've still got religion on my mind. "The St Patrick's Day Mass was alright, but the turnout was a bit poor," I say to Bob as he starts flicking through the bundle of mail sitting on his desk.

"Yes, but that's only a daily thing. It's boring," says Bob.

"Do you mean to say that you get the same people every day?"

"Yeah," says Father Bob. "These are people with nothing else to do: the nun from across the street, someone else from around the corner. They are Italians mainly. The Wogs love it."

"I used to deliver mail to the nun from across the road. Is she always referred to in such a formal manner: Sister Eugenia?"

"Oh yeah, it keeps her happy," drawls Father Bob laconically. "If we drop the 'Sister' she feels as if she's been defrocked. She came to Australia from Italy about thirty-five years ago to look after her mother and father."

I can remember going to the front door at Sister Eugenia's on occasions to get a signature for registered letters from Italy. The visitor is left in no doubt that this is a religious household: Sister Eugenia has religious pictures sticky-taped to her front windows.

"Do you have Communion every day after Mass?"

Father Bob who has turned his head to look out the window suddenly swings it back and looks directly at me. "No, you have it as part of. Your Mass is supposed to be an assembly of readings, prayers and Communion. That's what it's supposed to be. Traditionally its weekly," says Bob continuing. "Obligatorily it's weekly, unless you've got broken bloody legs or you're in a lunatic asylum or something, and even then we used to go and visit you and do it in your own institution, *but* after a while, three or four hundred years, they ended up doing Masses *every day* not every Sunday. Then in the sixties they said: 'By the way, since we are now living in a post modern civilised society we had better admit that youse can go to Sunday Mass on Saturday night!"

"Vatican Two," I state.

'You've come a long way since 'Vatican Who?' sneers Rene Descartes.

"That's right," says Bob raising his eyebrows. We could now have Sunday Mass on Saturday night just like the Jewish people have. The Jew's Sabbath starts at sundown the night before. The Catholics started to play around with that. That's what drives the obsessive compulsives mad in the Catholic Church. That's what drove 'em mad from the sixties into the nineties, until they won, because we are now back to obsessive compulsive observance of days, places and personages."

"In other words, pre Vatican Two?" I ask. Descartes sniffs loudly.

"Yes. Everything now has to be I's dotted and T's crossed, you bow at the right time and you kneel at the right time and you don't call His Grace, Denis. Call him: 'Your Grace.' " Bob drags out these last four words, stretching his mouth wide when he says 'Grace.' "You bless yourself before you genuflect, all the things that we decided were interesting Catholic practices, but non-essential. We, the Vatican Two-ers, divided everything into being essential and non-essential."

"So you no longer had to bless yourselves?"

"No!" answers Bob loudly, "We could do what we bloodywell liked. It was a free country, *but* we could avail ourselves of these optional extras. Prior to Vatican Two we won a reputation around the universe as being obsessively compulsively engaged in religious practices, devotional practices. After the revolution in the sixties we demythologised all of that and we were supposed to help people around the universe to understand that we weren't throwing out the baby with the bath water. Now, obviously, we didn't do as well as we thought we had done because in fact a lot of people, mainly at the top end, the hierarchy, the ruling classes of Catholicism many of whom were longing for the day that they could wind it back, have done so," he says, looking at me and shaking his head.

As Father Bob has been speaking, there has been a gradual increase in the level of noise emanating from outside. Excited, high-pitched voices just outside the window bring talk of Vatican Two-ers versus the ruling classes of Catholicism to an abrupt end.

"Look at all the kiddies out there!" exclaims Bob looking out the window to see what all the noise is about.

A class of young school kids with two teachers in tow has just invaded the garden.

"The kiddies are out there ready to have their re-enactment of Holy Week," Father Bob tells me.

"Is this going to be on now?" I ask.

"Soon," says Bob.

I'm disappointed because I've got to finish the round and will miss it. "What part are you going to play?" I ask.

"I dunno," he says casually, "I'm just going over as Jesus at twelve o'clock."

'Just going over as Jesus!' I smile and even Ronny is having trouble picturing Father Bob in the role of Jesus. God maybe, but given Bob's age and stature, playing Jesus will be like a middle aged person going out clubbing.

"Dear God, I'm worn out," sighs Bob as he picks up a script from his desk.

He might be worn out but he looks to me as if he is looking forward to playing in the starring role as Jesus. He reads the script aloud: " 'Today, we gather together as a school of the Parish community. Years one to six seated in the church leaving the first three rows on each side free for the press.' "

Three rows for the press! *Jesus Christ Superstar* would be going to fill three rows of press people on opening night.

Bob reads. "Narrator: 'Prep children follow Jesus to the altar and make a line across the altar and face the congregation. Hosanna to the Son of David.' That's all very nice," he comments.

Ronny beams a picture of Father Bob walking to the altar with the youngsters chatting excitedly following him up the aisle as though he were their favourite uncle.

"Are you dressing up?" I ask smiling.

"I dunno what I'm doing."

'He's dressing up,' states Rene with conviction.

Bob reads on: " 'Grade three to four. Jesus goes into the city and does this, that and the other thing. Father Bob stands behind the altar and the twelve apostles join him.' I say: 'Here is the loaf of bread; eat this, all of you; this is my body.' She (the teacher) is getting me into trouble with this because it sounds as though we are doing Mass."

I nod but can't see anything wrong with it. Even if they are doing Mass, Father Bob is an ordained minister.

I listen as he reads on: " 'I ask each of you to come forward now and share in the unconsecrated bread.' Well, you could argue that I've just consecrated it, but I'll have to stick a stopper in me gob I suppose," says Bob.

I smile as Father Bob continues reading: " 'We use it to symbolise the sharing community that Jesus wanted us to be part of. Father Bob will give the unconsecrated bread to the students and parishioners and return to his place behind the altar.' "

Getting into the spirit of the reading Father's voice rises just as if he were in church saying Mass, " 'After sharing the bread he took the cup, drink this all of you. When supper was ended Jesus and his disciples left to pray in the garden of Gethsemane. Father Bob and his disciples eat from behind the altar and nick off,' " adlibs Father as he puts the script down. "*The Age* bloody newspaper is supposed to be here for this."

"I've got my camera with me. Maybe we could go outside and get a few photos before I go," I suggest.

As we leave the study to join the skylarking kids in the garden Frank materialises from the bowels of the mausoleum and strolls out with us.

There are kids, many in costumes, all over the garden, talking excitedly in their high-pitched voices.

"Hi, Father Bob!" one little fellow wearing a burnoose and holding a sword calls out as Bob steps out onto the verandah.

"Hello, Uncle," Father Bob is beaming. "Does that sword light up?"

"Nah," the freckle-faced boy says with a cheeky grin.

Bob introduces me to the teachers and I am about to take a few candid photos but it's too late. Teachers and kids are programmed. Whenever they see a camera they get together in a group. Without being asked the children pose in front of the bluestone wall, smaller ones kneeling at the front, taller ones to the back with an 'Arab' kneeling on the wall looking for all the world as if he has just liberated the place. A small Vietnamese liberator in the front gives the victory sign with two fingers. The teacher, wearing wrap-around sunglasses, stands proudly with his shoulders back and hands behind his back like a soldier. The kids cheer after they hear the shutter click.

"Thank you," I say, laughing, as the group dissolves into a noisy, excited, swarm.

"I hope you don't mind us crashing your garden," says Lisa, one of the teachers.

"Do what you like," says Bob as the kids mill around him. We all have to talk fairly loudly so that we can be heard over the noise of the throng. Green parrots in the gum trees are competing too. Frank joins in and is a great attraction with the kids. He wags his tail gleefully, the sunlight glinting in his eyes, as they vie to pat him. There is a holiday atmosphere to the affair and I'm sorry that I will soon have to leave to finish the bloody round. Why couldn't I have been a teacher instead of a postie? I lament to myself. Descartes is about to make a smart-arsed comment but I shut him out.

Lisa and I try to cajole Father Bob into having his photo taken with the kids but he won't be in it. This is most unusual. Lisa pleads with him and gives him her most imploring smile, but maybe not wanting to be seen to be succumbing to the wiles of a pretty girl, Bob is already walking back inside with firm steps, his loyal companion at his heels.

"No, no, no. *No*, I've gotta work," he reiterates as the screen door bangs behind him and his dog.

"It'd be good for the book," I yell over the top of the bedlam, making one last attempt.

"No!"

"He's a devil," I say to Lisa, who asks me about the book as we watch the antics of the kids. I promise to give her a copy of the book after it's published. I'm going to have to watch myself. I've promised copies of the book to others as well. I'll end up being like Bob: I'll send myself broke.

Before leaving I go back inside to say goodbye and take a photo of Frank. He is lolling in his armchair like some sort of canine laird.

"I'll have to get going in a minute," I say to Bob. "The Post Office Fleas will be looking for me."

"You'll get through the day alright," he says smiling warmly. He gets Frank to sit up straight, which is not what I want. I want him stretched out in his chair with his head resting on the armrest, which is how he often sits. I'll have to get that shot another day because I'm running late.

"Say hello to your Uncle Ron," Father Bob says to his dog. "Uncle Ron's over there. Smile."

The doorbell rings just as I'm leaving. Father Bob introduces me to his visitor.

"Australia's leading auto electrician. Australia's leading postman."

'Uncle Ron,' adds Ronny.

"The green light is fixed on the bus," says the man without further ado.

"Oh, yeah," says Bob. "Will it flatten the battery? How long? How long?" he asks.

"Two days, two days," is the answer as we move out amongst the kids again.

"Goodbye, Father. See you in church tomorrow," I say as I mount my bike ready to ride off.

"Goodbye, Your Grace," he replies.

The kids yell out their goodbyes. Lisa smiles and waves as I ride away.

I pull a bundle of mail out of the bag as I head off, deliver to four houses in Dorcas Street and then turn into Nelson Road. The panniers are bulging: two bagsful. Junk mail that has to be delivered today in conjunction with the normal mail is unbalancing the bike and I wobble about like Luvy coming home from a Christmas party as I ride along. Many a postie has been sacked, over the years, for dumping this garbage down drains, burning or hiding it in the roofs of their houses, or soaking it in a bucket of water before putting it into their worm-farms at home. The man-in-the-street sees a postie riding around delivering mail on a nice sunny day and says: "Lucky bastard." He's got no idea. Spooks comes to mind again. He's looking much healthier and happier since he snatched it.

Riding along, I see George trundling his old pram down the street. He has probably been up and down Nelson Road more times than me or Flo. There is an enormous cardboard box that once held a TV lashed to the top of the pram with pieces of frayed yellow twine. His little black-and-white Chihuahua sits primly in the front of the pram with the enormous box behind him.

George, who is intellectually impaired, likes to stop and talk to me whenever he sees me. He's a nice enough bloke but I have to be careful when he's talking to me. He likes to get up close and it becomes a sort of waltz as I continually roll either back or to one side on my bike, moving my head from side to side like a boxer, trying to dodge the spittle that sprays from between the gaps in his teeth as he talks enthusiastically. He follows my moves though, taking up the slack, talking and spraying all the while, so close that I can see the tartar building up on the gums around his crooked teeth.

George wanders the streets picking up aluminium cans. Large bags full of these cans can be seen stacked on the front verandah of his Ministry of Housing house in Dorcas Street where he lives with his wife. When the bags of cans build up to such an extent that they can hardly get in their front door or see out of the windows, George ties them to the pram and takes them off to market. I've seen him, dwarfed behind a mountainous load, pushing the pram down to the scrap metal place in Graham St, Port Melbourne. Every now and again he has to peer around the side of the load to see if he is heading in the right direction.

Eric, whose house is not far from George's, jokingly called George's dog a fleabag one day when he met him in the street. Poor old George stormed off to the police station in Bank St. where he reported Eric for denigrating his dog.

Because he is on the other side of the road, we won't be dancing today. I call out and wave to him as I go by. George gives a small wave but doesn't answer. I shrug and shove a householder into a letterbox that sits in a fork of a tree near the front fence. For the umpteenth time the letterbox clatters to the ground. This time, I leave the bastard there.

## Chapter 35: Good Friday

*"We're mad about naked bodies.
Jesus's body was naked on the cross."*

*The Age* newspaper doesn't let Father Bob down. Browsing through the paper this morning, a few pages in, I see a large coloured photo of a young boy 'staggering' up the aisle of Sts Peter and Paul's Church bearing an enormous cross on his back and wonder about the load that is also being added to his young mind.

For the second time this week I'm off to Mass at the church. 'Who would have believed it?' I think to myself as I get into the Jag. I tried to talk Ladybugs into coming along but as you can see the passenger seat is empty. The motor, a 350 Chev that is nearly as old as me, fires on the second attempt and there is a pleasing rumble from the exhaust as I roll down the driveway. My mate Roger has just finished modifying the exhaust. Ronny loves it; he reckons that we are the oldest teenagers on the block.

Because of all the roadwork at the Montague Street end of the Westgate Freeway, I turn off once I get over the bridge and go down Todd Road through Port Melbourne and then up Williamstown Road. Less than half an hour after leaving home, I am slotting the car between two Catholic cars out the front of the church. Incongruously, there are two Aborigines clad in traditional loincloths following me along the path past the rectory to the church. The youngest one is playing a few notes on his didgeridoo as he walks. I look around and turn on my voice recorder but it's too late: he stops playing.

As I walk down the aisle through the nave, I locate my daughter Penny, her husband Matt, and her in-laws, Bill and Doris, sitting on a pew a few rows from the altar. I take my seat and survey what is a lively scene. Father Bob is greeting people like the host of a big party would do. He comes over and I give him the voice recorder to put on the altar.

The Easter Faithful, as opposed to the pious Catholics of St Patrick's Day, have flocked to the Good Friday Mass. There is an expectant buzz in the air; the joint is fairly jumping with excited Micks.

The booming sound of a didgeridoo stirs the dust mites in the church. The flock settles. Swivelling heads turn on bodies like inquisitive budgerigars as the congregation strains to see the show. The young Aborigine leads the way playing the didge as the two walk slowly down the aisle through the nave towards the little bright red light on my recorder. They walk up to the altar, the didgeridoo fades out and Father Bob takes over. It's like a confluence of the Dreamtime and Christianity.

Father Bob, once again dressed in the white alb and stole, introduces the two men to the congregation as Kutcaj (pronounced Kutcha), and his nephew Eric.

Kutcaj and Eric step up onto the chancel and Kutcaj moves over to the ambo to speak. He is a big man, slightly hunched, but his voice is warm and soft as he leans forward and bends down to talk into the microphone.

"For the past five years at Christmas and Easter, Father Bob has started his Mass with the sound of the didge.' Being a Mudgee Mudgee man from the Murumbidgee River at Balranald I have to *acknowledge* that old country. That is what Father Bob is actually doing here: *acknowledging* the prior inhabitants of South Melbourne. We thank him for that, especially now that the Prime Minister of this nation has apologised to indigenous people for forcibly removing us from our parents. Words are cheap though; there has to be action from the government now. Father Bob's actions are as strong as his words."

"We've got the Aboriginal flag flying out the front," says Father proudly, steering Kutcaj away from politics.

'Maybe we should have the Orstralian flag flying too,' chips in Rene in his Bob Maguire voice.

"Everybody have a safe Easter, and we'll see you at Christmas time," says Kutcaj.

There is sustained applause as the Mudgee Mudgee men leave by the side door. Maybe they've got another gig.

"We are going to tell the story now," says Father, "of *our* Dreaming, and part of *our* Dreaming is Jewish. If you can't see," he says to a couple of people right at the back, "I respectfully suggest you leave your places and come up here for God's sake. There's an acre of spare space up here," he says, meaning on the chancel with him! "If you want to come up here, feel free." Father Bob says something about the prophet, Isaiah, and then in a louder voice: "The lavatories are out to the side there, girls." He indicates the side door with a casual wave of one hand.

One of the 'Leaders', who I assume are laypersons playing roles in the Mass, reads from Isaiah. After the reading Bob is still concerned about a lady who is standing at the back of the nave and he asks that someone make room for her. "Otherwise," he says, "Jesus will say (he employs an Aussie drawl) 'You're talking about me down there but you've left me sister standing up at the back.' "

There is a smattering of laughter and the sister up the back gets a bit of colour in her face. As the Mass continues, I compare this carnival crowd with the pious regulars who attended the St Patrick's Day Mass and who attend many of the daily Masses. I wonder what the small congregation from last Monday thinks of this holiday crowd.

After the next reading, Father Bob, in his self appointed role of usher, directs latecomers to seats. "Up the front, girls and boys. There are some seats here. Don't be embarrassed."

There seems to be a role reversal of sorts here because it is one of the leaders who then directs the congregation to trace the sign of the cross over their hearts and not Father Bob. There is a short, sharp, flurry of activity as the congregation traces the sign of "mystery and contradiction," as the leader calls it.

A soprano then bursts into song. Her voice is captivating and the worshippers sit quietly, many reading the words of the hymn from a large screen. It's reminiscent of a karaoke night at the local pub. After a few lines some of the worshippers begin to sing along. They seem to be self-conscious though; there are no lusty voices like you'd get at a Presbyterian Church. Maybe they could hire the Choir of Hard Knocks next year. After the hymn the congregation prays 'The Way of the Cross.' There are fourteen Stations along the 'Way,' which are known as The Stations of the Cross. Father Bob has written a contemporary script that is read by the leaders in conjunction with the traditional. It is not something that the tail, that is currently wagging the dog, would appreciate.

A leader reads in a clear voice that rings out: "Jesus is condemned to death." He then reads Father Bob's prayer: "Remembering all those confined by imprisonment or ill health. What does it feel like awaiting trial in a prison cell?"

I can remember one New Year's Eve waiting in a cell down at Lorne, but I won't go into that. The congregation responds, reading from the liturgy, answering the questions asked by the leader. There is mention made of prisoners, sick and elderly, bedridden people and then Jesus himself is referred to.

"What does it feel like to stand before your people and hear them cry: 'Crucify him'?" the Leader asks.

"Jesus knows," is the response from the brethren.

As the story plays out two men carry a heavy cross slowly and solemnly up the aisle. They leave it leaning against the altar, with the red light of my voice recorder shining brightly just to the left of where it sits.

As I listen to the story of Jesus lumping his heavy cross to the Place of the Skull, which is just outside Jerusalem, I shift uncomfortably on the pew and think of the picture of the young bloke carrying his cross up the aisle. Hopefully he won't ever have to suffer like Jesus did.

An actor approaches the altar and places a wreath made of barbed wire on top of the cross. One of the Leaders bangs two sticks together repeatedly. "Jesus is nailed to the cross," he says as he hammers in another nail. I like Bob's tough description better: 'Jesus is nailed up.'

I sit upright, moving my weight from one cheek to the other as I watch an actor reverently drape a black garment over the cross.

As the Leader reads from the script about the final act of taking the body to a place of burial, the two actors carry the cross back up the aisle and leave it at rest, ready for the Adoration of the Cross.

'Christ Rises' is the last Station of the Cross. The Leader reads: "Then a light begins to shine within me as I await the Resurrection."

There is silence for a few moments then Father Bob steps on to the boards to begin his Homily. The 'theatre' erupts into applause for the crowd's favourite actor. "That was magnificent, wasn't it?" Bob asks the full house after the applause dies down. "To say anymore than that would be gilding the lily. Sometimes you have to know when to shut up. I've been yak, yak, yakking since this time last year."

Father Bob says that the Catholics are a bit peculiar. "We're mad about naked bodies. Jesus's body was naked on the cross," he tells the congregation. Yes, I agree with Father Bob: the Catholics are a bit peculiar. "So that crucifix is a strange, disturbing symbol," says Father. He tells the congregation that the Catholics started out with the sign of the fish. Maybe they handed it down to the Jehovah's Witnesses when they tired of it. The Joeys like to display the sign of the fish on their cars. I used to have a transfer of one, with a piranha chasing it across the back window of the Jag.' Father Bob talks about the Jews who used to get up the Roman's noses with some relish. "The Jews drove them mad, absolutely mad," says Bob, "whereas the Christians, for the first four hundred years were running around the place hiding from the police, the Roman senate. That's probably when we were at our best at not showing off. We used to hold meetings in the catacombs, which are cemeteries under the ground, built by the ancient Romans."

As I listen to the sermon, it is as if I am lounging in my chair back in the rectory with Frank flinging his hamburger-with-the-lot around the room and Bob is telling me another story about Biblical times and explaining what catacombs are, just in case I don't know.

The theme of Father Bob's sermon is hope. "I left the **Hope**Mobile out the front because I'm trying to say something symbolically, and that is you've got to have hope. Catholics have to learn to be hopeful so that others can derive hope from being part of our lives. Give 'em hope, hope, hope, hope, hope." Bob says imploringly. He relates the Greek fable of Pandora's Box that contains all the horrors of the world. Pandora releases them and they fly around the universe terrorising the human beings. It gets to the stage where there is only one piece left. 'For God's sake take that piece out and it will all stop and give us a chance against these furies,' the humans beseeched. "What was it?" Father Bob asks the congregation. Nobody answers. I'm about to call out but I reckon Penny will belt me if I do.

"Hope! The last piece in the box was hope; if you lose hope you've lost the lot," Bob explains. "That's what the disciples of Jesus tried to instill in people. What the Founder of the Firm recommended was to be unremarkable: like Himself."

Father Bob says that he wanted to put something remarkable on the notice board out the front of the church. "I couldn't think of anything," he says. He pauses and his audience laughs. "I thought, 'I'll just leave it blank.' Then it got the better of me, so I put up: 'Organ donor of the day – give your heart.' Whatdyathink? It's silly, I know, but it's got legs. We do silly things," he adds disarmingly.

"We are going to be very silly in July when the Pope comes to Randwick racecourse for World Youth Day. Now that seems bizarre doesn't it? Who would have thought? Stopping the races and paying fifteen million 'pounds' to the 'horses.' It's silly, but it's got legs."

"Of course the world will stop," Bob says flatly. "People will say: 'Oh my God! They're coming from everywhere. There's an Eskimo, there's an African, the Catholics are coming from the four corners of the earth, and they're coming from across the river. It's silly!"

A few people in the ranks are stirring. Penny's father-in-law, Bill, is muttering something about the priest making a joke of religion. His wife, Doris, nudges him with her elbow and tells him to 'shut up' in a hushed voice. 'You shut up!' Bill snaps back. I stiffen and cover my mouth with my hand.

Bob tells the gathered that we've already got most of the things that people kill for. We've had them for two thousand years, four thousand if you count our elder brothers and sisters, the Jews." I bet the tail doesn't look on the Jews as its elder brothers and sisters.

"It's all there. What we have to do," says Father Bob his voice gradually rising, " is do that thing in *our* way, not do that thing in *their* way but do that thing in *our* way! That's the multi splendid thing!" He concludes emphatically. That's what the dog should do. "We are going to do two things now," says Father. "One, which is a bit sentimental, is kissing the foot of the cross. If you wish; only if you wish," he reiterates. "It's not compulsory. It's silly, but it's Catholic. The second thing is Communion. We'll put the Host in your hand, or on your tongue if you want."

It is silly, but it's as Catholic as Monsignor Quixote's purple socks, I suppose.

"If you take the Host in your hands," explains Father, "you can look at that and say: 'Ha! That reminds me of the nails in the hands of Jesus, who was the founder of the firm.' You might even be able to see through that piece of bread and see what is the thing that's nailing you to a cross."

I can't work out what it is that's nailing *you* to a cross. I only know what is nailing me to a cross: the bank. The sermon goes on but I won't. I'll move on to where the congregation pays up.

"We've got to take up a collection now," says Father and I grin. It reminds me of my youngest granddaughter, Amy, who once brought out her moneybox when a visitor arrived. "Once a year the Roman Catholic Church says: 'We'll take up a collection,' Bob's voice rises dramatically, 'round the world because we are franchised all over the world. We're like Starbucks. We're all over the world so we'll ask the punters to give for the Holy Places in Palestine, that the Crusaders probably destroyed in their day and the US Marines, the British Army, the Italian Army and God knows who else destroyed in theirs. They've all had a go at the Holy Places in Palestine," he says frowning, "which is why St Francis of Assisi designed the Stations of the Cross. You don't have to go to Palestine. You can just go to your parish church and get a free trip around the Holy Places."

As the collection takes place, Father Bob says to one of his offsiders: "Can you understand these directions? It's a bit much for me. It says here: 'Communion will be distributed at the front of the church.' Where's the front?"

One of the Leaders announces instructions to the congregation so that the job can be done in an orderly manner. Communicants are to move out of the pews and come up the two outside aisles towards the altar. After partaking of Communion, they are to return to their seats by way of the centre aisle.

"Please watch your air hostess for directions," grins Bob mischievously. He holds out his arms wide to indicate the side aisles and then brings them together to indicate the centre aisle. "Use the side aisles to obtain Communion," repeats the larrikin priest. "If nothing works, the oxygen masks will drop from the ceiling." Most people laugh. "And the best of luck to you all. This is Virgin Airlines," he concludes.

Father Bob's quips and his fondness of an audience remind me of the late Graham Kennedy sometimes. He has that same larrikin-ness about him. It might be this type of larrikinism that endears Bob to the average Aussie but not to Penny's father-in-law whose face is now as black as the inside of a cow.

"Our Father who art in Heaven!" Father Bob begins praying very loudly bringing about a bit of shush. The congregation joins with him.

"They're standing up," says Bob grinning. "Look what you've done, Aileen (the air hostess). As we forgive those who trespass against us." The congregation completes the Lord's Prayer.

"The peace of the Lord be always with you," says Father. "Let's offer one another a sign of peace."

The worshippers turn to each other saying: 'Peace be with you.'

"Enough! Enough!" says Bob after a couple of minutes.

"Beautiful!" he declares. "Have a seat, girls and boys. Our home-grown choir will now sing *Lachrimosa* from Mozart's requiem."

Following the requiem, Bob chats about upcoming events and then launches into the last prayer for the day: "Lord, send down your abundant blessing upon us."

At the end Father Bob says, "Tat tar,' and then like a good host stands around talking to the guests who don't want the party to end.

My sleep is restless. Jesus is nailed to the cross. My Uncle Jack is working at the fish market. I've seen the resurrection but I don't tell him; he'll think that I'm mad. I pick up a snapper by the tail. As I proffer it to the fishmonger it comes to life, wriggling vigorously. Quicker than you can say Father Bloggs she grasps it behind the head with one hand and rips its head clean off with the other. Discarding the head the fishmonger wraps my fish then nails me with her brown eyes. She nods and solemnly hands me the fish. 'The body of Christ,' she says.

## Chapter 36: Post Mortem

*"You've got the Pope running around in pink shoes and Armani suits dressed up like the man outside Hoyts."*

It is now Easter Tuesday.

"Do you want a cup of tea?" asks Father Bob as I enter the rectory. There is a steaming cup sitting in front of him.

"No thanks, Bob, but you drink yours," I say.

'Big-hearted Ron,' says Rene curling his lip.

"I haven't got time," he growls, and I smile, "I'm flat out like a lizard." He is a bit crusty, like a lizard too this morning. I'm probably not helping matters either.

There is a message on the answering machine and Bob presses the button to play it. A lady is enquiring about a baptism that Bob is going to perform. As she talks, with a baby squealing in the background, he 'answers' her, coming out with comments such as: 'What!' 'No, bugger you!' 'Well what are you doing it for if you don't understand it?' The lady says something about 'dropping him an email.' Bob says: "Yeah, drop anything you like." He hasn't laughed yet but I can't help myself. "How many people would you estimate were at the Good Friday Mass?" I splutter.

"About three hundred. If you put chairs out you get five hundred. Put more chairs out and you get a thousand" Short sharp sentences are rattled off like bursts from a machine gun left over from his Army days.

"Do you ever get that many in there?" I ask.

"Yeah, Christmas time. We get a thousand." His staccato answers mean that I have to fumble for another question.

"People love Christmas time don't they?" Rene Descartes sniffs and shakes his head.

"They like Christmas because it is childish." Father Bob decides to drink his tea.

"Childish?" I ask.

'Yes, childish,' snaps Descartes, 'All those bloody Christmas cards!'

We are interrupted at this point when the front door bell rings. Bob talks on the intercom to his secretary in the office: "That'll be the dog, darling." Then he greets his dog: "Hello, Frank!" The dog comes bounding into the room, jumps up on Bob and nearly knocks him out of his chair. "Say hello to Mr. Burrows!" Frank charges around the desk to greet me in a similar fashion.

"He's boisterous. The long walk doesn't tire him out much," I comment as we laugh at the dog's antics.

"He's glad to be back," says Bob, "He likes it out there with the dog-walker but he feels that this place is his." I'm glad that he's back too.

Frank jumps up into his armchair and rests his head on the armrest as Father Bob starts opening the mail. There is a letter from Terry Monagle's publisher, saying that *The Rebel Warrior Priest. The Life of Bob Maguire* will be published on 1st March 09.

"We could all be dead by then," Father laughs. "Yes. That was a big show for you on Good Friday."

"It *was* a big day: and an even bigger turnout on Sunday. I thought everyone involved did very well, all told, on Friday. Those Stations of the Cross that you were waffling on about, I saw them last year and thought they were excellent. You showed up on St Patrick's Day too."

"Yes. I enjoyed that day more."

"Yeah?"

"I felt intimidated amongst that big mob of bloody Micks on Good Friday. I felt like an infiltrator. They all seemed to be looking at me as they walked down the aisle."

Father Bob laughs, "Oh, no. We're all the same. Well you were there. As long as we get the occasional significant . . ." His voice trails off and I laugh. "Who else was there of yours?"

"My daughter, Penny, her husband Matt, and his parents Bill and Doris, who are Catholics."

"What did they think of it?"

"Penny and Matt enjoyed it but Matt's parents . . ." I fade out this time.

"They would have been a bit . . ." He searches for a description. "They are traditional!"

"Yes. Bill said: 'The Priest is making a joke of it all.' He wasn't impressed."

"Yeah? Ah well," he says.

"Later on I played them some of the recording from the more traditional St Patrick's Day Mass and they were quite happy. Penny also explained that all you were doing was trying to de-mythologise the ceremony, not make a comedy of it."

"They were squared orf?" asks Bob.

"Yes, they were," I lie. "At the start of the Good Friday liturgy you asked if anybody knew why the body of Jesus on the cross is covered on Good Friday."

"Yes, I asked that because the bloody fool of an altar-server is a (there is a loud squeak from Frank's toy) whatdoyacallit." Father Bob searches for the word.

"A traditionalist," I supply. There is a sense of deja vu as the conversation is punctuated by Frank's rubber toy.

"Yes. That is one of those old-fashioned Catholic customs. It's very mysterious (squeak, squeak) the mysterious Catholics. It's one of the things that puts the wider community off. Yet *he* persists. I asked him why he had covered up Jesus, and he said: 'It's the rule.' I said, 'It's not the rule at all. It *was* the rule.' He said, 'Oh yes *but*.' Anyway I gave way to him. I can't fart and argue with him."

I laugh again. Bob grins. "Most of these ceremonies don't make sense," he adds.

"Is the Good Friday Mass held at three o'clock because the crucifixion took place at that time of day?" I ask.

"Allegedly," answers Bob. "According to the Gospels, he died on the cross. I don't know whether it was made up or not. It doesn't make any bloody difference, but it has come to mean something over the centuries."

"Would you say that it is more traditional than anything else?"

"I wouldn't use the word traditional. In the Roman Catholic context there is something stronger. The tradition would be the death (squeak) and resurrection (squeak) of Jesus. What you dress it up as is, to me, weaker than that. It's convention. To the ordinary human being though tradition is probably the same as convention: 'this is the way we usually do it.' "

Frank is now making a hell of a din, shaking the toy, launching it across the room, and then bounding after it. Bob raises his voice to compete. "The tradition was St Patrick but then they conventionally turned it into a procession up bloody Bourke Street. You don't have to have the bloody procession to keep the tradition," he explains. "It's the same with Anzac Day. You don't have to have poppies and things. You may well *have* to have the Last Post," Bob concedes.

"Yes," I reply, "It wouldn't be much of an Anzac Day without it."

"Even *he* cries at the Last Post," says Bob.

I look around to see who has entered the study. There's nobody there.

"Who?"

"The dog."

"Does he?"

"Yes. We were watching television on Anzac night when he howled for the first time."

I smile. "That would have been a bit unnerving, alone at night in this mausoleum."

"It was a bit spooky because I'd never heard a noise like that come from him before," says Bob.

"Gee, you must have been petrified," I say with conviction.

"Yes, a howling dog *in your room*." Bob points out with emphasis that it's the sound of the Last Post which is unnerving for ordinary human beings. The ritualistic Collingwood versus Essendon crowd on Anzac Day, for instance, is given an opportunity of going through a catharsis. "That's what you are supposed to get out of rituals," says Father Bob.

He tells me: "The early Christians started it off. Until that time the early Christians did all their stuff in 'ouses or underground in catacombs."

Father Bob's sermon from Good Friday must be still playing in his head because he is now going back over it. He smiles. "The Roman model got knocked about especially by your friend, Napoleon Bonaparte. He said: 'I'm the emperor.' We got our 'eads cut off in the 1700's. The rich clergy had their heads lopped off in France. The village clergy preferred to survive with their people so they signed a doco for the French Revolutionary Government that said: 'we swear allegiance to the French Revolutionary Government.' That was nice," adds Bob. "We are always considered piss-weak, the GP's, because we would usually go with the people. 'What do you want people? Do you want to have your heads cut off or what?' 'Nah, we don't want our 'eads cut orf.' 'Alright then, sign the doco.' Whereas the upper clergy, your pretentious Cardinals and Bishops wearing red tabs and stuff would say: 'No we're going to stand for the cause, which they will say was Jesus, but which in fact was the Roman Empire, so the Revolutionaries cut their heads off, just the same as they cut the King's and Queen's heads off. Now by the time Napoleon comes along, which I think was seventeen ninety something, he calms down all that revolutionary bloodlust but he still installs the secular system over the church, which was about time. The Frogs are still secularists. They've still got a long history of Catholicism but they've had to become secular."

"Is it a bit like Russia?" I ask when Bob finishes his monologue.

"More like Turkey. Turkey became secular. That's what they are fighting about now. Ataturk came along before World War One and said: 'This is frogshit. The Turkish Empire is falling over. It's all over the place like a dog's breakfast.' He said: 'This is no good to us. I think that we should go European,' so he made 'em all wear European clothes. 'Chuck that bloody hat away,' he said, 'that red thing stuck on your 'ead like a bloody potplant. Get rid of that! And get rid of those baggy pants! You're a laughing stock. Let's cut out this bullshit about Islam. You can do it in private but we're not going to be an Islamic State. We're going to be a Secular State.'

I start off with a smirk that gets wider and wider until the laughter bubbles out.

"They are still fighting about it now," explains Bob, 'because the Supreme Court in Turkey said to the Government: 'Hey! We think that youse are trying to install an Islamic Government and the Constitution says that you can't have it. So we're telling youse that you're acting unconstitutionally and you will probably have to get out,'" says Father Bob. He wraps it up by saying matter-of-factly: "That's the secular state."

From Turkey the track leads back to Rome.

"The Roman Catholic hierarchy around the world made its mind up with Vatican Two. 'Yes,' they said, 'we were wrong. We should have been working with the pooah and the young, not working for the rich and the powerful.' 'Oh,' said the world, 'what a lovely thing.' So when I came out of the seminary we took our collars off and we threw away the rich clothes that we wore in church and got down to the simple style of alb. Now the bullshit is back! You've got the Pope running around in pink shoes and Armani suits dressed up like the man outside Hoyts; he's buying heavily brocaded vestments dating back to 1208. Father Bob groans theatrically. "Oh God, it's all coming out again: the Latin language; he likes Mozart and all the upper class things which he will say is culture."

"Do you believe that Mozart is upper class?"

"Oh yes," Father Bob states emphatically, "in comparison with guitars and bloody drums in church." I think of didgeridoos. "We never had Mozart in church. Who's this bloody fool?" he asks as someone steps onto the front verandah. "Go away," he commands majestically but not very loudly.

"He has gone away too," he says gleefully. His eyebrows are raised.

"You must have the power."

"Do you think so?" Bob grins. "I got him with my laser." We

laugh like two kids. Just as Bob opens his mouth to speak again there is another interruption as his volunteer helper for Open House comes in to ask him a question. I've noticed that politics exists even amongst the volunteers who give their time to help feed the homeless. This lady volunteer, whom I shall call Jennifer, is conservative. It's highly probable that Jennifer loves the idea of singing Mozart in church.

Father Bob's sympathies lie with a volunteer named Maureen Johnston. A situation has occurred whereby a particular piece of equipment that would come in handy at this moment is not to hand.

"There's a rack out there," says Father Bob, indicating the car park at the side of the church.

"It's not there anymore," says Jennifer, "Maureen got rid of it."

There is silence. The seconds tick by.

"Thank you," says Jennifer. More silence. She leaves the room.

Bob looks at me and shakes his head. He says quietly: "Jennifer can't help saying that Maureen got rid of it."

"Ah," I say just as quietly. We are like a pair of safecrackers discussing a problem that has arisen during a 'job.'

"Jennifer is an anti-Maureen model," Bob states solemnly.

"Yes, I gathered that," I reply, my eyes narrowed as I watch the doorway.

"Maureen works on different days to Jennifer."

"Yes?" I try to arch my left eyebrow like Bob Hawke is fond of doing.

Father Bob's voice is conspiratorial: "Jennifer is upper class, practising Catholic," he whispers. "She is *also* feeding the pooah. Maureen is not a churchwoman. Maureen swears, Maureen smokes."

"Ah haa," I murmur again as if I've just cracked the safe.

"So we'd like to show that our form of feeding the pooah is just as good as Maureen's." Father says with his nose in the air.

"If not superior," I breathe.

"Patronising? 'Oh no, we are not patronising.'" Father Bob's voice rises slightly: "Well, I'm the conductor of the orchestra and I can discern a discordant note."

I let out a deep breath. Bob's voice increases further.

"Maureen has been seriously ill and may well not come back, but she deserves a medal for services rendered." Bob tilts his head to one side. "*Yes*, she has kept others away because she picks and chooses but, she's in command."

Maureen has been working for Open House since its inception and I make a mental note to pay her a visit. I know the lady concerned because I delivered her mail for seventeen years.

"If she knows that someone is a troublemaker or a fraud, cheat and liar, well that's personal. This lot here say," and here Father Bob puts on a plummy accent: " 'Oh yes, several people have complained that Maureen has kept them away.' Fair enough. They can come back now," he concludes matter-of-factly.

Bob opens another envelope and then says: "Here's the Roman Church asking for money again. I'm sick of it. The bloody Roman Church!" He grimaces.

"You should be asking them for money," I say cheekily as I stand up, ready to leave.

"Yeah," Bob laughs as I say goodbye and make my way to the door.

When I get to the flats in Ferrars Street, I see a pensioner named Arthur exercising his two budgerigars. They sit on his shoulder as he brings them outside, then he puts them down in the garden, where they are free to scratch around, as they would if living in the wild.

"I have to watch out for crows though, mate," Arthur explains to me. "They've got a nest in that tree there. The bastards will swoop down and grab the poor little buggers if I stray too far." I tell him about how I like to watch the crows soaking their stale bread in my birdbath. Arthur nods, turning his mouth down, and then continues the case against crows.

"The sheep farmers are dark on 'em, 'specially at lambin' time. They peck the eyes out of the new-born lambs ya know." He looks at me and adds: "That's nature I 'spose."

"If I had budgies or sheep I wouldn't be too keen on the blighters either," I say. Arthur grins, then promises to give me a young budgie at a later date, "I'm going to mate these two," he says. I don't tell him that I think it's cruel to keep birds in cages.

## Chapter 37: Catherine of Siena

*"You should go home and look up Wikipedia and see what this girl, Catherine of Siena, was on about."*

It has been estimated that there are five million Catholics in Australia but only fourteen percent of them attend Mass on a regular basis. I decide to call the remaining eighty-six percent who only attend at Easter and Christmas 'Holiday Catholics.' This will be my third Mass in less than two months. My grandfather would be appalled but I forgive myself: this is a different era.

There is a vase of white Gladioli and Tiger lilies standing on the chancel in front of the altar. I know the ropes now. I stop before the altar and bow slightly, my head tilted forward to show my respect (although I don't really know whether I should do this!), before stepping forward to place the recorder on the altar. Rene is disgusted.

When I sit down Sister Eugenia, dressed in her winter habit, hands me a book. I recall that about six week earlier, on St Patrick's Day, she had been wearing her summer outfit. On that occasion it was forty degrees; today it is fifteen. I read through the Catherine of Siena service whilst sitting quietly with the rest of the congregation that numbers eight or nine. I listen to the Town Hall clock ring out twelve times. A few minutes later, Father Bob dressed in his white alb enters by the side door chanting in Latin as he steps onto the chancel. Then he announces: "Mr Burrows is gracing us with his presence."

"Good afternoon, Father," I respond with a smirk on my face.

"Catherine of Siena!" he announces after looking at the book. He pronounces Catherine in Italian.

"God is light. There's no darkness in Him at all. We live life." Father Bob stops reading and then says like a university lecturer: " 'The Wisdom of the Desert', Mr. Burrows, 'The Wisdom of the Desert.' " He continues: " 'I'm writing this, children, to stop you doing the wrong thing but if anyone should do the wrong thing everything will be alright because we've got an advocate, a barrister.' " That's handy really. Do the wrong thing and the job's right. Just get onto your barrister. Father Bob looks up and then says to me "Catherine of Siena. What year, Mr Burrows?"

"1347, Father," I reply.

"Correct," says Bob, like the host of a quiz show. "She told the

Pope off, which is a good idea. Pope Gregory XI. These days, people think that the Pope is not to be told off. Catherine told the Pope off." He smiles serenely. "Yeah, she got stuck into him. 'You're making fools of us,' she said. We remember my cousin, John Maguire. Part of his ashes were interred last Saturday," says Father seriously. He is quiet for a few seconds.

"Yesterday the rest of his ashes were buried in a plot at a private cemetery owned by the Redemptorist Order in Perth, Scotland. John used to attend Mass nearly every day at the monastery."

"We also remember Virginia and Fiorina who are deceased, and whatever else is trembling on your mind. *Give that man a book*," he says, like a carnival spieler, as a late arrival enters.

'Step right up!' says Ronny, banging a big drum.

Father Bob reads again raising his voice at the beginning: "Here is a wise and faithful woman who went with lighted lamp to meet her Lord. Alleluia. In the name of the Father, Son, and the Holy Spirit. The Lord be with you," he chants.

The Mass continues and I wait to hear more about Catherine. I fold my arms and clamp my teeth together when they start chattering.

"In meditating on the ordeal of your Son, and in serving Church in the 1300's Catherine was filled with the fervour of Your kind of love. By her prayer, may we share in the mystery of Christ's death," his voice rises, "and also show a bit of form in reforming the church. That's what she did."

Father Bob surveys the congregation, looking around as if for someone who is missing.

"Who's gonna read this?" he asks knowing full well who's gonna read it. "Mr. Burrows, would you like to read? There's nobody else who can read. That's the problem with this."

'This,' being a congregation made up of old migrant stock. Reading English is not its forté. There could be a case for conducting the Mass completely in Italian during the week. Maybe Bob could send a missive to Rome asking for Italian books.

"We've got to have people who can read otherwise the priest has to do *everythink*."

Once again I step up onto the chancel and the duo is back. " 'A reading from the first letter of St John.' The blood of Christ cleanses us of all sin." The reading concludes with: "This is the word of the Lord."

'Proclaimed by the bloody postie,' adds the sneering Descartes and I can't stop myself from grinning.

"The Psalm!" says Bob.

I read the Psalm: "Oh bless the Lord, my soul." I wonder what these old Italians think of this business of the postie becoming part of the Mass. It's bizzarro.

I tune back in to the Mass. Bob is asking a question of the congregation: "How can you find out about it? Look at the stars, the moon and the sea. Look at the mathematical formula. Listen to Beethoven. *He* says another way you can find out is by listening to me."

There is a prolonged blast of a car horn out in Montague Street as we sit peacefully in church listening to Father Bob.

"Or listen to *you*," continues Bob. "That's your job. Go and *be* Jesus!" Father Bob looks down and reads again: "Come to me, all ye who work."

An answering horn with a deep note honks back. Tyres squeal.

"Learn from me. I am gentle and humble in heart."

"And my burden is relatively light. This is the Gospel of the Lord," says Bob closing the book vigorously.

Suddenly a woman screams. Dogs start barking outside the side door.

"And wine," continues Father without blinking. "Accept the saving sacrifice we offer." The intensity of the barking increases. "What the!" he exclaims, "Is that murder?"

The side door bursts open and a severely handicapped woman looking somewhat frazzled, hobbles in using two aluminium walking sticks to aid her ungainly progress.

"Page 221, Feast of Catherine of Siena," intones Father as the distraught lady picks up a book off the front pew and then remains standing, leaning against the back of a pew that runs north/south, beside the main body of pews which run east/west.

"By following her teaching and example, may we offer more perfect praise. In other words: let's get on with the business of *reforming*!" implores Father Bob. "We ask for this through Christ our Lord," he sings.

I look across and smile at the lady, who is now composed. She smiles at me and shrugs her shoulders. Suddenly I hear footsteps walking fast down the centre aisle towards the altar. A man dressed in faded blue jeans and denim jacket stops before the altar, kneels and thrusts his body forward so that he is almost prostrate. He rests his head on the chancel. His bum sticks up in the air like a Muslim at prayer. The man prays silently as Father Bob, standing before him, chants: "The Lord be with you. Lift up your hearts. Let's give thanks to the Lord our God."

The man in the denim 'suit,' circa 1965, hasn't moved. I manage to keep from smiling. Father Bob continues, barely glancing at the man: "Send the Spirit on this Tuesday bread and wine that they may become the body and blood of Jesus. Before he was given up to death which he freely accepted, He took the bread and thanked you and broke it."

At last, the man moves. He rises, stands before the altar, makes the sign of the cross, turns and walks briskly back up the aisle. I glance at the lady who is still leaning against the back of the pew. She raises her eyebrows and smiles, her eyes twinkling.

"Brothers and sisters gone to their rest in the hope of rising again," prays Father in his singsong voice. "Lavinia and Fiorina Avirginia gone to their rest. John Maguire a year ago.

"That's Wayne," says Father Bob of the man who has just left. "He comes in once every three months or so."

Silence. Then: "Bring them and *all* the dead into the light of Your presence. Finally, we pray, have mercy on us all.

After Communion, as the communicants file back to their seats, Father Bob says: "Of course we need a heater! We spent a lot of money on this joint in 1999. We had some sort of electric heating put under the floor. I don't think it works," he adds resignedly. "You should go home and look up Wikipedia and see what this girl, Catherine of Siena, was on about." I don't think many of the old Italians will be doing this.

"The Pope was no good. He was living in France," says Father.

Sister Eugenia says: "In Avignon, Father."

"Yes," agrees Father Bob. " 'Come back,' she said, 'you fool. What are you doing up there with the rich? Come back to Rome.' He said: 'I don't like Rome. It's falling down.' She said: 'Well, I don't give a rat's whether it's falling down or not. Come back to where you belong.' "

Father raises his voice. "We need a bit of that now. We haven't had much of that lately. Catherine wasn't a Commo. She was a Dominican Nun. If you talk like this you sound like a Commo according to . . ." Father Bob doesn't complete his sentence. "Almighty and ever-living God," sings Father getting on with the job. "Thank you for all the Catherines we've had over the centuries and please God, those who are the Catherines of Siena, these days, won't be *put off* by the criticism that they will receive. Keep criticising *positively*,' he adds.

As the Mass draws to a close, I wonder about the denim-clad man: why he feels it necessary to express his feelings in such an astonishing way. I am also pleased that, like a spinning wheel stopping on the right number, I landed on 'Mass' today to witness this act of praying in the extreme. I wonder, too, about the handicapped lady and her encounter with the dogs and who it was that called Father Bob a Commo..

Father sings: "God bless you - the Father, the Son and the Holy Spirit. Let us all go in peace to serve the Lord." He smiles at the congregation. "Grazie, grazie."

Father Bob leaves by the side door just behind the lady who was threatened by the dogs. I follow, fiddling with my voice recorder. Once outside, she accosts Bob.

It seems that someone attending Mass has left the dogs there. The lady is intent on retributive justice. Father Bob, however, prefers restorative justice. Unable to placate the lady, he kindly suggests that she write a letter to the Archbishop.

## Chapter 38: Tractoring

"*Ralph* has asked me to write a short piece,"

It's mid afternoon and I'm standing outside the foyer of the Fleapit, aka Australia Post Headquarters, in Exhibition Street Melbourne, talking to a couple of posties from the Disaster Centre. Blinking, I look closer at the features of a short bloke wearing a navy pea jacket and black hat, who is accompanied by a couple of younger, burly looking characters, approaching. The short bloke looks a lot like Father Bob.

"How are you, Your Grace?" Bob asks me as he walks up and introduces his mates from the Maritime Union of Australia. He has promoted me from Mobile Priest to Mobile Archbishop of late.

Joan Doyle, Secretary of the Communication Workers Union, who is standing on the back of a truck addressing a disappointingly small crowd, calls out enthusiastically to the visitors through her megaphone. The rally has been organised to support injured postal workers who are being unfairly treated by Aussie Post. Bob, and the wharfies who are now unfurling their flags are here to lend their support. There are only about thirty of us crowded around, including three posties from the Disaster Centre, on the footpath in front of the truck. The wharfies, with their MUA flags fluttering in the breeze, position themselves near the cabin like a pair of self-appointed bouncers as Joan roars into her megaphone. The generosity of the wharfies and Father Bob who are giving their time to support the rally only seems to highlight the poor turnout of postal workers, I think as I listen to Joan.

A pair of Fleas, talking and laughing, skirt the small gathering and casually nip through the open glass doors of the Fleapit. Where are the bloody posties, counter staff, mail sorters and drivers who should be here to support their mates and make life a bit more difficult for the Fleas? You'd think that they'd want to rally round given the threat to their future well-being and livelihood. I look around me at the pitiful crowd. It's not much of a turnout for a company with a workforce of thirty four thousand people. Sadly, they don't want to knock off work to attend rallies; they just want to go home and get away from all the bullshit.

I turn and glance disdainfully at the retreating backs of the Fleas in their dark suits as they walk through the foyer. Joan says that the union has many case studies of injured workers being returned to work when it was obviously not safe for them to be there and the one-legged postie leaning on a crutch on the periphery of the crowd adds a picture to her words. There is a placard around his neck that says: 'Ask me how I was injured at work.' Father Bob walks over to ask him. He introduces himself and they shake hands. I notice Bob frowning and shaking his head as the postie talks. Before coming back to where I'm standing Bob shakes the postie's hand again and says: "Good on ya, mate."

I'm wondering what Father Bob is going to say when they hoist him up onto the truck because this has been a controversial problem since someone at Aussie Post contrived a cunning way to cut Lost Time Injuries some years ago. According to my union informant, a person whom we shall call Dr. Nolove who runs a generic of GP's was contacted. "Help us get our injured workers back to the workplace without too much lost time and you will be handsomely rewarded," he says the Aussie Post schemer implored of Dr. Nolove. With biting sarcasm my informant said: 'As any manager knows, the ones who stay away from work are lazy malingerers anyway, making a meal of their injuries to rip off the company.' It's easier, and cheaper too, to reduce the 'lost hours' than it is to reduce the injuries or make working safer I suppose.

I remember a driver from the Disaster Centre who was involved in a road rage incident. After being informed that a 'driver was down' the manager rushed to the scene of the accident. He took the driver to one of Dr. Nolove's team who put his broken leg into a cast. The manager made sure that the driver was at work the very next day his broken leg propped up on a desk as he stamped up the posties' return-to-sender mail or sat around reading magazines. All that matters is that the boondoggler doesn't show up in the lost time injury results.

"*Ralph* has asked me to write a short piece," states Father Bob after Joan finishes her spiel and we wait for her to call him up to the stage.

"Who's Ralph?" I ask.

"*Ralph*, the magazine," he says simply.

"*Ralph*. I've heard of it. That's a men's magazine isn't it?"

"Yeah! What do you think of the idea?"

"I don't think that a man in your position should be associated with a rag like that," I say, actually sounding like an Archbishop counselling his clergy.

"No? You don't think it's advisable, Your Grace?"

"No, definitely not. What would people think?" I ask, looking at the poor soul.

"Alright. I'll tell 'em I'm not interested," he says as Joan gestures and calls him up to the microphone. A postie in a fluoro shirt is ready to give Father Bob a leg up onto the truck bed but he demurs and speaks from where he is standing. After warming up his audience with a couple of jokes and with the timing of a commercial television station promoting its own image, Bob slips a hand into his jacket and pulls out a couple of pages. He reads out a passage giving the manuscript its first public plug: the bit about his dog biting me on the arse, which he obviously still finds amusing. Everyone laughs and Bob then points me out and I'm left standing there like a leper with everyone gigging at me. He doesn't actually say anything about the Flea's behaviour but instead talks about something that he thinks we *all* should have. It's a word that he signs off his emails with: Respect.

'Well done, RJM!' says Rene enthusiastically adding the initials that follow the word 'Respect' on Bob's emails.

Before heading off to the Elms Family Hotel in Spring Street with a couple of the blokes from the Disaster Centre, Bob and I discuss the latest chapter which explores Bob's experiences of being a beekeeper at the Seminary. Some of Bob's stories, although told only as Bob can, sometimes stretch into lengthy monologues (or bobologues as I have come to think of them. Sometimes I do little more than offer up my ears). In trying to preserve Bob's apian experiences, the chapter has become bogged down in a beekeeping bobologue. I resolve to rectify the problem when I get home from the pub.

After dinner, I go over and over the bloody bees and the beekeeper. If I tractor up and down much more you will end up having to read the words through the furrows. You might even be able to see me, off in the distance, chugging along on John Williamson's *Beaut Little Ferguson Tractor*, black smoke chuffing out of the stack and bobologues, peeling off the sidewalls of the tyres, left to fallow in the literary paddock.

I park the Fergie in the shed, print the pages of The Beekeeper, spread them out on the kitchen table and take up my blue crayon. After I finish, there are paragraphs crossed out and others with blue circles around them with arrows pointing to circles on different sheets. There are sentences amended and pointers like this ^ with new writing squeezed between the lines above it. As I kick the clods away from the furrows and rewrite the chapter, it occurs to me that today was a momentous one as far as the manuscript is concerned. Until now we've had me, the postie, pedalling around peddling his story about the priest. There have been stories about Father Bob and stories about posties but this has been a story about Father Bob interacting with the posties. This is how it would have been when the priest conducted his Character Training courses with the young soldiers in his Army days. Today we had the not-so-pious priest in his role as a stand-up comedian and the not-very-religious posties intent on his every word.

## Chapter 39: The Beekeeper

*"I found it paid to become a bee whisperer, like a horse whisperer, where you don't force yourself on them."*

"Good morning, Father," I say to Bob as I enter the study.

"Be quick as possible," he says without the hint of a smile. He is seated at his desk working on his computer. I shrug off his brusqueness.

"Flat out as usual I see."

"Worse," Bob says gloomily, tapping at the keyboard. Tap, tap, tap.

I settle into my chair and look around for an ally but Frank is nowhere in sight.

"Worse," he repeats. Tap, tap. Then he looks directly at me and says accusingly: "You were supposed to come in and drive my bus and hand out DVD's."

"Do you reckon I can drive it?" I say, giving myself time to think.

"Of course you can bloody well drive it. Somebody's gotta do it. If it doesn't get done I'll be broke in a minute." The parrots are squabbling in the gum trees outside the study and I wish I were out there with them. I was 'supposed to come in and drive the bus' according to Bob but I never agreed to do so.

"I dunno about driving around in the bloody bus," I finally say as a wattlebird trumpets. 'The bus,' that Father Bob is alluding to is the **Hope**Mobile. He has had some humorous DVD's produced that explain the purpose of the Maguire Foundation and wants them distributed. He sent me an email suggesting that I drive 'the bus' into the city, stand on a busy corner, and hand out the DVD's. I was noncommittal at the time.

"Drive into town and park it and . . ." he starts.

"I'd never be able to park it," I say.

"What are you talking about? Not the big one. We'll get the blue one."

"I didn't know you had a blue one."

"Yeah, it's parked around the corner. It never goes out. I'll be broke soon," he grumbles. "I've got another appointment at 11 o'clock to talk about raising money." Bob's voice rises. "It's gonna take me more time and energy." Tap, tap, tap: one finger at a time.

"I've thought of a good awareness raising idea," I say lamely, wondering what he is doing on the computer.

"Yeah, but I've got other things to do…"

"I know, but…"

"Apart from bloody awareness raising."

"What's this about beekeeping?" I ask abruptly.

"Yeah, I was a beekeeper," Bob says just as bluntly, "when I was in the Roman Catholic Priest Factory from 1953 until 1960."

"Were you the only beekeeper?" I ask.

"No, no. It was a tradition. We had to feed ourselves, so we grew vegetables. We had chooks for eggs. There were 150 grown men together with staff at the old Chirnside Estate between Melbourne and Geelong," he says, swivelling in his chair to better see out the window. "It was a famous old joint," he adds, swivelling back.

"You said on your radio programme that it was one of the best times of your life."

"Well, only because it got me out into the fresh air." Father Bob gives me one of his detective stares.

"Yes, of course."

"And also," says Bob raising his eyebrows, "because it got you time orf from the boring routine of study and stuff." Just the mention of his beekeeping days has turned Bob's mood around.

"That sounds good."

"It *was* good,' he says. "It was something that I'd never have been experienced in. What would you call it, agriculture?" Father Bob asks.

"Yes, or animal husbandry maybe. It could be either I suppose."

"When I got there these bees had been around for quite a while," says Bob. "I called in the State Beekeepers to check, like I try to do with everything else that I come across, and that is, run an audit. 'Please tell me what's already here.' Just as I did in 1973 when I came here."

'The State Beekeepers! It sounds like an organisation that the Russians would have,' quips Rene.

Bob's secretary taps on the door and asks if he can spare a moment. "Don't go away," Father says dramatically as he gets up from his chair to deal with the problem. "The story of the bees will continue . . . when we return." I'm about to select a book from his bookcase when he returns and resumes his story:

"When I was in the Seminary with the bees, I took the same approach as I took in the fifties. I said: 'Thanks for the bees.' "

After a while I am almost transfixed by the droning voice, the air feels warm, I can smell daisies, and there is a definite humming sound in the study. I look around, cocking my head. Yes, it's the fan in Bob's computer.

"Well who the hell wants to go into a war zone?" asks Father Bob. "Everybody knows that all bees are armed? If you want to play with the bees . . . there are two ways of dealing with armed persons, or insects, or animals. I found it paid to become a bee whisperer, like a horse whisperer, where you don't force yourself on them."

I smile and think about Eric and his lavender: two bee whisperers on the round.

From the story of a bee whisperer Bob shifts seamlessly into an exposition dealing with the habits of the egg-laying queen and bees that fly off into the wilderness to fill themselves up with nectar (which Bob sounds out as nek-tar). The bodies of the bees become "little factories" in Bob's unfolding saga "and lo and behold, ladies and gentlemen," announces Father, like a shiny, top-hat clad magician pulling half-a-mile of knotted hankies out of his sleeve, "they put it in a little hexagonal cell and there you have it: honey!"

With nary a pause, Bob likens the life of the bee to a Shakespearian play. Act I is about bees that flap their little wings so much on a hot day that after a while the poor buggers collapse; they have "passed their use-by date" says Bob. I lean back in my chair, all thoughts of finishing the round gone as the bobologue builds. In Act II 'The Mating Flight,' Bob regales Ron the Listener with an account of the drones going after the queen. "The one drone that reaches the lofty heights to which the queen bee has flown, impregnates her. Whereupon the drone's reproductive organ is rrripped (Bob theatrically rolls the 'r' in ripped) from his body and he falls to his death." In Act III the gory story of a bee committing Hari-Kari is dramatically told. The worker bees have a sting that "if stuck into something hard and solid, rrrrips their guts out." They then die. "You may notice," Bob explains, "that if a bee stings you, it may go flapping around for a while but eventually it pulls its guts out."

'What a way to go!' exclaims Rene.

Father Bob tells me how to remove a bee's sting without the contents of its venom sac being 'injected' into my body, just in case I ever get stung:

"The worst thing you can do is grab hold of the sting and pull it out. It's got a sac of venom attached to it, so if you grab it you'll squeeeeze the venom into the skin via the sting. So, what you do is: you scrape it out so you don't touch the sac."

I nod.

Act IV is called 'The Night of the Long Stings.' If the food runs low the workers drag out the drones and mercilessly kill them "because they are *useless*," says Father Bob vigorously. "The workers' mob mentality has clicked into alert. 'We are running out of food. The queen and we, the workers, must survive; the drones are of no use and are now a threat. We will now drag the drones out from the hive and we will dispatch them.' " The 'talking bee's' voice is one of Bob's old favourites: Frank Thring.

Even bees can be a pain-in-the-arse according to Bob. After The Night of the Long Stings a swarm of bees will take off leaving the old lot with the worn-out old queen. There can't be anything much worse than being left with a worn-out old queen, I think as Bob says: "These are the ones that are a pain-in-the-arse because they've outlived their use-by-dates and they are all a bit narked."

Father Bob's phone buzzes in his pocket like a captive bee and I notice that he deals with the call faster than he would usually. "A nastier episode is when you have to eliminate the queen in the hive," he says after slipping his mobile phone back into his left pocket, "because you want to change her. That's when you get your little, sealed with wax, mousetrap-size block of wood that comes from Bruthen, with a compartment in it that is open to the air but is covered with gauze so air goes in but the creature can't get out. In that little compartment 'Bruthen' will insert a new queen bee and two or three little worker bees from the same hive so the trip to Melbourne will not be client-unfriendly. Queen bees have to travel in company. You can't have queen bees running around on their own because they are colony minded.

"Instinct governs all of this," he says. "I remember one mob whilst I was doing this. The Moody Bible Institute was an American evangelical mob who made a film about bees. 'If only *we* could all work together like this,' said Moody, and indeed it's a fine sentiment but you end up with a totalitarian state. Or even a church," says Father tellingly, "where you've got the 'queen bee' having to be kept in a position of eminence, allegedly because we have all invested ourselves, in our welfare and our futures, and our safety in this key person. The question is: Is the queen bee bigger than the hive or is the hive bigger than the queen bee." Bob puts on his Frank Thring voice again: "It's one of those delicate balances of nature," he says pontifically.

"Global warming is a delicate balance that may not be easily understood by us because we panic at the first stage of drought, or a prolonged drought, forgetting in fact that nature may well have droughts as part of, well, as part of nature. Anyhow, what else do you want to know?" asks Bob remembering my presence but, before I have time to answer, he launches into another story about a lady visiting the Seminary who wanted to come and see the bees. "A bee ran up her veil, so to speak," says Bob, "and stung her on the forehead. The poor lady ended up with two black eyes that lasted for days. If you don't look after your beehives you end up with these rogue bees. They get nasty," he states.

"What brings that on?" I ask as I straighten up in my chair, throwing a line to my wandering attention.

"Longevity. They shouldn't be allowed to continue like that. Something has gone wrong. They haven't gone through the natural cycles of going to work, coming back to regular tucker, leadership. The queen's too bloody old. It's this balance of nature."

"Does the beekeeper then have to bump the bees off?"

"He has to bump the queen bee off. The bees will be bumped off of their own accord because they'll die."

"I remember on one occasion," says Father Bob, "and it only happened once in my time, we had to get a truck and take the hives away to another spot." Bob's phone begins buzzing again and he impatiently fumbles it out of his pocket.

The bee-moving truck triggers a bee-moving memory from my bread-carting days. As chance would have it Bakerboy and I were delivering bread to the same shop in Ballarat Road, Deer Park simultaneously. Our vans were parked beside each other out the front of a milkbar. After coming out of the shop I went to the back of my van to shut the doors only to find that it had been invaded by a swarm of angry bees. Thanks to Bob I know that these were probably drones. They were buzzing around in a frenzied state. Neither Bakerboy nor I were bee whisperers so there wasn't much chance of us talking them into leaving peacefully. Bakerboy suggested that I drive along with the doors open, saying that he would follow and signal me if the bees flew out. I drove down Station Road towards St Albans accelerating gently and after about two kilometres Bakerboy flashed his lights.

"Where was I?" Bob asks uncharacteristically.

"Bee moving, Bob" I say, the memory of that morning as fresh as a bread roll.

"That's right," says Bob. "They had run out of nectar. Most of our bees were living off ground cover and gum trees but the supply ran low so we took 'em up to the You Yangs in a truck. Hello, Frank! Say hello to your Uncle Ron," says Father, as the dog bounds into the room, only to exit as quickly as he came in.

Isn't it funny the way animal lovers treat their pets as if they were human? Our elderly Scottish neighbours treat their terrier as if he were their little boy, which often amuses Ladybugs and me. 'Go and see your Mum,' says Ken, or 'Wait 'til your father comes home,' says Mary if the wee dog has been digging up the garden. We've even heard Mary refer to the dog as 'Stinky Bum.'

" 'Bugger Uncle Ron,' 'e says," Father Bob laughs and continues his bee-moving story. Frank runs back in and comes over to greet me. I pat the dog and then as Bob talks, Frank casually wanders over to his chair and settles down with his head in its customary position, flopped onto the armrest.

"We got a fair few gallon tins of honey out of that," says Bob proudly as he finishes his story. "We left 'em in the You Yangs for quite a while and they filled up the frames. When we brought them back we got many tins. That kept us going for a while, one hundred and fifty men, plus staff, in the joint. That's where I got my interest in honey and I'm still eating honey now."

"Are all Seminaries run like that? Self-contained?"

In responding to this question, Father Bob weaves together an analogy between bee and priest: "The idea was to go rustic so you were a bit like a bee yourself because they trained you as if you were monks in a monastery, and in fact you weren't monks in a monastery; you were men who would have to live on their own, or at most with two or three others, but you see, *religious orders* were in monasteries. They took vows of poverty, chastity and obedience and they were all in one house together. We, the secular priests, were meant to be trained as task forces of one, so there's two hundred and fifty parishes around Melbourne and beyond, and each boy lives on his own. That's why some of 'em got into trouble later, because they're living on their own and it's like a worker bee. The worker bee becomes a rogue. So," says Father Bob, "you get a clergyman, the secular priest, who is a drunk, a paedophile and God knows what else. Not many of them. Not many of them," he repeats looking pointedly at me. It certainly casts the poor old worker bee that becomes a rogue into a more favourable light when compared with the rogue priests, I think to myself.

"I see a figure today," says Bob, "which I am contesting in my Blog page: 'tens of thousands of cases of clerical abuse.' Now that's popped up this morning. Will the Pope come to Randwick and say: 'I'm sorry on behalf of the Roman Catholic Global Church?' " Father Bob says in his high-faluting voice. "I am saying: 'would our Melbourne headquarters mind checking this number: tens of thousands."

"That's an astounding figure."

"It's gross!" exclaims Bob.

"Does he mean just for Australia?"

"Yeah, he means just for bloody Australia! What does he mean by it? I'm asking our officers in charge, as in fact, with Abu Ghraib in Iraq, if some of the soldiers in the ranks committed atrocities, then the easiest thing to do by high command is to put the heat on the soles of their feet, water-board them, court-martial them, execute them, do whatever they do, but the high command itself will not answer questions as to how this came about. The Roman clergy is the same. They put the heat to the feet of Father Bloggs, lock him up in prison, strip him of his uniform, ridicule and humiliate him." Father Bob runs out of ideas for punishment. "Do whatever," he says lamely, but then comes up with more, "Flog and hang Father Bloggs!"

'Father Bloggs and Chaplain Bloggs could well be one and the same,' says Descartes. 'I wonder if in fact after leaving the army, where Chaplain Bloggs could always be found in his office, he took up as a parish priest eventually becoming a rogue padre.'

"They did all of those things to Father Smooch except for the flogging and hanging, " I say.

"What I'm asking of the bosses is: 'Where were you? Because this all happened on your watch' They'll say: 'Don't talk to us like that. How could we possibly know what was going on?' My answer to that would be: 'Well, you are supposed to be an organisation as well as a movement. That's what you pride yourselves on, with Roman diocese and headquarters, let alone little parish headquarters, but you've got a diocese and headquarters that is supposed to be responsible for two hundred and fifty clergymen. If you don't know what is going on, you should stop being an organisation and become something else!"

"You've got them by the balls of their flat feet!" I declare.

"I haven't though. They'll wriggle out just the same as the high command wriggled out of Abu Ghraib. No one at the Pentagon was sacked because of Abu Ghraib, only little Miss What's-her-name who was running around taking photos of naked men."

"I've got nothing against the bosses," continues Father, "I'm simply saying that as in all authoritarian models when things go well they accept the honour and the glory. When things go badly they say: 'We don't know anything about it.' You can't have it both ways. If your Archbishop stands up and says: 'Excuse me. That happened on my watch and I accept responsibility. Goodbye and good luck,' then he would be portrayed as an honourable man."

I wonder, too, what Father Bob's new secretary, Judy, thinks of all the palaver emanating from the study. Hopefully she is not an ultra conservative because by now she will have found that Bob is not your archetypical parish priest. Father Bob quietens down. "Well, I don't know where it is. I'm going," he says abruptly as he stands up: story time over. "I've got to go and see the *Leader* newspaper, then I've got to go to Mass, then I've got to go to the podcast, then I've got to go and meet someone down at Docklands, then I'm going to come home."

"And collapse."

"No!" Bob bellows. "Then I've got to go to JJJ to record with Safran."

Bob often seems exasperated by his many commitments: 'I've got to go here and I've got to go there'. Why does he *have to* go anywhere I wonder? Surely he is behind all of these commitments, the architect of his own unhappiness.

As I stand up, Frank jumps down from his chair and looks expectantly at us. The meeting is over, Frank, I think, but don't actually say. He has become an integral part of these talks. I say goodbye to Bob and pat Frank on the head before departing. Frank, as he so often does, follows me to the door, wagging his tail as I leave. 'Probably glad to see the back of you,' comments the nasty little bugger on the left.

# Chapter 40: The Fool-in-the-Grey-Flannel-Suit

*"Priest uses Bible is ok. Bible uses priest not ok."*

After dinner, I download the Moody Bible Institute's film: *City of the Bees*. The film, which was originally shot in 16mm, is about fifty years old and the sound track is a bit scratchy in places. As Father Bob said, the story of the life of bees *is* remarkable but it is the old-fashioned, somewhat stilted voice, delivered in a metallic American twang by the 'Man from Moodys' that makes me grimace.

The sting comes three quarters of the way through. The M from M, in a grey suit and dark tie, appears in front of the blackboard to lecture us on the difference between the Bee and Man. He is not there to recommend that we adopt the ruthless measures of the bee to regulate our society. No, he is there to flog the Ten Commandments. But, he says, the trouble is that Man is incapable of following the pattern of the Ten Commandments because God never locked him in, the way he locked the bee into its behavioural pattern. Man has free will, but, says the M from M: 'God offers to link Man to Himself in a warm, personal, vital relationship. Without this vital relationship Man is incomplete, insecure, disturbed,' he says. 'God has made no provision for Man's happiness or success apart from this relationship because God never intended that Man should live without it.'

Up to this point, Father Bob and the M from M would *probably* agree. I say this tentatively because I'm not Father Bob.

Then the M from M reaches for the book: the Bible. I hear Bob's voice clearly ringing in my head: 'The fools go to the book. They talk all day and night about the bloody book. The book fascinates the fundamentalist Christian. The book is not going to teach you. I'm saying the book will kill you.' I remember him saying on an earlier occasion: 'There are no cross-references; you daren't use it as a reference book as the clowns do.'

The M from M opens the book and says in his hard American twang: 'In John 1:12, we read.'

Smiling, I hear Bob's parody again: 'In Chapter fourteen, page such-and-such, He says...' I can remember Bob saying as we sat in his study that day: 'they go on and on, woof, woof, woof.'

Closing the book and holding it before him in both hands, the fool-in-the-grey flannel-suit looks directly at the camera and says in his nasally voice: 'This is God's solution to the problem of human behaviour. It deals with the problem at its source, not the group, but the individual. Can this relationship with God solve the problems?'

'Put the bloody thing away!' I hear Bob bark in his exasperated Aussie voice. 'Jesus will send you the Spirit and the Spirit will teach you *everything* you need to know. Now that means get away from that *bloody book.*'

I am perplexed though about Father Bob's relationship with the bible. How can a priest be a priest when staying away from the bible? What about Bob's use of the bible in the Mass? How is this different from the M from M? I dash off an email to Bob asking these very questions. His answer is short and to the point - just the opposite of his stories:

*Ron, good...priest uses Bible is ok ...Bible uses priest not ok. RJM.*

# Chapter 41: The-Man-in-the-Middle

*"The rich used smoke in their houses to make them smell sweeter. The rest of them had to put up with their own smell."*

At 9.53am, I send an email to Father Bob asking him for Maureen Johnston's telephone number so that I can ask her for an interview.

At 10.56am, Bob replies:

*Ron,*
*Too late! We bury Maureen TODAY at 1pm.*
*RJM.*

The traffic crossing the Westgate Bridge is travelling a bit faster than normal today as I drive to South Melbourne from Sunshine to attend the funeral. It was announced on the television news channels yesterday evening that the speed cameras had been turned off two years ago because the vibrations on the bridge were blurring the images!

When I arrive, I park my car in Dorcas Street and then join the mourners who are rugged up, many with scarves around their necks, standing around talking in the autumn sunshine. Henri Ser walks over to two girls standing to one side of the mourners. The cuffs of his jeans are turned up like a cowboy's in an old black-and-white movie and there is an enormous bunch of keys hanging off his belt at the back. His jeans ride low on his hips.

"How's your boyfriend?" he asks one of the girls.

"He's nearly dead," she falters. Tears well up in the eyes of all three and they hug each other as we start filing into the church.

Father Bob says in his Blog that Maureen Johnston wasn't religious. 'She popped up about 10 years ago,' he says, 'to volunteer to feed the local poor, both from the parish kitchen and backyard of the church, and from a food bus travelling through South Melbourne, Port Melbourne, and St. Kilda. She died last weekend. We'll send her off from this kitchen and church on Friday 23rd May 08,' his Blog reads.

When I enter the church, I find myself wishing that I were wearing a beanie and maybe a pair of long johns. There is a speaker high on a pillar in the nave five rows back from the chancel. It's not far from the head of Jesus, who is nailed up. I slip into this pew and turn on my voice recorder.

An old man wearing a grubby Gabardine overcoat slides along the pew opposite me; he sits for a few moments then stands up, genuflects stiffly, and walks up the aisle to the coffin. He puts his hand gently on the top and looks at the photograph of Maureen, which is sitting on the lid. After a few moments, he slips into a different pew and kneels, resting his arms on the backrest of the pew in front of him. He takes out his rosary beads, jiggles them and then bows his head, his lank shoulder-length hair hanging over his face. He is unshaven and his mouth is set in a grim line like a down-and-outer from the days of the Great Depression.

I hear Henri coming up the aisle before he comes into view. He walks up to the coffin, which is decorated with a large sheaf of flowers. Standing before it, his keys jingle gently. He then walks back to a pew.

Maureen's family comes down the aisle as one and sits in the front pews as Father Bob, in his customary white alb, enters from the side door. He rubs his hands vigorously. Uncle Jack's rabbit-skin motorbike gloves come to mind. Bob continues rubbing his hands together whilst standing in front of the pews talking to the family. He steps up onto the chancel and adjusts the microphone like the seasoned performer that he is. "Maureen would like this," he says his voice now rising. "You're all down the back!" There is a smattering of laughter. Bob tells the congregation that anyone who wants to speak after his eulogy is quite welcome. "These men might want to speak," he says indicating a few blokes sitting opposite me. "They can come up if they like, and if they get out of order we'll knock 'em out. Anyhow, we'd better show a bit of respect," he says.

"It's up to you," someone calls out.

"What?!".

"To knock 'em out, I mean," says the interlocutor who has a grizzly beard and is wearing a filthy Collingwood beanie.

"I think I'm beyond that," says the fellow Magpie supporter, but the laughter is drowning him out. "They know where I live too," he adds chuckling.

"Maureen was a serious woman but by the same token she could brighten up our miserable lives with her laugh," says Father, "because she had a *good* laugh. A bit smoky," he adds as an afterthought. "Peter Jackson Gold. In the old days it used to be Camels that'd give you that laugh."

There is quite a bit of Peter Jackson laughter and gurgling Camel coughs from the congregation following this remark. I smile and look around at the smattering of old men wearing ragged clothes, some with scarves around their scrawny necks. It was four degrees overnight and tonight's prediction is for a low of two.

"My job is simply to preside over your farewell to Maureen, but because I was intimately involved meself, not as the priest so much but as a friend, then I'm in the same position as you are. I welcome you all here on behalf of the family, because it's a family affair with me present, not *my* affair with you present. The family has got an ordeal to go through that none of us can go through."

Father Bob reads from the notes that the family has prepared. He tells about Maureen's voluntary community work. "This was her community, which she loved, and the community loved her. We all know there are two communities in South Melbourne," says Bob. "There's 'them' and 'us.' I'm the parish priest. I should be saying: 'There's only 'we,' because I've gotta put up with 'them' *and* 'us.' "

There is more cackling from the mourners. The other day I heard a blues singer named Buddy Guy singing *Hoochie Coochie Man* in which he substituted the words in one line with: 'She had one leg in the east and one leg in the west and I was in the middle doing my best.' Bob is a bit like the bloke in the song: he's in the middle doing his best.

'And now he is presiding over a secular funeral laying the dead to rest,' rhymes Rene.

"There *are* two communities," avows Father Bob firmly, "and the one being represented here today, in case anybody is in doubt and thinks they've strayed into somebody else's private property, belongs to you as much as it does to the church-going people."

That's right, I think, there are two communities. The church sits on the 'Dorcas Street divide' and is itself a house divided. Even the people who give their time to help feed the poor are divided despite working for the same cause. Jennifer and the middle class live south of the divide whilst helpers like Maureen come from the northern side.

"I don't want you to feel as if you are strangers," says Father Bob. "That's your church outside: the backyard is a church."

Descartes pipes up again: 'Very noble, but why do the homeless people have to be fed in the backyard? Were Archbishop Milingo or Bob Santamaria fed outside?'

As the service continues, I mull this over. Maybe feeding poor people out the back is peculiar to Australian culture. The farmer didn't usually invite the swaggy in for a feed after he'd chopped a pile of wood or mended a fence. No, he was told to knock on the back door of the farmhouse where the missus would either give him a feed or some provisions to take with him.

My reverie is interrupted as Henri jangles down the aisle. He sounds like a horse in traces as he goes by the pews. He too adjusts the microphone and begins talking. He tells of a time fourteen years ago when Maureen asked if he would drive the old so-called 'Graffiti Bus' around South Melbourne and Port Melbourne to give out toasted sandwiches and hotdogs to people in need. "Maureen lived for the community," says Henri, "although if you came from St Kilda, she wasn't all that happy about it." There is more nicotine and catarrh choked coughing and chortling. The old fella near me wearing the Collingwood football beanie slaps his thigh. Henri winds up by saying: "Maureen will be sadly missed by everyone who came in touch with her. She wasn't just a woman: she was a saint." There is heartfelt applause as Henri makes a musical return to his seat.

Father Bob's voice rises slightly. "We have permission from the family," he says, "to do two things that the Catholics do when they get together for their funerals, and that is, we are going to use water and smoke. They are both restricted substances, you're not allowed to use 'em so that'll appeal to Maureen. And the smoke smells better than the ones she used, I'm tellin' ya." He prepares the thurible for a bit of Catholic mumbo jumbo.

"They are symbols," explains Bob as he swings the thurible over and around the coffin. "We are here today and gone tomorrow, says the smoke. At least, that's what the smoke would say," he laughs, "if there were any smoke." For some reason the thurible is not smoking.

'I'd say Maureen has finally given up smoking,' quips Rene.

"It was also used in the old, old days," says Father undaunted, "to show respect for royalty. The rich used smoke in their houses to make them smell sweeter. The rest of them had to put up with their own smell." There is plenty of raspy laughter and coughing now.

Father sprinkles water over the coffin as he walks around it.

"And the water is a reminder of that, as well as these beautiful flowers, which *always* amazes me at funerals. When people suppose that they have to feel down, all of a sudden," he says, his voice rising in his trademark way, "we walk in with a bunch of colourful flowers and put 'em on the coffin for God's sake!" His voice drops slightly. "They're saying: 'Hang on! The best is yet to come. Death is not the end. It's only the end of the beginning. Because look at the flowers. The flowers are saying: 'There's still life in us even if we appear to die.' There is no flower without a dead seed."

'Darwinian or spiritual, you can't argue with The-Man-in-the-Middle on that one,' says Rene.

"The flowers grow and then die and another one takes over where they left off. Even the lawn outside here," Father elaborates, "looks like it's dead but a bit of rain and she's back. What we mean in this building is for everybody, no matter how much rain falls in our lives, and too much falls in some lives, there's always a payoff, and that is, some beautiful result. This family," says Bob as he indicates the family in front of him, "should not only be proud of their mother, their grandmother, but I hereby publicly tell them their mother, grandmother, was, is, and always shall be, proud of them."

As *The Rose* plays on the CD player, Maureen's family stands and then files out of the church.

# Chapter 42: The Icon File

*"Those of us working in the community sector over the past few years have watched the poverty and disadvantage swell and rise along with the property values of our city's real estate." Chris Middendorp.*

I've got sponsors on my mind. If the Father Bob Maguire Foundation could secure a major sponsor, Bob would have more time for working with the pooah because he would not have to be continually fundraising. A few days ago I wrote to Ardmona, owner of the iconic SPC label. To add a bite of levity, I mentioned that Father Bob had joked about needing "fifteen thousand tins of SPC Baked Beans and Spaghetti to feed the hungry little human-beans." Next I wrote to CHIKO, a legendary Australian company if ever there was one. I explained that I was not suggesting that homeless people should be stuffed with CHIKO rolls on a regular basis, but wondered if the company was interested in sponsoring the Maguire Foundation.

Shunting Vegemite to one side, I picture Open Family's Ford sponsored car and decide to add another company to my file: Ford's arch rival. Google tells me that the Executive Director of Sales, Marketing and After-sales for GM Holden is Alan Batey. I start jabbing away at the laptop keys again.

*'Dear Alan,'* I write, as if I know the bloke. *'I have recently written a biography about Father Bob Maguire. Helping the poor has been Bob's vocation since leaving the Priest Factory, as he calls it, in 1960. Whilst editing the book, I realised that Father Bob had mentioned a few Aussie icons such as Four 'n' Twenty pies, SPC baked beans and CHIKO rolls to name a few. These names had just popped up during discussions. As a volunteer working on behalf of the Father Bob Maguire Foundation I decided to write to these companies to let them know about Bob's work. Holden was not mentioned in any discussions but given that it is* the Aussie icon I decided to write to you.

*As with the other companies that I mentioned, your company could benefit by association with Father Bob's Foundation and vice versa. The Father Bob Maguire Foundation runs an old Ford food van called the* **Hope***Mobile, which travels from its base at Sts Peter and Paul's Church South Melbourne to St Kilda where volunteers feed homeless people.*

*By sponsoring the Foundation to the tune of, say, thirty thousand* *dollars per annum, and with your logo on the van, the public perception could well be that of a successful Australian icon supporting a battling Aussie icon. I'm sure there is a newsworthy marketing angle in there somewhere. Maybe you could hand over the keys to a brand spanking new Holden van, with "***Hope****Mobile proudly sponsored by Holden" emblazoned on the side, to Father Bob on Today Tonight or some such show.*

*The plight of the homeless is now in dire circumstances. Chris Middendorp of Sacred Heart Mission said recently in The Age: "Those of us working in the community sector over the past few years have watched the poverty and disadvantage swell and rise along with the property values of our city's real estate. Homelessness was a dire problem 10 years ago: it is now scandalously out of control and urgent intervention is now required."*

*Despite living a Spartan lifestyle, Father Bob has sent himself broke. He is supporting homeless people with money from his own pocket. He is in desperate need of corporate sponsorship.*

*Should you decide to sponsor Father Bob's Foundation, you will find yourself dealing with the battling Aussie icon in person.*

*Bob tells me that he would be tickled pink to be associated with* the Aussie icon, as I have dubbed it.'

After dating and signing the letter, I save it on file, and then print it ready for posting.

Sadly, all three Aussie Icons ignore my letters.

## Chapter 43: Flash in the Mud

*"The real heroes are the ones who give away income that is not disposable."*

As I ride along Dorcas Street towards the Church, I glance across at George's place. The bags of cans are piled up and cover the window. It's market time. Someone else will have to take them though because Eric tells me that poor old George died the other day. His Chihuahua will be lost without him I think, and then remember that George was married. It's a tragedy because his wife is mentally retarded and used to rely heavily on George.

After sitting down in Father Bob's study, I notice that the old Open Family map of Australia that has been there for years is missing from the wall. A white-board headed with the words: 'Father Bob Maguire Foundation' hangs in its place. There is a figure, an amount to strive for, words vigorously underlined and lines joining boxes to other boxes and amounts. There is mention of three hundred dependents. All scrawled in black texta; it's like one of those boards the TV detectives have hanging on the wall with vivid photographs of a murder victim and 'people of interest.'

Frank has followed me in and brings his orange rubber ball over for me to throw around the study for a while. He bounds around the room like a mad thing as I toss the ball about.

Bob looks at me and says grimly: "It's very hard for me at the present minute. I only need another six months of life. Three would probably do with a great burst of energy. That would take me through to the end of September."

'Christ!' That was Rene.

Father Bob looks as if a swarm of rogue bees has just knocked off his prized queen.

"You won't be able to go, though." I incline my head towards the white-board. "You owe your soul to the company store."

The tenor manages a smile and sings a couple of bars: "St Peter, don't you call me because I can't go . . ." He shrugs and his smile fades. "All this accumulation of 'let's do all the weddings in the universe, let's baptise everybody, let's anybody who is vaguely interested in having a religious ceremony for a wedding or a commitment, let's get in touch with the funny priest.' It's no wonder that Barry Moran thinks I'm a narcissist."

"Who?"

Frank lets the ball roll out into the hall and jumps up into his chair.

"Barry Moran: priest Moran. Because: it's on all-day-and-all-bloody-night. You've got Channel Nine's *Today* show. They rang and said: 'How about we cross to you a couple of times a week during the week of World Youth Day when the Pope's here?' I said: 'Fair enough.' *The Australian* newspaper rang and asked: 'What's your mobile phone number, because we might want to ask an expert opinion when the Pope's here?' Alright, that's all good fun. But one forgets, because one doesn't even have any experience of old age, that maybe one is doing too many of these things. Whilst one is doing all that, one can't run around trying to raise this two hundred and fifty thousand to keep this bloody project of three hundred people going."

'Maybe one should start slowing down before one has a heart attack or stroke,' says Descartes. Just as well Bob can't hear this cheeky bastard.

"Now if the Archangel Gabriel was to walk in the door and say: 'Listen, Bob,' 'Yes, Gabe.' 'Stop this project because it's a figment of your imagination, darling, and God has sent me to tell you to stop. Get back to church and say your prayers.' Well I might do it."

"You're trying to do too much."

"Yes, but in the balance of things, where's the objective commentator who says: 'what are you on about?' I still haven't had one. This has been going on for eighteen months now. If you were to make an appointment and then came in one day and said in a serious tone of voice: 'Bob?' 'Yes, Ron.' 'My research, and all the rest of it, tells me that in fact you're barking up the wrong tree, and I've come to the conclusion, and I'm telling you, personally, after all my research, I think that you should stop all this social activism and retire into a monastery and read the scriptures in Sanskrit and say your prayers, and I know you'd say you know a good cave in Syria where the early church fathers, the desert fathers, went."

"We're back in the desert again."

"Yeah. Back I'll go into that cave and live there until I drop dead. But, see, no one's telling me that."

"You're telling yourself that." I got in fast there before Rene and he is miffed.

"I'm only questioning because I can't get any negative comment. I can only get stabs in the back. You can't tell much if you're stabbed in the back. First of all you don't know who did it, and secondly you don't know why he or she did it."

I think of Luvy who sometimes turns his back to me and asks me to pull the knives out and then ask Bob: "What are you going to get done in the next six months before you die?"

"Well, over the next six months . . ." Father trails off and looks desperately at his whiteboard. "I've got to pay rents! I've gotta find two hundred and fifty thousand!" He sounds desperate, like a gambler who has got in too deep and can't punt his way out. Normally he would have said: 'two hundred and fifty thousand pounds.' I can actually feel myself frowning in sympathy, and yet a niggling thought intrudes. Ever since the day Father Bob gave me a copy of *The Tablet,* which had an article about the pragmatic approach to poverty, written by Margaret Hebblethwaite, I have been thinking about Bob and his work, and the work of others like him. According to Hebblethwaite, the fundamental rule is: 'Don't Give Money to Individuals.' I distinctly remember Bob telling me that he is sending himself broke by doing the very opposite. I remember him telling a funny story about meeting a skinny sheila, who asks him for a handout, whilst he is shopping in a supermarket. Bob has been creating dependencies by disregarding this rule. The people whom he helps literally become his dependents and he becomes their provider, sometimes for life. Take the hapless Margie and her forty years of dependence on Bob's handouts. Doesn't this serve to position Bob as the saviour and hero, putting the needs of others before his own? Perhaps his needs relate to being idolised as a heroic character of enduring self-sacrifice? I think of the old saying: 'Give someone a fish and you feed him today - teach him to fish and he feeds himself forever.' It is probably much more complex than this and perhaps Bob has been teaching some people to fish, I muse. Exasperated by my tardiness in responding to what he has just said, he says: "If you weren't sitting there and somebody else wasn't sitting there and Channel Nine wasn't on the bloody phone and my secretary didn't want signatures for cheques, I'd be able to sit here and pick up the phone to canvas support. All I need is the breathing space over the next six months because then I can personally, on the bridge of the battleship St Peter St Paul's/Father Maguire Foundation, see more clearly. Just now I'm surrounded by icebergs, but I know that on the other side of the icebergs there's a clear sea. That's what I've got to try to get through. It's no good writing books and going on the bloody television if there's a hole in the whole. All youse want to do is come around at the end and say: 'Excuse me, do you mind if we interview you why we go down, all hands on deck? You can give us a last few words."

'Or the last rites.' Smart-arse Descartes again.

"You might be able to get rid of some of the icebergs with the advent of global warming."

"Yes, that's right but then something else will creep up. There'll be crocodiles coming down from Africa in the warmer water."

I laugh but Bob doesn't even join in. Instead he hands me a black business card. A white cross is formed by the words, *fatherbob.com.au* printed horizontally and a slogan: *raise hope, not just money,* printed vertically. It is simple and starkly contrasting. I turn it over. The card, white on this side, is completely covered with nine lines of black print. The message reads:

> **Unconvenstitutional** (adj.) hybrid term *esp.* describing the belief that unconventional and institutional means are necessary to help the underprivileged; that social capital, as well as financial investment, is required in undertaking philanthropic acts; examples of the unconvenstitutional ethic can be seen in the work of Father Bob Maguire, through his three charitable movements, The Emerald Hill Mission, the Fr Bob Maguire Foundation and Open Family.

'Open Family?' snorts Rene. How would you like someone like him in your head all the time? He can be a nasty piece of work. Maybe the card was printed before Bob got the sack I think as I push Descartes to the back of my mind and look up as Father Bob says: "To be unconventional is to let the poor have the lion's share of time, energy and funds, but you can't be unconventional safely and over a long period of time unless you are also institutional. And institutional means that you've got to bloodywell have offices, and you've got to have professional people associated with you, if not in fact running your show, so you get a fine melding of the two ingredients. To do that I think you've got to be cashed up because you've got to be able to pay for separation, one from the other, occasionally. You've got to be able to pay for your church building over 'ere. If one of your departments, like in my case, the church, has got funds, it can then help the others to keep going in hard times. When the others have got funds they can help the Parish Church to keep going if *it's* having hard times. Now we're on the verge of the parish church having enough funds to keep itself going for the term of its natural life."

'That might not be much longer if some of these deviate priests don't start behaving themselves,' says Descartes crossly. I wish *he'd* start behaving himself.

"We are on the verge. That's what I've been aiming at over thirty-five years. But this next six months is gonna be hell for me because while you are on the verge, as you know, you can slip over the bloody edge one-way or the other. I'm seventy-three and whether I make seventy-four or seventy-five I don't give a bugger, but I wouldn't mind making it to the 1st of January 09. Whilst we are talking about all of these personal things, are we not losing sight of the bigger picture, which is: Why are people in these communities so closely in touch with one another and so widely separated from one another all at the same time?" Bob inclines his head and sits quietly waiting for a bloody answer.

Hell! I can't think of an answer to a conundrum like that at short notice. I'm an ex postie, not a philosopher, and bloody Ronny is never there when I need him. He has conjured up a graphic picture of a bluestone church, with slate tiles sliding off the roof, teetering on a precipice. "Les Twentyman tells me that you used to be a priest at Braybrook," I say without looking at Bob. Descartes curls his top lip like Elvis Presley and sniffs.

My sudden question in lieu of an answer to his question almost stuns Father Bob; he looks at me in consternation before saying: "Yeah! Working class suburbs were the places where we did our best work."

"I know the church in Churchill Avenue. What can you tell me about your time there?"

"What about it?" asks Bob loudly.

"Can you tell me what it was like working in such a poor area?" I ask.

Father Bob looks at me, hesitates and then nods.

"They were poor but they were fair dinkum," he says earnestly. "People in Public Housing are the most socially deprived in the community. At Braybrook they could see that you were on their side and they did whatever they could do with whatever little they had. All this other business for the thirty-five years since has been trying to convince people to help with what they had *left over*. At places like Braybrook they helped you with the little they *had*, because they knew you were trying to help their kids. In Braybrook we had a chance because we were so poor."

Not long after Richard Pratt found himself embroiled with the ACCC over price-fixing, I commented to Bob that maybe his philanthropy squared things. Bob replied that Pratt gave away disposable income. "The real heroes are the ones who give away income that is not disposable," he said at the time.

"Strangely enough," says Bob, "the Parish Priest at the time I was there, and who'd been there for a dozen years, Tom Murray, was an unconvenstitutional person because he did things very unconventionally." Bob glances out the window for a few seconds, turns back and says: "Not just strange. Mysterious. The way in which the brain works, I mean."

Yes. Ronny is alright most of the time but just listen to Rene Descartes! I vividly remember the first time I saw the twins: with the sides of their heads together and their strange colouring they looked like a cauliflower that had been perfectly divided.

"The Church hierarchy had stuck him out in the mud of Braybrook in the sixties. He was flash," says Bob who will probably be astounded when he eventually reads about the Cauliflower-twins. "He had taste this man. An Irishman. *They* knew he was flash, and they said in a kind of a perverse way: 'We'll teach Tom a lesson. He can be flash in the mud.' "

'Flash-in-the-Mud,' savours Rene, seemingly over his pique. 'I couldn't think of a better nickname myself.'

I snort and Frank lifts his head from the armrest of his favourite chair and looks quizzically at me.

"Tom, being flash, said: 'Thanks for nothing, but thanks for everything, because I'll now *be* flash in the mud. He then set about building in Braybrook, a precinct for Christ the King Parish, where all of a sudden, out of the mud, appeared a Catholic Primary School, magnificently furnished, a church elaborately furnished, with the best vestments and the grandest Church vessels. He also started to build a Catholic Secondary School in the middle of the mud."

Ronny is now drawing Flash-in-the-Mud trudging around the muddy quadrangle in a pair of gumboots and I'm not sure whether it is brought about by Bob's evocative storytelling or Ronny's vivid imagination.

"He invited a religious order of Brothers from Canada. He did all the flash things. Nobody in Orstralia talked of getting Brothers from Canada at that stage. But he did, and he did it!

"Now, lo and behold, the place burnt down! Everything! The whole precinct: an electrical fault. So there he was, flash in the mud, and ironically, brought to his knees in the mud. I don't think he ever got over it. I was posted there after the fire but was only there for a year because Tom and I fell out. No, *he* and I never fell out," says Father Bob, reconsidering. "He was probably suffering post trauma stress. He was stuck in a little Housing Ministry house opposite the school because his place had burnt down. I was stuck in the house with him," explains Bob, "in a room, and the housekeeper was fiercely devoted to Tom Murray's personal welfare. So she was going to protect him against any comers, including any upstart assistant priest who was posted there. If they thought, because he had been brought to his knees that they were going to stand over him, or her, or anybody else, they had another thought coming. The bloke before me had been chased out of the place, more or less, by her, and I was sent there to try to cope with that situation, with a fierce housekeeper who was Tom's personal bodyguard. The bosses do that. They don't think things through."

"Yes," I laugh. "It's an amazing world-wide phenomenon: the workers think things through and the bosses don't."

"When I first went out to Braybrook," continues Father Bob with a laugh, "I was shocked and 'orrified because of the state of the whole place, but I did what I had done in Ashburton and what I had done in Heidelberg, which was to try to appeal to the younger generation by setting up a Christ the King football team, under fifteens. If you could get them to kick footies around you saved them from getting into trouble. There wasn't much around for them to do. I remember one of the games: the full forward was drunk, and he was only fifteen. We were appalled, but he wasn't a *real* drunk, he only *got* drunk: the kid. The type of trouble that kids got into was pretty mild in comparison to these days," he says smiling. "We got football, basketball, and cricket teams going. We played in the Footscray District League and played on the muddiest football ground in the universe, which is in Churchill Avenue."

I know the ground and it's good to hear Bob call it a *ground* too. They are not called footy grounds anymore. Now they are referred to as football fields. Global warming has taken care of those glue-pots too, I think, as Bob goes on with the story.

"We tried to show a bit of form and show a bit of class. It was hard because everybody was that bloody poor. I was only involved for the length of a football season. Over the seven or eight months, I was there we managed to get the jumpers and the other gear, and we managed to get the oval. We had a lot of big, good quality kids.

"It was going well but then the woman must have detected a bit of flashness about me," says Bob. He shakes his head. "She told him, I think, that this wasn't on. He told 'town' that this wasn't on. Town buckled, because the Parish Priest has, in fact, the last word. I then left Braybrook and went to East Kew. Braybrook was a short sharp reminder to me of how you can get the people who are the least flash in the world to fight above their weight. There were such good blokes out there. I remember going to a fundraiser they put on in a little Braybrook Housing Ministry house, for God's sake. It would have been a sausage sizzle outside in the carport.

"Now, I could dance and sing in the nude here, out in the street, to try to raise a dollar for a specific purpose. Like I'm saying now: 'Excuse me, these people are starving. Excuse me, these people are freezing during the winter. Excuse me, these people have got to pay the rent or be thrown onto the street.' That's why I've got to exercise all this energy because I know now that I'm not going to get support from Church or State."

With the tail now vigorously shaking the poor old dog you would have to agree.

'The Roman Catholic hierarchy or the State couldn't give a rat's arse,' says Rene who is starting to learn a bit from Bob.

"I have to do it myself. I could sit down and argue for six months. Why is it so? Whether it's so. I haven't got the time any longer to argue about the why and the whether because I've been through it all for over forty years now, since I was ordained in 1960. I haven't got the time now to enter into discussions. People say to me: 'Why don't we make an appointment to see Mr. Bloggs of the Philanthropic Trust?' "

I grin, thinking of Father's burgeoning collection of Bloggs. That's the best one to date: Mr. Bloggs of the Philanthropic Trust. Rene adds it to the roll as Father Bob continues.

" 'Yeah, when do we go?' 'I've just rung Bloggs up and he can't see us until August.' 'Alright.' That's another month off. When we get there he will give us bits of paper and say make a submission. By the time we go through all that we will have nothing until January. Now I may as well be feral and try to raise the two hundred and fifty thousand or whatever it is by my means without going through the ordeal."

Bob stops talking to me to answer his mobile phone and thus talks to someone *else*.

"All I want is a bit of calm and a bit of respect, but I can't get it," he says as he slips his phone back into his pocket. "I'm not a bloody genius. I'm not made out of stainless steel. It's my own fault because I've let everybody in. That's why I'd go upstairs: to get away from all this. But I can't go up the bloody stairs until there's enough money to fix-up upstairs. The critics will say: 'Well, he doesn't want to go upstairs because otherwise he would do it,' and I'm saying to them: 'That's your interpretation of the facts. My interpretation of the facts is: 'We've spent the money on the poor and we haven't got money to go upstairs.' "

"Spending the money on the poor was your objective from the start, right after reading about Abbé Pierre wasn't it?" I ask, not meaning to water-board him.

"Yeah, but he's dead and I'm not. I want to go up the stairs because there are other things to do besides looking after the poor. I don't mind if the poor get the lion's share, which they have had for the last thirty-five years, but there are other things."

I wonder if the idea of 'going up the stairs' is a way of retaining his sanity? When referring to Brother Bloggs in the House of Hospitality Father Bob said that Bloggs 'has to be able to get away from the madness so that he doesn't become a lunatic himself.' At the moment, the only time that Bob can go up the stairs is at day's end; on Thursdays for instance he doesn't finish recording at RRR until 11pm; on weekends he is left to respond to the needs of people knocking on the door at any old hour.

'No wonder the poor bastard wants to go up the stairs!' says Rene with a shake of the cauli'.

Bob glances at the white board. "The Bob Maguire Foundation has got three hundred people up there on the bloody board, waiting. Am I gonna feed 'em, pay their rent, or what am I gonna do? The more time I spend talking, the less time I've got for fundraising."

"You're *responsible* for three hundred people?"

"Yeah!"

"How are you going to manage that?"

"Well, I'm managing it now. If I'm allowed to," he says pointedly looking at me. "I spend too much time talking. Hello, he's on the Denton show. Hello, he's on the bloody Neil Mitchell show. Hello, talk, talk, talk, yak, yak, yak. To what effect?"

"With Open Family you had more…" I can't finish the sentence because Bob belts it aside like a cricketer whacking a wayward delivery over the fence for six.

"Open Family, for me, died in the water in 2004," he says sharply. "This is not going to die in the water because I'm still alive. Once I'm dead it may well die in the water, which is why I've got to try to install the Father Bob Maguire Foundation with its three-hundred-thousand-a-year income to look after that mob on the wall."

I look over at the mob on the wall and then turn back to Bob. "That's a good effort: three hundred thousand a year coming in. You've only been going for four years."

"It's wearing me out. I've got other things to do. I've got books to read, I've got poems to write, songs to sing. I've got all that to do and I can't do it because I've gotta be a bloody fundraiser."

"I'm buggered if I know how you manage. There's too much pressure for one man."

"I don't know either. I'm telling the bloody story over and over again. I'm telling it to you, I've told it to Terry Monagle, I'm telling it to Greg Day. I've told it over and over and over and over and over again and it's not worth a dollar. It's getting late too! I've only got six months."

"What! Are you really going to be dead in six months or are you just going to pull out after six months?"

"No! I won't pull out after six months. This *thing* will either be dead or alive in six months."

"It'll be alive," I say confidently.

'Just like you,' adds Rene.

"Six months, which is why I have to get on with the business."

"I'd better get out of your hair then," I say.

The trouble is now Bob won't let me go. He has got one more thing to say.

"There is a St Vincent De Paul one-liner that says: 'Money is Love,'" he says, proffering a pamphlet. "I was reading about the Catholic Church in Melbourne. Prahran and South Melbourne were the first St Vincent De Paul Society groups in Australia. It says 'ere: 'The St Vincent De Paul Society was established in Melbourne by Father Gerald Ward to run the orphanage of St Vincent De Paul, first in Prahran, then in Emerald Hill, which is now South Melbourne. It was the first St Vincent De Paul Society in Orstralia.' All I'm trying to do is continue that original commitment to the poor. That's all I'm doing." He shrugs and looks at me.

"You've done a remarkable job," I say, rising to my feet.

"Now get out!" says Father Bob.

## Chapter 44: Chiko

*"It's not a perfect world. I'm hoping for the best without planning for the worst, which is probably the real story of my life."*

It could end there. The manuscript though has other ideas. The ride is not over until the manuscript says so. There is no getting off early. I wrote 'The End' last night but there has been a further development this morning in the form of an email from Father Bob. He says that Greg Day, a 'well known and respected author,' has been contracted by a 'well known publisher' to write a biography about him. He says that he has 'alerted Day to the existence of an unofficial concurrent work in progress.' Bob also philosophises: 'It's not a perfect world. I'm hoping for the best without planning for the worst,' and says that that is probably the *real* story of his life. He asks if I will contact Day 'with a view towards the best possible outcome.'

I am unsure what Bob means by 'unofficial.' It could be that he says it is unofficial because I do not have a publisher at this stage. The name Greg Day is instantly recognisable because Bob used it in conversation during our last talk.

'I remember his exact words,' says Descartes. He flashes them up for me:

"I'm telling the bloody story over and over again. I'm telling it to you, I've told it to Terry Monagle and I'm telling it to Greg Day."

Until then I had never heard of Greg Day and Father Bob has never mentioned him before but he has become a player. From Rene's worrying interpretation of the message it seems that he might be my nemesis, in the same way that I have become Terry Monagle's nemesis. With some trepidation I reply to Bob's email telling him that I'm not sure what he means by 'unofficial' and that biographies are usually tagged 'authorised' or 'unauthorised.' I agree to contact Greg Day.

Before contacting him, however, I Google him and find out that he has written an extremely imaginative novel called *The Patron Saint of Eels*, which now heads my list of books to read.

'The Patron Saint' and I converse by telephone. We seem to hit it off fairly well and are forthright with each other. He tells me that Terry Monagle is too ill to continue writing his book and it has been scrapped. He has been contracted by the earlier mentioned 'well known publisher' (WKP), he says, to write yet another biography! I can understand now why Bob was so upset the other day. The poor bugger is now engaged in telling his life story for the third time. No comers are refused. He just can't say no.

Rene Descartes doesn't consider Day to be a threat though because he reckons that my story is unique. 'A publisher could gather the finest writers in Australia, let's say Robert Drewe, Brian Castro, Martin and Richard Flanagan, Thea Astley, Peter Carey, Elizabeth Jolley, Tim Winton, David Malouf . . . ' Ronny butts in now. 'Take a large rolling-pin and roll out Don Watson as flat as a shit-carter's hat,' he enthuses. 'Then using him as a casing, roll Rene's writers up, after being pot-stirred by Mungo McCallum, into a huge Chiko Roll, a super writer, and then charge this being with the undertaking of writing Father Bob's biography.' Rene joins in: 'Will Chiko ride up to the church on his first day to deliver the mail and leave it on the altar? Will Bob's big black poodle ("The bastard's mad," says Bob) bite Chiko on the arse as he (the sexed possessive is appropriate given that he is in the shape of a Chiko Roll I manage to think as Rene continues) stands on the pedals to ride off after talking to Bob? Will he be there when Father Bob's protégé, Barnabus, with the mad black poodle loping along behind, charges down Dorcas Street trying to get the monkey off his back, yelling profanities at passing drivers who are gawking out the windows of their cars? Will Chiko be present when Father Bob disregards the Pope's orders and celebrates St Patrick's Day during Holy Week?' Descartes is getting louder and louder. 'Will Maria Orlando walk up to Chiko with the chalice after Communion and ask him to finish off the wine?' he laughs hysterically, obviously worried. 'Will Chiko be in the Church garden with a film crew on a stinking hot Friday morning whilst Formula One cars can be heard in the background screaming around Albert Park Lake? With all his panache, imagination, wit, sense of humour, sympathy, style and vast vocabulary, Chiko will be able to produce a decent biography,' says Rene as he calms down, 'but it won't have the same collateral as the story written by the postie about the priest he has known for twenty years. It won't have the same appeal to the book buying public as *The Postie and the Priest* either,' he declares emphatically.

Maybe it's time: time for me to send my manuscript to a publisher.

In the pre-dawn, my subconscious flicks the switch; my eyes spring open like the little electric shutters depicting the numerals in the bedside clock radio. I lie awake, hardly blinking, as the Cauliflower-twins compose this chapter in my head. I consider getting up and opening the lid of my laptop as I have done on other occasions when the twins were suffering from insomnia. No, it can wait, although I don't get back to sleep. I even make it wait until after breakfast, still considering the move. It could be too soon. The writing in Chiko seems evocative to me, it captures something essential about how I write. I polished this short piece for hours. The manuscript, especially the early chapters, is as rough as guts. It shouldn't see the light of day, yet. Chiko was mostly about me so I was able to give my imagination full reign. There is a lot of discipline in the writing of a biography. I have constantly had to hold myself in check. It's frustrating. I'm impetuous however and at 8.15am send Chiko to a friend of Henri's who manages a more obscure publishing company, asking if this whets her appetite. The lady from this more obscure publisher: (OP) takes a bite and asks for more. It's only 9.45am.

'Christ!' says Descartes. 'Some people just love Chiko Rolls.'

# Chapter 45: The Roman Catholic Thing

*"Why have I got two biographies on the go?"*

"If Barry Moran thinks you are a narcissist now, what's he gonna say when he sees this hanging up?" I ask, looking at the large framed photograph of The Grin (donated to the Church by Geoff) hanging on the wall behind Father Bob. Bob laughs and I give him the news that a publisher has asked to read the manuscript; he says: "Is she a human being? She might be a bloody communist."

"I don't care," I say.

'Cocky bastard,' Descartes declares.

Chiko, I muse as I run my hand across my chin.

Frank bounds into the room and comes over for a pat, and I smile as I ruffle the hair on his head.

"Why do these things happen to me?" asks Father Bob.

"That's a good point. Why do they?"

"Why have I got two biographies on the go?" he asks.

Why have I got two voices in my head? Rene Descartes is especially taking an extraordinary interest in the manuscript now.

"I think Day will pull out. He says he is not a hired gun for WKP, but where did he get the manuscript from then, if not the publisher?" I ask.

"He probably got it from me." Bob looks at me innocently and raises his eyebrows.

"Eh? You were in possession of Terry's manuscript?"

"Yeah! Most of it: it was about that thick," says Bob holding his thumb and index finger about five centimetres apart. "The craft is too complicated for me," he says wearily. "If Monagle's out of the picture, you're left with Mrs. Knight."

"Who's Mrs. Knight?" I ask,

"The lady from the publishers: WKP. What's the bloody protocol? I don't know what it is. Mrs. Knight suggested Mr. Day. She sends along Mr. Day. Mr. Day and I sit and talk a bit, then he goes back to Aireys Inlet. I like Day. The difference between you and Day (I smile), as far as I can see, is he comes from the inside: Roman Catholic ethos," he says, baring his teeth like a chimpanzee as he stretches his mouth across 'ethos.' "Well, at least, I think he does. Monagle comes from inside the Roman Catholic thing too, but he was a bit alienated by the Roman

Catholic *thing*. Nevertheless, he was still a practising Roaming Catholic whilst not being a slave of the Roman Catholic thing. Now Greg Day comes along from the Roman Catholic thing, but he hasn't been as cynical about the Roman Catholic thing."

"As?"

"Monagle. I think the Monagle family might have suffered from the split in the Labor party. I dunno."

"That was way back in the bloody fifties!"

'You're starting to sound like Bob talking,' notes Rene. Maybe he should listen to himself.

"Yeah!" says Bob as if to say: 'What's wrong with that!'

Apparently some Catholics have long memories and hold grudges for decades. Francis' mother comes to mind, not letting Francis fix the broken lock on the sideboard.

"You've been here for a long time but you come from a different angle," says Bob. "You don't come from the Roman Catholic thing."

The word 'but' seems to imply that Father Bob would prefer his 'official' biography to be written by an educated writer from the 'Catholic Ethos' with a separate, humorous, anecdotal story written by the postie. The Roman Catholic Thing is too much for me. I'm glad I don't come from that background. It's like a big club alive with petty squabbles, backbiting, jealousies and betrayals, with the tail constantly trying to wag the dog, as Bob says.

'The Roman Catholic Thing is evil,' shudders Ronny. 'It's a paedophile dressed in the trappings of a priest, like Father Smooch.'

'Yes!' agrees Rene Descartes somewhat surprisingly, 'and this Thing, the carcinogenic clergy, is gnawing away at the vitals of the Roman Catholic Church.'

'The dog is going down in the back legs; he's got distemper,' adds Ronny sadly.

"My question is, and I'm only a bloody cog in the wheel here," says Father, who is quiet partial to clichés, "because I don't understand the craft for a start and secondly I don't understand the legalities of it; what do I do?"

I shrug. The Cauliflower-twins are becoming too heavy but I despair for Bob who, like thousands of priests world wide, is being stigmatised by Ronny's version of the Roman Catholic Thing.

"There's nothing I can do," Bob bemoans as I struggle to focus on the topic.

"I said to Day: 'Here is Ron Burrows.' I then asked him: 'what do I do?' He said, 'You can't stop either of us.' "

'Does Bob *want* to stop one of you?' wonders Rene.

Bob looks at me, raises his eyebrows. "How do you see it?" he asks.

"All I know is that we might have a publisher." I smile. "I sent Chiko to OP and . . ."

"Yes," interrupts Bob not giving me a chance to finish, "but we have two books."

"We can have as many books as we want," I state unequivocally.

"Legally you can't, can you? One publisher is not going to publish if another publisher is publishing. Are they?" he questions. "I don't understand the craft," he says again.

"I'm not contracted to anybody. Anyone can publish my manuscript and that in turn would not stop another publisher from publishing another version of your story."

"Can they?" He shakes his head, "The vagaries of the publishing world."

'Being unravelled by the eponymous postie and priest,' adds Descartes.

"Yes, as far as I know," I answer.

"I said to Day," says Father Bob, "who would probably be . . . I can't think of the word. I was talking to an architect about renovating the back section of this old church. He came yesterday after five visits and gave me a poem. He said this sums up what you and I have been talking about. I thought: 'well, that's another way of putting it.' "

"Are you going to read it out to me?"

"No. He has drawn up the plans and this is another way of putting what the plans allegedly are going to portray. Now have I got two ways of putting the story, with Greg Day putting it one way and you putting it another way? You've both got different styles."

'Father Bob *does* want two books,' says Rene, 'the Greg Day 'official' biography and the Ron Burrows 'It's all bullshit' book.'

"Yes, our two styles would probably be *vastly* different."

'I'd stake my half of your brain on the bullshit book,' says Rene loyally.

"And," says Bob, "What, in the final analysis, has it got to do with me?"

"The final wash up is that the more books we sell the more people hear about The Cause," I say, wondering about all the people who Aussie Post employs. We've got a lot of potential readers there.

"What I'm alluding to though is: WKP is probably not going to publish Day's book if you are published."

Descartes thinks that I'm a bit slow. He points out that Father Bob seems worried that WKP might not publish the Official biography because the Bullshit book will be out first.

"That's up to them I suppose. Monagle wasn't sacked by WKP."

"No, he was too sick to continue. I don't know if he has died or what state he is in. I haven't heard anything. I'll send him another email today. He still answers emails. I suppose we can all answer emails even if we are dying."

"Yes, you're right."

"It's talking to people that's the bloody drag," says Bob, reiterating what he said on my last visit.

"It's really up to you whether you want to continue talking to Day," I say.

"I don't know what to do," he says again. "I haven't signed anything but does the WKP contract that I had with Monagle spill over to Day?"

"I don't know. You've got a copy of the contract though."

"Have I?" asks Bob.

"Yes, I was here the day you opened the letter. You wouldn't let me read it at the time because you said it was highly confidential."

"Can't I have both of youse?"

"Yes, you can. I can't see any reason why not as long as Day continues. His mind was divided when I spoke to him. He said that because I am so far advanced he might pull out."

"You're saying we've got two horses running 'ere and one of 'em might *pull out?*" asks Bob in amazement. Or is it dismay?

"Yes. One horse has just jumped out of the starting stalls and the other is coming down the home straight."

"I said to Day, 'you've got two styles here, one of them is . . . what's the word? it's like the architect's poetry."

'Bullshit,' supplies Rene.

"In the Aussie vernacular, maybe," I suggest with a smile.

"That's your style. I'm talking about his. His is, well I haven't seen his either."

"You've read *The Patron Saint of Eels* though, haven't you?"

"No, I read his other one about the sea of diamonds, about fishes."

"Richard Flanagan wrote a magnificent book about fish: *Gould's Book of Fish*, it's called," I say digressing slightly.

"I haven't read that," states Father Bob. "I asked Day if his book was gonna be fiction, because his other two were fiction. He said: 'No.'"

"The Patron Saint has got religious connotations though. He will be comfortable writing about a priest." He will see a different 'side' of Bob too because I think that he (Bob) will present himself differently. During our sessions, despite the fact that they are conducted in Bob's study, he generously steps 'down' to my level of comprehension. When being interviewed by a writer from the Catholic ethos (I can't help stretching my mouth across the word) he will step back 'up.'

"Yes," agrees Bob, "What am I going to do about all this?" he asks.

"You mightn't have to do anything."

"I'm going to get into trouble; I can see it. It's the story of my life."

"You won't get into trouble because of me. If OP knocks me back and Day quits, I will ring WKP if you'd like to give me a contact name and number."

Father Bob gives me the details and then asks: "How much does WKP have to be told? They know that you are writing anyway; Monagle would have told them that."

"What I can't understand is: why didn't the WKP ask if she could read my manuscript knowing that Terry was too ill to go on?"

"Publishers probably prefer known writers. She probably said: 'We know this man, this bloke who wrote such and such.' She had another bloke here before Day, who had written something about the mangroves in Queensland. He backed off after just one visit. 'Too hard,' he said, 'I'm not interested.' What am I going to say to Mrs. Knight?"

"Leave it all to them," I say with a shrug. The poor bugger does look concerned though. It might just be uncertainty that is worrying him. He has invested a lot of time in telling his story but there is nothing to say that it will ever be published. To continue Bob's horseracing analogy: he starts out on a performer from the Catholic ethos (Terry Monagle) who has wins (published works) to his credit. He also has a roughie (me) with potential on the training track but no form on a city racetrack running for him as well. His form horse crashes and is out of the race but the stable (WKP), undaunted, lines up another proven performer, also from the Catholic ethos. The roughie, well versed in track savvy, savages the favoured runner with scare tactics (Chiko), which sends the Catholic runner back through the field and leaves him with little chance of recovery.

"Bugger it!" says Bob. "It's too hard thinking about it."

When I arrive home about thirty minutes later, there is an email from Father Bob. 'Terry Monagle has died,' it reads. 'RIP.'

A few days later, there is another email from Father Bob saying that WKP would like to see my manuscript for assessment.

Once again, a few days later, my bike is resting: leaning against the fence whilst I'm sitting in Bob's study discussing publishers and manuscripts. Frank is nowhere to be seen. He must be out with the dog-walker again.

Bob tells me that Day rang him from Aireys Inlet the day before. "Day said to me: 'I don't think it's very nice for you to say that I am a writer of books and that Burrows is a postman who is writing a book.' He said: 'It doesn't matter whether he is a bloody postman or the Archbishop of Canterbury. If he's writing a book he's writing a book.' He also said that: 'Mrs. Knight did not let me know about Burrows until I asked her.' According to Day, she said: 'I know that Burrows is writing a book,' and Day was a bit upset that she hadn't told him right from the start. He now says to me that Mrs. Knight wants to see your material; I presume, so that she can then decide whether WKP will publish your manuscript."

"I'll send it to her but also let her know that OP is currently assessing it."

"Yeah, alright," says Bob, "There is a third sheila who sent a message earlier. She could well be a prospective bloody publisher. Now what did she have to say?" he says, as he starts sifting through old emails on his computer. "How long ago? Not long ago," he answers himself. "Jesus help me through the day," he prays softly. "What was her bloody name? This is all too much for me," he laments.

"It's all too much for me now too. It's a bit of a quandary," I say.

"We don't like quandaries," says Father as he scrolls down the page. We chat away as he peers at the screen, shielding his eyes against the light coming through the window onto the screen.

"Do you think Safran would be interested in writing an introduction to the book?" I ask.

"Oh, yeah he might do that," Bob says offhandedly, "I'll let him read that bit about Chiko. I said to Day: 'the bit Burrows sent to you (Chiko) is not necessarily in the tone of the rest of the bloody manuscript. He's got serious all of a sudden.' What would you say?" asks Bob fixing me with his familiar detective stare.

"The tone of the manuscript should indicate the 'tone' of you. That's what I have tried to portray. You're not serious all the time and neither are you in a humorous mood all the time. I've simply tried to capture you."

Bob nods his agreement. The 'tone of the rest of the bloody manuscript,' as Bob puts it, though has worried me for as long as I've been writing it. His deep personal feelings are guarded jealously by his persona. In his book *The Divided Self,* R. D. Laing writes: "A man without a mask is indeed very rare. One even doubts the possibility of such a man. Everyone in some measure wears a mask, and there are many things we do not put ourselves into fully. In 'ordinary' life it seems hardly possible for it to be otherwise." Oscar Wilde was also intrigued by personas: "Man is least himself when he talks in his own person. Give him a mask and he will tell you the truth."

'Maybe,' sniffs Rene Descartes, unafraid even to take on the might of Oscar Wilde, 'but will he tell you the whole truth?'

Trying to 'capture' someone is like trying to catch your shadow: you can get close but the shadow is always just beyond reach and often disappears. I look across the desk at Bob. It's not just about persona either; age has made him cynical and less prepared to put up with all the bullshit. I sense that he has a feeling of deep frustration at not having been able to fully accomplish the objective that he set for himself in 1973 and at the antics of the tail continually thwarting the dog.

"Where's this sheila?" Bob is still scrolling. "We keep staring at these bloody things;" he says grimacing, "they're supposed to make life interesting for us."

"Yes, they're simple but can take up a lot of your time," I say, smiling as I watch him. One hand is above his eyebrows shading the light coming in from the window, his head is tilted back and he is looking through the bottom section of his glasses.

"You'd say: 'You should have put the woman's name in the address book.' I don't know her bloody name. I can't just write in: 'unknown author: please find' because the thing's not Mandrake the Magician.'"

"Who was that bloke at the Catherine of Siena Mass who threw himself down in front of the altar whilst you were conducting the Mass?" I ask Bob as he taps a couple of keys?"

"That was what's-his-name." Father Bob sighs heavily.

"It was rather bizarre, I thought."

"Oh, yeah, he's a bizarre kind of bloke. I've known him for years. He's a street worker. Whether his piety is insanity or not, I don't know. What's his name now?" Bob goes still and looks into the middle distance like a fortune-teller. "Wayne Neilson," he declares.

"Wayne Neilson! I recall you saying after he left the church, that his name was Wayne, but I never twigged that they were one and the same. I never got a look at his face."

"How do you know Wayne Neilson?" asks Bob.

"You introduced us. I went out with him one night not long after that looking for young prostitutes."

"In St Kilda?"

"Yeah. We went to the Peanut Farm too. He's not a bad bloke. That is one of the earlier episodes in the manuscript," I say. Bob hasn't given up on the scrolling.

"He's alright! I don't mind Wayne," says Bob. "He's a pain-in-the-arse when it comes to spiritual things. Where's this bloody sheila? If I ever find her again," he says giving her a name: "the Third Woman." She is the Third Woman and as far as WKP is concerned I was nearly the Forgotten Man.

Bob reads aloud as he scrolls. "Nah, we're buggered," he says. "If I find her name later, I'll email it to you. She was an interesting woman who showed a bit of interest. I told her that there are already people in the market place. I'll go through this again," he says. He sighs deeply once more, reading names out as he scrolls down the page.

"From what Day said yesterday do you think that he is still interested in going on with your biography?" I ask.

"I wouldn't think so. He said: 'She'll have to make up her mind.' But she's going to have to make up her mind after seeing your stuff. She might say this bloke's well and truly into it, therefore we'll pay him."

"Maybe," I say hopefully.

'Good old Chiko,' crows Rene.

The search continues: "Wedding bloody booklet. You're gonna waste your time sitting here. Bendigo Spirituality Meeting, Kate's wedding ceremony appointment. Aaah, thank you, Jesus: Linda Williams. 'I would like to discuss with Father Bob Maguire the possibility of putting some of his life experiences into a book,' reads Bob. The writer adds a few contact details and signs it: 'Linda Williams, publishing agent. He reads a bit about Linda Williams' profile. " 'Linda adds her personal touch. You have a different hook to excite clients and media alike.' She might do these things," he says then reads out one of the adverts: "'Rebecca Beazley: inventor of Bedazzle teeth-whitening products,'" and we both laugh; it's as if we have just realised that all this drama is no more important than a tube of toothpaste.

"I'll send the manuscript off to WKP first to see how it goes," I say, rising to my feet.

"Oh, yeah. You don't want to miss out on WKP," says Bob. We are both still smiling broadly.

A crow sitting in a gum tree near the tap caws mournfully. On that note Father Bob sighs deeply and, like a couple of auditors who have had a torrid session unravelling a paper track, we declare an end to business for the day.

"Can you find your own way to the door without the dog?" asks Bob.

'Not if he's anything like Ronny,' Descartes says.

"Yeah. I'll manage thanks, Bob. Hooroo."

As things turn out, we do miss out on WKP. Maybe I'm a bit gullible. Mrs. Knight gratefully accepts the manuscript and replies by email. She says that she wants to make it plain that WKP is still going ahead with a biography by Day who has been contracted to write it. Mrs. Knight says that she only wanted to read my manuscript 'to make sure we aren't clashing or writing along the same lines.'

Rene sniffs. 'Nonsense! If two people are writing about the same person . . . ' He doesn't even bother finishing his sentence. It doesn't matter because I reckon Bob might be right: Mr. Day is about to pass judgment on Mrs. Knight.

I am reluctant to contact The Third Woman because I still haven't heard any more from OP. I send an email to Father Bob and tell him that I won't contact her until I hear from OP.

A few days later someone from OP does indeed contact me and writes that he 'got an odd feeling of déjà vu when reading one of the chapters relating to one of Bob's sermons. "It turns out Mum used to take me to South Melbourne to see him sometimes when I was little." He also says: "I still remember one sermon more than all the thousands of others that were given by regular priests over the years." He tells me that he has read the manuscript and has recommended it to his boss, "who has sent it to the next person up the ladder to read." He offers to send me the Reader's Report, an unbiased opinion of a person contracted to review and critique my manuscript, by email.

You can be lucky sometimes. I've struck a Catholic who has fond memories of Father Bob. I fervently hope 'the next person up the ladder' isn't a Bloody Protestant.

## Chapter 46: The Roaming Catholics

*"I would like to think that local Catholicism is not just a franchise of global."*

Leaving aside the publishing side of things, I ask Father Bob: "Do you want to say anything for the manuscript about the Pope, George Pell, or World Youth Day?"

"No." Fair enough.

"It's probably appropriate that you do say something about World Youth Day," I persist, "since that's what this interview is supposed to be all about."

Bob picks up a magazine off his desk. "Look at this:" he says. *"Who* magazine." He starts reading out bits of a letter to the editor. " 'Who better to give an interesting and spiritually informative opinion about World Youth Day than Father Bob?' I can't see the point. The Archbishop or the pilgrims, as they are calling them, aren't knocking at my door. 'We would very much like to interview you on the lead up to Pope Benedict's visit to Sydney for World Youth Day. We only need twenty minutes,' he reads. That's alright I s'pose," says Bob, but to be honest I just want to be left alone."

"What do you think of World Youth Day?" I ask.

"World Youth Day." he says, "I really should shut my mouth although I'm writing it for the SBS Blog. This Jesuit has got a nice thing here," says Bob reading from a page that he has printed from off the Internet: 'World Youth Day Blooms Beneath the Aphids.'

"That's poetic prose."

"The Jesuits are good at this type of thing. It appeals to me. It's saying that it's a sensible approach and that something good is going on. There *are* spots on it but he's saying: 'take the proactive positive approach and concentrate on the bloody rose and not on the aphids.' "

"It's a good metaphor. What's your personal opinion of World Youth Day?" I prod again.

"I rang around yesterday to talk to a few priests, ordinary working priests, and they're all saying: 'It's marvellous, it's marvellous, this has given us an injection.' It's like here in South Melbourne: we said the Grand Prix's no bloody good. It's gonna wreck this, wreck that, and wreck the other thing. Then the visitors come, walk up and down Clarendon Street, as you would know better than I do from when you are delivering the mail, and lo and behold, ladies and gentlemen, it's all very interesting and exciting."

"These pilgrims have certainly come a long way and would have spent a fair amount of money to attend." This word 'pilgrim' appeals to me. John Wayne used to call people 'pilgrim' in his laconic voice.

"Yes," agrees Bob, "We are so far away that it should be an experience, I think, for them to come to the land of the Southern Cross, which was the last to be discovered, or settled by Europeans. It should also be an experience for us because it's a reminder of that kind of patchwork quilt of cultures that we are missing out on, because it's so easy for them to go from one country to another in five or ten minutes. We can't do that; we've missed out on that but at the same time we've also missed out on the horror stories. We had to go overseas to get into battle, and then, on behalf of somebody else. 'No foe shall gather our harvest or sit on our stockyard rail.' I don't know where I learnt that. I think we used to sing it."

Then we both say in unison: "It could be Banjo Paterson."

"Or Lawson," I add.

"One of 'em," says Bob.

Father Bob continues his discourse: "It's hard, and we're caught a bit short, the Roaming Catholics."

'These bloody pilgrims must be Bob's fair dinkum *Roaming Catholics.*' It sounds like Rene is warming up.

"This World Youth Day week at the top level, thanks to the media, is now like a bloody virus. At the bottom level, on the streets of Melbourne and Bendigo and Tatura, it looks like it might be a vaccine," says Father Bob whose metaphors are as good as John Updike's.

"Most of these young people would be clean living types."

"Yes," he agrees, "but they may well be lost in a kind of: 'what's the world all about?' so they're grabbing hold of this World Youth Day. If they are European visitors they may well have been through all of the horrors. Not them, because they're too young, but their families. The German Pope will be here, a man who was in the Hitler Youth. The last Pope who started World Youth Day, a Pole, Karol Wojtyla suffered the Germans and the Russians. Here we go, global Catholicism and local Catholicism. What am I doing here?" Bob moves his head from side to side and then says: "I suppose I'm local. I would like to think that local Catholicism is not just a franchise of global."

"Be that as it may," I say, "You are answerable to the Pope, aren't you? And he is the head of global Catholicism."

Father Bob looks at me quizzically. "The Roman Pope is often presented by his middle management as being more than first among equals; he is presented to Catholics all over the world as being the supreme ruler. I was just thinking yesterday, we might have the same problems as the British Queen. If she says she's the Queen of Orstralia, is the Pope the chief Bishop of Australia? Is George Pell working for the Pope? It comes out now with the media coverage of George and his problems. Who's working for whom? George Pell is saying: 'You can't sue us because Mr. Goodall (a disgraced paedophile priest) wasn't working for us.' You'd say: 'But he was a priest in a parish.' 'Yeah, but the relationship between the priest and the diocese is not one of employer and employee." Father Bob raises his voice substantially, making me jump. "Now what the hell is it? *I* don't know and I've been in the priesthood since 1960!"

I sit up straighter.

"I asked them once," says Bob. "I said: 'Who am I? Am I working for you or what?' and they ummed-and-arred."

"Nobody knows then?"

"Nobody knows," he affirms. "I want to know if I'm working for you because I want to know, do I have to do as I'm told or am I an independent consultant or what.' They all went away and rolled their eyes and God knows what. I said maybe we needed a union."

"Do you think that the Pope will apologise for the predatory behaviour of the paedophile priests who have ruined peoples' lives?"

"I don't know. I don't know what is going on. I said to a priest this morning. We are both old diggers. I said: "Here is the general being pilloried. Do you take Sir's side? 'No, No,' he said, 'You get him sacked.' That's the Aussie attitude to leadership. If he's no bloody good, well then, get him sacked."

"What's this priest's name? Maybe I could ask him for an interview."

"I'm not saying nothing!"

"You're getting cagey in your old age, Bob," I declare laughing.

"Yeah! I'm not saying nothing." He reads from another page that he has printed from the Internet: 'In Australia, connection and meaning are problematic. From the tabloids, to the scholarly quarterlies, observers remark on the superficiality of connection and meaning in Orstralian society. Binge drinking, gangs, and a selfish materialism are only a few of the phenomena attributed to the young as evidence for these weaknesses. It's no wonder that many fear that Australians will risk losing any strong sense of national identity.'"

"This is not some modern phenomenon. Young Aussies have always been binge drinkers if they've had the wherewithal to buy the grog."

'You certainly were! I don't know how many times you dried us out with alcohol.' How can I shut him up? Where the hell is Ronny?

"Have they?" asks Bob. Then he says: "You just have to think of the Aussie soldiers in Egypt during World War One I suppose. I'm just saying, and God knows it could turn and bite me on the bum, this superficiality of the *Orstralians*," he says screwing up his mouth, "may well be another sign that we have an a-cultural identity which means we're multicultural but at the same time we're a-cultural, which means *we haven't got any!*" The last four words leave his mouth like projectiles. And the next sentence is just as fast and just as loud: "*And we don't want any!*" Frank lifts his head from the armrest of his chair and looks at Bob as I laugh. He jumps down from his chair arches his back (the dog), and then wanders out into the passage.

"We've seen what it's done around the world," says Bob. "Somebody pops up and says: 'I come from Kurdistan or somewhere and my culture says this, this, this, and that,' and we're saying: 'Jeeze we don't really want the end product of that culture because look what it's done. Blood soaked all over the world. Everybody's living in blood stained territories. In Orstralia, with all these tourists, there's no blood anywhere. We might be like babes in the wood. There's no one here raping and pillaging, apart from say, the corporates. This is not a rape and pillage society and we don't want to slip into it."

Father Bob's secretary, Judy, announces that there is someone at the door to see Bob. He glances out the window and says: "Yeah, he's been around for thirty years." He withdraws ten dollars from his wallet and gives it to Judy to give to the beggar. "He used to get as drunk as an owl. He's one of those who came back from the dead. He comes here looking for a dollar. And also, I suspect, and if I were a woman I'd be able to work it out, that he's also looking for a place where he can occasionally drop in."

I asked for the silly bugger and now Ronny's singing a Gladys Knight and the Pips number: *If I Were Your Woman*.

> If I were your woman
> If you were my woman
> If I were your woman
> If you were my woman
> And you were my man

I smile inwardly. "Have you and Safran interviewed the lady who wrote *The Honey Spinners* yet?" I ask indicating a book sitting on top of the pile on the conference table. I'm still smiling.

"Yes, she was very difficult to interview," says Bob. "I wanted to talk to her as a beekeeper but she's not a beekeeper. She wrote about blind beekeepers and bees all over the world. Safran wanted to know if there are any electronic transmitters being attached to bees so they can monitor troop movements in Afghanistan. I was more interested in the bigger question of why the bees are disappearing around the world. I shouldn't be interested in it though because what the hell's it got to do with me?"

"And the frogs," I say. "I'd like to know how we are going to stop the frogs from being wiped out."

"And the frogs," agrees Bob.

"Once the bees and the frogs go, that's it," I declare, like some eminent scientist predicting the end of mankind.

"We probably used to be frogs," says Bob, "or something that came out of the water. I don't know where it's all gonna end, Ron, that's all I'm saying."

"Are you going to retire and go up the stairs before that happens?"

"No; unless it gets too much for the old brain. Because of the constant pursuit of looking for money, I can't make executive decisions on certain things that would drag me into the next episode of parish life, neighbourhood life, and personal life. I don't know if there's anything else. It looks a bit bleak, but still . . . "

We decide to leave matters hanging there because Father Bob has a busy schedule. Besides, I don't think Father Bob would be suited to retirement.

## Chapter 47: Cuban Cigars

*After some confusion about page numbers, he tells one of the worshippers to "snap out of it!"*

This is to be the last church service for me. I'm also having a sickie from work. I've bought a small gift for Father Bob and attached a small card. It is sitting on the front seat of the car as I drive over the Westgate Bridge. It will be spring in ten days time but there's no indication of it today. It's about nine degrees at the moment and has rained for most of the morning.

Poor old Bob is buggered. He sent me an email last night that said: 'Ron, I'm just exhausted. Remember that baby who I discovered on the parish house doorstep twenty years ago? Her adoptive father who lives in Canada wants to see me. How's that!' It is signed with his trademark: 'Respect. RJM.' I recollect Father Bob telling me about it one day, years ago, outside the church. It would have been a chance meeting in the street. The discovery took place about a year before I started delivering mail to Bob and he must have told me about it not long after I started as a postie.

The three drenched flags of resistance are hanging limply from the verandah of the rectory, I notice, as I slot into a parking spot, which seems to have been reserved for me, beside Father Bob's old van. I wonder what has happened to the Falcon sedan that he used to drive.

There's an army tent, with a small blue tent beside it under the eucalypts in the front garden. The kids from Galilee school pitched the little blue tent. They were concerned that there might be homeless kids looking for a place to sleep.

'Canvas Town Returns for South Melbourne's Homeless,' is the heading for Father Bob's latest Blog. In it he notes that despite showing interest earlier in doing a story about 'my problem of paying rent for the people who depend on me for health and safety, *A Current Affair* isn't interested any more. They've got Didak and the Shaws (Collingwood footballers) or the Beijing Olympic Games to keep the channel cashed up,' laments Father Bob. 'My union mates have stepped into the breach,' he says. 'Kevin Bracken, parishioner and Maritime Union State Secretary, and his mates have put up a sizeable tent, a symbolic gesture, to depict our willingness to share church land with my dependants.'

In the Blog, Bob says that South Melbourne was called Canvas

Town in the early 1850's and that Eureka happened in 1854. He writes: 'The Eureka tower, with its splash of gold (wealth) and slash of red (labour) looks down on our corner of Dorcas and Montague. Two Eureka Tower entrepreneurs, Bruno and Nonda, are regular contributors to the care of the poor emanating from our parish precinct.'

Bob's Blog is a relatively short piece but I'm willing to bet that even the older residents of the area would be ignorant of these facts. He writes: 'Our very street, Dorcas, is named for a Christian biblical woman of the 1st century of church history. She was an entrepreneur, too. She wove and dyed cloth to sell to make money to help the poor.'

History of the Parish Church and South Melbourne shows that dedication to helping the poor in this area started long before Abbé Pierre was even born. The Bloody Protestants get a mention in his article too. 'The local Anglican Church was named Dorcas before its current St. Luke,' he tells us.

'Not much of a mention,' sneers Descartes.

Father Bob says: 'It's time for me and this Catholic parish and our associates of all faiths, all social classes, who've cared for the poor for the last thirty-five years, to proudly present our efforts as a unique, urgent and flexible response to social exclusion, the toxic imprint left by laudable progress.'

I've got ten minutes to spare before the noon Mass so I get my camera and wander over to the tents. The showers have eased but big drops fall from the eucalypts as I take a couple of photos. I probably shouldn't pry, ('well, why are you doing it?' asks Descartes) but I do. I console myself by saying that I only want this information for the manuscript. Peering through the window in the tent I see that I am looking into someone's home. A thin mattress is in the corner with a rumpled blanket on top. There is a pair of shoes, in reasonably good condition, near the bed and a half full plastic container of orange juice beside them. I step back.

'What if someone had been home?' asks poor old Ronny with a shiver.

'Peeping Tom,' declares Descartes. I feel shocked but have a quick look over my shoulder and then quickly take a photo. What am I becoming? Maybe I can get a job with *News of the World*.

It's very cold in the Church but I'm well rugged up.

'The Pope is running around in Armani suits and red Italian shoes and poor old Bob in his worn out alb has to suffer like Jesus did,' says Ronny.

I put the gift on the altar and sit down with my camera beside me on the pew.

The usual crowd is in attendance: about a dozen, mainly Italians, of Bob's vintage. They all know each other. It's like a kind of club and once again, even in such a small gathering, I feel out of place. This is the last time so I try to put the thought out of my head.

When Father Bob steps up to the altar, he looks questioningly at the gift. "Did you put this here, Ron?" he asks.

"Yes, Father," I reply meekly.

"I gave 'em up three months ago, thank God," he growls. After some confusion about page numbers, he tells one of the worshippers to "snap out of it!" I put my head down like a worshiper and grin like the devil.

The Mass celebrates Pius X. "Giuseppe Sarto was his name. 'To defend the faith, and make all things new in Christ.' That was his motto," says Father. He repeats it in Latin. It is a tradesman-like performance, the type that Penny's father-in-law, Bill, would appreciate.

"Some good news according to Saint Matthew," chants Father. He reads a parable and finishes with Peter asking Jesus after they had eaten: 'Do you love me more than all the rest?' Peter was upset, see?" asks Bob looking at the parishioners. "You've got to get upset sometimes to get the facts. We're too comfortable." He reads a bit more and says: "Pius X, Global Pastor. Down to us at the corner of Dorcas and Montague, we're supposed to be the neighbourhood pastor. But unfortunately we look after ourselves," he says grimly. "See what I mean?" he asks the old Italians. "That's not the contract. The contract is to look after the others. This is the Gospel of the Lord."

When the Mass is over, Father Bob picks up the packet and asks: "Ron, am I to take this?"

"Yes, Father," I reply.

Ronny the romantic says: 'I hope he gives it to the bloke who lives in the tent.' He says that he likes the thought of a grizzled old bloke sitting back like a lord in the tent, smoking a Cuban cigar.

"Thank you," says Father Bob. He turns and walks out the side door.

Father Bob is a bit like Cranky Franky, I think, as I walk down the path, past the tents, to my car. When all is said and done, he takes all the blows and does it his way.

'I've got a better one,' says Rene Descartes: 'Life is meant for living. Even when my chips are low, there's still some left for giving.' '

## Chapter 48: Exponential Growth

*"I came into this organisation four years ago with the purpose of turning it around. It had been making losses for some time and I was recruited for that purpose." Ms Sue Renkin.*

You may remember the occasion when Bob was talking to the Archangel Gabriel. He said wistfully that he'd like to run Open Family again but thought that the odds were against this ever happening.

Ronny is confused; he thinks that Open Family is the name of a racehorse. The radio is on in the background and the race-caller just mentioned the sire, Family of Man, in relation to a runner in a later race.

Open Family has continued to perform poorly over the last eighteen months, unlike Family of Man. Father Bob says that Open Family was a charity based movement and was running as such until the division between him and the Board when he was callously bumped over the rails. The Open Family Board employed Ms Sue Renkin as Chief Executive Officer. Ms Renkin, who took over the reins of the volunteer run movement and turned it into an organisation run more on commercial lines, was recently reported in *The Age* as saying: "I came into this organisation four years ago with the purpose of turning it around. It had been making losses for some time and I was recruited for that purpose," Ms Renkin said.

'What? To make losses?' asks Descartes incredulously.

However, with the organisation now a million dollars in debt, corporate sponsorship receding, and morale ebbing like a gambler's lucky run, it's possible that Open Family will founder.

Father Bob told *The Age* that he wants to "take the charity back." He says: "This movement, founded in blood, sweat, and tears and made in Australia for Australian conditions, is being reduced to an old hack, which may still look good but is not doing much. It's terribly sad."

'Father Bob could organise a coup d'état,' says Ronny enthusiastically.

'A coup d'état,' sneers Descartes. 'That's a contusion caused by your half of the brain making contact with the skull.' He sniffs. 'Anyway Bob's too old; he's seventy five.'

Don't forget that he's already managing that mob-on-the-wall with its yearly turnover of three hundred thousand dollars. He's not too old at all. Bart Cummings was eighty-one when he trained Viewed, winner of the 2008 Melbourne Cup. Bob doesn't have to hang around the streets in order to run Open Family anymore than Bart has to run around the track to train a winner.

Rene listens to my argument and then says condescendingly: 'Yes, but Bart Cummings trains thoroughbreds. Bob Maguire would be working with a broken down old nag: about as useful as the sit-on-your-arse Catholic priests.'

Things go quiet in my scone for a few moments and then Ronny presents a possibility: 'What if the sit-on-your-arse Catholic priests *were* to become involved.'

Descartes doesn't respond. I mull the idea over. It's reasonable to suggest that they get off their collective arse and do something useful. Providing a spiritual oasis, as Bob described it, may be welcome to their parishioners but there are hungry, drug-dependent kids sleeping on the bloody streets and these priests are in a position to offer help. The Catholic Church owes a lot to society. Priests like Father Bob Maguire are the only ones in the Church who can do anything towards regaining the respect of society after the incredible amount of damage done by the Roman Catholic Thing and the 'tail' that protects it.

Ronny is bubbling now: 'With the sit-on-your-arse priests, as well as all *their* contacts, working for The Cause, Bob could work towards that exponential growth that he has always wanted: an explosion of street workers.' He smiles broadly. 'At Meekathara . . . '

Rene Descartes groans theatrically (à la Bob Maguire) and says to me: 'Tell Ronny he's dreaming.'

## Chapter 49: The Gladstone Bag

*"We don't give a rat's arse what happens to one another and we think everything should be left to the government."*

Frank is lying on the floor gnawing on a raw chop. He looks up as I enter the study and appears to be weighing his options. The chop wins.

Bob, who as usual is sitting behind his desk, takes the bundle of mail, greeting me with: "I'm sick of it. Oh God, it's all too much for me."

Rene Descartes warns me about wasting Father Bob's time: 'Consult your notebook, ask your questions and then get out! Bob has to go to a funeral,' he says brusquely. His persona has changed somewhat since I first started writing Bob's story: there is definitely a touch of the Maguire about his side of the cauliflower now.

"Is there any real chance of getting Open Family back, Father?"

"No, I'm not interested, although Twentyman wants to keep up the struggle. The bloody thing is probably dead and buried anyway. The modus operandi should have been to get involved with the nuts and bolts," he says as if he were talking about a Meccano set. "If I had it back though I wouldn't have to reinvent myself, like I do with my Foundation. The Foundation is a reinvention. I have to go around begging again. I've got no infrastructure this time." Bob shakes his head. "The point that Les Twentyman and others have made, and I think it's trivial, is that if people think that I am Open Family they will support Open Family because they think they are supporting me. At that point I probably should withdraw from the discussion because it becomes too political for me. I'm an activist but I'm also a clergyman so I don't give a rat's arse about who's doing what to whom. I haven't got the time or the energy to *work out* who's doing what to whom. Once you are involved in the Church, you become a bloody self-sacrificial person. If you're in the real world with a business and a wife and a reputation and a future you have to defend your patch. I don't defend my patch; if they want it they can have it."

I consult my notebook as Rene nods his approval and Frank wanders out of the study. "You will be seventy-five next week which is the mandatory retirement age for priests. I know that you want to continue in the job but do you really think that the Romans will try to force you out?"

"They can do what they bloodywell like. They're Romans. I've been waiting to see what dirty tricks are in the offing. It's been a big week for me. Phone rang Wednesday: 'It's the Archbishop. I'll be there in twenty minutes,' " says Bob in his Archbishop voice. "I didn't have time to call for help because before I knew what hit me he was knocking on the bloody door. Luckily Judy was present to take notes. By the time he left, I was feeling ninety years of age, not seventy-five, the age of statutory senility. He gave me two dates for compliance: one was my birthday: he expects a letter of resignation. The other is a month later: he expects me to vacate the premises."

"Are you going to resign?"

"No. I won't resign. There's more things to be done; the job isn't finished." Then he prays in a whisper: "Jesus, Mary and Giuseppe."

"If you are pushed, what do you think is the future for this parish?"

"If, by that time, the locals haven't got a committee dedicated to the immediate future, including my position, then there's nothing I can do. And as you know, the Orstralians, even when it comes to bushfires, would prefer to wait and see what happens. If someone presents them with a warning saying that we could be heading into a terrible fire season, they say: 'Yes, but we might not be.' They might send me notification saying: 'Please vacate the premises within one week's time.' If it happens, it happens. One has only been a reactor over one's lifetime but one will battle on. One will eat one's vegetables and take one's pills."

"Is there any possibility of them sending you to a quiet parish in the scrub?"

"No; my understanding is that they don't do that. I can't be sure though because the hierarchy speaks with a forked tongue."

"You haven't got a razoo to your name and you'd have nowhere to live. Surely they won't turn you out."

"The simple Roman solution would be: 'We've got places where old priests like you can go. Collect the key for a unit off Mr. Bloggs.' "

Rene Descartes clears his 'throat.'

"How do you see your future panning out if you don't get kicked out?"

Father Bob leans back and hitches his trousers up over his potbelly. He looks directly at me and says: "The answer is to battle on regardless of all this palaver, in which case you end up involved in the opening of the Regional Catholic Primary School by the end of the year; you end up, hopefully, in the lease of 'alf your empty school buildings to the State of Victoria for thirty public housing units; you end up trying to plan what the parish Church should be doing to pastorally care for the Southbank Catholics, St Kilda Rd Catholics: all those on the periphery in the new towers; and I presume you would try to clean up this House of Hospitality so that it becomes available to both the socially well placed Catholics who are safe and secure (they should be able to drop in too and do whatever middle-class Catholics do: read books or drink tea) and the other lot, the pooah. The backyard where we feed the pooah should be revisited and renovated. We are in a fairly efficient feeding mode: we've got forty or fifty coming to be fed now, four times a week and we've got two buses going out to feed 'em on the street," says Bob.

"It sounds as if things are going well as far as the parish is concerned."

"That's the interesting thing," says Bob enthusiastically. "This year I may well get what I've been looking for over the past thirty-six years: enough resources, owned and managed by the parish to be able to do the things that the parish feels it is called to do. This year, this very day, we are in the throes of talking to your State Government about the lease of those empty school buildings."

Judy ushers in a lady named Muriel, from Middle Park, who has called in to give Father Bob a hundred dollars for the poor.

"The Spring racing season is nearly upon us," says Bob as he takes the cheque and reaches for his receipt book.

"Yes, good luck," laughs Muriel. "I hope it does well."

"In the old days, I would have spoken to one of the leading parishioners up the back lane: he was a big time bookmaker as well as one of the pillars of the church."

'Fleece the pooah on Saturday, and thank the Lord on Sunday.' Rene sniffs.

"God bless your heart and soul, Muriel."

Muriel smiles at Bob, turns to leave and steps on the half-eaten chop with its straggly white sinews hanging off the bone.

"That's my lunch," quips Bob as quick as you like. "Goodbye, Mother," he adds as Muriel leaves laughing.

Bob inclines his head and says: "The rich like her should be able to come in without fear or favour but it may be an impossible task to have a Catholic parish that is doing both. I'd like to think that you could, but in reality . . . if she walked in and came across Barnabus." He screws up his face. "Well, you'd say in principle she should be able to put up with it, but in practice it may be too much to expect. Whereas if the place had been like this for one hundred years and you *knew* that it was half madhouse and half monastery, it would be a different thing but this has only been going on for about thirty of the last one hundred and fifty years."

"Do you think that the bosses have got a plan for your future or for the future of the parish?"

"I'm probably paying headquarters too big a compliment by thinking they have a plan because I've been told a hundred times in the last month: 'Don't think that headquarters has got a plan. Don't fuel your paranoia by thinking that there's a plan to get rid of you *or the parish* because they haven't got one.'"

"No plan at all is better than a plan that is against you."

The dog bounds in then, pounces on his mauled chop and starts flinging it around the room, charging around the study like a mad thing.

"Yeah. But being an old digger . . . although I should have known that even the diggers battled on in the face of no-plan-generals. That, then, is the position we are in: we are in a state of flux. If I could get say fifty out of the two hundred Sunday churchgoers to form a Catholic think tank that could go from thinking to doing that would be the best solution in the world but the lack of interest by the parishioners now is as stunning as it was when I first got here."

"Nothing has changed. That must be disheartening."

"It's a different quality of disinterest. It's not opposition. The disinterest when I first came here was due to the fact that the Catholics were blue collar. They didn't want to go to a meeting. It would have been like going to a union meeting."

"Yes."

"They didn't want to do nothin'. Over the years we've prodded the dead horse several times. I was a romantic; I thought that the horse wasn't dead: it was only playing dead. Bob grimaces. "Maybe the bloody horse *is* dead. Now, if the horse is dead . . . " He leaves the sentence hanging like a bridle on the wall. "You'd hate to be doing something just for the sake of doing it because you would have institutionalised your own chaos although I said to Judy the other day when we were discussing this: 'You need a job. I need a place to sleep. If we accept the fact that the horse is dead well then we just carry on as though it were alive."

Bob starts talking about football and checks his diary to see if he is going to be able to make it to the finals. "If God is good, this will be off," he says referring to an old entry in his diary.

Descartes pulls out his cattle prod. I nod imperceptibly and say:

"You started your vocation as an assistant priest. Where's *your* assistant, the man who you are mentoring?"

"There aren't any priests. You can only get 'em from Indonesia or somewhere."

"Don't the Catholics operate a priest factory anymore?"

"No. It's a dying art. There's nothing in it. There's no ethos. In the old days you thought you were being commissioned to come and bring good news to the pooah and to heal the broken hearted but these days the Aussies go to the clinic to be healed. We are in danger of losing civil society, meaning the civil society where we all look after one another more or less. There is a collapse of civil society: we don't give a rat's arse what happens to one another and we think everything should be left to the government. Whereas the old style was: 'we'll have to do it ourselves.' How the hell can you do it yourself in a city? I'm saying to the bosses: 'Leave us alone for Christ's sake. Get out of the road. Let us trade on our own merits and we will develop.'" Bob looks at his watch. "Come on, Ron, get out! We mustn't keep the dead waiting."

As I'm about to walk out of the study door, I turn like Lieutenant Columbo to ask that one last question. "What will you do if the Archbishop does force you to leave the premises, Bob?"

Father Bob Maguire shrugs. "If it does happen I've got a Gladstone bag. I'll put a couple of things in it and go out to the nearest bus stop."

# Chapter 50: Father Bob and the Clerical Cliché

> *"When I took over the parish in 1973, there was no money. I went around finding the real estate assets because Headquarters was always reluctant to tell me where they were."*

It's September 2009. Father Bob hasn't begun to pack his Gladstone bag yet but the Archbishop probably wishes that he'd get on with it.

"He's been stalking me since 2002," says Bob grimly like a complainant talking to the sergeant of police. "At 75, I feel as if I am a condemned man."

Bob is now embroiled in what is becoming a public and acrimonious fight with His Grace, the Archbishop of Melbourne, Denis Hart. The drama, which is playing out on the morning shows on television and on the nightly newscasts, is as popular as *Neighbours*.

In the latest development, the Archbishop is claiming that Father Bob has financially mismanaged the parish. The Archbishop is not accusing Bob of impropriety he says, but between March 1980 and 2004, when money has been tight, Bob has seen fit to sell off seven parish properties for three million dollars to cover operating expenses.

'Bloody bewdy,' says Ronny, wiggling his grey eyebrows and flashing up an image of Grandfather Maguire reciting Othello onto my 'screen.'

Yes, the words hit home because the Archbishop, by accusing Bob of financially mismanaging the Parish, is filching from Bob his good name and making him poor indeed. (With apologies to The Bard.)

Father Bob's private reaction to the Archbishop besmirching his good name should be interesting so at our next session I become the Archbishop's attorney: "You've been selling off the firm's real estate," I accuse.

"That's all bullshit!" Bob bristles. Frank jumps out of his chair and skulks out of the study.

"He's signed off on those deals. What are you talking about? It was of no earthly use anyway. I write a letter saying: 'Dear Sir or Madam, The South Melbourne Parish needs cash to keep trading; however, I have a little piece of collateral across the road which will sell for $300,000 and will cover our present debts and our spending for the next twelve months. Yours faithfully.'"

"What are they worried about then?" I glance out the window at the little pieces of collateral across the road.

"Nothing!"

"All that's got nothing to do with forcing you out then?"

"Nooo! It's an illusion." Bob roars. "The more you get into the murk, the more you become disillusioned as anybody does who starts to peel away the layers of an institution. You go into it and ask yourself if this is all there is. 'I've wasted a year. I thought that I was going to end up with a dark conspiracy.' It's like Dan Brown's novels: he depicts the whole show as being a bloody global conspiracy. Wrong; it's just made up of mutts: dills thrashing around making a mess; more like a global conspiracy of children."

"They're novels though."

"Yes, but yours is almost a novel too," he grins as he manoeuvres the conversation around to the manuscript.

I smile sheepishly and agree. He never took this much interest in the manuscript before he became aware of the Cauliflower-twins.

"What I'm saying is: would this bit about Archbishop Hart not spoil the story?" Bob says, shifting from protagonist to publisher.

"No. I think that it will put an end to the story. After the fight, if you win, you will be more or less reborn as a Parish Priest and you can start again in the position that you were about to be kicked out of."

'Which is what he always wanted to do,' says Ronny, 'start over again, just like Jesus. On the corner of Dorc-arse Street,' he adds with a laugh.

At this stage in the serial, Father Bob's 'stalker' does not want Bob to start again. He reveals that between 1998 and 2008 the parish incurred deficits for eight of the eleven years totalling $1.191 million and only made a profit for 2000, 2003 and 2004 because he sold property assets to the value of $1.5 million. The Archbishop, unlike Father Bob, appears to be a dour man showing little warmth in his media outings, but he knows how to play up to that media. He tells *The Age* that: "Outgoings have been considerable so that basic bills can't be met and we (the diocese) have had to help with that."

Father Bob counters with: "That's very naughty of Denis. We have had our suits working with Headquarters trying to raise bridging finance until we get this lease of the empty school sorted out with the State Government." He says that when he took over the parish in 1973 "there was no money. I went around finding the real estate assets because Headquarters was always reluctant to tell me where they were."

Bob also tells *The Age* that he has "personally kicked in $360,000, or $200 a week" since he became parish priest. "That's the spirit in which things are done around here. It's only since Denis, with his economic rational attitude, was appointed in 2002, that issues of assets being sold became a problem."

Tony Long, chairman of the South Melbourne Parish Council, rejects the Archbishop's statement that the parish is no longer financially viable. "The Archbishop doesn't believe spending money on the poor and homeless is a reasonable use of the church's capacities." He says that the parish and the archdiocese have different philosophies about appropriate ways to use the parish's assets. He also says that the Archbishop's comments are "an outrageous mis-description. Bob's view is that if assets are surplus to need they can be sold and the monies used."

The public seems as enthusiastic as a picture-theatre full of kids at one of those afternoon matinees of years ago where they paid ninepence to get in and spent much of the time rolling Jaffas down the wooden aisles much to the chagrin of the ushers. Father Bob in his role as the white knight can be seen beaming amiably as he banters with the 'morning crew' of a television station. At one point, he has everyone in hysterics with a melodious rendition of the John Lennon classic "Allll we are sayyyyinggg, is give priests a chance". Bob's comic but mischievous response to his predicament and his up-beat breakfast bonhomie is extra cream for the presenters' Corn Flakes: Bob the Battler taking on the establishment ("And we're all behind you, Bob, aren't we, everyone?"). There are flashes of the Archbishop, portrayed as the black knight scowling under a black mitre.

Readers will no doubt know the result of this sacerdotal scrap: The public elect, white knight, is wounded but not done in (yet). It's a clichéd story that has already been told in newspapers Australia wide, where at the end of the day everything 'moves forward,' is 'melted down' or 'rolled out' and where people who have suffered adversity just want to 'get on with their lives'. In this priestly power-play, the Archbishop asks Bob to step down and move on before St Peter (or St Paul) finally calls him up to the Pearly Gates of Heaven.

At our increasingly frequent sessions, Father Bob enthusiastically talks about the manuscript and the struggle to get a publisher to sign up, but despite the way he seems to embrace the media he is reluctant to talk about his public battle with the Archbishop.

"I can't see that what we've got isn't enough: we've got the postie and the bloody priest. I like the fusion of the two worlds. I don't really want too much bullshit about the Archbishop. Except in passing. I suppose I'm just blotting it out because it's too wearying to think about. They're meeting here this morning, the dumb suits. 'Let's build up his profile so that at least we will have the Bob Maguire champion horse running in the race against the heavily backed Diocesan authority horse, but I could drop dead and there'd be no bloody horse left. "

"*The Postie and the Priest* is another horse that could still be running on after you drop dead."

'Jesus,' groans Ronny and this time it is Descartes who laughs.

Bob laughs also. "This is a friendly horse too. He's not out there slagging Denis. There's no value in doing that. But, you are the author."

"Yes."

"How do you see the story up to date?"

"I'm hoping that it finishes with you mounting up again."

"I was attracted to that other idea you had, but it's too hard. I think we all might have to end up talking in parables."

"Do you mean turning it into fiction?" At one stage I thought about doing a Frank Hardy and fictionalising the story as Hardy did with 'Power Without Glory.' Father Bob Maguire becomes Father Bill McGoo or somebody, Henry Nissen is replaced by my old mate Caz, an ex boxer who marries a Russian bride with comical consequences. True stories become fiction, which would really let Ronny off the leash.

"Yeah! But it'd be too hard," says Father who once confessed to liking book characters more than real life people, a man who learns by osmosis, a man it seems who would prefer to be protagonist in a novel: a character of the third person.

"Maybe I could do it but I don't really want to."

"What's wrong with fiction?"

"I love fiction; in fact I reckon I'm probably better at writing fiction than doing this. My interviewing technique could be better, but I'd rather persevere."

"If we want to go into the marketplace why couldn't we go to an ordinary printer and print a batch of the manuscript?"

"Because it's too hard to distribute. We'd have to personally visit the bookshops and convince each manager to stock it."

"But say we put it on Twitter or somewhere like that?"

"Not enough people would read it."

"Say we didn't want to make money though," says Bob. We are starting to sound like two school kids inventing a new game.

"In that case we could publish it as an ebook, I suppose, but what's the point?"

"Isn't it better for the point of art, for art's sake, to get the story out and then if it's that bloody good . . .?"

"It's probably not that bloody good."

"But it may be that bloody good. The genre . . ."

"Maybe that's the problem: the genre. It's not a normal biography."

"No, it's creative and innovative."

I laugh, but Bob insists that it is. "The publishers are simply not adventurous," he states emphatically. "I sent you a couple of prospective publishers from people on Twitter."

"Yes, I got them thanks but let's just *please* stick with this publisher for a while longer eh?"

"But we will be dead before . . ." Bob stops talking, raises his eyebrows like Ronny and we laugh. "Could it be published this afternoon, as it is?"

"No; we have to finish this bit about the Archbishop. I've sent him a letter asking for an interview."

"You'll have to take strong medicine before you go near him."

"I'd like to hear what he thinks about the way you have both made use of the press."

"Ron, I could turn religious at any minute and say: 'I'm leaving it in the hands of God,' but that's not going to sell," says Father Bob sounding like a pulp fiction writer who is more interested in marketing than writing prose.

"It's probably because you've developed such a good relationship with the press."

"They come to me. I don't go to them. What the hell would I be doing going to them? I wouldn't be smart enough. My enemies, though, think that I'm that media-savvy. No! No! Now put that in print: 'He never goes near the press. He never goes near the press; the press comes to him.' "

"But you are well prepared; you got up this morning at 6am to argue your case in front of the bloody cameras."

Father Bob says: "Arrrrrrrrrr," as if I'm a doctor checking his tonsils. "I made a tactical decision; I said to meself or somebody said to me," he says stopping to think. "Say it was Mother Mary McKillop; that'll go well in the book: 'Mother Mary McKillop said to 'im: "take every phone call; say yes. Trust in me," Mother Mary McKillop said.' "

"It's turning out to be a good strategy."

"Do everything or nothing and then trust in . . ." he stops mid-sentence again. "You'll have to leave it blank because the Aussies won't want to hear 'trust in God.' You'll have to leave it blank," he says again. There are four of us writing the story now: me, Ronny, Rene Descartes and Father Bob Maguire. "Trust," he says, "that's all I can do. I've got no hope in hell of fighting against headquarters. Forget about it! But then the phone rings; and then the phone rings; and then the phone rings; and then the phone rings; and then the phone rings, and away it goes. It's got a life of its own. You'll have to explain that. If I were writing a pious pamphlet I would say: 'He is putting his trust in the God whom he has served faithfully for fifty years and this is the outcome. For those who believe in God an explanation is not necessary. For those who do not believe in God an explanation is not possible."

"That sounds like a pretty good explanation to me."

"That's what's happening. Do they think I'm sitting here like some kind of a bloody entrepreneur working out a strategy? No. I just know what not to do."

"That on its own is a good strategy: to know what not to do even if you don't know what to do. If you know what not to do you can't get into too much trouble."

"No. Therefore if somebody pops up on one of those web pages wanting to do Denis in then I'm saying: 'If you want to take this kafuffle as an opportunity to air your own grievances about child abuse or something then you'll have to fight me before you get near Denis. I was reading a book the other day about Global Catholicism where the author talks about the Roman church being the global corporate versus the local church, especially the Irish local church, and I suppose that this is a clash of cultures between Denis and me. This is a clash of cultures, not a clash of poor little Bobby Maguire and Denis Hart, the Archbishop of Melbourne; it goes beyond that. I'm saying that if I could, like the Watergate man, forensically, track down the evidence, look at all the papers, Archbishop Hart would come out crying his bloody eyes out saying that this is a terrible travesty of justice. But I just haven't had the time or the energy. I can do bits of it; if you follow me around today I can pull bits out that'll show beyond any reasonable doubt that this is a clash of cultures. This is not offensive behaviour by a rogue Roman Catholic priest."

The global juggernaut with his grace Denis Hart as Goliath and the redoubtable Father Bob Maguire standing in as plucky local hero David, minus however, the crude armament which balanced up the odds. It may be a travesty of justice but the little man rarely prevails in the long run. Bob will eventually leave the parish one-way or another and as the late legendary race-caller, Ken Howard, might have commented: 'you can bet London to a brick on' that his replacement will be quieter and less of a nuisance to those at the top. Meanwhile the real villains in this clichéd Catholic cliffhanger, the paedophile priests (who are themselves so common as to be platitudes), slip back behind the skirting boards as Father Bob yet again cops the treatment from headquarters.

As a decision becomes imminent, it is hard for Father Bob to spare me any time for an interview so I'm reluctant to even ask. I resort to posing questions by email and occasionally ring his mobile phone. The two camps now have their lawyers talking to each other.

'The prominent Catholic marriage has broken down and the courts will now have to decide,' says Ronny. All this business about priests, parishes, dioceses and Archbishops has been white sauce to Ronny's side of the cauliflower and he is licking dollops off his chin.

"No," laughs Father Bob when I ring him. "We've got pro bono and friendly lawyers: just because they can talk, not because they've been hired to defend me, and because they can talk the language of the bureaucrats in town: so I end up with my suits talking to their suits. Never again Denis and me."

The show goes on; the suits become the spokespersons and Father Bob even refers some press people to them. He has hopes that the Archbishop will "back orf entirely," he tells me by mobile phone as he travels into town in the back of a car with his solicitors "to sign the bloody document." It's 25th September 2009, eleven days after his 75th birthday. Before saying: "Goodbye, Your Grace," he amends his 'condemned man' metaphor, saying quietly: "At 75, I feel like a felon who is about to be convicted."

Bob goes in hoping for five years and comes out with two-and-a-bit, which is comparable to a felon going to court hoping to get two-and-a-bit and getting five. "Two-and-a-bit is not very long to do anything but my suits said: 'Darling, this is all we can get just now, short of going to VCAT to contest the whole question of age,' he tells me over the phone. "There's more to it than age though," says Bob. "I can't argue with Denis Hart personally because I'm part of the institutional Church, a big part of which is the administration of property. I've agreed to let the Archbishop run the place and I've agreed to resign in February 2012 but I don't know whether the public will want that," he adds.

The floorboards are reverberating; the white knight has won for the moment. Father Bob Maguire remains priest of South Melbourne Parish for another two-and-a-bit years. At least that's the colourful clichéd image that is presented by the press. The black-and-white print is more revealing: in reality the black bishop has demeaned the white knight by making the knight's tenure as priest conditional on him handing over financial management of the Parish. The black bishop is now dominating the white knight.

'It's nearing endgame and bishops are stronger than knights 60 percent of the time,' says Rene sounding like one of the Friday night Channel Seven football commentators, who churn out useless statistics and drool over the physical exploits of young players.

'But it's what the knight does in the game that's important and the knight's strategy is sound,' continues Rene brushing aside the image of constipated commentators grunting out statistics.

"I don't mind getting knocked off in a fair struggle, but not by stealth," comments the white knight when I ask him about the black bishop's crafty move.

'A knight should always be in the centre of the action, moving preemptively rather than reactionary and defensively . . .' Ronny interjects mocking Rene: 'A knight on the rim is grim,' and cops a clip over the ears from Descartes for his cheek.

# Chapter 51: More Tea, Vicar?

*Bob is very outspoken but he's very loyal to the Church.*

Imagine my surprise one morning when reading the local paper, *The Advocate*, to discover that perhaps there is a bit more flexibility in the retirement rule than the Archbishop would have us believe. It seems that the 75 and you're out caper doesn't apply equally to all the foot soldiers in the Roman legion.

Father Peter Carrucan (pronounced ka-rew-can), a contemporary of Father Bob's, has just hung up his cassock and he's seventy-eight. Father Carrucan has worked in the western suburbs for the past 20 years and has just retired from Holy Eucharist Parish St Albans South, home to a branch of the Shiny Suburban Catholics, although the parish is mainly made up of migrants. On reading of Father Peter's retirement I was surprised that the reporter didn't make more of Peter's age. After all it was only eight months since the Archbishop tried to force Father Bob out at 75 and the press was indignant. So how could this bloke stay on three more years and apparently retire when he wanted? Curious, it wasn't long before I had the good Father's contact details and tapped out an email to him via his old parish.

Yesterday, when I told Ladybugs that I was going to bake some scones for today's afternoon tea with the priest she said: "What do you want to do, kill the poor old bugger?" This morning she was up baking scones before going to work.

Father Peter is a tall softly spoken priest: another stranger who is willing to go out of his way after being asked to talk about Bob. To compare the two Catholic priests is a bit like comparing the two Jewish street workers: The little bloke with the bent nose is a different man to the one who reads from the Torah at Father Bob's services.

"There are a lot of others who would know Bob better than me," Father says after he sits down.

"Would you like a scone, Father Cacurran? (Pronounced Ka-curran)"

'You bloody idiot,' hisses Descartes. 'His name is Carrucan.'

"A scone. Oooh, I'll have a scone," says Father with obvious glee.

I then tell him the story about Ladybugs making the scones and he says:

"I'll always say 'yes' to a scone." His eyes barely leave the plate.

Peter was ordained in 1962, two years after Bob and agrees with Bob's description of life at the 'semetery.' "We did anything we could to keep ourselves occupied;" he laughs, "otherwise we would have gone mad."

Peter doesn't remember Bob as a beekeeper though he does remember another of Bob's occupations. "In the seminary he was always a very strong personality. I remember that Bob was a football and cricket umpire." This is news to me, I think to myself: Bob had not mentioned this stint as a rule-keeper. "He umpired a lot and was certainly good at it. But they hated him too; they hated all umpires," he says matter-of-factly with a laugh, as if unsurprised that the universal rule of hating umpires should apply to the clergy too. "Bob walked off the field one day I remember. That was the end of that game! I took it on for a little while when I had a crook leg but I couldn't stand the abuse. I thought: 'Bugger it; I'm not putting up with this!'"

Ronny is shocked. The thought of a mob of trainee priests abusing one of their own is disconcerting. Maybe it's a testosterone stopcock, I think.

Whilst I'm boiling the kettle and breaking out the best china from the sideboard ('otherwise know as bunging on side,' notes Descartes with a cliché of his own) Peter asks me if I've interviewed Father Bob's mate Paul Garland. I tell him that I would have liked to but thought it prudent not to try after being told that he had had a breakdown.

'People do recover from nervous breakdowns!' says Rene Descartes in exasperation.

Peter gives me Paul Garland's address and says: "It would be a good idea to talk to Paul; he's like Bob: he never stops talking. Tell Bob that if he wants a decent biography then you'll have to talk to Paul," he laughs.

Whilst the cauliflower ponder this further I set the table, put some scones on a plate, with the jam in one dainty container and the clotted cream beside it in another (all set out especially by Ladybugs) and make the tea. As I'm pouring it into the cups, Father Peter says: "Bob has always been an inspiration. I admire him very much for his commitment to the principle of justice and fairness. He's fearless when it comes to issues that he feels very strongly about. For all his maverick behaviour he's got a great sense of loyalty and faithfulness to God and to the Church and to people."

'Even to the Archbishop,' Ronny chips in laconically.

"What else would you like to ask me?" says Father, as if making it easier for me to come to the point, so I do just that.

"Bob was asked by the Archbishop to retire at 75. That doesn't appear to have happened with you."

"According to Canon law, when a priest turns 75, the Archbishop contacts the priest to find out whether he wants to retire or whether he would like to continue. That's what happened in my case: I decided not to retire. I don't know why he insisted on Bob finishing at 75. It's really up to the priest to make the decision, unless the bishop has good reasons."

"Bob seems to think that your case was different because you had never been any trouble to the Archbishop," I say as I pour the tea.

"Yes, that's right. People like me wouldn't cause the Archbishop any trouble at all because we don't make waves. Rarely does he even come into our thinking because we are busy about our work."

'Like one of Bob's bees.' Notes Ronny helpfully.

Placing Father's tea in front of him, I comment: "He comes across to me as a man devoid of feelings."

"Every person brings whatever they can to the job," says the diplomatic priest after sipping his tea. "It's a huge job that he's got. He has his own way of operating; you have to respect that. I think that Bob respects him very much. We all respect the Archbishop. It doesn't necessarily mean that we like everything he says but we all respect the position that he holds and the sign that he is to us. Bob is very outspoken but he's very loyal to the Church. Frank Little used to say that ninety-five percent of priests don't bother him at all and the other five percent drive him mad. It wouldn't be people like Bob," he hastens to add. "There's nothing wrong with what Bob's doing," and I smile. "You'd have to ask the bishop why Bob wasn't afforded the same treatment as me," he says quietly, resting his cup back on the saucer.

"That's what I hope to do. He's only given Bob another two-and-a-bit-years. Were you allowed to stay on indefinitely?"

"I felt a little bit of pressure to finish but still felt as if I was being respected even though they were putting pressure on me. I must have mentioned retirement at some stage though because they never let me forget it. The Archbishop's a good man. Like all of us, we try our best but we ask God to forgive us for the harm that we've done. Bob's the same. He does the best he can and his best is very good. I've heard him say: 'God forgive me for the harm I've done today.'

I too have heard that little prayer. "Jam, Father?" I ask as the priest breaks open a scone.

'More tea, Vicar?' asks Ronny with an invisible grin. It doesn't elicit much of a smile from me though because I'm busy doing my arithmetic.

Seventy-five plus two-and-a-bit equals seventy-seven-and-a-bit: not far from seventy-eight. Financial mismanagement aside, maybe Bob's sentence is not so harsh after all. When I had first read the article in *The Advocate* I wondered why Father Peter was allowed to priest-on until he chose to stop. Not so it would seem: subtle pressure was also brought to bear on him to retire.

"Yes please. I can't believe I'm having scones," he says, picking up his teacup. "We know our ancestry when we have scones."

"Yes I suppose we do; I've never thought of it like that," I say, wondering what he thought of the chapter entitled: 'Father Bob And The Mobile Priest' that I sent to him in my introductory email. Uncannily he says: "What I like about Bob is that he's not afraid to be the figure of Christianity in all kinds of things. He talks about the brothel in that chapter you sent me. He's got people in South Melbourne and St Kilda who are into the common pastoral care of disadvantaged women. They've got access to the women and the women can talk to them about the education of their kids. He does so much good to embrace everybody.

"When I was in the Belgrave parish, we had an old house that we wanted to convert into a home for homeless girls. It created a lot of opposition in the parish when we were debating it. I turned to Bob for help. He gave me the courage to push ahead and set up the house. He sent up this guy whose trousers were held up with string, and who had rings all around his ears and in his nose," says the priest as we both reach for another scone, "and he couldn't have sent anyone better. This guy just sat there until it was time for him to talk and then he said: 'I don't know what you are arguing about. Why wouldn't you want to help these kids? If they come to the city they will die. Why wouldn't you want to help them stay alive? That changed the whole tempo of the meeting. We started the house for the girls."

"Is it still going?"

"No. It lasted for quite a while though; it outlasted me. It was still going when I left the parish some years later. The care of the girls was always a problem; sometimes we were going well and other times we were struggling but it did help to change the mentality of the parish."

The ability for the local priest to shape and influence the mentality of the parish has probably been a lot easier since the relaxation of the rules with Vatican Two and I ask Peter what he thinks about Father Bob's metaphorical 'tail' taking control of the 'dog' again.

"Nobody can stop the Spirit," he says after considering for a few moments. "They might try to impede the Spirit but all this sexual abuse that's coming out of the Church is going to bring change and that vision coming from the Vatican Council will eventually fall into place. It's not a newness of teaching; the whole purpose of the Vatican was about practice: to bring Church into the world, not change the doctrines. It's about presenting the doctrine and our vision of life in a world that's rapidly changing. I don't think you can stop that because things are happening; no matter how much you exert the push to go backwards it's not going to happen."

"You mentioned earlier that you are going overseas next week."

"Yes, I'm off to Christmas Island tomorrow: a little dot in the middle of the Indian Ocean."

"Anything to do with the detainees?"

"Yes."

"What are you going to do?"

He sighs. "Well, I'll soon find out. I've just spent an hour with the director of the pastoral care. He's painted a pretty good picture of the work that I'll be trying to do. Ask me when I come back."

"How long will you be there for?"

"Two and a half weeks. It's not long but apparently you can't stay very long because the work is too exhausting. One of the teachers told me today that one of the nuns came back; she was supposed to do an eight-week stint and she only did three weeks. It's not only the terrible stories you hear from these poor people but also the weather: it's very oppressive."

"Well, you'll get away from the cold weather for a little while and provide pastoral care to some distressed people whilst you're there."

"I hope so, Ron. Tell your wife the scones were lovely," he says as he lays his knife neatly on the plate.

"Thank you. I will, Father."

"This has turned out to be a better afternoon than I'd expected," he says. "My mother used to make scones just like these every Sunday afternoon when we were kids. Roast lunch and afternoon tea with scones. I was amazed when I went to England: they still have the Sunday roast and high tea at five o'clock. It's a bit different in St Albans with the migrants: they don't know what scones are."

"No. There would be more Afghans in St Albans than Poms, I should think."

"Yes. One of the nicest things that ever happened to me in all the time that I worked at St Albans concerned a woman from Afghanistan who was a member of the Hazari tribe. She had four kids and couldn't read or write in her own language or in English. In Afghanistan, the Taliban had attacked her home; she lost a few front teeth when they knocked her out. Her husband was taken away and thereafter she didn't have any idea what had happened to him. Shortly after that, a man came and asked her if she was interested in getting away from the place with her children. Convinced that her husband was dead and afraid that she, her children and mother-in-law would be killed if they stayed, she paid the people smuggler. The family travelled across Southern Afghanistan and Pakistan by truck. From Pakistan they travelled into Karachi, Kuala Lumpur and into Jakarta. From there they came by boat to Port Hedland. They were released from Port Hedland after three weeks and we found a place for them amongst her own people with another Afghani family in St Albans. Both families had lost the husband/father figures." The priest smiles and continues: "Whenever we wanted to take a photo of this woman, she would put her head down. Gradually she tried to find out what had happened to her husband. She would often go from our place to different areas where it was rumoured that Afghanis, Pakistanis or Iranians were gathered.

"Early one morning, she came into the office with a row of numbers on a piece of paper. She asked me whether I would dial that number; it was a Pakistani number. We sat down and I dialled the number; we had a speakerphone so when a male person answered I looked at her and she nodded. I left them. About forty five minutes, later she came out of the room absolutely transformed."

"She wouldn't have been worried about her teeth."

"By that time her teeth had been fixed. She hadn't seen or heard of him for four years and found him through all these contacts. Her face was just suffused with joy. That's the nicest experience that's ever happened to me. The guy who was working with me said: 'That's the end of you as her number one man.' She worked for another couple of years and eventually got him out. That was the end of me; she no longer needed me. That was great; it's a lovely story."

"It sure is."

"I told that and another story recently at my farewell. This is such a good story, one that's connected to the Christmas story of the Catholic Church." Father Peter recounts that two days before Christmas, a Christian woman and her two sons were released from Port Hedland but had nowhere to stay. The authorities contacted him at Holy Eucharist and asked if he could accommodate the family. "We thought of the connection with Jesus and his parents with no room at the inn and were determined to help them." Christmas drew nigh and the NO VACANCY sign outside the 'inn' shone brightly. Father said a prayer and rang a Muslim family: a husband and wife with three children. "On Christmas night, the Immigration Department brought the Christian family to the Muslim family's home," says Father, his eyes shining. He pinches the bridge of his nose and wipes his eyes with his thumb and index finger before quickly shifting attention away from his own work back to Father Bob. "Well, Ron, I'll have some great stories to tell when I get back home but we should get back to Bob Maguire." What would these 'great stories' be about? I wonder: stories about persecuted people who have endured terrible hardships, people who have heard about *The Lucky Country*? The only problem is they won't have heard about our Prime Minister Kevin Rudd or the leader of the opposition Tony Abbott, two devout Christians, the former a Proddie and the latter a Mick, who want to shut the door and send them 'back to where they came from'.

'The only difference between the two is that the Proddie will burn in hell,' says Ronny mischievously.

'What a hypocritical nation we are,' scoffs Descartes and he begins humming our National Anthem: Advance Australia Fair, bursting into song when he reaches the second verse:

'For those who've come across the seas

We've boundless plains to share.'

Who will Father Peter regale with these tales when he gets back home? Other retired padres?

'Where is home for a retired priest?' asks Ronny who projects a picture of Bob morosely packing his Gladstone bag.

Untroubled by my silent wonderings, probably not saddled with such a fertile cauliflower, Father Peter continues: "I would think that Bob has done so much good: good for the Church, good for the people, good for community and I think that his whole attitude has been to try to bind the people together and to speak the truth as best he could in charity. He's a great reader; he's a great thinker; he's a marvellous communicator."

"I wish we could all be like that, although some of his communications tend to be rather lengthy," I add with a grin.

Peter laughs. "Some of the people who work in his Parish have been listening to him for years. They listen to Bob weekend after weekend, and during the week; they never tire."

I tell him about how most of the interviews with Father Bob were conducted whilst I was midway through the delivery of the mail.

"I remember during a theology class at university: there was a guy there who was a postie. He'd been a postmaster but went down the scale to a lower wage and took on the job of postie to give himself more time to do his degree on theology," says Father Peter.

"It's often easier to climb down the ladder than up."

'That sounds like another cliché,' sniffs Rene, his literary radar sensitised by the previous chapter, 'and we've had enough of your clichés.'

"His name was John Paul. I remember thinking: 'fancy a Protestant having a name like John Paul.' All he wanted to do was get his theology degree so that he could be a minister in the Protestant Church. I really admired the guy." Peter pushes himself forward in his chair then and says: "Well, I don't know whether I've helped you at all. Thank you for your hospitality and thank your wife; tell her they were the best scones I've had since the ones my mother used to make."

"I will. Good luck on Christmas Island, Father," I say as he walks down the steps off the front verandah.

"Thank you, Ron; say a prayer for me."

As I go back inside my thoughts wander back to the idea of retirement. Why is the tail obsessed with the dog retiring at three-score-years-plus-fifteen? The pontiff does not have a use-by-date; the year of *inauguration* of a pontiff is usually about the time they ask the priests to retire.

'And that's all done with chimney smoke,' says Ronny.

If the hierarchy is worried about the capacities of priests diminishing with age then why is it that the pontiffs are excluded? The only time a pope retires is when he expires. The last one could hardly hold himself up at the window to bless the masses and he wasn't asked to retire.

'And who would ask him to go?' chortles Ronny. 'God?'

What does it actually mean to retire anyway? I ask myself, ignoring Ronny's interruption. Father Peter Carrucan is retired and he's off to Christmas Island to minister and support the poor refugees. And what about Bob? When he retires, what will he be retiring from? And why is he so worried about it? What will happen at St Peter's and St Paul's when he is gone? What will happen in the parish of South Melbourne? Maybe Bob will have more time to concentrate on his good work unimpeded by the demands of clerical office and the surveillance of the hierarchy. However, without the constraints of the church what would Bob be resisting?

'Old age,' answers Descartes disdainfully with a brush of the grey matter.

## Chapter 52: The Hard Sell

*"It's all too much love, isn't it?"*

Father Bob wasn't available until late in the afternoon so I drive to the church after work. 'The Jag' has been retired for over two months now and its replacement, a new orange SS Holden ute, looks incongruous sitting beside Father Bob's old Falcon sedan outside the church. Somehow it looks too flashy beside the workmanlike Ford with its 'In Bob We Trust' placard on the door, a bit like the Pope in his Armani suit and pink shoes standing beside a parish priest in a white alb, or the Prime Minister in a silk suit talking to a road worker.

I'm about to walk up the big step that leads from Dorcas Street onto the path that goes up to the rectory when I'm accosted by an intense looking young bloke who is dressed in black leather motorcycle gear. "People say I look like Bruce Lee," he says with a stony, challenging stare. Even Ronny has trouble with this one; all the silly bugger can do is laugh. The bloke is a redheaded Aussie with a ginger three-day stubble on his chin! More like weedy pop star Billy Idol than a martial arts master.

"You do look a bit like him," I say as I walk away and step up into the Church grounds.

Today's meeting is held in the big dining room where the Delta Taskforce was conceived and where Father Bob entertained Bob Santamaria and Archbishop Milingo. The players present for today's performance other than Bob and me are:

- A film crew from GHOST, a Melbourne based production company that is making a documentary about the life and times of Father Bob, led by Andrew De Groot, cinematographer and Lynn-Maree Milburn, director.

- Someone we shall refer to, perhaps hopefully, as The Editor: a woman, who works for a prospective publisher, who has come to meet us and talk about editing the manuscript. (OP decided some time ago that it did not want to publish our story and in my mind has now faded into obscurity like a single pixel in a ten-mega-pixel picture.)

- And Geoffrey, who flogged his post-office horse to a standstill so that he could get here on time this afternoon.

Unfortunately, Frank is not in attendance, much to the chagrin of The Editor who had read all about him in the latest draft of the manuscript and was looking forward to meeting him.

The manuscript, double-spaced, printed on one side of each page and separated into two spiral-bound volumes, runs to 474 pages and Father Bob is astounded at its size. It sits on the polished table in front of The Editor like a prized exhibit. The priest fervently extols the virtues of the tome, like an encyclopaedia salesman from a bye-gone era. The film crew quietly moves its cameras to different positions as Geoffrey sits unobtrusively at the furthest end of the table taking candid shots.

"Ron's thing's alright. I like it better than . . . what was the name of the bloke who died?" he asks me.

"Terry Monagle."

"His book was a bit deep and meaningful."

"What's happened to that manuscript?" asks The Editor.

"I've got a copy of it, but I prefer Ron's because it is the postie and the priest. It's not hagiography. It's more of a comic biography, which I think is more interesting," he says as the Ghosts set up their cameras again.

I think that Bob is making a point with his remark: 'it is the postie and the priest.' He's saying that it is not a straightforward biography about the priest, in the classic sense. Instead it is the unlikely story of a postie who is writing a biography about a priest to whom he delivers mail every day. That's what Bob likes about it: it is not just about him. We not only have to convince The Editor of this but the publisher as well.

"Dear Jesus, I don't know how you are going to do it," Bob says with a sigh. As he utters the sentence, I think for an instant that he has been reading my mind and is responding, but it is The Editor who answers with a short laugh.

"How I'm going to do what, Father Bob?"

"Get on the train with that!" says Bob as he once again looks at the manuscript.

"There's a lot to tell about you, isn't there?" she laughs.

"No! I keep telling people: No, no, no, no," says Bob.

"That's been a problem," I say to her, "He won't even tell what there is to tell."

"I've never been anywhere," says Bob.

"Or done anything," I add.

"I haven't got any money or friends," continues Bob, who could go on for longer if only I could think of a line.

"Isn't the Archbishop an old mate of yours?" asks The Editor.

"Denis?"

"Yes."

"No, not an old mate. He was the costume manager . . . not an old mate . . .was he?" Bob's acting is so good that you'd swear he is confused.

"Were you in the seminary together?" The Editor asks.

"No, that's George Pell. He was in the semetery with Hart. They're both younger than me. I've got no friends and he's not one of 'em," he says sounding just like Spooks who once claimed that he only had three shirts and that they were both in the wash. "This is one of those things that you lay people will discover with the Roman clergymen: they've all been castrated."

'Have they all really been castrated?' exclaims Ronny.

The Editor laughs. "Do you mean alienated from normal society?"

"Mmm," says Bob, "Socially castrated. Where are they going to go? I was at a meeting the other day with Army chaplains and I thought: 'These blokes have been to war; they've been all over the place. They should be bright eyed and bushy tailed but they're not. That's the result of being forced into a position over a period of time of years. When you get older it, must be a terrible realisation that you are now a permanent resident in the Clerical Asylum. You've got nowhere to go. That's if you sold your soul along the line to the Church and the Bishop. We ourselves (excuse the Royal plural) decided we'd be ourselves, and the Church and the Bishop could have what's left, whereas these other boys have decided that the Church and the Bishop will have the first call and they will have what's left. And I don't know that there's much left. I saw them the other day and I was very disappointed because they're all very talented men. What's next?" asks Bob.

"Have you leased the school next door yet?" I ask.

"No I'm still waiting for the Archbishop to sign. I'd like to get rid of that half of the school for forty units of public housing." I think that it was thirty last time but what the heck.

"I think that's a worthwhile project," I say sounding like the Victorian Planning Minister, Justin Madden, must have when he approved the destruction of the back half of the historic Windsor Hotel to make way for a 91metre tower.

"Yeah! The parish would then have identity for the next hundred years. We decide to look after the poor first. It would be there. It would be etched. Maybe the bosses in town are wavering on whether to sign because they don't want it etched or maybe they are hoping that it will go away," says Bob. He reconsiders and says in his Frank Thring voice: "That's paranoid. They are simply taking all the right steps to make sure that the legalities are attended to." He now sounds as if he is trying to cover his own arse and I grin. He looks at the manuscript again and says to The Editor: "What are you gonna do, take all that on the train?"

"Yes, Bob," she says and asks him about his win over the Archbishop."

"Well did we win? By the time this gets published it might be all over. We're gone in February 2012."

"What happens after that?" I ask.

"Who knows? Who cares? It depends whether that (he nods toward the manuscript) gets published and whether this bloody documentary goes to air." Laughter from both The Editor and me but there's merely a ghosts of a smile from the film crew. "Because if they get published, I've got a wild card," says Bob.

"Have you heard anymore from the Archbishop since the battle ended?" I ask.

"He disappeared!" exclaims Bob. "I signed the bloody document and he installed a micro-manager of Parish monies and then patronised me by saying: 'I admire the work that you are doing,' which denied the work that he had just done."

I marvel at Bob's lyricism as Descartes, with Ronny leaning over his shoulder, starts composing a letter to the Archbishop seeking an audience for us.

"It costs $120 an hour to micro manage our money. It's cost us more, since the intervention, to manage than it did before. I told 'them' that."

"What did they say when you told them that?" I ask. Descartes nods his approval. It's like getting an elephant stamp on the back of your hand from the teacher.

"They just brush me aside. I let the others talk: the suits. It's no good talking to 'em."

"Surely you are not referring to the money for the everyday running of the show? The petty cash?" I'm dumbfounded.

"Yes! He comes in and looks at the books. 'Where's the money? Is it the church money feeding the dog? The presbytery money shouldn't be feeding the dog!' 'I'm sorry about that.' All that micro-bloody-management!" exclaims Father Bob in a high-pitched old man's voice. "The micro-manager sits in there and thinks . . . " He decides not to go on. "Someone said to me: 'You don't talk to him' and I said 'Why would

I want to talk to 'im?' " There is a bit of laughter from The Editor but Bob's face is dark. "He should ring the Archbishop and resign because it's an insult."

"Yes. The Archbishop is making a mockery of your position," I say.

*

"The whole bloody show is ridiculous, darling," says Bob, back as Mr Thring. "As your Pope is sounding more and more as though he thinks we'd better repent. We'd better grind to a halt and regroup. Maybe he's looking for Vatican Three."

"'I think he's looking to fix it," comments The Editor, who sounds like she is from the Catholic ethos.

"As Peter Kennedy has said: 'Don't fix it. Let it collapse and start again," says Bob. (The Archbishop of Brisbane kicked Peter Kennedy out of St Mary's Catholic Church for violating the tenets of Catholic dogma.)

"Why don't the priests start pushing for Vatican Three?" I ask.

"Because," says Father Bob succinctly, "they've sold their souls to Mother Church and Father Bishop."

"You haven't," I say.

Rene Descartes gives one of his customary sniffs: 'Be careful or you will be smeared with the schmalzy hagiographical spatula.' I shudder involuntarily as if I've just swallowed a fly.

"No," says Bob, "but it's tempting. If I keep meeting clergymen who have sold their souls to Father Bishop and Mother Church I might say to myself: 'What the . . ." he lets the last word drop and says: "I'm walking around the place like the sole representative of Creative Roman Catholic Chaos. Safran and I interviewed a bloke on the wireless last night named R. R. Malloy who wrote: 'The Globalisation of God.' The cover took me: a nest with a chick in it (Bob gives a couple of squeaks) and edging an egg out of the nest. As Malloy explained last night, this little chick is in fact a cuckoo chick that is kicking out the egg that belongs there and then will take over the nest. Roman Corporate Catholicism has in fact, especially in Ireland because of the Celtic spirituality, kicked out the egg that was already in the nest: the spiritual egg. Malloy would contend that that happens all around the world where there is a spirituality that is indigenous to an area. That sort of behaviour should be encouraged by the Roman Centralist Church but it's not; it's like Kennedy: his egg has been kicked out of the nest because the Romans won't admit that there was another egg there in the first place. I read the book and I said: 'Yeah, I agree with you.' Kennedy was a priest practising in his own environment; the silly Church should have allowed that to happen. But it didn't. He (and this man who incidentally excommunicated the Church before writing his book) decided to go the next step. I don't know that I'd go the next step coz I can't see why Mother Church can't be converted. It was converted back in Vatican Two but then (Bob cheeps) like that chick, the ten-percenters who were the ultra conservatives kicked that egg out, so all we've got now is the Corporate Church. He puts it in stark terms, which I'm not prepared to do, although I probably would if it were safe to do so. The Roman Catholic Church is the first example of global corporate and all the other global corporates have learnt from the Romans. Presently you've got the cultural clash of a continuing Roman global corporate versus local or indigenous Catholic spiritualities. Malloy says that even as a Catholic priest he was quite happy say with the plurality of all those bloody saints and things in the Roman Church. There's plenty of variety. It's a trouble to you if you have to sign on the dotted line every now and again to say that you believe in God the Father Almighty Creator of Heaven and Earth, and there's three of them."

By this stage in the bobologue, The Editor and I are reduced to the odd Mmmm or yeah as Bob forges on: "So there's a bit of plurality at least hinted at and the Mother, Mary, is almost promoted as God anyway."

"Yes," agrees The Editor. Ronny and Rene Descartes can't work that one out but then we're not from the Catholic ethos.

"So the woman's in there. Admittedly the proof of the pudding is in the eating so you end up with no woman, in practice, ('mmm' from The Editor and Ronny scratches his cauli') and no plurality in practice, but it's there in principle. This is where the Romans get caught. That's why they can have self-reformation any time they wish or when they want to turn it on because they've got all the bits and pieces lying on the bloody table; all they have to do is put it all together again like Rubik's Cube. I believe in that but some of my colleagues would be saying . . . " he grimaces and starts again. "They take it that damn seriously that if the bloody cube can't be put together the boys are gonna bleed and do something else."

Father Bob is directing most of his dialogue at The Editor and again she replies: "Mmmm," and I smile, seeing myself sitting there. I have been putting my muted responses during interviews with Father Bob down to a lack of technique but I see now that that's not necessarily the case because if one is caught up in a bobologue, the topic of which is not one's forté, one is reduced to monosyllabic answers, such as yes, yeah, or mmm.

"I'm sorry about that," says Father Bob, once again as if in response to my reflection, "because I thought: 'well, I probably would adhere to . . . '" He stops again and takes another approach. "Like in the Monty Python film 'Life of Brian' and 'What have the Romans ever given us?', when who is it tells off the critics of the Roman Empire? 'They gave us aqueducts; they gave us water; they gave us this and they gave us that, and everyone cheered saying: 'That's true, that's true.' He then asked: 'Well, what the hell are you having a revolution for?' See?" says Bob then goes on even as The Editor is mmming: "The Roman Church has given us law and order and things like that but the trouble is," laughs Bob, "the price you pay for it seems to be too high because you lose the local and you lose the personalities of the locality and you don't show much respect for the history of the localities. The Irish are awake up to this because they've been banging on (I shut Descartes up before he gets a chance) about their localities for five thousand years."

"Yes," I manage. I remember my history of the Irish Church as told by Bob in his study one morning.

"The Irish Church and the Roman Church were nicely tolerant of each other for the first six hundred years and then the Roman invasion and later the Vikings who had become Roman Christians invaded Scotland and Ireland."

"Yes," says The Editor who may or may not be good at history.

"So you ended up once again with: 'Excuse me, would you mind conforming?' The Irish replied: 'Excuse me, but we've already got our own Catholicism based on monasteries', and occasionally there's a woman like Brigid (Saint Brigid of Kildare) ('Mmmm' from The Editor) who was allegedly a Bishop." (Another 'mmm'). Father Bob looks askance at me and says again: "Allegedly. Home made. But that's what the Irish were like."

"Yes," responds The Editor.

"Mmmm," from me.

"The Romans said: 'What the hell's going on here? You can't have a woman Bishop for Christ's sake; it's not right. You've got to conform!" Bob drags out the word 'conform' until it's nearly a metre long. "So you end up clash, clash," says Father as if describing a scene from the film 'Gladiator.' The Romans eventually seduce Patrick ('Mmmm') who becomes a Roman Bishop, so to speak. He's their patriarch and the only one you hear about in Irish Catholicism is Patrick, whereas the other one would be Brigid."

'One of the stained glass windows in Sts Peter and Paul's Church is of Brigid of Kildare,' says Ronny.

"Yes," says The Editor who goes to say more but she is not quick enough.

"You should be hearing about Brigid and you should be hearing about the non-Roman Irish like Saint Columba. I found it fascinating because that's what I have been banging on about but can't do it in such lyrical terms as that bloke who wrote the book. What I'd be looking for in Orstralia is for the Orstralian Catholics to do what the Aussie commanders did in Gallipoli: they saluted but they get on with the business in their own way."

"Mmmm," The Editor and I in unison like a pair of school kids responding to the teacher's tuning fork.

"They salute, 'Morning, Sir,' and get on with the business. Now that would be the perfect solution but then the Catholic bosses won't be satisfied with a bloody salute; they want to micro-manage the platoons and the bloody sections etc."

We both go: "Mmmm." The Editor looks to be stunned and Ronny is banging his tuning fork on the desk.

"And that's the Roman model until Vatican Two comes along and says: 'Excuse me, the Roman model is meant to be that Romans have the services of each regional diocese at least, because to go to the next step and say that the Roman Church is at the service of the individual Parish is going a bit far, but that would be the ideal. 'Anything we can do for you?' says the Pope to the Parish Priest at Middle Park," only Father Bob doesn't say it, he almost bellows the question and there is a fair bit of movement as well as laughter around the table. " 'Yeah, I'd like a dispensation for Muslims to marry for the third time a Roman Catholic for the first time.' 'Oh, that's alright. Do you reckon it will help?' 'Yeah,' 'Alright, here's the paperwork.' "

The Editor laughs as the phone rings.

"What's that a phone?" Asks Bob as he reaches for it: "Yes, yes, but I'm in the middle of something, how many minutes? What do you want me to do? Not as long as there are three hundred de-frocked priests in the diocese of Melbourne, I can't do anything about that Carl Williams? The funeral? I've heard nothing, I don't expect anything, he's on the other side of town, yeah, that's right, what'd they say? No, he'll be in the Coroner's Court for ages won't he? They have to find out how he died, it might take a while, I've heard nothing, what about Les Twentyman?

No, he knows more about Roberta than he does about Carl, righto, Your Grace," he says and hangs up. "Bloody newspaper wants to know about Carl Williams' funeral." He says 'Carl Williams' harshly and through the side of his mouth, the way in which John Elliott is reported as saying 'pig's arse!' but which he has always denied. I guess things are easier to deny if you say them out of the corner of your gob, better than crossing your fingers behind your back.

"Won't you be doing his funeral?" I ask.

"No, why would I be doing Carl Williams' funeral?" ('Carl Williams' growled in that same voice.)

"You've done a few of the other underworld characters."

"Nah, not from that side of town."

"Victor Pierce."

"He was local.

"I just thought . . ."

'Maybe it'd be better if you don't think,' says you-know-who.

"No! I've done Painters and Dockers and all that, but I won't be doing Carl Williams. Pierce's lot got buried from St Monica's, Moonee Ponds. But Carl's body will be in the freezer for weeks won't it?"

"Yes, I suppose so." I reply.

"That's the other aspect of the locals burying their own without having to answer to Central Headquarters who might prefer us not to bury crims, but I would say: 'locally you are obliged to bury your own, Your Grace.'"

"Yes," agrees The Editor.

"I could be mischievous now if they rang up and said: 'Excuse me, will you bury Carl Williams?' I might mischievously say: 'Ring Bishop Tomlinson at the diocese and ask him if it's alright. Ask him. Ask those fools in town."

The Editor laughs but doesn't say anything and I still see myself in her because her behaviour is as mine had been at some of the sessions: an audience at the Bob Maguire Show. I'm also amazed because despite their close proximity, Andrew and Lynn haven't given so much as a peep. I heard Geoff's shutter a few times early in the session but the crew from GHOST is well named. At one point Father Bob directs a question to Lynn who is sitting with her camera positioned on a tripod between The Editor and me. Lynn, who is a softly spoken woman leans forward and almost whispers in my ear as she answers. Ronny starts fidgeting.

"They criticise when you've done it. He should make proactive attempts to get headquarters to face the facts. What are they? Are they a Global Church or are they a Local Church? Anyhow listen," says the monologist suddenly, "you've had enough. We've all had enough." He looks at the Ghosts. "You've had enough." He looks at me. "You've had enough. He's had enough," he says indicating Geoffrey who is sitting quietly way down at the far end of the table like a vegetarian at a barbeque. "More than enough!" he reiterates. "You've had enough, Editor. What time's your train?"

"I don't really have to catch a train."

"Don't you?" he asks as if amazed.

The Editor laughs and makes her move: "We'd like to hear from the Archbishop if possible."

"Oh Jesus!" exclaims Bob and The Editor laughs delightedly.

"What do you think?" she asks.

"I don't give a rat's . . . you know." The Editor and I both laugh. The Ghosts and Geoff sit quietly, respectively filming and observing.

"Who's asking him?" asks Father as he glances out the window behind Geoff. "It's starting to rain."

"I'll ask him," I reply.

Bob puts the next question directly to The Editor. "How do you want us to do this?"

"Well . . ."

"You want us to work it ourselves," Bob declares. "You want Archbishop Hart."

"'Denis,' as you call him," jokes The Editor.

"Yes! You want Hart. Make a note," Bob says to me, sounding like a busy executive directing his stenographer.

"I think I can remember that."

'The stenographer crosses her legs as she jots it in her notebook,' quips Descartes.

"Can you remember that?"

"I think so."

"Well, you better get onto Hart," Bob says. "Anyone else?"

"He was the one I had in mind. Do you have anyone in mind?"

"God no," says Bob but changes his mind. "Eddie Maguire. You could question Eddie Maguire," he says to me. "He might know something."

"Do you and he get on well together?" I ask

"He went to the old school, Christian Brothers College, St Kilda. He keeps waffling on as though he knows me. That'll do, won't it?" he asks as he looks at the manuscript again.

"Have you read any of that?" he asks The Editor.

"I've read all of it," she replies.

"What do you think of it?" he asks giving her his detective stare.

"It's got a lot of potential."

"It's comic, isn't it?"

"Yes."

"An' he writes good," declares Bob as he picks up the ringing phone. "Yes? yeah, yeah, yeah, I'm here, yeah, wait a minute, that's St Paul's, mmmm, yeah, I need a loan too, how much do you want? yeah, well, we do our best but I'm broke me-bloody-self, no but if you can find out where I can get money we'll all have it, you should be able to get money if you're in a wheelchair, what do you want electrics or something? yes, yes, sounds reasonable, can you write or send an email? tell 'em to send me the details, yes but you haven't got the address, darling, can you write or what? can you remember? does he? who is he? James Grant the Anglican at Preston, alright, well get him and send me a note, yeah, they should be able to, either that or they're duck shoving, no good, I'm being questioned by experts here, cameras and recorders, go and get it done and send me something, righto, Your Grace." Bob hangs up. "He'll now go and get his minister to send an email."

"Do you get people ringing all the time like that?" asks The Editor.

"Yes."

"Usually on the mobile," I add and ask Bob if he has turned it off. He replies:

"No, but Judy has gone home for the day. I don't like the idea of having phones and then not answering them. Don't like it," he emphasises. "Last year for self-serving purposes, I *daren't* not answer them because the Press was often on the phone, and in general they were offering to help. It's no good half-answering them because they won't come back."

"Yes," agrees The Editor.

"So I decided: 'Darling, whatever the time of the day or night it is you'd better answer the damn thing and do whatever they want done. If it's good enough for the Press it should be good enough for the other punters, except the Press is usually simple: 'Be outside the house at 6.30am for *Sunrise*.' 'Alright.' That's easy. This bloke wants help with the bloody wheelchair, not to give him the money but to arrange somehow that his pension will pay instalments on a $1500 wheelchair. That should be simple enough for the minister of the Presbyterian Church in Doncaster but it's all too hard for some people."

"He's over at Doncaster and he's ringing you at South Melbourne?" I chip in.

"No, he's in the city now; he was talking to the someone at St Paul's bloody Cathedral. It's all too hard for 'em."

"Then he rings you?" I ask in amazement.

"Yes! Why wouldn't you?"

We laugh. "He must think that you will get the job done," I say.

"Yes, with me and Les Twentyman the general impression is that you will get something done. Whether it's true or false is another thing; you can't get it done if you haven't got any money. He doesn't want money though; he simply wants a connection to a lender."

"I saw Les the other day; he looks terrible," I say.

"He always has," Bob replies, "since birth." I'm sure I heard one of the Ghosts laugh this time and Geoff couldn't help himself either. In fact the volume increases as Bob says: "Are we gonna finish now or what, Ron?"

"Yes, thanks, Bob."

"Did you get enough, Cameras?" he asks the Ghosts and Geoff. "It's still raining outside."

The three Cameras reply in the affirmative. Bob turns to The Editor and asks the same question.

"Yes, enough to go on with. Thank you very much for your time," replies The Editor.

"Not at all. I've got no wife or children. How did you get here, darling," asks the considerate priest.

"My husband dropped me off and is picking me up," she replies.

"Well, as long as it's your husband," says Bob.

Bob's mobile buzzes for the first time this session: "Are you there? yes, yes, but the woman's not here, she's out drinking, ring her on Tuesday, Judy 9.15am to 4pm, she knows everything, yeah, they're all lazy, ring Judy, alright, tat tar.'" Father sighs heavily: "'I can't find anywhere to get married on a Sunday,'" he mimics. "I don't know what these boys are up to. They just won't do things that they don't feel like doing."

"You're lucky that you've got a good secretary," I say.

"Yes, she's alright. She'll lose her wits soon though working here."

"Judy used to work for a publisher in London: Penguin," I tell them.

"Did she?" asks Bob. "If we publish ourselves . . . I got a strange book the other day from a woman. The writing was awful but the presentation was excellent. It had a fancy cover. There were lots of typographical errors and silly little things. Knowing it was her, I thought: 'I like what she is saying but it's awfully put."

"It wasn't Margie, was it?" I ask.

"No. This woman must have published it herself. How much do you need to self-publish?" he asks The Editor.

"I'm not really sure; I think that it depends on the quality."

Father Bob plucks an exorbitant figure from the stratosphere. "$20,000?"

"No, I wouldn't think it would be that much."

"We'd have to be able to promote it and sell it ourselves," I repeat. This is deja vu.

"And distribute it. It's not easy to get it into bookshops." says The Editor who commented earlier that maybe the story of finding someone to publish the manuscript should be left out of the book because everyone knows how hard it is to get a manuscript published. Do they though? I wonder. Everyone who tries to publish a manuscript would know but only a small percentage of readers write manuscripts.

"That's probably where she fell over," says Bob and once again my thoughts seem to segue seamlessly with what he is saying. "All she wanted was for me to read it and see what I thought of her spirituality. From her experiences and everything I though it was alright. Hopeful. She was attacking Mother Church a bit but not viciously or maliciously. Then she wrote me a letter thanking me for reading it, but I don't think it's going to get anywhere. Come on, let's get out of here."

As we are leaving the dining room, The Editor asks: "How many years are you a priest now, Bob?"

"Fifty, coming up this year," he replies. "That's why this (indicates the manuscript) should be published this year."

"Yeah, definitely," replies The Editor.

"Fifty years; all by the book. All by the book," he reiterates. "I joined another thing this week, Ronny (the twin on the right pricks up his cauliflower ear). Some woman stooged me into becoming the face of Grief Line. Nothing bright and chirpy: Grief Line!"

"A weekly show?"

"No, only once on the wireless: the new station, which is 3 Melbourne Talk Radio. They're saying that the signal can hardly be heard in Melbourne. Grief Line. While we were speaking almost the government decided to give them $120,000."

"That's not a bad effort."

"Yes, that's very good. When we went into the studio they were afraid that they were going to be closed down. By the time we came out of the studio, not due to anything we'd said or done, the government had given them one hundred and twenty thousand pounds. Listen, kiddies, do you want the lavatory or what? The lavatory or the mirror?" he asks The Editor. "It's all too much love, isn't it?"

"Yes," she agrees with a laugh.

On the way out, as I am talking to the Ghosts, Bob asks if I am going to contact Denis Hart and I say that I will. He also says to the Ghosts that they should also ring him.

"Do you know Denis Hart?" I ask them.

"Nobody knows Denis Hart," says Bob. "I can't even find out who his best friend is; but then you might say to me: 'We'd like to get in touch with your best friend and I'd be hard-pressed to tell you who my best friend is. I would have thought that your best friend is somebody who would stand by you right or wrong. Is that right?"

We all agree that he is right and he says: "I don't know that I've got any of them."

"Yes, you have," I assure him.

"Well, name one," he says loudly as The Editor, who has preceded us out the door, turns around and waves goodbye.

\*Despite the hurt caused by the Archbishop's installation of the accountant to manage the Parish funds, Father Bob only manages to give the 'micro-manager' the silent treatment for a short time. The priest's natural empathy washes away the bitterness. He flabbergasts me one morning by referring to "that nice man, the micro-manager." Seeing my look of astonishment he grins and says: "I used to ignore him but I now think he's alright. He's doing as he was told: he's micro-managing, and he now knows there's no frauds, cheats, and liars here; we may be creatively chaotic but I realise now, and you know this better than I do, that people who've got a craft can only be expected to pursue their craft. His brief is to dot the I's and cross the T's accountancy wise."

## Chapter 53: Follow Me

*"That woman! Have a look at that woman. She's got a baby and about four children. Did they all fall out of the bus?"*

Bob closes the security door behind The Editor and we walk into the study. He turns to the Ghosts and says: "It's alright him knowing who my best friend is. What's the use of him knowing? He's a nice man and would naturally think that one would have a best friend."

Occasionally, the mask slips to reveal the vulnerable organism beneath. The man who has to 'help people, help people, help people' is in need of some love himself. With the mask down he allows his disappointment to show. "The Editor's not showing anything but then I suppose she's not the publisher," he says. We wander back into his office so that he can check on his appointments for the Ghosts who are going to follow him around quite a bit over the next couple of years.

Bob reads out a few engagements and then says: "Dental appointment. Do you want to see the dentist pull me tooth out?"

"Do you have to have one out?" asks Lynn, although I doubt that she wants to watch.

"This swine's after it. I was sitting in the chair and I said: 'You're not to pull any out.' 'Oh, but I might have to.' You're old and then he brings in the strange man who reminds you that infection in teeth and gums can affect the heart. Now what can you say? The old bloke is probably lying," he jokes. *

"There's Shirley Shackleton's book launch next Thursday night at Vic Ave Bookshop. It's 6pm for a 6.30 start.

"Are you going to launch the book?" I ask.

"No, I'm just going there because we are in love," he quips as he pushes the mask back into place. He reads on: "John Safran back in town on 20th May."

He continues leafing through his diary. "What are you gonna do, Ron? Go out drinking? It's five after four on a Friday."

"I'll probably go and have a beer with Eric."

"This event will come on soon: Mick Gatto and Jerry Lewis are going to hold a telethon to raise money for muscular dystrophy, and we'll get a cut," says Bob rubbing his hands.

"Speaking of cuts, he could be the next one to go," I say.

"Well, I hope he doesn't go before May. He's an old boy of this school."

"Has he got a strategy to help raise some money?" asks Andrew.

"He's part of this telethon idea which will raise $800,000 for muscular dystrophy and he'll give us ten percent."

"Gatto is behind the fundraising?" Andrew enquires.

"Yes. He's promoting this man," says Bob waving a sheet of paper about.

"So he's actually raising money for you too?" Andrew persists. I've got to learn to keep asking questions like him.

"Yeah! Yeah! Yeah!" Bob exclaims sounding like one of the Beatles. "Everybody will fight and argue about it but they can fight and argue about it until they are blue in the bloody face. I'm saying he's an old boy of the school. Simple." It sounds as if Bob is getting dirty just discussing it with us so I wouldn't want to be one of the ones with a blue bloody face because I reckon that he'll really stick it up 'em as Teddy Whitten used to say.

"People will say: 'it's blood money.' 'Go and talk to the bloody Archbishop then.'" He uses this as a segue: "You can talk to the Archbishop about all that, Ron: Tell him that you are going to give him a chance to expose this corrupt priest, Maguire, who is getting mixed up with Gatto. It won't matter to me what you put in the book because the way things are going I'll be dead when it comes out!"

On our way out of the study, Bob picks up a book: the winner of the 2009 Crime Thriller of the Year and says: "What about *The Girl with the Dragon Tattoo*?"

"Are you reading it?" I ask.

"No, I just carry it under me arm. I got interested because one of my clients said: 'Just say all these people who are sponging on the State and on Maguire are all duds.' She said: 'Here's a book where the main character really should be a dud, but she refused to be a dud and she became a crusader. I'd like to be out there in a bloody uniform. Any duds come near me, I'd erase them."

We finally step out onto the front verandah and head towards the street.

"Whose is that? Is that yours, that orange ute, Ron?"

"Yes, Father."

"When I got back earlier I drove around the block a few times assuming that there was a hoon loose in here and . . ." Father Bob stops in mid sentence and exclaims: "That woman! Have a look at that woman. She's got a baby and about four children. Did they all fall out of the bus?"

Lynn runs towards the bus shelter where a bus, its doors open, is idling; a woman is picking up her handbag and its contents from the gutter. We all follow Lynn. There is a little one about 12 months old in the pusher who flashes a couple of milk teeth. The other three children, all with chrome-plated scooters, range from about 3 years old to about 6.

"The bloody driver won't come and help," says Bob.

"No, he's just sitting there." I glance at the impassive face of the driver.

"Is he gonna lock her out, that man?" asks Bob. As if in answer, the pneumatic doors close with a whoosh and the bus drives off leaving the woman and Lynn picking up belongings from the gutter.

"I'll take 'em home," says Bob to me, "Will I be able to fit that pusher in the boot? The pusher, not the girl."

"Did the driver refuse to let you on?" I ask the woman.

"We couldn't get on. The pusher wouldn't fit. It's an old bus."

"Is there a modern one coming?"

"Probably." She is unflappable and the children's manners are exemplary, especially under the trying circumstances.

"Why can't you get on the bus?" Father Bob asks.

"Because the bus is old and the pusher won't fit. There's a bar in the middle so the pusher won't fit. This morning I had to let three go by before I could get on a bus. They were all old. I don't understand why those buses are still running."

"The driver couldn't work anything out then? There's no way?" asks Bob.

"He wouldn't even let me try. He said: 'I know it doesn't fit so I'm not even going to try.'"

"Put it in my car. What have you got, about twenty children?" We all stand around getting wet and laughing.

"How many? One, two, three, four," says Father Bob sounding like he is reciting a nursery rhyme. "Four and that pusher."

"Yes."

"Does the pusher fold?"

"Yeah, it goes flat."

"Does it?" he asks in amazement. "Will it all fit in my car?"

"Everybody will fit in but you haven't got any child seats," I say.

"We're only going down to Port Melbourne. Don't worry about car-seats; the children are more important than bloody car seats."

"It's just that it's the law. If I have to wait, I have to wait." says the lady resignedly.

"The law! We'll just have to break the goddamn law," says the priest. "These children want to go home. How long have you been there darling?"

"For the last hour."

"An hour! The baby wants a feed. This one wants to go home and watch Sesame Street."

"Yea," says the little girl as she balances on her scooter. The rest of us cheer loudly.

"You can put the pram and the scooters in the ute if you want." I say, laughing as the little girl scoots towards the cars.

'It's a Father Bob parable: Don't Leave Me Behind, Cobber,' laughs Ronny excitedly as I head towards the ute. 'Like the parables Jesus told in the Gospels: Christ and the Prostitute, Jesus and the Family, The Woman with the Ointment, The Stranger, Joseph Greets his Son, The Temptation of Jesus.'

Geoffrey and the Ghosts help load the gear into the back of the ute and the lady and her kids pile into the Falcon. "Follow me," says Bob, sounding like one of his heroes, as he gets in behind the wheel. With the kids laughing excitedly, Father, mother and the four billy-lids roar off down the road like a 1950s family out for a Sunday drive.

*From Father Bob's Facebook the following week:

Been to dentist who won't pull out tooth. Now wants to install crowns! OMG thousands $'s!

## Chapter 54: The Fish 'n' Chip Eaters

*"It turns some people off but he really speaks the language of the Fish 'n' Chip Eaters."*

We've just plucked a letter from the letterbox. This one is personal correspondence from the black bishop. Ronny is practising his 'Your Graces' but Descartes is wearing his turned-up Elvis Presley lip ('Why would he let *you* grill *him*?') as we walk back into the house. I don't know that I want to grill him although there is one question that might cause him some discomfort that I intend to ask just before I walk out the door, one of those Colombo type questions: 'Oh by the way, why . . .'

'You won't get the chance,' Descartes interrupts as we sit down at the kitchen table to open the letter. Slipping a knife under the flap, I cut the paper with precision, as if my correspondent's eminence within the Catholic Church decrees scrupulousness on my part, and read the letter. After the formalities there is mention of an 'extremely heavy schedule of commitments.' 'Regret' stands out. I shrug. The letter ends: 'With every good wish for the success of your book. Yours sincerely in Christ.' The black bishop has drawn a cross before signing his name: 'Denis J Hart,' above the capitalised words 'Archbishop of Melbourne.' This is a knockback from a stranger.

'You've staggered into the Archbishop's camp and he has lopped *our* head off,' laughs Ronny with unaccountable glee.

'Bob was right when he commented on The Stranger parable: 'The natural instinct is to chop the head off the bloody stranger because he's strange and he may cause harm.'

'The question?' I hear the Father Bob in my head ask. He's definitely in there with the bloody twins. The question: Pocketing my voice recorder after shaking hands with the black bishop I would have headed for the door, half turned, looked back over my shoulder and asked: "Oh, Archbishop Hart, one last question: why did you find it necessary to belittle Father Bob by sending in an accountant, to micromanage the books?"

That's The Editor's nomination scratched, I muse, as I push Ronny to the back of my skull. One person who is willing to talk though is Peter Carrucan's nomination, Father Bob's old mate: Paul Garland. Over the phone I tell Father Paul that Bob reckons he (Bob) hasn't got any mates but ask if he will talk to me regardless. Paul gives me directions to an address, a group of villas set aside for the exclusive use of 'senior' priests.

'Imagine a *precinct* (a catch-cry word that he has picked up from the television news or from newspaper reporters) for retired posties,' laughs Ronny. No, I won't.

"Welcome to Justin Villa, and as some people reply: 'You're welcome to it, too,' "says Father Paul as we shake hands. He describes the place as being "a bit strange" and I laugh when he says: "That's why it suits us." Father Paul Garland, a neatly dressed man with silver hair, is not much taller than Father Bob I estimate as he leads me into a small sitting room at the front of the building. He apologises for having cancelled a couple of earlier interview appointments but says that he is one of the able-bodied around the place and is often called upon for help. Only last night he tells me a ninety-five-year-old priest, who still plays golf, fell out of bed and had to be carted off to hospital. "We get a bit of drama like that," he says.

"Father Bob will be pleased that I've met you after all this time."

"Oh, good; how's he doing?"

"He's going as well as can be expected after all the brouhaha with the Archbishop. I suppose you followed all of that as it unfolded."

"Not really," he says, surprising me. "The last time I saw Bob would have been 1995 when he came out to our church at Mooroolbark to hold a funeral for a baby who had died."

"I see," I say, only now starting to believe what Bob said about not having any mates. "If that was your last, what was your first memory of Bob?" I ask, somewhat dismayed at this new information.

Father Paul tells me that he first met Bob in 1949 at CBC St Kilda where they were in intermediate level. "I palled up with Bob. He was a humorous kind of fellow, or just starting to appear that way." He says that Bob used to play handball and that they were both in the under 15's football team.

"Was he a bit reserved when you were kids?"

"He might have been a bit shy but he overcame that. I had a lot of mates in the school; I came across to CBC with a lot of fellas from St Thomas More's, which was a central school; we were a big band together. The next year was when Bob's mother died. I think that would have been 1950. We used to go to the pictures together around that time on a Friday night. He used to come down from where he was living in Peet Ave, Glen Iris, with Betty and Jimmy Maguire. Jim's a funny man," he adds, smiling.

"Yes, I've spoken to him on the phone; he lives in Queensland."

"That's right. I haven't seen Jim and Betty for a hundred years. Bob used to come down to my place in Greville St, Prahran. My mum and dad used to ask him to come and have tea with us. He would turn up eventually; he was always a bit late."

"Did you both decide to become priests at the same time? Was it a pact?"

"No; as far as I knew he was going to join the Christian Brothers. I wasn't gonna join the Brothers. I thought: 'No, not interested in them.' I must have said to him . . . I forget the sequence of events."

"Had you made up your mind to become a priest by then?"

"Oh, I just thought: 'That's what the Lord wants you to do.' So we went down there to have a look at the seminary with Bernard O'Connor, the parish priest from Glen Iris, and I think he also drove us down to Werribee when we entered."

"That would have been a big step for both of you, going in for eight years."

"Yes, although we used to be home for three months each year so we could work to help pay for our fees and stuff like that."

I ask him if he remembers his holidays with Bob at Pat and Brian's place at Dimboola.

"Yes, that was a *thou*sand years ago," he laughs.

'Gee, that *is* a long time!' exclaims Ronny.

"What do you remember about the bee keeper?" I ask, as our conversation seems to ebb.

"Oh, yes, the bee keeper. Bob was also supposed to look after the herbarium but I ended up digging it for him most of the time. It wasn't very big: one-and-a-bit longer than this and a bit wider that that," he says indicating the length and width of the room. "Bob was a bee man though; he was a bit wrapped up in that."

"Peter Carrucan told me that he was football and cricket umpire too."

"Yes, and a wicket keeper. He enjoyed handball as well," Father Paul, obviously trying to think of something to say, adds: "As far as I remember at school, Bob used to barrack for Essendon and I barracked for South Melbourne."

"And now he barracks for Collingwood."

"Yes, and I'm very wary of people who change their footy allegiance," he laughs.

"He used to barrack for Essendon because his sister, Kathleen, used to take him to the Essendon matches at Windy Hill."

Paul nods and looks at me for a couple of seconds. "Have you got any other questions?" he asks suddenly.

Oh, I'm running on empty too and Descartes must have gone to sleep. I check my notes but haven't got anything else written down to prompt me. I steer my way back to the imaginary pact. "I thought that when you both joined on the same day that there was some sort of agreement in place."

"No. It was a year-by-year commitment at the seminary to see how you were getting on and to see if there was any future there for you. It wasn't as if we had . . . well, not as far as I'm concerned . . . a great light on the hill."

"That's similar to what Bob said about his own commitment."

"I used to say to some of the blokes: 'If anyone here doesn't want to get married they shouldn't be here.' I was only eighteen then but that's what I thought."

"That's right; if you wanted to get married, you wouldn't want to be a priest."

'You bloody drongo,' sniffs Rene Descartes, coming out of hibernation like a polar bear leaving its cave, as Paul reiterates.

"You would hope that those who were joining up would have made good husbands. It wasn't a rejection of marriage."

I can see Paul's reasoning but wouldn't that only make things unbearable for a young man going into the seminary? You would have a man who wanted to get married but who was now taking a vow of celibacy and subjecting himself to a lifetime of sexual frustration, and as recent history has shown, it's a commitment that many priests can't sustain. I don't mention my thoughts, but comment instead that Bob would most certainly have made a good family man. I think back to that day when the schoolkids took over the garden and how popular he was with the kids.

"He's got that gift with kids," says Paul. "You mentioned on the phone that he said he didn't have any friends."

"That's what he said, although I didn't believe that to be so. At the time," I add.

Father Paul nods and says in a serious tone: "Yeah, well a lot of people over the time have really made efforts to be with him, but there was no great give and take in all of that. Unfortunately."

I remain silent.

"There seemed to be some . . . something there that he really couldn't . . . I don't know if it was privacy . . . I know so many lay people who wanted his friendship but . . . " He leaves his sentence to infer what he doesn't really want to say and what I really don't want to hear.

"For years we used to have a little confraternity of about six or eight priests who would meet on Sunday nights. Originally Bob was part of that and then he dropped out. He had his own reasons. A lot of people really went out of their way. I used to have to drive from Billyo to Billyo. We had a good group of priests there. He's been in various groups but he's moved in and moved out of them as he's gone along. A lot of people do that."

'Maybe Bob should have said that he didn't have any mates *left*,' says Descartes grimly.

"Yes, although you usually hang on to your old mates," I say to the priest, thinking of More.

"Bob's got his tremendous support but, as I said, I haven't spoken with him for so long. Whether he didn't want to be hurt by being close to people or something like that I don't know. But he's able to give of himself. He used to speak about the Fish 'n' Chip Eaters. He's got very interesting use of language," he laughs. "It turns some people off but he really speaks the language of the Fish 'n' Chip Eaters. Friends of mine for example: they've got association with young blokes: early twenties, drugs, the whole bit, but they've heard these blokes comment after seeing Bob on the telly: 'If only they were all like him.' He's an acquired taste," says Father as Ronny sprinkles salt all over a big parcel of fish 'n' chips, "but if the Fish 'n' Chip Eaters needed him he'd be there. My mum and dad were fond of Bob; they fitted into the Fish 'n' Chip Eaters: the salt-of-the-earth crowd."

'Salt-of-the-sea,' chips in Rene but he is not enthusiastic, seemingly preoccupied.

"Bob reckons that there's a lot of talent amongst these people."

"Oh, God yeah; he reaches them. He did that funeral for the little baby whom I mentioned. The Fish 'n' Chip Eaters all thought it was terrific because before he got up there they would have had these stereotypes of priests and ministers of religion that weren't necessarily right." Paul ponders further. "I saw him on one other occasion in 1995. It was my 60th birthday and the blokes had gathered; I didn't know that it was going to be on and I saw Maguire at the back of the church so I went around and he said: (and here Garland does a Maguire impersonation in Bob's Aussie twang which is pretty good) 'I'm not stayin', I'm not stayin'. He came in but wouldn't stay, said he had things to do. That's the way he is and there are probably reasons for it."

We are both silent for a few moments and then Paul says: "I think he worked as a postman like I did." This is almost 'a Maguire:' something you don't expect, like the first time I heard Bob use the 'f' word: I was sitting on my bike outside the church talking to him and remember him saying: "I was just watching that f…ing taxi driver trying to do a u-turn."

'A postman!' exclaims Ronny.

"A postman!" My response is identical.

"When we were younger, during December, helping out. I was at the Prahran post office."

"Delivering parcels?"

"No; letters. I had my round. This all took place while we were student priests on leave for three months to find out whether we wanted to go back or not. We weren't in a religious order or anything like that at the seminary; we belonged to the troops."

It's not much but I reach out for the segue like The Marlboro Man used to stretch out for his oxygen mask. "Bob enjoyed being with the troops when he was in the army."

"Yes. He was an officer. When he was up at Seymour as a priest I went up to see him once or twice. I remember going to see him when he was in hospital; he did his Achilles tendon playing squash, another game that he played; he was good at that. He had so many visitors in the hospital that he was getting worn out," he laughs, "so I took him out for the weekend."

There are voices in the hall outside the room but Paul is oblivious. "One year, about 1964 I think it was," he says "we went to Sydney in my EK Holden. Maguire was driving along, with a cigar in his mouth. There was a furniture-van coming towards us and out from behind the van appeared this car: a Karmann Ghia coming straight at us. Maguire kept going and the Karman Ghia went across in front of us onto the grass. We could have been bananas, wiped out. He just said: 'Did you see that?' and kept going. I remember the ash from his cigar falling down the front of him as he drove. I hated the smell of those cigars."

Paul considers for a while and then continues his analysis of Bob: "He developed his own personality and this has gone on. He appealed to some fellas and didn't appeal to others. He's approachable and all that but some people don't like the way he does things." The priest smiles and says: "Maguire's got humanity: he was always concerned about the Fish 'n' Chip Eaters; he identified with working people." Another Maguire impersonation follows: " 'You've got to look after the Fish 'n' Chip Eaters haven't you?' " he barks, "'All of 'em!' " Garland considers further and says of Maguire: "In some sense he's a late developer. He's always had a lot of talent. It's a pity in a way he didn't get back to Scotland for a look for his own self. It's a bit late now."

"He could even end up living here," I say.

"It would drive him up the wall."

"Do you think so?"

"Oh, yeah."

"He'd fix 'em up,"

"No! They'd fix him," says Father Paul with conviction.

Rene Descartes flashes an image onto the screen: Escher's 'Ascending and Descending,' with Escher's own description of his intriguing lithograph retrieved from Rene's recently renovated 'library':

*A rectangular inner courtyard is bounded by a building that is roofed in by a never- ending stairway. The inhabitants of these living quarters would appear to be monks, adherents of some unknown sect. Perhaps it is their ritual duty to climb those stairs for a few hours each day. It would seem that when they get tired they are allowed to turn about and go downstairs instead of up. Yet both directions, though not without meaning, are equally useless. Two recalcitrant individuals refuse, for the time being, to take any part in this exercise. They have no use for it at all, but no doubt sooner or later they will be brought to see the error of their nonconformity.*

'There's Father Bob!' says Ronny pointing to one of the recalcitrants who is sitting on the steps, looking outwards. 'There's no telling what he's thinking there…'

'Yes, believe it or not, Ronny is right,' says Descartes. 'Father Bob is a recalcitrant. If he lived here they'd pressure him into conforming. It's probably what happened with the confraternity.'

Father Paul says that he'd "better get cracking" so we head for the door. As we walk outside I tell him about the recently retired Father Peter Carrucan's visit to Christmas Island and his mission to offer pastoral care to the refugees.

"I don't know what we are going to do about that. The fact that it's just a political football is awful," Paul says. "Someone asked me: 'What are we going to do about the boat people?' I said: 'Send in the fighter planes and napalm 'em. Don't have to worry about 'em then,' says Father with a mix of sarcasm and resignation. "That's what Bob would say and that's what I say. It's a raw nerve with many so-called Australians. The poor things, particularly the Sri Lankans and the Afghans."

"Yes, and our new Prime Minister, Julia Gillard, is also in favour of strengthening our borders, as she puts it."

"It's all politic talk, Ron," adds Paul. "The percentage of refugees who come by boat is minimal so I don't know what is worrying them." At the gate we shake hands and as I walk towards my car, Father Paul calls out, as if I might have missed the point: "Don't forget the Fish 'n' Chip Eaters."

## Chapter 55: The Civil-Bloody-War

*"I don't mind talking about the Civil-bloody-War, especially with somebody who knows something about it."*

A few weeks after meeting with Father Paul Garland, I manage to arrange another session with Bob. It's cool outside and I'm glad to be off the bike for a while because it's nice and warm in the study; the heater behind the desk is glowing and Bob is sorting through some papers on his desk. There is something odd about the scene though: it's the pair of long legs poking out from behind and to the side of Bob's desk. There is no movement from the legs' owner either as Bob, who is unperturbed by my puzzled look, grumbles:

"I wish they'd leave my bloody desk alone. My desk is covered with shit." Then he adds: "It's sad. All this swearing and cursing going on."

"I wouldn't worry about that," I say, looking pointedly at the legs as I sit down.

"I'll start sounding like Kevin Rudd."

"No, I don't think so; he's abusive when he swears."

"We're just discursive."

"Yes, discursive," I agree but I'm more concerned about the legs poking out from behind the desk. I glance at the legs again. There has been no discernable movement since I entered the room and I'm having trouble concentrating on what Bob is saying. Bugger it: "What's the matter with the dog?"

"Arthritis: he's gone in the back legs," says Bob. "He was worse after I took him to the vet."

"Did they work on him?"

"Yes, they gassed him and he hasn't been any good since. He wouldn't move at all for about a day. He wasn't that bad when I took him but I'm giving him pills." He reaches into his jacket pocket and pulls out a plastic bag of grey pills. "We're taking pills for it, aren't we, Frank? We're happy; we're still playing a bit. I don't know if we'll be able to walk properly again." Frank lifts his head, turns and looks at Bob, then disconsolately lowers it again.

It's time for a bit more discursiveness.

"You hadn't seen Paul Garland for fifteen years before I went to see him. Did that help?"

"Buggered if I know. You never know with Garland. See, Garland .

. . ."

"I meant did it help with you? Were you able to contact him again?"

"Oh, I'm beyond help. I rang him the night before my Golden Jubilee dinner, a clergy only affair, and it was just as if we had spoken the day before."

"Well, that's good."

Bob doesn't indicate whether he thinks it is or isn't, so maybe it isn't. "With Garland I think it's more of a psycho-technical problem," he says. It's like a diagnosis from R. D. Laing. "I don't think it's anything else. Garland was always inscrutable. Garland always wore protective clothing: psychosocial, protective clothing. He must have felt vulnerable."

"Psycho . . ."

"Psycho-social. I'm saying he wears a protective cloak. If you put him and me together in school he became dux of the college. He was brilliant. He could also talk funny: dark humour. He would have felt vulnerable because his family wasn't the stock-in-trade Catholic family. Garland was counter-cultural because his father, Don, was a card-carrying Labor man who didn't believe in the Labor Party during the split. His mother was a Baptist so she was counter-cultural for a Catholic, and as far as the school was concerned. He had to balance all that. Now both of those components went into Garland's personality. He had to defend himself against any charges, especially after the split in the Labor Party, 'cause we were in the seminary during the split. We weren't fascists you see. The Catholics were going the way of fascism. They were going the way of Bob Santamaria: a form of fascism. That was a natural habitat for Christian Brothers, Nuns – and the Archbishop," he adds with a flourish and I laugh.

"He had to balance all that. It was hard because we had to become double agents; in the seminary at the time you had lots of visiting speakers on behalf of the movement, on behalf of that continental fascist Catholicism: lots of 'em. Because of the dominance of that particular opinion we had to be careful; we had to be clandestine Commos," Father Bob declares honestly. "That was an undercurrent through most of those years."

He wonders too if that effort over the years didn't catch up with Paul Garland because: "he had to live a double life." Bob says that Vatican Two would have helped him because: "Vatican Two said: 'bullshit to fascism.'

"Garland came out of the seminary at 26 with an acquired persona:

he was an actor, and the actor had become the person, or the person had become the act. He was always entertaining but unnervingly entertaining. He played the part of a stand-up comedian for years: entertaining, laughing, impersonating and all the rest of it but you might have had a sneaking suspicion that he was protecting himself against imaginary, or real, threats to his psyche."

'Bob could equally be talking about himself and his own protective cloak,' adds Descartes.

"Maybe it caught up with him so he took time off from it. The only way to take time off is to leave the stage, which is what he did," says Bob. "I rang him and he said blah, blah, blah, and I said blah, blah, blah. Before hanging up I said 'I'll see you at the Golden Jubilee Dinner,' and that's what happened. He's still talking highly intelligently, still black humour about Mother Church; the only way to deal with Mother Church if you're a critic and you're a cleric is to have black humour. You daren't be an outright critic because they'll arrest you and throw you out. There's an old saying: if you can't convince them then confuse them. We were great confusers. Anybody that thoughtful and still in service can't be the enemy; it just sounds like he is the enemy. People would be saying to the Archbishop nowadays: 'Maguire is harming.' Denis would deny that but would say: 'it merely looks as though he is, and sounds as though he is, but he is not.' So, he's confused. Maybe Garland has got a Masters in something," laughs Bob.

"Were all those at your table at the Jubilee dinner from your era?"

"Yes; 1960's. We were a pain-in-the-arse."

"How many pains-in-the-arse would you say were there?"

"There were five at our table. There was Charlie Borg, a small Maltese who joined us in the semitary and paid for it because he was small, Maltese and pious. Poor little Charlie: actual name Karmelito: Karmel. That made the Aussies laugh: a man named Karmel. He became Australianised to the extent that now he's got more 'bloodys' in his language than I have."

It's an infectious word. I've noticed that it has snuck up on me and the twins too.

"And poor old Frank Arnold, who already had a bachelor of science when he went into the semitary in 1953, was there. He's still parish priest at North Blackburn; won't resign. Denis put it to him that he would like him to resign."

"He must be nearly 80."

"Frank is 78. He more or less eyeballed Denis and said: 'Yeah, well

I'll see you later.' I could have said the same thing but Denis cooked up this 'reason for asking for his resignation.' I could have taken that seriously and taken it to a tribunal, or a court."

"Do you mean a civil court?"

"Yeah."

"I didn't think that was a possibility, not with a priest fighting the Archbishop."

"Why wouldn't I take him to court?"

"Catholic priests just don't do that sort of thing." There I go, counselling the priest as if I *am* the Archbishop. "Would any of your peers do that?"

"No, they wouldn't because they're Catholic priests."

"That's what I'm getting at."

"They wouldn't, but I would!" he says loudly.

"You would?"

"Yeah! Bugger him. I would now: for honour."

"That accounts for four of the five; who's the last bloke?"

"Moran. I don't know what Moran's up to. Moran . . . same Moran . . . same Moran as ever."

"I've never met him, although I've heard his name mentioned by a few people."

"Same Moran," he repeats. "Moran hasn't spoken to me for a while. Spoke to me nicely at the dinner. I don't understand it."

"You've lost four old friends."

"Oh, well," he hesitates, "we've never been friends in the sense of ordinary human beings."

"What about Garland?"

"The question is whether I've lost their friendship or they've lost mine." Bob seemingly interjects himself. "They haven't lost mine! I'd go into battle for them," says the old soldier, "but I don't know they'd go into battle for me."

"Did any of them go into battle for you during your dispute with the Archbishop?"

"I don't think so. I don't know that any of them rang me."

I frown at this damning indictment of his brethren. There seems to be apathy amongst them, reminiscent of posties.

"Garland's now saying to me that over where he's living in that home where there are other old priests – on the side he's saying this: 'I'm now the resident expert on the American Civil War.' "

"Is this a metaphorical civil war?"

"No, *the* Civil War. You wonder if that is a comment; oh no, he's telling me that to survive there he has had to . . ." Bob considers and then says: "It's a third language. He can talk American Civil War until he's black in the face over there. Every time he meets them in the corridor, or at lunch, or anywhere, which means that they'll never be getting through to him and he'll never be getting through to them."

"Is he really interested in the American Civil War?"

"Oh yes, he's always been interested in it. He will use it as his . . . if they want anything to do with him they'll have to talk American Civil War."

"That's incredible!"

"If he wants to have anything to do with them it's only on the level of the American Civil War."

"It's bizarre."

"It shows the depth of his alienation. If you don't share any ideas in common whatsoever therefore to coexist you'd better have something that other people need. What have you got that they need? You've got something that you know that they don't know. It's either that or we'll all have to deteriorate into gossip."

"That's an amazing strategy, then."

"Brilliant," Bob declares, further describing it. "You could therefore be considered to be mad. Eccentric would do. 'Don't go near Paul Garland because all he will talk about is the American Civil War.' Alright. You might like to go and talk about the Civil-bloody-War. 'Paul, how many actually died in the Civil War?' I don't mind talking about the Civil-bloody-War, especially with somebody who knows something about it."

At this stage there is movement from the body. He springs into life and jumps up attempting to charge around the study like he used to but his back legs aren't up to it; he hobbles for a few strides and then returns disconsolately to his place behind the desk in front of the heater.

"The five of you would have had a lot to talk about, reminiscing about the old days."

"No, it was a bit hard. There's a table there. There's a bloke at the end who makes a speech, eventually."

"Was it a bit like a wedding reception where everybody moves around?"

"No, you don't move around. You don't know who's the enemy. If you move around you don't know if you'll come back in one piece."

'The poor bugger sounds as if he is paranoid. Maybe he is suffering from post-traumatic stress now that the clerical war is over,' muses Rene.

"You said to a reporter after the do that one of your regrets was that you hadn't made friends with people."

"Arr," says Bob, "I'm saying that I could have been a better friend. The paedophile thing didn't help much because you ended up with people you liked but with whom you almost daren't associate with in public because others would then say (not clergymen so much, but others: outsiders) 'Oh, yeah, he's had Father Bloggs up there at his place,' and then later they find out that Father Bloggs has been to court for being a child abuser. That would then muddy the waters because people would then say: 'Oh, Jesus.' "

"Guilty by association."

"Yes! So you've got to stay away from them in public."

"Isn't that what happened with Kiss? You liked him."

"Yes; I didn't mind Kiss as a human being. Brian Coffey has been to court; not gaol I don't think. Nice bloke, poor bugger. His mate Pat Flanagan was there. Pat Flanagan's the parish priest at Red Cliffs up near Mildura."

"Any relation to the Flanagan writers?" I ask making a mental note to check with *Broken Rites* to find out just what this 'nice bloke' fronted court for.

"I don't think so although Flanagan himself is a very articulate man, ungainly as a human physical specimen, but very talented. He was there, thank God; he's friendlier."

Just then we hear Barnabus talking loudly in Judy's office. Sounding like a character out of a Carter Brown paperback I murmur: "I'd like to get the lowdown on Barnabus." As far as the Father Bob story goes, what we have up to this stage is the life story of a priest with very little about his forty-year mentoring of Barnabus. "You'll never get it," Bob says quietly. "You've got no hope. It's too tender with him. You're not gonna get it outa me either."

Barnabus walks in. Father Bob looks at the set of my jaw and says: "You won't get his story."

I ask Barnabus anyway. Maybe I'm getting the hang of this reporter caper.

Barnabus says: "No, I can't even give the story to myself. I *won't* give it to myself. How could I give it to you?"

These two really are close I think as I check to see if Bob has got his hand up Barnabus' back. This is the old ventriloquist Ron Blaskett and his dummy Gerry Gee. Father Bob has used these words. I was pestering him one day, trying to get him to talk Barnabus into telling me his story. At the time Bob said: "He can't even give the story to himself. He *won't* give it to himself. How could he give it to you?"

## Chapter 56: Broken Rites

*"Footballers are found drunk and disorderly;
the priest is found paedophiled."*

When I get home after work, I look up *Broken Rites* on the Internet, (a group that helps the victims of church-related sexual abuse), to follow up on the story of a rock-spider disguised as a rector. As I read from the website, I wonder how any parents could trust a Catholic cleric with their child any more. In the past, the deviant do-gooders were moved from one parish to another as if, incredibly, to extend their reach and impact.

However, it seems that a nomadic existence was quite common in the early years of a priest's career. In explaining the reason why he was moved around in his first thirteen years as a priest, Bob gives up the story in snatches: "It would have been: 'this bloke is young, eccentric, trustworthy. We will therefore send him to half a dozen places.' Places where the old man is performing poorly. . . he's cracked or too old or whatever . . . they would have had a complaint about him." Bob's stint at Braybrook is the likely source of this story. 'Who will we send to these places?' Bob asks on behalf of his imaginary interlocutor. "Often times it was me," he says with some exasperation. "When I got to South Melbourne in 1973 I said 'thank you, Jesus,' because I could now settle."

Unlike Father Bob, Brian Coffey, who was also ordained in 1960, remained an itinerant priest and moved on from parish to parish over a period of thirty-seven years. Moved on it seems by the Catholic Church to cover up his paedophilia. During his time as a priest from 1960 until the 1990s he offered pastoral care and 'ministered' to the children in Western Victoria, and like a train stopping at all stations: Horsham, Koroit, Terang, Port Fairy, Ouyen, Charlton, Colac, Sea Lake, Gordon and Stawell, his dastardly stays were brief. During the 60s and 70s the Archbishop of the diocese covered up all reports of Coffey's nefarious deeds in the usual way: he bought him a one-way ticket to the next parish down the line where he could continue as before. Incredibly, according to Broken Rites, none of the allegations from his victims was reported to the police. In fact it was December 1997 before the train was stopped in its tracks: the police dramatically arrested the sixty-four year old priest, dressed in his vestments, at the altar one morning in front of the congregation. The predator priest was shunted into the Ballarat County

Court where he pleaded not guilty to the molestation of ten boys and one girl aged between six and eleven over a period of fifteen years. His lawyer shrewdly applied to have each charge heard separately so that each jury would be ignorant of the other charges but Judge Kelly ruled that a single jury be sworn in.

The assaults began as tickling games and playful spankings and ended with Coffey fondling the children's genitals, the court was told. One of Coffey's victims, who was abused when he was eleven, said the assault had "a profound and devastating effect" on his life. In an impact statement read to the court he said that he had become an alcoholic and regularly visited a psychologist because of 'what Coffey did to me.' Police were told in 1997 that, after growing up with problems, at least two other Coffey victims had committed suicide.

Coffey was duly convicted and sentenced to three years gaol, wholly suspended! An appeal by the Director of Public Prosecutions against the leniency of the sentence in September 1999 was dismissed. Coffey left the court to back slapping from a group of male supporters; a West Victorian priest, a fellow seminarian from the late 1950's, who had been accompanying him to Court each day bizarrely pointed his camera at Coffey's victims in the street, allegedly taking photos.

Coffey had luck on his side and escaped conviction on more serious charges too: after being charged with five counts of buggery, allegedly committed against a boy at Ouyen in 1975 and 1976 the charges lapsed: the boy was so shy and ashamed that he couldn't be coaxed into Court.

This man's paedophilia does not appear to be the result of sexual frustration brought on by years of celibacy. It's my conviction that he chose a career as a priest so that he would have a smorgasbord of children to pick from for the rest of his days. He broke his rites at the first opportunity. At a house in Ballarat in 1960, he molested an eleven year-old child at a party held to celebrate his ordination. For the lewd and lascivious priest, the feast lasted for thirty-seven years before he was finally dismissed from priestly duties.

Coffey was invited to Father Bob's dinner to celebrate fifty-years as a priest and was readily accepted by his former brethren.

"Not a bad bloke, poor bugger," said Father Bob of this monster.

Judy ushers me into her office when I next arrive because Father Bob is still talking to a visitor in his study.

"You must have seen and heard a lot since you first started working for Bob, Judy. How have you found it?" I ask as I plonk the bundle of mail on her desk.

"Bob's a lovely man to work for. He's funny; he can be . . ." Judy leaves the end of the sentence to my imagination. He can be hilarious? He can be...

"How have you fared since you first started here? It must have been a bit of a shock." I ask this because Judy's job seems to be not just one of secretary but of problem solver and confidante to Father Bob.

Judy laughs. "It was an inspiration. I've always either worked for myself or for bigger companies. I worked in shipping for a long time, dealing with people worldwide, so it was a bit different coming here. You know, I'm not a Catholic," she confesses.

"Neither am I." I laugh.

"It is much different working for Father Bob; it is *so* busy, Ron, I can tell you."

"Do you feel as if you're under pressure a lot of the time?"

"Yes, definitely. All the time! The phone never stops. For the first hour today there was a meeting in the dining room, the doorbell kept buzzing, the phone kept ringing at the same time, and I've got things to do; I just have to plough through it. I've got the church noticeboard to do now and a few other things for the church whilst the phone's ringing and the door is buzzing."

We hear Father Bob's guest leaving and Judy announces me: "Here's Ron to see you, Bob."

"Yes. Do you know where that book is, or has somebody stolen it? The book with my face on it," he asks Judy. "It might be in the dining room unless Barnabus has pinched it."

Judy goes in search of Bob's book. I smile because it reminds me of home. Women often seem to be much better at finding things or telling you exactly where something is in the fridge.

Barnabus who has come to ask his mentor for money, enters stage right and declares: "Nice to see you," as he proffers his hand. "You look wonderful."

"You're looking alright too," I rejoin as the dog starts barking.

Bob says: "That's his job, to drive us all mad." At first I think that he is referring to the dog and I laugh, but he exclaims: "Yeah!" Reduce us to his level."

"I wouldn't do that at all. Thank you very much, Father," Barnabus says as he leaves with his hundred pounds.

"You know exactly what you are doing," Father calls after his ward's retreating back.

"I hope so," replies Barnabus, missing the point.

"Yeah, that's the one," says Father to Judy who produces a large black rectangular book. Geoffrey's black-and-white picture of 'The Grin' is in the centre of the cover with the title 'In Bob We Trust' in white writing underneath. I leaf through the glossy pages of the album, which contain many of Bob's old black-and-white photos as well as a few present day images. As I look at a group photo of freshly ordained priests I say to Bob: "The last time we talked about the priests who were present at that do of yours you said that Brian Coffey wasn't a bad bloke."

"Mmm."

"I looked him up on *Broken Rites* . . . "

"He sinned."

"He more than sinned. He was a paedophile before he went into the seminary."

"He wasn't a paedophile in the Semitary."

"He molested a boy on the day of his ordination and then continued molesting children for 37 years. I just wonder how you could call him a good bloke."

"Well he was. I knew him in the Semitary for eight years."

"Mmm," from me this time.

"As far as I know . . . I saw a bloke the other night when I was making a speech. I recognised his features and thought: 'that looks like Des Gannon.' Then I thought: 'No, it can't be Des Gannon,' because I though Des Gannon was dead. Not so: he'd been in prison.... poor old Des Gannon. He told me that he was not long out of the nick. But he was in gaol for that too."

"Poor old Des Gannon?"

"Mmm."

Bob doesn't seem too perturbed about having to associate with these paedophile priests. "It's hard for me to understand how you and your peers can have any sort of feelings for these bastards. The only thing that I can put it down to is that priests have never had children of their own."

"Never had anything of our own!" Bob says loudly. Then, more quietly: "Ah, well."

"Is there anything else you can say about it? You found him to be alright whilst you were in . . . "

"I found him alright nothing!" he snaps. "I'm just saying that they were in the Semitary and that they were fellow clergymen. That's all I can say."

"They've ended up on the dark side."

"Yeah."

"Are you saying . . .?"

"I'm saying," he interrupts, "they are emotionally to themselves no good. They can think alright, but EQ says they don't feel alright. It would be the same with Coffey."

"How are they going to fix the Catholic Church?"

"They will have to do what they were supposed to do after Vatican Two, which is hand it over to the lay people, who probably will be as stupid as the bloody clergy because the institute itself is too big and too powerful. Decentralise it or abandon it altogether."

"Wouldn't it help if they got rid of celibacy?"

"I don't know."

"I doubt if celibacy had anything to do with Coffey's problem anyway. He was more than likely a paedophile right from the start and he targeted . . ."

"He wasn't a paedophile in the semitary because there weren't any children."

"Maybe he wanted to be a priest because that gave him the opportunity to access children."

"Nah, nah, he was alright; I knew his father and his mother and his brothers and sisters."

I smile. "What went wrong then?"

"The institution, I'm telling you. Send him to Red Hills and send him to . . .

"Yes, but he started right from the day he was ordained."

"That's what *Broken Rites* says."

"Yes."

"His colleagues might say otherwise: Mr Moran and Mr Hodgkins, and the nice priest at Ararat, Davey, who was a mate of his. I don't think anybody's going to be a bloody paedophile, a practising paedophile," he amends and then says: "Practising diabetic."

"What! Diabetic?"

"Well, it's the same thing. If you are buggered psycho . . . what's the bloody word?"

"Psychologically."

"Psycho-socially. These are immature people. I've said a thousand times: these are immature people. These are like league footballers. If you promote them to a position beyond their capabilities emotionally they become dysfunctional. Footballers are found drunk and disorderly; the priest is found paedophiled." Bob's phrasing makes it sound as if it is the priest who has been wronged! "The only access he's got to possible undetected vice . . ."

"But is it fair to make excuses for the priests?"

"I'm not making excuses; I'm giving reasons."

"Yes. What of the Church then? All it does is send the offender off to another parish where fresh possibilities for paedophilia are presented."

"Yes. That's an administrative problem. It's up to the bloody community to say what they want done with corrupt policemen, publicans, prostitutes, parliamentarians and priests." He rattles off all of these p titled people with such lingual dexterity that I am astounded for the umpteenth time by his effortless use of language. However, by lumping them all in together does Bob attempt to lessen the sins of his Fathers by planting them in amongst a crowd of sinners? I am not sure that we expect the same of publicans and prostitutes as we do of priests. "All institutions will become dysfunctional," he states with authority.

As if to summarily end the discussion, the old fax machine starts squelching loudly. Bob says: "Maybe it's sending me good news: I don't get much of it. One sheet of good news would get me through the next five years. It's making noises like it could be good news."

"How's Frank going now?" I ask as the machine starts spitting out paper.

"Frank's a lot better, thank you, doctor."

"He just about seemed to be his old self when he greeted me at the door."

"Yes, they jabbed him with steroids. Who's this?" groans Bob as the phone rings.

"There's one more question that I'd like answered about Coffey if you don't mind, Bob," I say when he terminates his call. "Why do the rank and file priests accept the paedophile priests back into the ranks once they return from prison or court?"

"They don't accept them back into the ranks; they just retain their friendly relationships with them. It's no business of mine who gets back into the ranks: it's headquarters."

"Not necessarily the ranks then, but social occasions like the one that Coffey attended."

"Friends, friends! If you knew a bloke who was a paedophile, and a friend of yours, are you never going to talk to him again?"

"No, probably not," I say leaving aside the challenge that he has said he has no friends.

"Wouldn't you?" Bob seems to be amazed. "We have to. We remember that the person is not a born paedophile. There's a strange man out there," he says pulling the curtain back, the better to see.

"I don't think there'd be many other groups who'd accept such a person back into the ranks: a mob of posties, for instance, or a grid of electricians."

Bob lets the curtain fall back into place. "Ah, well, coppers! Not paedophiles. A corrupt cop. Paedophilia is only a form of illness. Corrupt dentists. He groped Mrs Smith whilst she was in the chair. Are you going to talk to him again or what?"

I laugh at Bob's quip.

"What do you do? he asks. "You either ostracise them forever . . ."

"That's what I'd do."

"Which is tribalism: banish them."

"Isn't that what most groups would do though?"

"Yes, but your Christians can't do it because your Jesus keeps saying: 'There but for the grace of God go I, judge not thou shalt not be judged.' I know that in practice you might want to spear him. I don't care what you do to him, but you can't stop me from going home and saying: 'Sorry, Bryan, I couldn't stop Ron from spearing you, but whatever you've done, we're still mates."

Bob changes his analogy. "Now I'll say Ron is in charge; he's got the uniform on. He wants to take 'em all away and put 'em in the oven. Off you go. Tat taa. 'Help us!' they cry. 'I can't help you; Ron's in charge of the oven. Off youse go.' You then say to me, Ron: 'And what's more, I don't want to hear you say anything good about these people, ever.' I'm saying: 'you put 'em in the oven but I can't undertake not to say anything because I knew this man when he was a child and his mother was lovely. Kiss had a lovely mother and a lovely sister who was a nun. Now your lot would say: 'Once a bastard, always a bastard.' I don't know if that's true."

"I think that they've got a lot of gall coming back and socialising with those who have not offended."

"Most of them are suffering from emotional immaturity. They might be six years of age in a body of fifty-four. It's an awful affliction but you'll say: 'the oven: put 'em in the oven. Now get out," he directs, and Frank lifts his head from the floor.

Leaving, I mull over what Father Bob has said. The graphic idea of Ron Burrows as the head roaster has had the effect that he intended I suppose: getting me to think objectively about the matter; but social immaturity is still no excuse as far as I'm concerned.

'Stick with tribal justice,' declares Rene Descartes.

## Chapter 57: The Flat Daddy

I shake my head in exasperation: the publisher wants to crucify the Cauliflower-twins. I am devastated. Rene Descartes is so pissed off that he won't even talk to me as I lay awake all night mulling things over. Ronny, the big sook, is inconsolable and there are tears on our pillow. This morning, after an ultimatum from the publisher, I betray the poor bastards and agree to nail 'em up. They haven't done anything wrong but I want to get published so I sell my soul to a woman whom I have never even met: the all-powerful publisher.

There are limits though. Even a traitor balks when he realises that the screwing has only just started. "Cut out all the Bobbywaffle and the swearing," the publisher orders as she stiffens her knees. "It's too long," she moans. "Cut it back to the size of one of those old two-bob westerns!" I groan. The publisher wants The Editor to suck the life out of Father Bob: flatten him, turn him into a cardboard cut-out, and stand him in the corner. She wants to chop and channel the manuscript and turn it into a bog-standard biography. I can't imagine Father Bob as a Flat Daddy though. It's been said that the best part about beating your head against a brick wall is when you stop, so I ring the publisher and tell her that I've had enough. Father Bob and I now need another publisher but at least I've got the twins back.

The dentist's waiting room is not usually a place of inspiration for me; the same morning show is playing on the wall-mounted television set: 'Mornings with Kerri-Anne' on Channel 9. Sorry, lady, but all I want to do is get it over and done with and go home for a cup of tea. Nothing changes in the waiting room from one six-monthly visit to the next: a huge wooden toothbrush, at least three metres long, hangs on an angle above the hatch. The receptionist on the other side of the hatch . . . hang on, there's a sign below Gargantua's toothbrush: 'Ask your dentist how you can get whiter teeth.'

I sit up straighter in my moulded-plastic chair. 'Rebecca Beazley inventor of B'dazzled teeth whitening products,' I think with a yellow smile. But it's not Rebecca Beasley whom I'm thinking about so much as Linda Williams. How could I have forgotten about her after all the trouble Father Bob went to that morning, scrolling relentlessly, looking for her email? Linda Williams, Publishing Agent. I wonder if she is still interested.

## Chapter 58: The Unknown God

*"He didn't want to trust us. He couldn't afford to trust us because, God, he'd have an example of a Roman Catholic parish that actually knew what it was trying to do."*

It *should* end here in the study I think as I walk in with the mail a few days later. After all, this is where it started: the postie, the priest and his dog. As Bob talks on the phone, the landline this time rather than its frequently buzzing pocket cousin, Frank climbs to his feet and limps over for me to pat him. The poor beast is remains in considerable pain but his tail is still wagging. A bit like the troubled body of the Catholic Church belied by the positive swish of its public relations tail.

Bob hangs up and I'm about to ask him a question when his moby buzzes in his pocket like one of his old bees. He glances at the caller's name and snaps: "Are you ringing me? What do you want? What? Yeah, what do you want? No, there's no money. No you don't. You just want to get out of the house because you don't want to do anything."

I smile. He sounds like a husband ticking off his lazy missus for not doing the housework. "I'll stick a hundred pounds in your letterbox. No, twenty minutes," he says roughly. Father Bob returns his phone to his pocket and says to me: "It's these veterans you see. That was Barnabus. Hundred pounds. The Turk will stagger in, in a minute, wanting money. Mr X in another minute: 'Can I go back home this afternoon.' Righto. Hundred pounds."

"What about Margie?" By now I feel as if I know her and wonder about her circumstances.

"She's been telling me that she's had her teeth out and her face is swollen. I've sent her money."

I nod and we are silent for a few moments. "What do you think of having an atheist as our Prime Minister?" I ask, with genuine interest in Bob's take on a heathen head of state.

"I couldn't give a rat's arse," Bob barks back with the dismissiveness he reserves for any of my questions that he thinks have missed the point. "We're all atheists. I've said in here: (he tilts his head back and peers at the monitor's screen through the bottom half of his bifocals) 'The early Christians were classified as atheists because the Roman upper classes said these people are Bogans. They won't accept the Roman Emperor or the Roman cul-cha, (he pronounces culture in the

Aussie way) as divine and so they were charged with being atheists.' It's the same now: Gillard could well be a follower of the Unknown God," Bob forcefully contends. "As St Paul said to some smart-arses in Greece: 'You've got a lovely museum here with all these gods in it.' And they said: 'Yes, it's nice.' Then he said: 'There's an empty pedestal over there. Who's that?' 'Oh,' they said, 'that's the Unknown God: in case we've missed one.' So he said: 'Oh well, I'll go for that. I'm a disciple of the Unknown God.' 'Ooh Jesus,' they said, 'we like that.' He liked that and they liked that so they both had a mutual talking point. I'm now saying that we are followers of the Unknown God."

There's time for another of my trademark non-sequitur quick changes of subject, apropos of nothing in particular, as our session draws to a close:

"Have you leased the school building yet?"

"Yes. You get two developments: one for the Friends of the Earth, and ours, which will be forty one-bedroom flats. This will do what I told the Archbishop it would do. I said to him: 'Give me credit please while I go to work.' He said: 'No, you can't have credit; you're under arrest.' He didn't want to trust us. He couldn't afford to trust us because, God, he'd have an example of a Roman Catholic parish that actually knew what it was trying to do. It was offensive to him and maybe even more offensive to his advisers."

"It's such a worthwhile project and yet it's become so political."

"Yes; it's *only* political." He sighs. "I'll go and stuff a hundred pounds in that boy's letterbox now," he says, as he comes out from behind his big tidy desk. We walk out the door together, the postie and the priest with Frank tagging along behind. As I mount my bike Father Bob says: "I'll love you and leave you." He climbs into his car and drives off to stuff a hundred quid into Barnabus' ever-greedy letterbox.